African American Historic
Burial Grounds and
Gravesites of New England

African American Historic Burial Grounds and Gravesites of New England

Glenn A. Knoblock

McFarland & Company, Inc., Publishers
Jefferson, North Carolina

LIBRARY OF CONGRESS CATALOGUING-IN-PUBLICATION DATA

Names: Knoblock, Glenn A., author.
Title: African American historic burial grounds and
gravesites of New England / Glenn A. Knoblock.
Description: Jefferson, North Carolina : McFarland & Company, Inc.,
Publishers, 2016. | Includes bibliographical references and index.
Identifiers: LCCN 2015040412 | ISBN 9780786470112 (softcover : acid free paper)
Subjects: LCSH: African Americans—New England—History. | African
American cemeteries—New England—Guidebooks. | African Americans—
New England—Biography. | New England—Guidebooks.
Classification: LCC E185.917 K58 2016 | DDC 305.896/073074—dc23
LC record available at http://lccn.loc.gov/2015040412

BRITISH LIBRARY CATALOGUING DATA ARE AVAILABLE

ISBN (print) 978-0-7864-7011-2
ISBN (ebook) 978-1-4766-2042-8

Front cover: *top to bottom, left to right* view, Meetinghouse Cemetery,
Princeton, MA; Gravestone, Pompey Lyndon, 1765, Common
Burying Ground, Newport, RI; Gravestone detail, Phillis and
Prince Lyndon/Stevens, 1773, Common Burying Ground, Newport, RI;
detail of view, Venture Smith Family Plot, First Church Cemetery,
East Hadddam, CT (all photographs are from the author's collection)

Printed in the United States of America

*McFarland & Company, Inc., Publishers
Box 611, Jefferson, North Carolina 28640
www.mcfarlandpub.com*

In memory of
William A. Allison, friend, fellow historian
and World War II veteran, 1921–2014

Table of Contents

Acknowledgments

I first conceived the idea for this book over twenty years ago, and it was at that time that I began gathering research materials and visiting sites. During the course of its actual writing, which took place off and on from 2009 until 2014, I received help and encouragement from many individuals. First and foremost among them is my wife Terry, who put up with my many absences away from home and hours at the library and computer, among other things. Without her loving (and sometimes stern) encouragement and support, my career as a historian would not have been possible. Thanks, too, go to my daughter Anna for her silent support. In addition, I'd like to thank my parents, Bill and Ceil Knoblock, for accompanying me on several cemetery expeditions during their visits to New Hampshire to get a sense of what my fieldwork is like. Finally, on the family front, I cannot forget the long-distance support and encouragement of my sisters, Lisa (herself an occasional poet) and Debbie, who have always taken an interest in my work.

Very seldom does any historian work alone, and that is certainly the case for my efforts to produce this book. Though much of this book is based on my own research and observations in the cemeteries discussed herein, the bibliography at the end is indicative of the many historical works I've consulted to gain the proper perspective and context. The individuals listed below were especially helpful or supportive during the course of my research and writing, making contributions for cemeteries in the states in which they are listed:

New Hampshire: Dr. Kathleen Wheeler, Independent Archaeological Consulting LLC (Amherst and Portsmouth); Dr. Bruce Jackson, professor and chair, Department of Biotechnology and Forensic DNA Science, MassBay Community College, Wellesley, MA (Amherst); Dr. Jamie L. Wilson, post-doctorate fellow, Department of Biochemistry, Boston University Medical School (Amherst); Valerie Cunningham, Portsmouth Black Heritage Trail (Portsmouth); Candace Daigle, cemetery trustee, Town of Gilmanton (Gilmanton); Richard Alperin, president, New Hampshire Old Graveyard Association (Newmarket); Jackie Marshall (Amherst); Carolyn and Tom Ramsbotham (Lee); David Moore, community development director, City of Portsmouth (Portsmouth); Kelvin Edwards, vice president, Seacoast African American Cultural Center (Portsmouth); Leigh Webb and the Franklin Historical Society (Franklin).

Rhode Island: Letty Champion (Newport), Julie Nathanson (Bristol, Providence), John Sterling (Providence, South Kingstown, Newport), Susane and Greene Gardner (South Kingstown).

Maine: Barb Desmarais (Brunswick), Marion Barrett Smith (Warren), Kay Kimball, Assistant Provost for Academic Services, the University of Maine at Machias (Machias).

Vermont: Randy and Wayne Smithhay (St. Albans); Hardy Merrill, president, Grafton Historical Society (Grafton); Maureen Fletcher, administrator, Grafton Historical Society (Grafton); LTC William R. McKern (Colchester); Pam Johnson and Jim Davidson of the Rutland Historical Society (Rutland); and the staff at the Rutland Free Library (Rutland), Barb Destromp (St. Albans and Burlington).

Connecticut: Karen Parsons, Jennie Loomis Family instructor in history and archivist, Loomis Chaffee School (Windsor); Deborah Shapiro, executive director, Middlesex County Historical Society (Middletown); Janis L. Franco, Local History Librarian, Meriden Public Library (Trumbull and Norfolk), JoAnn Rice (Norwalk); John Edwards (New Haven), Cathy Rimcoski (Hartford).

Massachusetts: Margaret Marshall, Barre Historical Society (Barre); Christine Comiskey (Georgetown); Eddie Johnson, president, Parting Ways (Plymouth); Susan Harnwell (Worcester); John Speer (Nantucket); Tammy Foley (Martha's Vineyard); Dr. Elaine Cawley Weintraub, department chair, Social Studies, Martha's Vineyard Regional High School (Martha's Vineyard).

While I have tried to give everyone who has helped on this project their proper recognition, I apologize in advance to anyone whose help I've received but forgotten to give proper mention. I also here make the standard historian's disclaimer that, though I've consulted many works of history and spoken with many individuals, any mistakes that have crept into this work are solely my responsibility.

Introduction

One of the most poignant quotes about African Americans in New England comes from Jaffrey, New Hampshire, historians Albert Annett and Alice Lehtinen, who, in 1937 wrote of the town's black population and a lack of historical details concerning their lives that "the earth has closed over them like the waters over one lost at sea." The history of African Americans and many aspects of their lives in New England from early colonial times down to the present seems often to have been lost, but has actually been documented over the years in general historical works on the subject, specialized local or regional historical studies covering such cities and towns as New Haven, Connecticut; Portsmouth, New Hampshire; Newport, Rhode Island; and Hinesburg, Vermont; and in anecdotal form in numerous town histories.

The African American presence in New England has a long history, dating back to at least 1629, when enslaved individuals were first brought to Massachusetts. Though this is a well-established fact, it is still little known among the general public. Adding to this perceived lack of African American history in New England is the fact that the region as a whole, for many reasons, is not particularly diverse. New Hampshire, Maine, and Vermont, despite having vibrant black populations in such urban locales as Portsmouth, Bangor, Portland, and Burlington, are some of the whitest states in the nation, with black populations that average about one percent of the overall population. While black population numbers are considerably higher in the remaining southern New England states of Connecticut, Massachusetts, and Rhode Island, they are in general concentrated in the large urban areas of Boston, Hartford, New Haven, New London, and Providence. Outside of these areas, in numerous small villages and towns, the black presence is much less pronounced.

Given these demographic realities, where, then, is the evidence of the region's African American past? Where are the historic churches and homes of notable African Americans turned into museums in the communities in which they resided, or where are the statues erected in their honor? What historical artifacts that they have left behind are enshrined in local museums? In point of fact, it is through these traditional historical remnants, with but few exceptions, that we can view only the white or European ancestral past in New England.

However, a small population and a lack of visible reminders from the historic past doesn't mean that the African American presence in the region was insignificant. In fact, black men and women in New England, including Anthony Clark in Warner, New Hampshire, Phebe Ann Jacobs in Brunswick, Maine, and Prince Hall in Boston, had a significant impact on their communities, more so than is usually taught in local schools or covered in general history texts. This is because the African American history of New England has had to be recovered and reconstructed, both literally and figuratively, and it is an ongoing process to this day.

However, there is one type of historical artifact indelibly etched on the landscape that serves as a strong reminder of the African American past. These are the picturesque and quiet, often overgrown or even abandoned, burial grounds and cemeteries of New England and the gravestones found within. Here is where some of the African American history of New England lies hidden. This aspect of New England black history, with all its societal and cultural implications, is one that is not only fascinating and well worthy of study, but also one that has an immediacy and direct connection to the past unlike almost any other artifact or historical site. Indeed, the details of black lives in New England, or a fragment thereof, can be found in the many mossy and time-worn town, family, and neighborhood cemeteries that dot our regional landscape in countless numbers. These sites have been there all along, some merely hidden in plain sight until such time as they were rediscovered, while in some rare instances they have been, both literally and figuratively, dug up from the past. From these historic burial grounds and gravesites, some well publicized, many obscure, there is much yet to be learned about the African American experience in New England from the early colonial days down to the early twentieth century.

Historical documents of similar age are often lacking or lie buried in library archives, while historical buildings have often been greatly altered or exist in settings that have grown and changed over the years so as to change their original context. However, old burial grounds and cemeteries, and the gravestones found within them, can serve as open-air museums. True it is that the areas where many of these sites are located have changed and grown over the years too, and most cemeteries have undergone periods of decay and revival, perhaps several times over. But when one steps into that immediate space, say, in front of the gravestones for Quash Gomer of Wethersfield, Connecticut; Elizabeth "Mumbet" Freeman of Stockbridge, Massachusetts; Pomp and Candace Spring of Portsmouth, New Hampshire; one is transported back in time, both in space and, with the right mindset, spirit as well. Though a work of this nature might be expected to have a supernatural element, you will find no ghost stories here, but the truth about these cemeteries is more interesting than any fiction I could manufacture.

To visit these places is fascinating and profitable not just to the historian, but also to the genealogist and any casual history lover. To understand the history behind (or buried at, if you prefer) these sites, can offer clues, if not outright answers, to such interesting questions as to why African Americans were buried where they were, why some individuals have gravestones to mark their passing while most others do not, and what funerary practices may have been observed. To the British statesman William Gladstone is attributed the quote, "Show me the manner in which a nation or a community cares for its dead. I will measure exactly the sympathies of its people, their respect for the laws of the land, and their loyalty to high ideals." I have applied this wisdom to this topic, for the dead, though they cannot speak, can nonetheless tell us much.

Indeed, within these sacred grounds we can rediscover the stories of those enslaved and of those who broke the chains of bondage to make a whole new life for themselves and their families, the remarkable deeds of courage and valor of those men who fought to gain our nation's liberty in the American Revolution, to help preserve it during the War of 1812, and to preserve our union during the Civil War. Also to be found are some incredible women, including one who fought for her freedom through the civil process and won, and a humble and kind woman, formerly enslaved, who served as an inspiration to Harriet Beecher Stowe. These and many other humbler, but no less important, stories await rediscovery by a larger audience.

The narrative portion of this work begins with several sections that discuss the introduction of slavery in New England, followed by details on the aspects of the lives of those who were enslaved, as well as what life was like for those slaves who gained their freedom and subsequent generations of free blacks. This brief background is crucial, for to understand how African Americans were treated after their death, we must first understand how they lived, both within their own communities, as well as in the midst of the white world at large in the region. Where possible, I have offered as examples in this discussion about African American life a number of individuals whose burial sites are known. Finally, relating to our subject at hand, burial practices, and details on the several types of burial grounds and cemeteries in which African Americans were interred, are also discussed, as are the many sites that were lost over the years, and some that have been rediscovered. The second part of this work is a selective, state by state listing of some of what I consider to be the most important or representative examples of African American burial sites and cemeteries.

Notes

Several important matters regarding this work that may offer the reader some insight are here mentioned before moving on. First, this work, with several notable exceptions, covers the time period from the pre–Revolutionary War days down to about 1910 and thus does not generally include a discussion of twentieth century individuals and burials. By this time period African American burial practices in New England were generally consistent with society as a whole, though, as we will see, racism and discrimination in the cemetery would never vanish completely.

Additionally, though many individual burial sites and cemeteries are discussed and highlighted, this book does not contain a comprehensive listing of all known African American burial sites for the time period under discussion. This would, of course, be a massive undertaking that would take years to compile, and while I have visited many sites and know of many others, there are others of great local interest, I'm sure, that have escaped attention. Instead, it is my hope that the sites listed and described herein are a representative sample of the African American experience in each New England state. This listing, by its very nature, is subjective in form, and necessarily dictated by time and space constraints, and while I realize that some communities may be disappointed that their own site was overlooked or thought to have been somehow less important, let me assure those readers that, in fact, I deem all such burial sites important and worthy of documentation and preservation, and encourage you to contact me via the publisher with any unmentioned African American burial sites for the time period covered in this work and any supporting documents, photographs, and details in the event that an expanded edition might appear in the future.

It is also here appropriate to make some clarifying remarks regarding some of the racial terminology used in this book. I use the terms "African American" and "black" interchangeably, while the word "Negro," which is now outdated, is used only in historical context, such as when discussing Portsmouth's early "Negro Burial Ground" or in quoted material. Derogatory and offensive names, such as "Nigger Hill" or "Nigger Point" are also given in their historical context to denote the older names that were assigned to the places where African Americans once lived and were buried. Thankfully, these names have now disappeared from the map and are no longer in general common usage (though, sadly, they still crop up from time to time), but it is my feeling, and that of many other historians, that New Englanders of today cannot be shielded from elements of their racially insensitive past.

Additionally, there is the matter relating to the terminology used to describe the institution of slavery. Both in the scholarly field and within the African American community itself there has been a debate for more than a decade now regarding the use of the word "slave." On the one side, there are those who would like to see the use of the term "slave" discontinued because enslaved individuals of the past are still degraded to this day by being defined as slaves, the word implying that the sole defining character of those held in bondage was the very condition in which they were forced to live. After all, it is clear from the historical narratives and accounts that have been written, whether that of Frederic Douglass, Venture Smith or Jeffrey Brace, that these men, and probably most other enslaved men and women, had their own conceptions of personal identity that didn't include the word "slave." However, in today's politically charged environment, others view this change in terminology as a bit of political correctness or historical revisionism, arguing that substituting terms like "captive" or "person held against their will" for "slave" is not only confusing to the general reader, but also sugarcoats the horrors of the institution of slavery. Also, those who prefer the word "slave" point out that this term is not meant to degrade enslaved individuals, but rather describes a degrading state of servitude, where the real horror lies. One of the best discussions about this issue may be found on historian Ryan Poe's website: http://ryanmpoe.com/wordpress/slave-or-enslaved/. But even here there is no consensus.

As for this work, though I see merits in both sides of the argument and have discussed the subject with the editors, in the end I decided to use the word "slave" as it has been used by previous scholars. My determining factor in this decision, as with such racially charged terms as "Negro" or "Nigger," was that, rather than shield my readers from the past by using more nuanced and perhaps confusing terms, I would stick with the word "slave" because it effectively evinces the reality of the institution of slavery. To do otherwise would, at least in this work, apply the same hypocritical gloss to the matter that the slaveowners of old New England did when they referred to their slaves as "servants." I also trust that readers will recognize by the tone of my discussion that "slave" is meant solely to describe their living or legal status, not their true character.

Finally, early on in this work I discuss the fact that our knowledge of early African American history in New England is mostly told through a white prism, so to speak, due to the paucity of African American accounts. Given this fact, it seems only proper to note that this history, too, is by a white author whose Connecticut colonial ancestors (the Sillimans) were slave holders. While the white viewpoint has often negatively skewed the historical accounts of New England slavery and the later free-black experiences that were written down to the mid–twentieth century, such an effect in this work, as with most modern histories, is a thing of the past. Then again, that is ultimately up to you, the reader, to decide.

I. The Enslaved in Colonial New England

The Introduction of Slavery

The African American presence in New England has a long history, dating back to at least 1629, when enslaved individuals were first brought to Massachusetts. The numbers were small at first, but quickly grew as the New England economy expanded. Most influential was the development of the triangular trade between the New England colonies, the West Indies, and Africa. Though there were many variations of this trade, the most common involved sugar, molasses, and rum. The former products, along with enslaved individuals, were imported from the West Indies by New England merchants in exchange for lumber, usually in the form of bundles of shakes (wooden shingles), and codfish. The sugar and molasses were then turned into rum in the many distilleries that operated in New England, especially in Rhode Island. This rum, along with many iron products wrought in New England foundries, was often then shipped to the West African coast, where it was subsequently exchanged for African slaves who were then transported to the Americas. During the Middle Passage from Africa to the Americas, as many as two million slaves over the years died, mostly due to the cramped and disease-ridden conditions aboard the transport ships. Others died by committing suicide rather than serve a life in captivity. No matter how they died, those African slaves who died during the Middle Passage had a lonely "burial" in the deepest depths of the Atlantic Ocean, far from home.

Though the largest numbers of slaves were shipped to the West Indies and the Southern colonies, many African slaves were brought directly to New England. The merchants of Rhode Island, Connecticut, and Massachusetts were heavily involved in the trade, but even northern New England imported its share of slaves. Maine, which was a part of Massachusetts prior to gaining statehood in 1820, imported slaves in small numbers and its ships and sailors were active in the trade, while New Hampshire imported a considerable number of African slaves relative to its small geographical size and population. Despite the fact that New England was heavily involved in the trade in African slaves for over two hundred years, and had plantations in some parts of the region that rivaled those in the South in terms of the number of slaves working them, up until the 1980s there had been a collective amnesia about the topic among Northern white historians. The trade was either denied to have existed altogether or, in those areas where its existence could not be denied, its impact was deemed to be minimal. Either the numbers were claimed to be insignificantly small or, more often, it was rationalized that enslavement in New England was a benevolent institution, nothing like the brand of slavery that was practiced in the Deep South or the West Indies. Local research has shown both these notions to be entirely false. Noted Harvard historian Clifford K. Shipton, for example, stated in one of his works, "Fortunately, Portsmouth [New Hampshire] had no part in the slave trade" (Shipton, Vol. 12, pg. 384). He would have discovered the real truth had he only perused the pages of the *New Hampshire Gazette* issued anytime during the 1750s through the 1770s and seen the many notices for the sale of slaves individuals and the many advertisements for runaway slaves.

To sum up New England's involvement in the slave trade, historian Lorenzo Greene succinctly states, "There was no stigma attached to trading in Negroes before the Revolution, for the slave trade was as honorable a vocation as lumbering or fishing" (Greene, pg. 57). To give some further idea of the slave trade and the evolution of the institution of slavery in New England from early beginnings to abolition, below are thumbnail sketches for each state.

MASSACHUSETTS

This was the first colony in New England to import slaves from Africa, beginning sometime between 1624 and 1629, when merchant Samuel Maverick arrived in Boston with two black slaves in his household. Here he operated a farm that later grew substantially when he was granted 600 acres in 1640. In 1638 he imported cattle and seed corn from Virginia, as well as other slaves, undoubtedly to work his large land holdings.

The institution of slavery received a big boost during the Pequot War in 1637, fought between the colonists and local Native American tribes who began to push back against the European settlers. Joint military campaigns of Massachusetts and Connecticut militia forces against the Pequots resulted in many captured native warriors who were subsequently enslaved. Because these militant slaves, especially males, were too dangerous to keep, beginning in 1638 they were shipped to the West Indies, here exchanged for African slaves and other commodities. Thus the trade was set, and for most of the rest of the century Boston merchants controlled the New England slave trade.

Their first direct importation of slaves from West Africa to the West Indies (where they exchanged new slaves for those already trained) began in 1644, and by 1676 Boston had originated the slave trade with Madagascar. Prior to 1700 Massachusetts traders were supplying slaves to all the other New England colonies, with the greatest number being sold in Connecticut and Rhode Island. This trade would only increase in the 1700s as the New England economy grew, and with it the number of slaves in the colony increased exponentially. There were fewer than 600 slaves in 1708, but by 1715 the number had more than tripled to about 2,000. By 1764 the number of African Americans in the colony, many of them slaves, had increased to 5,235, totaling over 2 percent of the total population, and closer to 5 percent of the overall population in the seaport towns like Boston, where the enslaved were employed in a wide variety of maritime-related and other manufacturing trades.

Among those families that made their fortune in the slave trade were the Faneuils, Andrew and his nephew Peter. The profits they earned from being one of the colony's leading traders in African slaves would later build Boston's famed Faneuil Hall marketplace and meetinghouse. However, merchants were not the only ones involved in the slave trade. From earliest times many clergymen and government officials were prominent owners of the enslaved, including the Mather family (the Reverend Cotton and the Reverend Increase), Royal Governor Thomas Hutchinson and Judge Samuel Sewall (of the Salem witch trials fame), and leading Revolutionary War figures James Otis and John Hancock.

Interestingly, despite several Massachusetts court cases (to be discussed later on), the institution of slavery was never abolished by law in the state until the passage of the 13th Amendment to the U.S. Constitution in 1865. While it is traditionally believed, and reinforced in many town histories even to this day, that the enslaved were free after serving in the Revolutionary War, or that slavery ceased to exist by 1790, as no slaves were enumerated in the first federal census for Massachusetts, this is incorrect. While many masters did free their slaves so that they could serve in the war, some did not, and there was no law guaranteeing such freedom as a result of military service. Similarly, though no enslaved individuals are listed in the 1790 Census, there is anecdotal evidence which shows that slave owners were encouraged not to list their servants as such, as it would reflect poorly on them and the state, undoubtedly in contrast to the spirit of freedom and liberty the state had exhibited in the recent War of Independence. Further evidence of the continued existence of enslaved individuals in the state can be found as late as 1807, when Winthrop Sargent of Boston placed a front page ad in the *Columbian Centinel* for his runaway slave man named Sancho.

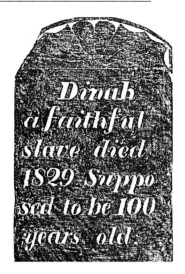

Gravestone rubbing, Dinah, 1829, Oxford, Massachusetts. This gravestone can still be seen today in Oxford's South Cemetery and is proof that the institution of slavery lasted in Massachusetts for over thirty years after its prohibition by the state's constitution (Gillon's *Early New England Gravestone Rubbings*).

CONNECTICUT

In the Nutmeg State, the institution of slavery grew much as it did in Massachusetts, but in time it would grow to make the colony the largest holder of slaves in all of New England. Enslaved individuals are first mentioned in Hartford as early as 1639, when Louis Berbice, a black slave from Dutch Guiana, was killed by his master at the early Dutch settlement there, and in the separate New Haven Colony five years later. As in Massachusetts, slavery became a fixture in Connecticut with the advent of the Pequot War and the treatment of Native Americans captured in the war who were subsequently transported to the West Indies in exchange for more tractable African slaves.

Connecticut merchants do not seem to have begun participating in the slave trade until the early years of the 18th century, and the trade grew slowly at first. By 1730 the state had a black population of about 700, totaling just under 2 percent of the overall population, but the numbers would increase drastically from the 1750s to the eve of the American Revolution. This increase was in keeping with the growing pace of the colony's economy. The maritime economy of coastal towns was booming, as was the agricultural economy in the eastern part of the state where some large plantations were located. Indeed, by 1774 African Americans, some free, many still enslaved, comprised 3.26 percent of the overall population, but were a much larger percentage of the populations of such important towns as Groton (9.4 percent), New London (8.87 percent), Fairfield (6.55 percent), and Stratford (6.37 percent) (Greene, pg. 345–346).

As in Massachusetts, but perhaps on a slightly larger scale, upper middle-class families, including lawyers, government officials, clergymen, and businessmen, were able to afford the purchase of a slave or two to help out on the farm or with business and household duties. By the American Revolution, one historian notes that half of all ministers in the colony and a third of all doctors were slave owners (Main, pg. 177). Among these ministers were some of Connecticut's leading lights, including John Davenport, a founder of New Haven. Many public institutions were also the beneficiaries of the slave trade in Connecticut, including Yale University, which has had to come to grips with its past in the last two decades. Its first professorship was endowed by Philip Livingston, one of the colony's largest slaveholders, while of its twelve residential colleges, eight are, or once were, named after those who owned slaves. Among these is Ezra Stiles College, named after a prominent minister, slave owner, and president of the university.

Because of the large number of slaves in Connecticut, the ideas of emancipation and freedom which came to the fore during the American Revolution were worrisome to slave owners. The legislature did pass a law in 1774 halting the importation of enslaved individuals, but in 1777, 1779, and 1780 rejected proposed emancipation bills. In 1784 a compromise was reached when a gradual emancipation bill was passed which stated that black and mulatto children born after March 1, 1784, would gain their freedom at the age of 25, which age was reduced to 21 in 1797. There were still 54 enslaved individuals listed in the 1840 federal census for the state, many of them aged, and it would not be until 1848 that Connecticut finally abolished slavery in full. By this time, however, it was too late for many of those still enslaved, not to mention the generations that had preceded them, as they were now too elderly to live on their own.

RHODE ISLAND

This colony, though the smallest in New England both in terms of population and land area, was the most heavily invested in the slave trade. By the early 1630s, slaves had been transported to the state by Massachusetts traders, and in 1652 the General Court even passed a law strictly limiting black servitude to ten years, but this seems to have been ignored, as was a statute passed in 1659 prohibiting the further importation of African slaves. Indeed, within less than a hundred years, Rhode Island would have the dubious distinction of being the leader in terms of the numbers of slaves held in the colony as a percentage of the entire population, as well as being the leader in importing slaves from Africa. The numbers for this state are quite startling: by 1749 the colony had 3,077 African Americans living there, the vast majority enslaved, comprising some 9.4 percent of its entire population (Greene, pg. 344). The ports of Newport and Bristol were the leaders in the slave trade, importing over a thousand slaves a year from Africa to America beginning in the 1720s and down to 1808, when the trade became illegal, on over a thousand ships.

Because of its heavy involvement in the slave trade, rum distilleries were a major factor in the Rhode Island economy, dotting the landscape around Bristol and Newport and producing thousands of gallons of spirits that were a major commodity in the triangular trade. Because Newport, many of whose citizens invested in slave trading voyages, was the center of the slave trade, the city's black population grew to be one of the densest in all New England and included men and women who performed both household and farming duties, but also those who worked in more skilled trades, many of them maritime related. It is estimated that by 1807 black sailors made up over 20 percent of the crews of ships sailing out of Newport.

However, while Newport may have been the center of the trade, another large group of slaves, surprising to many today, lived in the more rural areas and worked on the large plantations of a wealthy group of farmers known collectively as the Narragansett Planters. These large plantations in the southern Rhode Island towns located west of Narragansett Bay, including South Kingstown, North Kingstown, Westerly, Exeter, and Warwick, consisted of anywhere from 3,000 to more than 5,000 acres of excellent farmland. Here it was in a Southern-style economy that hundreds of slaves were put to work raising wheat and vegetable crops, tending to hundreds of head of sheep and cattle, as well as serving as household servants in large manor houses. The slaves who worked these plantations were supplied by Newport merchants, and they produced the agricultural and dairy products that were sold to Newport merchants, who then traded these foodstuffs in the West Indies as part of the triangular trade. Newport may have had the largest number of African Americans living and working within its boundaries, but in terms of overall percentages, some plantation towns were larger. In 1749 South Kingstown alone had 380 African Americans, most if not all of them enslaved, among a white population of just 1,405 whites.

As with other parts of New England, Rhode Island has had a difficult time confronting the past. Those in Newport have been sensitive about how its past involvement in the slave trade might affect the modern tourist trade, while in Providence, the state's capital, prestigious Brown University has had to directly confront its past. Originally named the College of Rhode Island and located in Warren, it moved to Providence in 1770, its funding and construction underwritten by the Brown family of that town and other slave holders. Slaves were even employed building the new college. The Brown family, including brothers Nicholas, Moses, John, and Joseph, were wealthy merchants who ran one of the largest slave trade businesses in all of New England. Though they were eventually split over the issue of slavery, they ran their operation from 1736, when they started the slave trade in Providence with their first voyage, until 1794, when state law banned the importation of slaves. The College of Rhode Island changed its name to Brown University in 1804 due to the family's largesse. In 2003 the university, under pressure to recognize its links to the institution of slavery in the past, published a report and instituted educational programs acknowledging its past history.

Though the town of Bristol is not as famous as Newport, it too was heavily involved in the slave trade, with the DeWolf family, beginning about 1769, being the major merchants. In fact, the DeWolf family imported some 11,000 slaves into Rhode Island during the many years they were involved in the trade, continuing the business for decades even after importation was outlawed in America in 1808. At his death in 1837, Captain James DeWolf, the prominent former U.S. senator for Rhode Island, was said to be the second richest man in America.

As for the abolition of slavery, Rhode Island's first serious, albeit limited, action came during the Revolutionary War. Desperate to raise soldiers for their Continental Army quota, the colony formed the 1st Rhode Island Regiment, which consisted of African Americans who were given their freedom in exchange for their military service. In 1784 the Rhode Island legislature, in a compromise between Quaker abolitionists and Newport merchants involved in the slave trade, passed a bill allowing for gradual emancipation only for those enslaved individuals born after March 1, 1784: girls would become free at the age of 18, while boys would have to serve their masters until the age of 21. This was as far as the state would go, however, and aging slaves were still held in the state into the 1840s.

NEW HAMPSHIRE

This colony, though independent, had many close ties with Massachusetts, so it is not surprising that, like elsewhere in colonial New England, the institution of slavery got its start in the Granite State with the help of Massachusetts slave traders. The earliest known account of African slaves in New Hampshire dates to 1645, when Captain William Smith from Massachusetts sold several African slaves to gentleman Francis Williams, a resident of "Piscataquak," modern-day Portsmouth and the Piscataqua River area, who had the year before been granted 1,000 acres of land in New Hampshire. Interestingly, one of these slaves was enslaved after a raid on an African village that resulted in the death of about 100 villagers. When the Massachusetts General Court learned of this incident, they had Captain Smith arrested and ordered Williams to return one of his slaves so that he could be returned to Africa (Greene, pg. 67). Despite their outrage at this incident, there is no record of any further actions by the General Court, and it seems likely that Williams kept his slaves.

From this violent beginning, the slave trade, and the number of enslaved individuals resident in the state, slowly expanded. By 1682 the wealthy and prominent Portsmouth merchant and ship-owner John Cutts was even carrying on correspondence with a Virginia merchant about supplying him slaves in return for tobacco (Samson and Cunningham, pg. 16). Whether vessels owned by Cutts made slave voyages direct from Africa is unknown. The idea of New Hampshire supplying Southern colonies with slave individuals seems unusual, but it makes perfect sense when it is understood that New Hampshire was one of the few colonies that had no tariffs imposed on imported slaves, and thus could supply them at a better price than colonies which did charge such tariffs.

How extensive the New Hampshire slave trade was is not fully documented, but many of Portsmouth's most famous mercantile families, including the Odiornes, Wentworths, Longs, and Pierces either owned ships involved in the slave trade or captained ships on slave voyages. William Whipple, a native of Kittery, Maine, and one of New Hampshire's signers of the Declaration of Independence, was actively involved in the slave trade as a ship's captain beginning in the 1750s and owned slaves right up to his death, after the Revolutionary War, in 1785. New Hampshire's other signer of the Declaration, Dr. Josiah Bartlett, was also a slave owner who was active for the patriot cause during the American Revolution. While he was away attending the Continental Congress in Philadelphia, his slave Peter was left home to run the Bartlett farm operations in Kingston.

The number of enslaved individuals in New Hampshire, because of its small size, was never very large, there being 674 held in bondage on the eve of the American Revolution. Most slaves were held in the coastal towns of Portsmouth and Exeter (the Revolutionary War capital) in Rockingham County, as well as smaller numbers in Strafford County in such towns as Dover, Somersworth, and Rochester. However, many slaves were scattered in small rural towns throughout New Hampshire, from Haverhill in the north to such southern-tier towns as Temple and Amherst.

As in other New England colonies, the upper-middle class and elites of society, clergymen, lawyers, and government officials were the usual owners of the enslaved. Clergymen especially were quite prominent in this regard, among the slave owners being the reverends Arthur Browne of Portsmouth, Jeremiah Fogg of Kensington, Timothy Walker of Penacook Plantation (modern day Concord), Josiah Stearns of Epping, and Jonathan Leavitt of Walpole, the later being dismissed from service for the way he treated his runaway slave. Private efforts toward emancipating New Hampshire's slaves began in the 1770s, including the sermons of the prominent minister Jeremiah Belknap of Dover, who preached about the incongruities of enslavement at the very time that the colonies were fighting for their own independence from Britain's tyrannical rule. As a result, some local slave owners manumitted some individuals. As also occurred in the other New England colonies, some slaves also gained their freedom as a result of their service in the army during the American Revolution. However, this was not mandated by law and occurred strictly at the slave owner's will and conscience.

Efforts by enslaved individuals to gain their own freedom were also initiated when a group of twenty enslaved African Americans in Portsmouth, including Prince Whipple (owned by Declaration signer William Whipple), petitioned the New Hampshire legislature on November 12, 1779, to abolish slavery in the colony. This measure was tabled without action by the government and went unanswered for 234 years until 2013, when Governor Maggie Hassan signed a symbolic bill that granted freedom to fourteen of the original petitioners who never gained their freedom.

In reality, though the institution of slavery eventually died out in New Hampshire, enslaved individuals were still listed in the federal census as late as 1840, and were possibly held even later than this. In 1841 the church at Mont Vernon voted to exclude slaveholders from the pulpit and Lord's table, while in 1843 the church in Boscawen passed a resolution declaring "that as a church we will not hold Christian fellowship with those, who for the sake of gain, continue to hold, buy or sell human beings as slaves" (Lawrence, pg. 354). These measures were almost certainly political in nature, but whether or not they also applied to any members of their congregation directly is unknown. Whatever the case, the formal abolition of slavery in New Hampshire would not come until 1865 with the passage of the 13th Amendment to the U.S. Constitution.

MAINE

This state has an interesting history when it comes to the institution of slavery, and is filled with contrasts. Because Maine was admitted to the union in 1820 as a free state as a result of the Missouri Compromise, while Missouri was admitted a year later as a "slave" state, many in the general public are under the impression that Maine never had enslaved peoples within its borders. However, before Maine became a state it had been a province of Massachusetts since 1652, and before that, from its first settlement in 1607, had several small, independent settlements. No doubt because of the influence of Massachusetts slave traders, enslaved individuals had been present in Maine, albeit in small numbers, since at least the 1670s, possibly even earlier.

In 1667 the early settler Humphrey Chadbourne and his wife Lucy had five servant men and women in their household, but it is possible that these were white indentured servants. But when Thomas Wills, the second husband of Lucy Chadbourne, died in 1688, a "Negro man" is listed in the inventory of the estate (York County Probate Records, Vol. 1, Folio 7).

However, the slave trade began even earlier in Maine, as in the southern New England colonies, when Native American slaves were taken by the Boston ship *Endevor* at Machias and Cape Sable in August 1676 (Noyes, Libby, and Davis, pg. 1). Another early example is found in the probate inventory for Nicholas Shapleigh of Eliot in 1682, which included five "Negroes," three men, one woman, and one child, valued together at 90 pounds. One of the enslaved men was likely "Coffe," a "Negro man" from Barbados, sold to Shapleigh by Edward Bushell of Boston in May 1676 (Suffolk County Deeds, vol. 9, pg. 336).

The numbers of enslaved individuals in Maine was never very high, probably under 400 at its peak. In 1764 there were 322 enslaved individuals in Maine (Thomas, pg. 26). Most lived in the southern part of the state in York and Cumberland Counties, though slaves were found in northerly coastal towns like Machias in small numbers. Among the leading towns holding the enslaved were Falmouth (modern-day Portland), Kittery, York, and Berwick.

As elsewhere in New England, almost all were owned by citizens of standing, including wealthy merchants and clergymen. When the Rev. Samuel Moody was called to preach in the settlement of Agamenticus (modern day York) in 1733, the parish voted to supply him a slave to labor in his household, which they did in 1736, purchasing an enslaved female African American named Phyllis. After the American Revolution, the largest number of slaves and free African Americans were largely concentrated around Portland, where they were employed in the maritime and other related trades. Though the institution of slavery may have almost vanished by the time statehood was gained in 1820, Phebe Ann Jacobs remained the slave of William Allen, the president of Bowdoin College, and his wife Maria Wheelock Allen until gaining her freedom in 1828.

Even after this time, Mainers still had a large connection to the slave trade; Maine ships and the captains and sailors who manned them were still heavily involved in the trade right up to the time of the Civil War. While a federal bill passed in 1807 prohibited the importation of slaves, enforcement of this law was sporadic. The slave trade was made even more dangerous with the passage of the 1820 Piracy Act, which declared that any captain caught trafficking in slaves was committing piracy and thereby subject to the death penalty. Only one captain was ever subject to this harsh penalty, Captain Nathaniel Gordon of Portland, Maine. His ship *Erie* was captured by the USS *Mohican* off the Congo River, West Africa, in August 1860 loaded with nearly 900 slaves. Gordon was tried and convicted for his crimes in trafficking in slaves in late 1861 and was subsequently executed by hanging at New York in February 1862.

VERMONT

The Green Mountain State is the state in New England with the fewest ties to the institution of slavery, though slaves were held here, as everywhere else in the region. The area of Vermont was largely a frontier area and was but sparsely settled until the 1740s. From that time until 1777, when the territorial government declared its independence, the land that comprised the future state was claimed by the colonies of New Hampshire and New York. New Hampshire's Royal Governor Benning Wentworth began making land grants in 1749 in the area between the Connecticut River west to Lake Champlain and New York territory. The New York colony responded by making land grants of their own. The New Hampshire Grants, as the region came to be called, were made on the traditional town model and resulted in the founding of over 100 towns, including Bennington, Brattleboro, St. Albans, and Woodstock. In contrast, the New York grants were made to wealthy, absentee land owners and were towns that merely existed on paper. While disputes among land grantees and the two colonies would continue, the area declared its independence in 1777 and thereby became known as Vermont. The state was entirely independent and operated as such until it was admitted to the union as our 14th state in 1791.

Vermont was the first state in the nation to abolish slavery, which was done so in its original state constitution drafted in July of 1777 and reiterated in its 1791 constitution. However, as in several of the New England colonies, this abolition was not without its conditions: enslaved girls in the state would gain their freedom at the age of eighteen, while males would have to serve until the age of twenty-one.

When the first enslaved African Americans were brought to Vermont is uncertain, possibly as early as the 1740s, but certainly by the 1760s as more settlers began to settle in the land grant towns. Just how many slaves came to live in Vermont prior to the Revolution is unknown, but the numbers were low, probably fewer than a hundred individuals. The number of enslaved individuals who lived in Vermont after the American Revolution is also unclear. The 1790 federal census numbers for Vermont are somewhat disputed. Contemporary news accounts states that there were 36 free African Americans in Bennington County and no enslaved individuals anywhere in the state, but the official census report published by the U.S. government in 1870 originally showed 16 enslaved individuals in Bennington County. This report was subsequently changed by the chief clerk of the Census

Bureau, Vermont native George Harrington (Slavenorth.com). While this discrepancy gives the historian pause for consideration, it is known for certain that enslaved individuals were purchased from outside its state borders and were transported to the supposed free state of Vermont, in direct violation of its original constitution abolishing slavery. It is also known that slaves were held in the state at least into the early 1800s, as will be discussed later on.

Captive Life in New England

The life of the enslaved was many-faceted, complex and seemingly contradictory. For the newly arrived slave in New England, it was surely bewildering, and in the case of those arriving direct from Africa, it was a continuation of the terrifying experience that began when they were captured on their native continent. Those who were transported directly to America from Africa—men like Prince and Cuffe Whipple in Portsmouth, New Hampshire, and Occramer Marycoo (aka Newport Gardner) of Newport, Rhode Island—surely felt some measure of instant relief after stepping foot, bound though they were, on dry land after having spent several months aboard a cramped and dirty slaving vessel. However, this was but a fleeting moment of relief, as the true reality of their situation, that of being a slave far from home, a stranger in a strange land, further set in. For those slaves who were transported from the West Indies, the voyage to New England, was a continuation of the experiences they had already undergone.

Besides the humiliation of being sold on the auction block like so many cattle, several other aspects also loomed large in their new "home." In order that we may better understand how African American slaves were treated after their decease, it is here quite appropriate to give a brief account of the lives they led in New England.

CLIMATE AND LANGUAGE

The first and most obvious of the conditions facing slaves on arrival was the climate of New England, vastly different from that of tropical Africa and the West Indies. Those slaves arriving in the summer months would have a brief respite before cold weather set in, while those who arrived at any other time of the year had a harsh reality to deal with from the start. When Jack, the slave of merchant Benjamin Deland, died in Salem, Massachusetts, in September 1807, the Rev. William Bentley stated that though Jack was only 64 at his death, having been brought to the town from Africa at the age of eleven in 1754, he looked about 90, claiming that "negroes in our climate soon take the appearance of age" (Bentley, vol. 3, pg. 320).

The second factor was that of language and communication. Those slaves arriving from the West Indies, already "broken-in" as was the common practice, had by this time learned some English to varying degrees and at the very least could usually communicate in some form of "pidgin" English. However, for those slaves arriving direct from Africa, it was like landing on another world altogether. In order to survive, they had to quickly learn the English language in some form. Thus it was that forced acculturation to their new lives began, learning the language and ways of the white New Englander. For those slaves sold to masters living in the larger towns, this difficult adjustment was somewhat eased by the many other slaves, and later on free blacks, from whom they could gain some help in understanding the English language and the expectations of life in captivity. There was also the added benefit of being able, perhaps, to communicate in their native tongue. Though there were many different dialects from the area of West Africa where most of the enslaved were captured, there was often enough some similarity so that slaves from differing locales could understand each other.

However, for those slaves who were purchased by masters living in small towns where few or no other slaves were held or, worse yet, those slaves taken to isolated New England frontier towns, their adjustment and circumstances were surely both terrifying and lonely. Such slaves were forced to learn the English language *and* their duties and expectations as they went along on their own. Their masters may have had some patience during this learning process, but there can be little doubt that many of these newly enslaved individuals were "whipped into shape." For these slaves, their isolated situation was probably relieved only sporadically, perhaps, when they accompanied their master and mistress on their periodic journeys to larger towns for business or social purposes, where they might gain some contact with a larger population of slaves.

NAMING PRACTICES

While the enslaved were physically controlled by their master, this control was also psychological in nature right from the start. The New England gentry who held slaves had no interest in learning the true names of those they held. That these names were too hard to understand and pronounce was one consideration, but the biggest factor was that these enslaved people were considered savages from a dark continent, and thus the first step toward civilizing them once transported was that of changing their names to ones that were generally more classical in nature (and thus more civilized) and easy to understand. Thus it was that Broteer Furro became Venture Smith, while Occramer Marycoo became Newport Gardner. Those enslaved were now forced to use their master's surname and a new given name as well. Many of the given names for the enslaved came from the Greek and Roman classical period, including Plato, Hercules, Scipio, Cato, Corydon, Caesar, Pompey, and Prince. Others were geographical in nature, like Boston, Cambridge, Hampshire, Newport, Bristol, and London, indicating where these men were usually bought or sold. Still other names, like

Gravestone, Fisherman Cahoone, 1760, Common Burying Ground, Newport, Rhode Island. This name is likely indicative of the work in which he was employed in by his master in this seaport town.

Venture and Fortune, were indicative of their owner's financial status or hopes. For enslaved women, the trend was toward Biblical names, often from the Old Testament, like Dinah, Lydia, and Chloe, though classical or mythological names such as Phyllis, Phoebe, and Venus were also common. In addition, many owners went with such simple and classic English given names as William (often shortened to "Will" and, perhaps to distinguish him from a white member of the master's family, "Black Will"), John, Tom, Peg, and Mary. Finally, there were other names that were conferred on the enslaved that are more unusual in nature. One such example is Song Haskell, the slave of the widow Haskell in Bristol, Rhode Island; he was so named because of his fine singing voice.

Though the enslaved were forced to accept these English names, those who came from Africa sometimes kept hold of their original names, remembered and cherished them, both as a way to hold onto their past identity and in subtle defiance of their owners. For those later generations of slaves born in New England to parents who were originally transported from Africa, native naming practices survived to a great extent. One example of such an African tradition that survived was the practice of naming children for the day of the week on which they were born. Thus, for those boys born on a Sunday we see the name Quashee (often shortened to Quash), for Monday Cudjo, for Tuesday Cubbenah (often shortened to Cubbe), for Wednesday Quaco, for Thursday Yarrow, for Friday Kofi (usually spelled as "Cuffee" or shortened to "Cuff"), for Saturday Quamin. African girls, too, were given names based on the day of the week on which they were born, but these do not seem to have been commonly retained in New England. One such survival is found in Bristol, Rhode Island, for Adjua DeWolf, a favored slave owned for many years by one of the largest slave-trading families in America. Her given name comes from the Akan people in Ghana for girls born on a Monday.

In some cases, those who were enslaved and took the names forced upon them by their masters, sometimes reverted to their African name upon gaining their freedom, one notable example being that of Arthur Flagg (1733–1810) of Newport, who upon gaining his freedom changed his name to Arthur Tikey, the last being his African name. By using these names African slaves found yet another way to retain their culture and identity in an otherwise white world.

Gravestone, Solomon Nuba Tikey, 1785, Common Burying Ground, Newport, Rhode Island. The middle and last names of this young boy are indicative of attempts on the part of his parents, Arthur ("Author") and Rose Tikey, to maintain their African roots. All were owned by the Flagg family.

SHELTER, CLOTHING AND SUSTENANCE

The brand of slavery that was practiced in New England was vastly different from that of the American South and the West Indies. Under Puritan influence, the New England colonies practiced a patriarchal form of slavery that was based on an old Hebrew model dating back to biblical times. This was entirely in keeping with the prevailing religious ideals in early New England and thus provided white masters with a moral justification for their actions. In this system, the slave, though enslaved for life, was a part of the family structure. Occupying the lowest rung in the family order, the slave was expected to work long and hard, but in return he was given the clothing, food, and shelter that was the due to all family members.

As to housing, most slaves lived in the same houses as their owner, usually quartered upstairs in a small attic or garret room that was cold in the winter and hot in the summer, but also sometimes in the cellar. In some cases the enslaved slept on the floor in the same room as the master and his family. Only the very wealthy families had separate buildings, usually directly behind or adjacent to the main house, where their slaves were quartered. This was likely most common housing arrangement in southern Rhode Island on the plantations of the Narragansett Planters, but was also practiced in larger towns like Boston, Portsmouth, and Newport.

There is only one type of structure like this known to have housed slaves remaining in all of New England today. It is a two-story wood and brick structure that lies just behind the main house of Isaac Royall, and it housed as many as sixty slaves during the forty years that the Royalls owned this 504-acre farm-estate overlooking the Mystic River in Medford, Massachusetts. Today it is historical site, open to the public.

One other site in Plymouth, Massachusetts, a small shed located at the back of the house of merchant and slave holder Colonel George Watson, located on North Street, may also have been used for housing slaves. The site has been the subject of archaeological investigation, and while the evidence is intriguing, it has not yet been conclusively determined that the structure was used to house slaves.

Slaves in general seem to have been well clothed in New England, as is evidenced by the many runaway slave advertisements in regional newspapers, when Seneca Hall departed from his master Samuel Hall in Portsmouth in 1776, he had with him over a dozen articles of clothing, including two pairs of leather breeches, two coats, a red and a blue one, as well as a blue pea jacket, and a fur cap (Knoblock, pg. 10). There is nothing in the ad stating that these items were stolen. Likewise, when Sancho Baxter ran away from his master in Yarmouth, Massachusetts, in 1763, he had with him a cloth colored jacket and a flannel jacket, a checked flannel shirt, breeches, and a beaver hat (Landi, pg. 40).

However, many runaway advertisements do mention old, patched, or worn clothing, suggesting that many slaves may have worn discarded clothing from their masters. In a day and age in New England where clothes were passed down from generation to generation, such worn clothing was common. But, the many descriptions of frostbite among runaway slaves reveal that clothing, and especially protective footwear, was often inadequate.

RUN-AWAY the beginning of last Month, from Merrimack, a Negro Man named Exeter, from his Master *Samuel Wentworth*, — a lusty strong Fellow about 30 Years of Age, a Cooper by Trade—Had on when he went away a Pair of Trowsers, Frock and Shirt—He was born in the Country. Whoever takes up said Negro, so that his Master may have him again, shall be well Rewarded.

Runaway slave advertisement, Merrimack, New Hampshire. Notice that the figure in the ad is clothed in what appears to be native African dress (*New Hampshire Gazette*, August 12, 1768).

It should also be here mentioned that in their clothing style, African slaves also retained some semblance of their native identity, and therefore offered yet another form of subtle defiance to their masters. Though black slaves usually emulated their master and mistress's form of dress (and really had no other choice) and even hair styles, they also enjoyed wearing brightly colored coats, shirts, breeches, and dresses, often combining these outfits in a way that brought ridicule from their masters. In African culture these bright color combinations were the norm and thus allowed the slaves to retain some semblance of the culture taken away from them.

In regards to feeding and nutrition, anecdotal evidence from white sources once again suggests that the enslaved were fed adequately, and in many cases dined at the same table and consumed the same food as the master and his family. However, as there is little direct evidence of this, historians must be careful about the conclusions that they make; what little archaeological evidence we do have, especially that gained from the examinations made of the remains discovered at the New York African Burial Ground in Manhattan, paints an entirely different picture. Many of those interred in New York (and there is no reason to believe New England was greatly different) suffered from the effects of poor diet and malnutrition, with diets largely consisting of corn-based foods that probably did not offer the needed calories for the amount of energy they were expending. Fresh meat was not unknown, but rare, while fresh fruit could only be consumed for a short time during the year. Dairy products in some areas of New England were available in abundance, but because Africans have a genetic characteristic that makes these foods difficult to consume, they were probably not a viable option for all slaves. Further, the essential nutrient Vitamin D may also have been lacking because, in addition to dairy products, it is also gained through the absorption of the sun's rays on the skin. For African slaves, their dark skin combined with New England's northern climate may have limited the production of this vital element (*The New York African Burial Ground*, pgs. 70–72). All of these dietary factors, combined with a heavy workload, meant that New England slaves, even if they did eat at the family table, were probably not as well nourished as traditional historical accounts lead us to believe.

WORK AND TRADES

The work of the enslaved in New England comprised a wide variety of tasks, much larger in scope than the brand of slavery practiced elsewhere in America. Slaves in the South were largely employed in agricultural pursuits, producing such commodities as indigo, rice, tobacco, cotton, and sugar cane. However, in New England it was a different story. Male slaves were employed in a surprisingly wide variety of occupations. As in the South, they were employed in agricultural production, animal husbandry, and other related tasks, including clearing the land and lumbering, fence building and barn and house construction. Slaves were also heavily involved in the maritime trade, serving in ropewalks and in iron foundries where anchors were made, as well as serving aboard ships as cabin boys and skilled sailors. On land, African American slaves also served in a variety of skilled trades, including tailors, cordwainers, tanners, blacksmiths, silversmiths, coopers, portrait painters, silversmiths, masons, printers and, at least in one instance, as a gravestone carver. In fact, there were probably but few skilled trades in which slaves were *not* employed. Because of the versatile trades in which they were employed, slaves in some towns were even prohibited by law from certain trades, so as not to take work away from white tradesmen. This prohibition is ironic indeed when we consider that these trades were not chosen by the enslaved, but rather taught to them by their white masters.

As far as household duties are concerned, male slaves also served their masters (often in addition to more physically demanding duties or trades) as coachmen, butlers, and cooks. Female slaves were also employed in a wide variety of tasks, including cheese-making, churning butter and making soap, spinning and weaving, as well as servant duties indoors that involved cooking and housecleaning, not to mention helping to take care of infants and children.

In most cases, no matter how they were employed, African slaves were in close contact with their masters for most of their lives. They not only slept in the same house and had a close proximity at mealtimes, but often worked side by side with their masters in performance of their duties. Those who learned a skilled trade often did so at the hands of their masters and usually worked under his guidance at their workshop, while farm owners and their slaves usually worked outdoors close at hand to one another. Inside the house, it was the same, with slaves working under the close supervision of their master or mistress. Though the work performed by slaves in New England was often performed alongside that of the master, this does not mean it was any less difficult. Not only did slaves usually work longer than their masters, they also suffered many injuries.

The many runaway slave advertisements listed in the region's newspapers in the 1700s are a clear indication of the hardships that they suffered. A sampling of these include Job Samson of Plymouth, Massachusetts, who ran away in 1764 and had a weak left hand and wrist, probably from his blacksmithing duties. Cuff Congdon of South Kingstown, Rhode Island, was advertised in 1769 as having a large scar on one foot and a stooped posture, probably from his work as a farmhand. Jack Lester of Newport, Rhode Island, in 1773 had a large scar on his neck that was made by a scythe, while Cesar (alias Hanover) Wady of Dartmouth, Massachusetts, in 1774 had a scar on one of his big toes that had once been split by an axe. Yet another man, Sam McClister of Enfield, Connecticut, in 1770 had a frost-bitten toe. These are but a few examples of the wear and tear that New England slaves suffered during the course of their servitude.

Education

The slave experience in this area, which was almost always intertwined with religion, varied widely depending on the master and his status, the work to be performed by the slave, and also whether the slave lived in a large town or in a more rural area. Those slaves held in rural areas who were employed in agricultural work, and in such workmanlike trades as basket makers, blacksmiths, farriers, and the like, tended to be less educated and often could not read or write, as is evidenced by the many men who signed their name with a simple x when enlisting to serve as soldiers in the American Revolution. In the larger towns, where specialized trades and shopkeeping duties were more the norm, slaves were often taught to read and write as part of the normal tasks they performed.

It was also in the large towns, where more slaves were held, that formal education programs were first proposed. The idea of educating and, perhaps even more important to the Puritan mind, catechizing African slaves began in New England as early as 1674, when the Rev. John Elliot of Roxbury, who gained fame for his missionary work with Native Americans, proposed the idea of a local school for the enslaved, but died before it could be established. His successor in this regard was the Rev. Cotton Mather of Boston, who not only wanted to teach slaves and Native Americans to read scripture, but also wanted to keep "wicked books" (Greene, pg. 237) out of their hands. In 1717 he established his school, and others later followed in the Boston area. Later on, ministers in particular were the leaders in teaching both their own slaves, and those in the towns in which they were settled, how to read scripture and write, including the Reverend McSparran in Narrangansett, Rhode Island, and the Rev. Samuel Johnson in Stratford, Connecticut.

However, it was not just the clergy who taught their slaves how to read and write; many wealthy merchants also did so for a variety of reasons. Phyllis Wheatley, later to be a famed poet, was purchased by merchant John Wheatley as a companion to his wife. Others educated their trusted slaves so that they could help manage their businesses in a more efficient manner and even conduct business on their own behalf. Among such slaves so taught and respected was Prince Whipple of Portsmouth, New Hampshire, who not only conducted financial transactions on behalf of his master but also served as a sort of aide-de-camp to General Whipple during the American Revolution.

Of course, many slaves were taught to read and write primarily for Christianizing purposes, and some slave women (and men) became devout Christians. The best known of these individuals was the previously mentioned Phyllis Wheatley, brought to Boston directly from Africa in 1761 and purchased by merchant John Wheatley. Phyllis was subsequently taught to read and write and soon showed her intelligence to the world. This frail young girl began to write poetry and had published her own volume of poems in 1773, she was even taken to England to meet a number of noble families.

Phyllis was preceded as a poet by Lucy Terry, the slave of Ebenezer Wells of Deerfield, Massachusetts. Lucy was first brought to Bristol, Rhode Island, as a slave at about the age of four, and was here sold to Wells. Subsequently taught to read and write in the early 1740s, when she was baptized as a Christian during the Great Awakening, she composed a poem entitled "Bars Fight" in 1746 that remains today the best contemporary account of a massacre of settlers in the town by Native Americans and makes her the first known African American poet in America.

Though this poem was only preserved by oral tradition and not published until 1855, Lucy Terry's sharp mind is well documented. After gaining her freedom in 1756 when she was purchased by, and subsequently wed to, a black man named Abijah Prince, Lucy Terry Prince and her family moved to Guilford, Vermont, and purchased land which later became the subject of legal difficulties with rival white claimants. The case eventually made its way to the Supreme Court of Vermont, where Lucy argued and won her case against some of the state's top lawyers.

Lucy Terry and Phyllis Wheatley were not just exceptions to the perceived norm. Indeed, many slaves became highly literate and used their keen intellects not only to try to better their own situation, but also to help others in their community. Outstanding examples of this are the several freedom petitions composed by African American slaves during the Revolutionary War. In January 1777 in Boston, "A Great Number of Negroes who are detained in the State of slavery" (Kaplan and Kaplan, pg. 26), including Prince Hall, a free man, Newport Sumner, Jack Pierpont, and others, petitioned for an end to the institution of slavery. In the spring of 1779, African Americans in Stratford and Fairfield, Connecticut, including two men known only as Prime and Prince, petitioned the General Assembly in Hartford asking "whether it is consistent with the present claims of the united States, to hold so many Thousand ... in perpetual Slavery" (*ibid.*, pg. 27). On November 12, 1779, a group of 20 enslaved African Americans in Portsmouth, New Hampshire, including Nero Brewster, Prince Whipple, and Pharaoh Shores, also petitioned the state legislature to end slavery, only to have their finely crafted petition tabled with seemingly little thought and no action.

Phillis Wheatley portrait, 1773. This portrait is thought to have been painted by Scipio Morehead, a slave artist of Boston and appeared in Wheatley's book *Poems on Various Subjects, Religious and Moral* (London, 1773) (courtesy National Portrait Gallery, Washington, D.C.).

RELIGION

While it is commonly thought that most slaves were baptized and thereby had accepted the Christian faith, many African American historians, including Lorenzo Greene and William Pierson, have shown that, in actuality, few of these slaves became confessed converts. There are a number of reasons for this, including those based on the masters' views and those from the viewpoint of the slaves themselves. For the slave holders, from the beginning there was much theological debate among ministers and colonial leaders about the baptism of African slaves: Were such slaves indeed human beings or mere beasts, and were they even worthy of conversion?

However, the most important factors involved practical and social matters. There were some fears that the religious conversion of slaves might make these slaves feel more like their masters' equals (especially in the eyes of God), and thus less willing to work as slaves. Perhaps a greater concern for the practical New Englander was the time and labor that would be spent in Christianizing slaves, taking them away from the primary tasks for which they were acquired in the first place. In addition, once converted and baptized as church members, they would no longer be permitted to work on the Sabbath, as was the norm for all churchgoing white members of society, thus further reducing the amount of work to be gained from the slaves.

From the viewpoint of enslaved individuals, the form of worship that prevailed in New England from earliest time down to the 19th century had nothing to offer African American slaves. For those slaves who were born in Africa and had a remembrance of their homeland, the white man's brand of religion was not only strange, but largely devoid of the joy, emotion, and musical celebration that were vital elements in African worship. The New England Sabbath day sermons, on the contrary, were of several unappealing types, some ministers' orations were so dogmatic and dry, and thus so boring, that white and black attendees alike often struggled to stay awake. Other ministers offered the hellfire-and-brimstone type sermons that were designed, literally, to put the fear of God into the congregation, making them fraught with worry about the destination of their souls and offering but little chance for redemption. These elements alone seldom appealed to African slaves, but since religion was also used to justify the holding of slaves, the result was a religion that held but little appeal to African American slaves.

Further adding to this lack of attraction is the fact that when African Americans did attend church services, they were almost always either forced to stand or were seated on benches within segregated areas of the meetinghouse, usually at the end of the building farthest away from the minister (the most affluent members of New England congregations had pews that were closest to the minister's pulpit), and usually in a balcony or loft area near the rafters if the building was large enough. In the meetinghouse in Torrington, Connecticut, the African American section was even boarded up so completely, much like livestock in a pen, that its occupants could not be seen by other (i.e., white) churchgoers (Steiner, pg. 20).

The genuine conversion of African slaves to Christian worship did increase during the Great Awakening of the late 1730s and 1740s, when the dour brand of New England worship was challenged and reformed, with the addition of music to sermons preached by the more animated and joyful "New Light" ministers. Some of these conversions to Christianity by African American slaves were undoubtedly sincere and heartfelt, including that of Lemuel Haynes, born in West Hartford, Connecticut, in 1753, who was brought to Granville, Massachusetts, afterward as an infant. Though he worked hard for his master, Deacon David Rose, by day, at nights he received an education and became an avid Bible reader, and was converted after witnessing the Aurora Borealis one evening. Haynes subsequently began composing his own religious sermons and as a young man even served occasionally as the town's minister before gaining his freedom in 1771. After serving in the Revolutionary War, Haynes later received private instruction and in 1785 was ordained as the first black minister in the Congregation church.

While Lemuel Haynes's conversion was unique in its ultimate outcome, New England church records are filled with the names of African American slaves who were baptized and married by local clergymen. In Middletown, Connecticut, an enslaved couple, Harry and Hagar, as well as their children, Jane, Hagar, and Gift, were all baptized on September 1, 1734, while the piety of Phebe Ann Jacobs of Brunswick, Maine, is also well documented. In Newport, Rhode Island, a number of African Americans were noted for their church standing and piety with inscriptions on their gravestones, including Belinda Miller (died 1807), an "esteemed" and "worthy member" of the Second Baptist Church; Toney Taylor (died 1799), also a "worthy member" of the same church; and Primas Deblois (died 1775), who "died in the faith."

Despite these examples, while many African American slaves may have attended church services, probably less than five percent were baptized as true church members. As one historian commented about black church membership in New England, as "Christians in good standing ... nowhere was the record impressive" (Piersen, pgs. 49–50). Many African American slaves did attend church, either because they were forced to, especially those slaves held by clergymen, or because such attendance may have provided some measure of relief from the physical labor normally required of them.

While there can be no doubt that many of the religious conversions were genuine, white Christian ideals about being "saved" did not always line up with the African-American mindset. When Caesar Webber, the slave of Thomas Webber of Hopkinton, New Hampshire, joined the Congregational Church about 1790, he was asked by his minister after his conversion how his renewed life

Gravestone, Primas Deblois, 1775, Common Burying Ground, Newport, Rhode Island. The fact that Deblois "died in the Faith" is a good indicator of his conversion to Christianity.

appeared in comparison with his past career in sin. "Well," said Caesar, "I never was very bad, and I will leave it to Deacon Kimball to say if I was" (Lord, pg. 272). It may be, too, that the conversions of some African Americans, not unlike the actions of many agnostic whites, were gained under dire circumstances, perhaps as a way to hedge one's bet, so to speak, rather than as a full acceptance of Christianity. When Vance Coit, a free black of Newport, New Hampshire, in the late 18th century, was offered by his neighbor a pound of sugar in exchange for helping him with his hay harvesting on the Sabbath, Coit responded by declaring, "Do you think I would have my soul fry in hell to all eternity for a pound of sugar? No! Give me two pounds and I will risk it" (Wheeler, pgs. 252–53).

Whether or not this story is true is unknown, but the church records of Middletown, Connecticut, provide a true and tragic example of a deathbed conversion. Rose, a free black in that town, was married to Salem (likely enslaved) on December 7, 1789, on the same day that Salem also was baptized and died, he being buried the following day. We may imagine that Rose and Salem were married at their minister's urging so that their unborn child would not be considered a bastard. The tragic events were repeated six months later, on June 16, 1790, when Rose (aged 29) was baptized at home, and died that same day after giving birth to two sons, one of whom was stillborn, and the other dying soon thereafter. Despite their baptisms and acceptance of Christianity, the remains of Salem, Rose, and their two children (who were likely buried in Rose's arms) lie in unmarked graves at an unknown location somewhere in Middletown.

PUNISHMENT

Because of the patriarchal nature of New England slavery in general and the close contact slaves had with their masters, it has often been characterized as being much more humane than the slavery practices of the South and the West Indies. Overall, in a narrow sense this is a true characterization; however, the collective New England mindset, aided by many generations of historians, has viewed New England slavery since its demise as a benevolent and helpful institution, really not a true brand of slavery at all in comparison to the American South. This we now know, and the evidence was there all along in plain view, to be a false portrayal. Going beyond the simple idea of depriving an individual of his personal freedom by force, there are the darker aspects of the institution of slavery in New England that are often overlooked.

Harsh punishments were the norm in Colonial New England for anyone, black, white, or Native American, who committed a crime. Punishments ranged from the humiliating and tedious (time in the public stocks, the scarlet letter, or sitting on the gallows with a rope around one's neck), to the painful (public floggings and branding), to outright death (by fire or by the noose). However, discipline was also meted out quite liberally when a slave did not perform his duties or did not recognize his "proper" place in the family hierarchy by master and mistress alike. It is, perhaps, all the more shocking when we realize that those doling out such cruel punishments were members of the genteel class of New England society, greatly in contrast with that traditional image of the cruel, uneducated plantation overseer of the South.

Indeed, in New England it was just the opposite, it being the judge, the wealthy merchant, even the town minister who was administering these punishments. Judge Asa Porter of Haverhill, New Hampshire, flogged his own enslaved girl, who was so terrified that she attempted to jump into the nearby Connecticut River. The Rev. James McSparran of Narragansett, Rhode Island, whipped his enslaved woman Maroca, and was helped by his wife in administering the same punishment to their enslaved man Hannibal (Greene, pg. 232). Though there are few records that document these types of punishments, they were almost certainly the norm.

Once again, runaway slave advertisements that appeared in the *Newport Mercury* also are suggestive of the end results of such harsh treatment. Dick Miller of Warren, Rhode Island, is described as having a facial scar when he left his master in 1758; Robert Hunter of Newport had a burn scar on his cheek in 1761; Jack Sole of Tiverton, Rhode Island, a forehead scar in 1765; Caesar Sweet of Newport, Rhode Island, a scar on his cheek in 1767; Bristo Wilcox of Middletown, Connecticut, a runaway in 1769, had one finger on each hand cut off; Peter Hale of Newbury, Massachusetts, a large scar on the back of his neck in 1771; Quash Weeden of Newport, Rhode Island, a very large scar over his left eye in 1771; Cesar Hazeltine of Mendon, Massachusetts, a large scar near his left eye in 1773; Dick Paine of New Shoreham, Rhode Island, large scars upon both legs in 1774; Prince Miller of Newport, Rhode Island, a large scar on one side of his neck in 1774; 19-year-old Francis Denny in 1793 is described as having a blemish in one eye and a scar across his chin; and Biram Browning, a runaway from Hopkinton, Rhode Island, in 1797, is described as having scars on his left cheek and forehead. While it is not certain that these injuries were all inflicted by their New England masters (some possibly resulted from treatment received at the hands of their captors or prior treatment in the West Indies), it can be reasonably speculated based on available anecdotal evidence that some of these scars *did* result from such cruelty practiced in New England, and were probably a factor in the decision of these captors to flee from their masters.

Harsher punishment was not unknown, even though a 1686 law enacted by Sir Edmund Andros, the governor of the Dominion of New England, declared that the "willful killing of Indians and Negroes be punished with death" and imposed a "fitt penalty for the maiming of them" (Greene, pg. 233). However, no white person is known to ever have been successfully prosecuted under this act. In 1695 Nathaniel Keene, a carpenter in Kittery, Maine, beat to death his enslaved woman Rachel (her burial site is unknown) without punishment. In Sandwich, Massachusetts, in 1719, Samuel Smith beat to death his enslaved man Futin and was brought to trial but was found not guilty, though he fully admitted the act, as his slave had died in his sleep afterward (Greene, pgs. 234–235).

While masters were more likely to beat their slaves to death, mistresses were also perpetrators of such crimes. Sarah Bradstreet of Newbury, Massachusetts, killed her female slave in December 1714, and while the deed was "much talked of" (Sewall, Vol. 3, pg. 32) in town, Mrs. Bradstreet does not appear to have been prosecuted. New Hampshire was probably the only colony that enacted its own law that prohibited masters from cruelly punishing or killing their slaves, but here again, there is no known incidence of the prosecution of an offending master. However, this is not to say that there were no social repercussions on such behavior; when the Rev. Jonathan Leavitt of Walpole, New Hampshire, was witnessed dragging his runaway slave woman back to his home at the end of a rope tied to his horse's saddle in 1764, this inflamed the town's sensitivities and provided a cause for his dismissal after having served just three years. Interestingly, several of Leavitt's grandsons would later become ardent abolitionists, operating stops on the Underground Railroad in Massachusetts.

Legal Rights

Like so many other aspects of the institution of slavery in New England, the status of African American slaves before the law was rather contradictory. On one hand, the enslaved could be, and often were, held for life and were thus legally considered as property, listed and valued in estate proceedings the same as farm animals and household contents. When a master died, his slaves were either willed to another family member; if a master died without heirs, a slave was often sold at auction. Some slaves were even given a verbal promise of freedom by their master after his decease, only to find that the master's heirs had other ideas, resulting in continued captivity. The enslaved could also be seized from their master and sold (often meaning they were taken away from their wife and children in the process), just like any valuable goods, to satisfy a debt.

In contrast to this, the enslaved also had a number of legal rights. Slaves could own personal property, including land, and could enter into contractual business agreements.

Slaves could also serve as witnesses in court proceedings, offering valid testimony regarding people of color and whites alike in both civil (including probate and business matters) and criminal cases, unlike in New York and colonies in the South, where by law no slave could testify against a white person. Additionally, the enslaved could bring suit against their masters for abusive or unfair treatment, and even to gain their freedom on legal grounds. Such cases are rare prior to the American Revolution, when a heavy conscience and the plain hypocrisy of colonists fighting for freedom against British tyranny while still holding slaves began to turn the tide.

Significant examples of this change of heart include the *Quock Walker versus Nathaniel Jennison* case and that of *Bett and Brom versus John Ashley*, both of which played out in Massachusetts courtrooms in 1781. In the former case, an enslaved African American named Quock Walker, who had been promised that he would gain his freedom prior to the American Revolution, ran away from his master Nathaniel Jennison in Barre, and upon being returned was severely beaten. Walker subsequently sued his master for assault and not only was awarded 50 pounds in damages, but was also given his freedom after his lawyer argued that Quock Walker had previously been promised his freedom. Jennison later appealed Walker's award of freedom but lost, and was himself, in 1783, charged by the state attorney general and found guilty of assaulting Walker and was fined yet again.

In the other case, Mum Bett and Brom were the slaves of John Ashley, a lawyer in Sheffield, having been brought there from New York in the 1760s. After the Revolution began, Mum Bett heard recited the first article of the Massachusetts Constitution, which stated the ideal that all men are born free and equal, and the following day, realizing the implications of this statement, consulted a young attorney. This attorney accepted her case, as well as that of all the Ashleys' slaves, and the case was subsequently heard at the County Court in Great Barrington in August 1781. Mum Bett and the others indeed won their case, and not only won their freedom, but were also awarded damages as compensation for their past labor. Mum Bett, who subsequently took the name Elizabeth Freeman, thus became the first African American woman to gain her freedom under the Massachusetts Constitution. While it is commonly and erroneously thought that the Walker and Mum Bett cases effectively ended slavery in Massachusetts (slaves were held in the state even after 1800), they were very important precedents in that slave owner's claims could no longer be effectively argued or upheld in a court of law in Massachusetts.

However, not every enslaved individual in the state could sue for his individual freedom, and court cases like these were rather the exception than the rule. Slaves who committed serious crimes were also entitled to a trial by jury and, depending on the evidence against them, might be found guilty or innocent. Records of convictions for African American slaves can be easily found, and the penalties for those convicted of serious crimes usually were a lengthy prison term, death, or a forced sale out of the colony, usually to the West Indies. Because of the tropical environment and the harsh work that the slaves there were subject to, being sent to the West Indies for most slaves was likely just a delayed death sentence.

Examples of these convictions include eighty-seven-year-old Prince Mortimer of Middletown, Connecticut, who was convicted of trying to poison his master in 1811 and was sentenced to a life term at the infamous Newgate Prison. In a similar crime, three slaves of John Codman of Charlestown, Massachusetts, Mark, Phyllis, and Phoebe, were convicted of killing their master by poisoning him with arsenic. Mark and Phyllis were executed in front of a large crowd on September 8, 1755, the former by hanging, the latter burnt at the stake, while Phoebe was deported to the West Indies. Mark Codman's body was afterwards hanged in irons at a prominent spot on Charlestown Neck to serve as a grim reminder to other like-minded slaves and remained in place, according to local lore, even up to the time of the American Revolution.

On the other hand, instances of slaves being found not guilty of serious crimes, or having their convictions overturned, are much more rare, but are not unknown. In 1757, Bristo, the slave of the Rev. George Beckwith in Lyme, Connecticut, was accused of rape by a white woman, Hannah Beebe. Bristo was subsequently tried, convicted, and sentenced to death, the standard penalty for this crime. However, before Bristo could be executed, the "conscience-stricken" victim confessed to a justice that the testimony against the slave was false, and it soon came out that the accusations against Bristo were all part of a plot by her parents to extort money from the Reverend Beckwith (Greene, pg. 166). Bristo's sentence was subsequently suspended (not overturned altogether) after an appeal to the governor, and Bristo was set free, though it seems that his white accuser was not punished for her misdeeds. In the end, it must be remembered that though slaves had some rights according to New England law, the vast majority had no way of exercising those rights that mattered to them most: to be free of masters who abused them physically, the freedom to remain with their families (forced separation, usually by sale, was often a motivator in capital offenses), as well as the very right to be free.

MILITARY SERVICE

New Englanders today can take much pride in the fact that the region, albeit because of practical necessity and not generally by design, had liberal ideas when it came to military service. This was in direct contrast to the South, where it was against the law for African American slaves to bear arms in any circumstances. To be sure, the New England colonies also passed these laws early on; in 1656 Massachusetts barred blacks, Indians, and any servant from military service due to their fears of an armed uprising. Likewise, in 1660 Connecticut also passed a similar law, and in 1693 Massachusetts went a step further, likely for economic reasons rather than fearful ones, by excluding slaves (as well as ministers and schoolmasters) from taking part in any militia training exercises. In 1719, New Hampshire also passed its law barring African American slaves from state militia service (along with "lunatics" and "idiots").

While such laws were on the books, they were almost always ignored in times of need, and from the 1690s onward many black slaves, in small numbers at first, served in local and state militia units on land, as well as at sea aboard privateers and state and later Continental Navy vessels. In 1710 a slave named William served during Queen Anne's War in the New Hampshire regiment commanded by Col. Shadrach Walton at Port Royal, Canada, while in 1716 Nero, the slave of the Reverend Swift of Framingham, Massachusetts, served as a trumpeter in the company of Captain Isaac Clark. Though the numbers were at first small in these minor conflicts, they grew in size beginning with King George's War (1742–48), increasing further in the French and Indian War (1756–63), and reached their peak during the American Revolution (1775–83). During the former war, John Gloster, the slave of Theodore Atkinson of Portsmouth, New Hampshire, saw real action when his gun was "Shot to pieces with a Cannon ball" during the Siege of Louisburg in 1745, while during the French and Indian War, Solomon Sipio served as a ranger in the New Hampshire company of Capt. Joseph Wait in 1761 (Knoblock, pg. 313–314).

In most cases, African American slaves were paid the same as white soldiers, though it was sometimes the case that these wages went to a slave's master and, in the case of the Revolutionary War, the bounty money paid to a newly enlisted slave sometimes went to his master in exchange for his freedom. During the American Revolution, many African Americans, both slave and free, served in the Continental Army and state militia regiments, with Rhode Island leading the way with its all-black 1st Rhode Island Regiment, formed from slaves who were granted their freedom upon enlistment with the consent of, and compensation to, their masters.

This and other New England units that employed black troops, especially in Connecticut and Massachusetts, were often the cause of some hand-wringing at home, for both practical and political reasons, as well as among some regimental commanders and generals who worried about their capabilities as fighting men, but their enemies recognized them early on as "able-bodied" troops and "strong and brave fellows" (Aptheker, pg. 34). Before the end of the war, even General George Washington, a wealthy plantation owner who had slaves of his own, was convinced of the effectiveness of black troops among his New England regiments. Indicative of this change of heart from 1776 is the fact that, at the end of the war, Washington personally signed discharge papers for his soldiers, white and black alike, honoring them with the Badge of Merit for their years of faithful service, including three men from New Hampshire, Cato Fisk (Epping), London Dailey (Exeter), and Caesar Wallace (Rye).

As to their duties, African American soldiers, whether slave or free, served in a variety of roles, the same as white soldiers did, including duties as drummers, fifers, rangers, artillerymen, and hospital workers. They were in the thick of every major engagement fought in the northern campaign in such places as Fort Ticonderoga, the Battle of Bunker Hill, the Battle of

Gravestone, Jeremiah Crocker, 1836, Center Cemetery, Henniker, New Hampshire. Crocker served several terms of service during the war and at the time of his death was celebrated both for his service and his advanced age.

White Plains, and the Battle of Trenton. African Americans also fought in the southern campaigns, but in much smaller numbers and usually in the hit and run, guerrilla warfare type units. African American troops, indeed, were present in the American Revolution from the very beginning to the very end, from Lexington and Concord to Cornwallis's surrender after the Battle of Yorktown. Though not assured of their own freedom (some remained as slaves even after their military service), these black soldiers not only helped to gain America's independence, but did so without problems or incident and with a lower rate of desertion than that of white soldiers. Many of these African American veterans would later be honored at their deaths and eulogized for their service as a well-respected "soldier of the Revolution."

SOCIAL LIFE

While the lives of the enslaved in New England were strictly controlled by their masters and regulated by the many laws that were passed, African American slaves in many areas were able to develop their own society where they could exercise at least a small measure of independence. Once again, the circumstances depended on where the slave was held. For those slaves held in extreme rural areas or frontier towns, typically in the New England interior away from coastal areas or major rivers, the life of a slave could be a lonely one with little chance for socializing with fellow slaves. In these areas, it was typically the case that a slave was held by the town minister, judge, or another prominent individual. If he or she were the only such slave held, this could mean a life of isolation and loneliness, though if well-treated it was often the case that their master and mistress, and perhaps even their children, were their greatest friends and a warm bond developed. If there were multiple slaves in the household, or slaves held by multiple families in these small communities, then we can be sure that these slaves found time to meet and gain some measure of comfort from each other's company.

One example of such a situation was that of Thomas, Flova, Nero, and Jack, who were owned by Moses Gill in rural Princeton, Massachusetts. Flova and Jack were previously enslaved by Nicholas Boylston of Boston, a relative of Mrs. Rebecca Boylston Gill, and willed to her upon his decease in 1771. Brought to their new country home, as the only slaves in the area, they at least were able to face their newly isolated situation together with the help of Thomas, an older "Negro man" who was probably already serving the Gill household. Indeed, just as they subsequently served together day by day in life, so too were they laid to rest beside one another at the Meeting House burial ground in Princeton after they died.

The best chance for socialization for many slaves likely came on the Sabbath day, when all prominent town members, along with their slaves, would gather together in the local meetinghouse (or a large barn or the minister's house if there was no meetinghouse). The segregated seating situation for African American slaves offered a chance for quiet socialization, while in between the day-long services, meals were prepared and whites and blacks alike could socialize before returning home in the evening. In some of the larger towns like Boston, not all African Americans attended church on the Sabbath, and instead socialized about town. Laws were eventually passed regulating the movement of the enslaved while their masters were attending church.

Another factor in socializing, in both large towns and rural areas, was the practice of masters hiring out their slaves to those who needed extra labor. This was done on a short-term basis, perhaps during harvest time or for a specific task in which heavy labor was required, but also on a long-term basis, perhaps during planting season or to make a sailing voyage. Whatever the case, while the master was the primary beneficiary by being paid for the labor of his slave, the enslaved sometimes benefited with the opportunity that they might come into close contact with other slaves and develop a social bond. However, those masters who constantly hired out their slaves also ran the risk of their running away, sometimes because of their too frequent change in living and working arrangements and the resulting inability to develop a lasting social bond.

The most intimate of all social experiences, that of marriage, was also frequently experienced by the enslaved, albeit with many complications that those who are free never had to contend with. Slaves could marry one another, but only with the consent of their master, or masters if the two parties were enslaved in separate households. In yet other cases, free black males courted enslaved women and even purchased them and gave them their freedom in order that they could be wed. One well-known example of this involved Amos Fortune of Woburn, Massachusetts; he was manumitted by his master in 1770 and in 1778 purchased the freedom of his first wife, Lydia Somerset. However, she died after only a few months. Later, in November 1779, Amos Fortune purchased the freedom of his second wife Vilot. They are buried side by side in the Old Burial Ground behind the meeting house in Jaffrey, New Hampshire, where they had moved to start a new life in 1781.

While interracial marriages were against the law, these too were not unknown, especially in areas where few African Americans lived, and usually involved enslaved men and white females. One interesting example of such a marriage took place in Machias, Maine, between London Atus and Eunice Foss, a member of one of the town's founding families, Local tradition states that Eunice had worked as a maid for the Rev. James Lyons, London's master, and that through close daily contact the two fell in love. Their first child, Betsy, was born out of wedlock in 1789, and a second child, Louisa, was born in February 1791. The very next month, Eunice Foss was hauled into court and found "Guilty of the Sin of Fornication by having a bastard" (LiBrizzi, pg. 28) and was fined six shillings. Soon afterwards, London Atus and Eunice Foss were married and would have ten more children together. Their family would serve as the basis for Atusville, a small black community within the town of Machias that would last until after the Civil War.

In many cases, just as with marriages among whites, intentions to marry, so called wedding banns, were also published, and most New England ministers, as was the tradition, both performed and carefully recorded these marriages, just as they did those of their white parishioners.

Though marriage was allowed among slaves, in keeping with the strict ideals of Puritan morality, the workings of a marriage could be problematic to African Americans and their masters alike. The time allowed for a courtship was likely brief as slaves had but a limited time for such activity in their "off-duty" hours. Once officially married, those couples who had different masters and lived apart from one another often, quite literally, had to steal moments when they could be alone together, and the arrangements among all parties could be difficult. For those married slaves who belonged to the same master, the logistics of married life were greatly eased and daily contact could be enjoyed, though usually only after their long day of laboring had come to an end. As for masters, their primary concern was in making sure that their investment continued to pay off, so their slaves' work production always held priority over any social arrangement, and these arrangements could be changed at any time, without notice or any recourse to the enslaved. An owner, albeit a

Gravestone, Domine Dyre/Bull, 1740, Common Burying Ground, Newport, Rhode Island. This young boy, aged four at the time of his death, had parents who were owned by two different masters.

cruel one he would be, could sell his slave man or woman to out of town parties, or to those in another colony altogether, resulting in a forced separation between man and wife. As we have also seen, the death or indebtedness of a master could also result in a slave's sale and resulting forced separation from the one that he loved.

For those wedded slaves who had children, this added another layer of difficulty: masters could and often did sell the children of enslaved couples (not wanting to pay for their care) with sorrowful results. Even when they didn't, there was always the concern among masters as to who would financially support the enslaved mother and her children. One Maine historian, commenting on the practice of selling off enslaved children away from their mothers, states that this was "the real cruel part of Maine slavery," but also makes the strange comment that, when the daughter of an enslaved woman, Phyllis Hobbs of Wells, was sold, "The mother was unusually fond of her child and a great deal of heartache ensued" (Thomas, pg. 27).

As to the practice regarding married names, enslaved women who had a different master from that of their husbands usually still retained their old names, while children usually took the surname of their father. Thus, we see some seemingly confusing name combinations on some of the gravestones in the God's Little Acre section of the Common Burying Ground in Newport, Rhode Island. One stone marks the grave of one-year-old Caesar Tillinghast (died 1763), the son of Sharper Tillinghast and Violet Sisson, while another pair of stones may be found side by side for Mark Wanton (died 1769) and Flora Coggeshall (died 1766), the wife of Mark. In this case, Mark was formerly a slave to the Tillinghast family, but he was later sold to the Wanton family and had his name changed yet again. Of course, many among the enslaved had relations outside the framework of traditional marriage and, like whites who practiced the same "sins," male slaves could be punished under the law for "fornication," while females slaves who bore children out of wedlock could be punished for having "bastard" children. While some historians believe that common-law marriages among slaves were commonly recognized by their masters, the evidence regarding this is lacking.

In addition to marriage and the opportunities for social activity in conjunction with religious observances and various aspects of the work they performed, African American slaves also had varied opportunities to participate in community activities, albeit within an already restrained framework. In rural areas, harvest celebrations, church and barn raisings, maple sugaring season, and a whole host of similar activities offered a chance for some diversion among slaves. Likewise, just as with whites, many African American slaves in their off-duty time enjoyed such activities as hunting, fishing, wrestling, horseback riding, and storytelling. This latter activity was important in that it provided a vehicle for African Americans to pass on stories and traditions from Africa to later generations that were born enslaved in America. Games, music, and dancing were also important to African Americans and were surely performed clandestinely as a way of keeping their culture alive. Not surprisingly, in Puritan New England such leisure pursuits as card-playing and gambling, as well as most dancing, music, and theatre or plays, were banned to all members of society, though they were indulgences that were nonetheless often enjoyed. However, by 1740 the old-time Puritan culture was fading, and slowly more leisure pursuits were becoming acceptable, one of the most argued being the introduction of music in the traditional church services.

In both rural areas and the larger towns where a greater number of slaves were held, such as Hartford, Newport, Boston, and Portsmouth, Training Day (also known as Muster Day), Election Day, and Lecture Day were important events that offered an opportunity for merrymaking among the enslaved, and at the very least a reduced workload. Training Day was an annual celebration, at first a serious one, later almost purely ceremonial, where males of age mustered together on the town common or parade ground to perform militia drills in order to provide some semblance of training in case they should be called out to defend hearth and home (early on, from attacks by Native Americans). These drills were witnessed by the town's residents, many dressed in their finest outfits. While African Americans, slave and free, were prohibited by law from taking part in militia training, many did so anyway, including Prince Walker of Woburn, Massachusetts, who wore a red coat and rode in the mounted troop for many years. After the training exercises were over, there was often a great feast, and, of course, much rum, ale, or hard cider consumed by the men.

Similarly, on Election Day, held at various times throughout New England when a new governor was inaugurated, the enslaved were often given the day off and permitted to go to town, where they could eat, drink, and be merry with one another, often on the town common. As will be discussed shortly, this was also a time when enslaved African Americans in some of the largest towns elected their own governors and officials to hold and exercise power, albeit in limited fashion, among their own people.

Lecture Day, in contrast, was a sober reminder to the populace of the Puritan ideals, almost a day of shame. On this day, usually a Thursday, no work was performed except by the local sheriff, whose job it was to administer punishments to those who had committed minor transgressions. These punishments (meted out to white and black alike) might include a flogging, temporary confinement in a cage or in the town stocks, or being chained to a post, and took place on the town common, at the meetinghouse, or in front of the local prison, all witnessed by the local populace. A long sermon, similar to that offered on the

Sabbath, was also given by the local minister, all meant to serve as a "lecture," so to speak, on the dangers of bucking society's laws and etiquette. It was also on this day that wedding banns were often posted, and in some locales elections were also held.

In addition to these traditional holidays, many states and towns had specific events or a periodic fast day or a day of thanksgiving to commemorate specific events that offered a chance to socialize. On days when a public execution was held, these grisly events were well-attended by local citizens. On a more positive note, in coastal towns the launching of a large or celebrated ship was also a day of celebration for shipyard workers and townsfolk alike that offered a pleasant diversion from everyday life.

Despite the many festivities that offered temporary relief, not all of these New England holidays could be attended by the enslaved. In Boston, an important event was Artillery Election Day, when the Ancient and Honorable Artillery Company of that town elected its officers and held a formal parade. One historian has commented about this event that "no black face dared to be seen" on that day, while on Gunpowder Day in Boston in 1765, no blacks were allowed to enter the town common (Greene, pg. 248).

Indeed, while in comparison to the Southern brand of slavery, the enslaved in New England seemed to have a great amount of freedom, there were actually many laws enacted to curtail their movements and activities. In Massachusetts, a law was passed in 1693 which prohibited all citizens from buying any goods from the enslaved if there was any suspicion (reasonable or otherwise) that they might be stolen. One of the most common type of laws were those restricting the movements of the enslaved. Most colonies had laws against their being out in public after 9 p.m., unless they had a pass, nor could they be on the streets during the Sabbath day services. The penalty for violating the curfew law was usually a severe whipping.

Other laws were also passed regulating the public activities of blacks and other enslaved peoples, including serving them drinks in public taverns and inns, disturbing the peace, carrying on "pageants and other shews" in the streets, setting bonfires, and bothering the public with "horrid profanity, impiety, and gross immoralities" (Greene, pg. 134). In Rhode Island, it became a crime after 1703 for the owner of a house to allow a gathering of black or Indian slaves in their home after 9 p.m. without the permission of each of their masters. In 1750 this law was made even harsher when owners were prohibited from permitting the enslaved to not only gather, but also to dance, gamble, "or any other diversion whatever" (Greene, pg. 136), which violations were punishable by both a fine and time in jail for the owner.

Most laws like these, especially in the largest slaveholding colonies, were enacted as a means of preventing slaves from gathering to-

ALL MASTERS or Owners of any *Indian, Negro,* or *Molatto* Servants or Slaves, are hereby Notified, that the JUSTICES of the Peace within the Town of Portsmouth, are determined to cause to be strictly executed the LAW of this Province, entitled, An ACT to prevent DISORDERS in the NIGHT; therefore whoever shall think it necessary to send out any NEGRO, INDIAN, or MOLAT-TO Servant or Slave after Nine o'Clock at Night, will do well to give such Servant or Slave a Ticket, whereby he may escape the Punishment inflicted by the LAW abovesaid.

Servants and slaves notice advertisement, 1764. Slave movements were strictly controlled by laws in all the colonies, especially during the nighttime hours (*New Hampshire Gazette*, November 2, 1764).

gether and formulating plans for an uprising against their masters. The most severe laws were enacted on the local level in those areas where the number of enslaved peoples held was considerable. In South Kingstown, Rhode Island, in 1718 it became illegal for an enslaved black to visit the home of a free black, and in 1726 laws were further passed there making it illegal for slaves to hold any outdoor gatherings. Thus it can be seen, that even when African American slaves did have the chance to socialize, they always had to be on guard so as not to offend white sensibilities, and in some cases had to take great risks to even be with their families and fellow slaves of color.

BLACK GOVERNMENT

One of the most intriguing aspects of African American society in New England and its development within the confines of the institution of slavery was the development of a separate government and power structure that was largely modeled after that of their white masters. As was mentioned above, on Election Day it was common in some towns beginning as early as 1740 for enslaved African Americans to gather together to elect their own leader and governing officials. In some colonies these leaders were referred to as "king" (Massachusetts and New Hampshire), while in others (Connecticut and Rhode Island) they were called "Governor." Connecticut, where nine towns are documented as having followed this tradition, was the most active in this regard. Here, the tradition seems to have begun in Hartford by 1755, and continued for 100 years or so. In Rhode Island, the towns of Newport, South Kingstown, and Warwick are towns noted to have had black governors, but this tradition did not seem to have been widespread until after the American Revolution.

The tradition, from what meager accounts have been thus far found, of electing a black government started in Massachusetts with the election of King Pompey in Lynn in the 1740s, and perhaps may have begun even earlier in Boston, though the names of any elected black leaders there have been lost to history. Two other towns in that colony, Salem and North Bridgewater, are also known to have elected kings. In New Hampshire, only one town, Portsmouth, is documented as having a black government, and though the tradition lasted for many years, only one king is known to us by name. It is highly likely that New Hampshire's other large slave-holding town, Exeter, also had an elected black government, but no evidence of this has yet been found. However, despite an overall lack of documentation in New England, it is certainly likely that some power structure, even if one more loosely organized, had probably been formed among enslaved African Americans in some of the larger towns well before the 1740s.

Indeed, we only know about these black governments because of their mention in several sources, including 19th century town histories and a few 18th century diary entries, all written by whites. Perhaps the most interesting source, however, are those few still extant gravestones, such as that for Boston Trowtrow of Norwich, Connecticut, that mention their title as governor. For many years, white historians assumed that these elected black kings and governors were merely a case of the enslaved mimicking their masters, and these black officials were thus often ridiculed by earlier generations, if they were mentioned at all. However, a careful study of these black governments and their leaders by modern historians has exploded these earlier myths, and clearly demonstrates their serious intent and purpose. The election of black kings and governors clearly grew out of not just the Election Day festivities, but also out of those informal festivities celebrated by black slaves to honor those of royalty among them, including such men as Pompey Woodward of Lynn, Massachusetts, and, perhaps, Prince and Cuffee Whipple of Portsmouth, New Hampshire, all of whom had been the sons of royalty in Africa before they were enslaved. From these celebrations of honor and respect among their own people, combined with the traditional Election Day holiday festivities, the tradition of electing a black government grew into reality.

Just as in white society, though under much greater time and freedom of movement restraints, black candidates campaigned for office with a lively spirit, often accompanied by music and boisterous voices that frequently annoyed white members of society. Several qualities stand out about these kings and governors, the first being their physical size and strength and overall imposing countenance. The second characteristic, especially important after the American Revolution, was their standing as a result of their achievements. Guy Watson of Kingstown, Rhode Island, was noted in 1790 for his prior service in the American Revolution as a member of the all-black 1st Rhode Island Regiment, while Peleg Knott in Hartford, Connecticut, was well respected in 1780 for supervising his master's large farm (Piersen, pg. 131).

However, it was not just their own character and achievements that brought them to prominence, but also the status and standing of their white masters. In fact, many of those elected as the head of their government were enslaved by the town's wealthiest merchants and other elites, and it was their financial support that allowed them to campaign and supply their supporters with food and drink. Indeed, white masters took some measure of pride in these black elections, because of the status afforded them by having their own slaves elected as king or governor. Once in power, black leaders received no pay for serving and sometimes appointed other officials to serve under them. In Portsmouth, New Hampshire, Willie Clarkson served as King Nero Brewster's "viceroy," while Jock Odiorne served as sheriff, with Pharaoh Shores serving as his deputy (Brewster, vol. 1, pgs. 212–13).

Though the functions of the black governments in most locales are but little documented, it is known that some, if not all of them, performed some judicial duties as well. In places like Portsmouth, Newport, and Hartford black governors and kings held public trials for fellow African Americans in the community accused of minor crimes where the evidence was presented and, if the accused was found guilty, corporal punishment (usually a whipping) was meted out. In this way, African Americans served to police their own communities without white involvement.

LIFE EXPECTANCY

The institution of slavery, no matter where it was practiced in America, was always about getting the most work out of the enslaved that could be had for as long as possible. Thus it was that enslaved African Americans seldom had a long life and often died at a young age. A trip to the Common Burying Ground in Newport, Rhode Island, New England's largest and best preserved colonial African American burial site, easily bears this out. Here may be seen the gravestones for Peg, "a Negro Servt" to Henry Bull, who died in 1740 at the age of six, and Adam, the "servant" of Elizabeth Miller, who died in 1792 at the age of 12. These youthful death dates are far from uncommon, as this burial ground contains 48 surviving gravestones for enslaved African American children under the age of seven. Few of the enslaved lived to a ripe old age as many white New Englanders did, and the average age at death, based on the extant gravestone data available from Newport, was about 33 years of age. This was probably about average for all of New England's slaves, as this above-ground evidence is corroborated by the study of the remains of African Americans excavated at the site of Portsmouth's African Burial Ground (12 in number). This is the only such site that has been archaeologically studied in all of New England, and the results show an average age at death of about 36 years, with ages ranging from as young as seven to a maximum of 50 (Sorg and Crist, pg. 12). While many of the enslaved died of the same diseases and common maladies that affected whites, their weakened state due to overwork and less than ideal nutrition often was a contributing factor to their early death.

A rough life filled with hard work, often accompanied by harsh treatment, was bad enough in and of itself, but there could be an even worse fate for those enslaved who were "lucky" enough to survive and live a longer life. Frugal Yankee masters were not averse to the practice of cutting loose their aged slaves by giving them their freedom when they became too old, infirm, and unable to work productively anymore. In other words, in the accounting books of the master, an asset had become a liability. This was a cold, dollars-and-cents approach that is a little-known aspect of the slavery in New England.

To be sure, government officials were aware of this practice and did pass laws to help prevent the practice, but not necessarily for the direct benefit of the enslaved. Connecticut was the first colony to pass a law of this nature, doing so in 1702 when it made the master legally responsible for any African American who became indigent after being manumitted, later, in 1711, the colony amended this law to provide means for recovering the cost of care provided to those indigents who had previously been freed by their masters. In 1703, Massachusetts passed a similar, but more detailed, law which required masters to post a 50 pound bond prior to manumitting an enslaved individual, and that no slave so freed without such a bond posted would be considered free. In addition, should the freed slave become a public charge, his former master was to be responsible for his care. Rhode Island, not surprisingly, passed a similar law in 1729, though here a posted 100-pound bond was required.

Gravestone, Peg Bull, 1740, Common Burying Ground, Newport, Rhode Island. As this stone demonstrates, it was quite common for young slave children to serve their masters.

These laws are quite interesting in that, in theory, on one hand they ensured that a master would continue to care for an enslaved individual who was sick, infirm, or elderly, but the requirement of a bond was also an added financial deterrent to manumitting a slave. As far as enforcement of this law goes, some masters were sued by local authorities to recover such expenses, but African Americans were usually caught in the middle of these disputes; their overall welfare was not the prime concern of the towns involved. In fact, many of the formerly enslaved freed in these situations remained public charges right to the end of their lives, and they often died a poor and lonely death.

It is interesting to note that disputes among white parties regarding the care of aged slaves who had been recently freed became somewhat more problematic after 1800, by which time the institution of slavery found no support in any New England courtroom. In Massachusetts in 1808 there was the case involving the towns of Winchendon and Hatfield, one suing the other over who was responsible for the care of former slave and Revolutionary War soldier Eden London, who had lived in both towns in an impoverished state. The court ruled that neither town was responsible for London's support, as slavery had been abolished in the state's constitution in 1780. While this case really marked the death knell for the institution of slavery in Massachusetts once and for all, the question of who would care for London would seem to have fallen to Winchendon by default, as London died in that town in March 1810 and there was buried, though his grave remained unmarked for over a hundred years.

While many of these disputes over who would support impoverished African Americans involved neighboring towns, the case of Cuff Chambers (formerly Blanchard) is an interesting and long-distance one. Cuff had served as a soldier in the American Revolution, as did so many others like him who later became poor, from Andover, Massachusetts. After the war, he and his family moved from Massachusetts north to Amherst, New Hampshire, and from there to Leeds, Maine, by 1808. While there the Chambers family needed town support, which they received for three years beginning in 1814. Part of this money was reimbursed to Leeds by the town of Andover after the former town made application and Andover town officials verified that Cuff Chambers and Cuff Blanchard were indeed the same man. Cuff Chambers died several years later in 1818 and is buried in a secluded spot in the Dead River Cemetery in Leeds.

It is in an earlier case, however, where it is clearly shown that a Vermont master skirted his moral obligations with the help of the courts. In July 1783, Jotham White of Charlestown, New

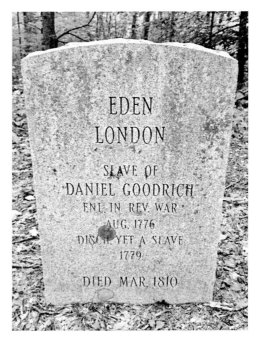

Gravestone, Eden London, 1810, Old Center Cemetery, Winchendon, Massachusetts. Eden was a soldier of the Revolution, but in old age the charges for his care became the subject of a court case between two Massachusetts towns. This stone was placed in modern times.

Hampshire, sold his "Negro Woman Slave, named Dinah, about thirty years of age" (Wardner, pg. 80) for forty pounds to lawyer Stephen Jacob of Windsor, Vermont, just across the Connecticut River. Jacob was a prominent man in the state, serving as town representative and a number of other government posts, and subsequently appointed as the first district attorney for the state of Vermont by George Washington. This was a man who, "being a lawyer by profession, of course knew well what the State Constitution had to say on the subject of slavery" (Wardner, pg. 81). In 1801 the selectmen of Windsor, in their role as overseers of the poor, sued Judge Stephen Jacob, chief judge of the county court, to recover the costs incurred in supporting the aged Dinah, whom Jacob had released in 1800 after she had become sick and blind. Judge Jacob not only fought the lawsuit, but sat as the presiding judge on his own case, hearing evidence with two other assistant judges, and with no jury empanelled. Not surprisingly, the case was dismissed on technical grounds by the court and Jacobs was reimbursed for his legal expenses.

The case was appealed to the Vermont Supreme Court and a jury was formed. The one key piece of evidence was the bill of sale from 1783 which proved that Dinah was enslaved and the property of Judge Jacobs. Jacob's defense attorney argued that this bill was inadmissible, claiming it to be "incompetent and void because, under the Constitution, no person could be held as a slave in Vermont" (Wardner, pg. 85). Despite this baseless argument, this piece of evidence was indeed denied admittance for the very reason argued, and thereby the case was dismissed as there was no proof of Jacob's ownership of Dinah. Thus it is that, though well hidden, the institution of slavery did cast its shadow even over the free state of Vermont.

As for Dinah, her living situation at an advanced age, by now "blind, paralytic, and incapable of labour" (*ibid.*) was not changed one iota, court case or not. Instead of living in comfort with her master in the only home she had known for the previous seventeen years, Dinah remained a public charge, living either at the town almshouse, or possibly farmed out to the lowest bidder, until her death in March 1809. Her final resting place is unmarked.

II. The Free Black Experience in New England

From the late 1600s going forward there were a number of free blacks living throughout New England, though the exact number of this population is unknown. When they were counted during various local and state censuses taken before the first federal census in 1790, they were always included with the numbers of those enslaved, and often with the Native American population as well.

One of the first free blacks in New England was John Wham of the New Haven Colony. He and his wife were freed by their master in 1646 (Greene, pg. 290). Since there were various laws in the beginning, especially in Massachusetts and Rhode Island, that limited servitude to a set number of years, some of those enslaved in the late 1600s were set free after reaching the limit of their servitude, thus creating a small free black population. Many others who were enslaved were manumitted by their masters after serving an agreed-upon number of years, while yet other masters manumitted their slaves for their faithful service or for reasons of conscience, including the Rev. Ezra Stiles of Rhode Island, who liberated his slave Newport in 1718.

In the early 1770s, as the tensions between the New England colonies and Great Britain quickly grew, and words such as "freedom," "independence" and "tyranny" gained a new meaning, many slaves were emancipated for obvious moral reasons. Still other slaves gained their freedom based on provisions in their masters' wills that provided for such after their death. In the latter half of the 18th century many enslaved men, like Amos Fortune of Jaffrey, New Hampshire, purchased their own freedom and that of their future wives by the money they had earned working in their so-called off hours. One man, John Quamino of Newport, Rhode Island, was able to purchase his freedom in 1773 with his lottery winnings (Youngken, pg. 50). Finally, as has been previously discussed, there were those aged and infirm slaves who, despite laws to the contrary, were "given" their freedom and were forced by their frugal masters out into the world all alone and dependent on others in the community for their support.

After 1800, other African Americans from the South, some free, many runaway slaves, also made their way to New England. Many found temporary haven in the Underground Railroad network of safe houses during their voyage to their ultimate destination of freedom in Canada, while others, such as William Grimes of Litchfield and James L. Smith of Norwich (both in Connecticut), stayed in New England. It was from all these groups of individuals that free African American communities both large and small developed throughout New England. Some lasted for a short time, maybe a generation or two, before their residents either died out or moved elsewhere, whether it was north to Canada or to seek a new life in western America. Others, in such places as Norwich, Connecticut, and Portsmouth, New Hampshire, have survived to this day.

Earning a Living

No matter whether an African American was born free or had somehow broken the chains of bondage, life was still difficult in New England well into the 19th century. Unlike white indentured servants, who could gain full societal status after their servitude had ended, African Americans (along with the smaller numbers of Native Americans) always occupied the lowest rung in a white dominated society. With rare exceptions, this continued to be the case for those subsequent generations of African Americans who were born free in New England; one historian notes that economic gains for African Americans remained stagnant, "tending to keep negroes in the same types of occupations which they had in colonial times" (Warner, pg. xii). Because of this, opportunities to gain wealth, and thereby a comfortable living, were often hard to come by.

African American men worked at a wide variety of skilled jobs, including tanner (Amos Fortune), carpenter (Jeffrey Hemmenway), cooper (Barzilai Lew), cordwainer (Prince Hall), rope-maker (Arthur Tikey Flagg), music teacher (Newport Gardner), baker (Pomp Spring), contractor/builder (William Lanson), and even as a veterinarian doctor (George Blanchard). However, most men made a living performing more common work as simple laborers, domestics, and hired farmhands, or "a precarious livelihood" (Washburn, pg. 267) with less steady work like basket weaving and chair-caning (Peter Salem).

With the coming of the Industrial Revolution and the rise of New England textile mills beginning in the 1820s, there might have been a promise of new and better jobs for African Americans, but these never materialized due to the large influx of German, Irish, and French-Canadian immigrants who would hold such jobs. In fact, "Negroes participated least in the new and most significant mode of production, factory manufacture" (Warner, pg. v), and their continued occupation on the lowest rung of the economic ladder led many African Americans out of New England to seek greater opportunities.

For African American women, their occupational opportunities were even more limited. Chloe Spear of Boston, along with her husband Cesar, ran a boarding house for laborers and seamen. Dutchess Quamino of Newport, Rhode Island, and Margaret Dailey of Exeter, New Hampshire, were noted for their baking skills, while Dinah and Rebecca Whipple of Portsmouth, New Hampshire, the widow of Revolutionary War soldier Prince Whipple and wife of his brother Cuffe Whipple, respectively, established the Ladies Charitable African School. These notable exceptions aside, the majority of women found employment as either laborers or domestic servants and, just like their male counterparts, often performed the same backbreaking work that they had done when they were enslaved, with low-paying wages to match.

Just how difficult the lives of free African Americans could be in the early 19th century is often starkly demonstrated in the pension record applications for those black veterans who had served in the American Revolution over thirty years before. Veteran James Huzzey, formerly enslaved in Massachusetts and later a resident of Townshend, Vermont, stated in 1818 that he was "very infirm-wholly destitute of property" (Quintal, pg. 138), while New Hampshire veteran George Knox, later a resident of Thetford, Vermont, was described by a local official thusly: he "has been a very hard working man but lately he cannot labour in consequence of having lost the use of his right arm.... His home is a mere hovel and has not any furniture at all and I really think he is as poor as a man can be and live. The small piece of land mentioned in his schedule, on which he and his family are buried in a small enclosure, is very poor and stoney [*sic*] and will provide nothing without great labour and is worth but little" (Knoblock, pg 134).

The difficulty African Americans had making a living in a largely white society continued to the end of the 19th century for the simple reason that backbreaking labor for low pay remained the norm. In Bennington, Vermont, Harriet Greenleaf, the daughter of former slaves Nimrod and Margaret Greenleaf, made a living as housekeeper for many years; in March 1883, as is noted on her death certificate, she died of exhaustion at the age of 62. Her grave is unmarked and likely lies in the Bennington Village Cemetery, perhaps near that for her mother.

Though many black families were economically challenged despite their hard-working efforts, there were some African Americans who were able to break through the many social and economic barriers in their way and make a successful living without feeling the effects of poverty, albeit also with a great amount of hard work. In Connecticut, the formerly

Knox family burial plot, Thetford, Vermont. A former slave, George Knox served extensively in the Revolutionary War but died in an impoverished state. This overgrown burying place for Knox and his wife Catharine is located in a field on private land, the gravestones now almost indecipherable.

enslaved Venture Smith, later a resident of East Haddam, was a prodigious worker who made both a comfortable living and a name for himself, while Amos Fortune of Jaffrey, New Hampshire, achieved the same results.

One of the highest achieving African Americans of his day in New England, although he was only known locally, was Wentworth Cheswell of Newmarket, New Hampshire, who was of mixed ancestry and had a pale yellow skin color that often caused whites to refer to him as the "yellow man." Cheswell's grandfather was "Black Richard," who had been freed by his master in 1709 and had subsequently purchased land in 1717 in Newmarket, the earliest known instance of an African American owning land in New Hampshire. Wentworth Cheswell was highly educated and not only served in a gentleman's regiment during the Revolutionary War, but later served as a town official in Newmarket in a number of capacities. His family cemetery, with its elaborate wrought-iron entrance gate, is perhaps the only surviving one of its kind for any African American born before the Revolution in all of New England. However, the above success stories were the exception rather than the norm for African Americans.

LIVING ON THE EDGE

One of the most significant factors that contributed to the economic inequality of African Americans in New England for over a hundred years was the poor quality of their small landholdings. Indeed, this was often the main factor for those who lived in an impoverished state. Just as with anyone else in free society, African Americans could buy and sell land, but they were often only able to afford the cheapest land available. This usually meant establishing a farm or homestead on an acre or two on the edge of town where the land was swampy and unproductive for farming, or a rock-filled plot that required backbreaking labor just to eke out a small harvest. Thus it was that in many areas throughout New England small communities of African Americans lived, figuratively, geographically, and economically, on the edges of society.

The hardscrabble nature of veteran George Knox's farmstead in Vermont has already been described, but he was not alone in this regard. In Concord and Lincoln, Massachusetts, there are the woodlands surrounding Walden Pond, made famous by the transcendentalist Henry David Thoreau and today a Massachusetts state reservation and a National Historic Landmark. In order to conduct an experiment about simplified living, Thoreau lived alone in the woods at Walden Pond for several years, and afterwards published his groundbreaking book *Walden; or, Life in the Woods* (1854). However, as he notes in his book, long before he chose to live there, the area had previously been the home for a small community of formerly enslaved African Americans, some of whom had purchased land that was deemed undesirable by whites, while others stayed on this heavily forested land with the permission of its owners.

Among the inhabitants around Walden Pond were Charlestown Edes and Brister Freeman, along with his wife Fenda, and her daughter Nancy, who together purchased a 12-acre lot of land, eleven of which were wooded, the other being a worn-out field; William Fillis, who settled on a small plot of land without making a purchase; and Jube Savage, who had purchased a small parcel of land and was paid by the town of Lincoln to board an impoverished black woman, Lucy Oliver (Lemire, pg. 123). Also a resident in these woods was Zilpha, Brister's sister, a woman who made a living by spinning linen and was known for her "loud and notable voice" (Thoreau, pg. 199), and Cato and Phyllis Ingraham, along with their daughter, Nancy, who squatted on land owned by his former master beginning in 1795. They were probably allowed to settle on this land as Cato's master had essentially abandoned him because he had married Phyllis, since he did not want the extra expense of supporting Cato and his family (Lemire, pg. 125). Of this marginalized society, where other African Americans would come and go over the years, as well as some whites, Thoreau comments, "Neither were they rich in worldly goods, holding the land by sufferance while they lived; and there often the sheriff came in vain to collect the taxes" (Thoreau, pg. 202). Though Walden Wood's black inhabitants were likely buried on their homesteads, no cemetery or marked graves are left today.

Another interesting landholding situation can be found in the history of the Parting Ways community in the town of Plymouth, Massachusetts. Here, in March of 1792, the town offered a 94-acre lot of land located on the edge of a town pasture to anyone willing to clear it within three years. This land was subsequently granted to Revolutionary War veteran Cato Howe, who, along with three other black veterans—Plato Turner, Prince Goodwin, and a man known only as Quamany—proceeded to build a small settlement. Here, in soil that today is "gravelly and singularly unfertile" (Deetz, pg. 140), the four men and their families laid out their own homesteads and scratched out a meager living. Most of the men, despite their hard efforts, remained poor, as is demonstrated by their applications for a government pension for their Revolutionary War service. Cato Howe's personal belongings in 1820 were valued at twenty-seven dollars and, significantly, included no real estate holdings. When he died in 1824, Howe's estate was valued at a meager $61.82, including $15 each for his home and barn (Deetz, pgs. 140–141). Once again, no land value is listed. The town of Plymouth, in fact, authorized the sale of land, but allowed the families of the original settlers to continue here, which they and their descendants did as late as 1895 and likely well into the 20th century. To this day, the land formerly occupied by these black veterans and their descendants is owned by the town and is now an important historical site.

One final interesting aspect of the Parting Ways community is the close-knit nature of the housing situation among its original settlers. While Anglo-American settlements adopted a spread out approach with each family settling on its own land, here the four African American men built their homes in close proximity to one another in the center of the 94 acres granted to them, each tending his own parcel of land (Deetz, pgs. 150–52). Whether this was specifically done for reasons of mutual security and support, for cultural reasons, or due to a combination of both is, of course, unknown, but highly likely as the layout of Parting Ways closely resembles that of the close-knit living arrangements that were typical of the West African villages from which some of these men likely came. Just as they were close-knit in life, so, too, were they in death, as there is a small cemetery at Parting Ways, the study of which has yielded some important and interesting information.

The African American communities around Walden Woods and at Parting Ways were not the only ones of their kind, but rather several of many that existed throughout New

England. While the number of their inhabitants and quality of the land varied, and most are but little documented, they all have one thing in common: all occupied grounds that were on the fringes of society, if not in the outright wilderness, away from mainstream white society. Some of these areas were integrated in that both poor whites and poor blacks lived in these compact communities side by side, while some were areas which had a largely African American population. Local place names that have survived even into relatively recent times, even those that are offensive to the modern era, often give these latter locations away, and all indicate some connection to an African American person, whether it be a single settler, a family, or a small community of individuals, some known, many long forgotten. While Congress in the 1960s banned the use of the word "nigger" as part of any place name designation on published maps, the old terms were still often used verbally and, in some cases, may have been replaced with the more acceptable term of "negro." For instance, it is unknown whether or not such locales in Connecticut as Negro Brook Hill (Burlington) and Negro Brook (Stratford) were original place names or ones that have changed in the modern era, while in the local records for Ridgefield, Connecticut, there is one 1855 deed that mentions the "Negro Rocks" area of town. Finally, off the coast of Maine there is Curtis Island, located at the entrance to the harbor of Camden, up to 1938 the island had been known as "Negro Island." This island was said to have been named after the African cook serving on the vessel carrying James Richards and his family, the town's original settlers. The black sailor pointed to the island and exclaimed "Dare—dat's my island!" upon their arrival on May 8, 1769 (Locke, pg. 26). In this case, the name of the island may be more reflective of a colorful anecdote than indicative of an actual black community, as the island was deeded to a white settler and in 1834 a lighthouse was built.

Further examples of the oft-isolated communities of African Americans that once existed in New England include the following. In Hinesburg, Vermont, there is the Hill, once commonly called "Nigger Hill," where Shubael and Violet Clark purchased 100 acres of farmland on the southeastern edge of town in 1795. They were the first of a small African American community established on the hill, whose land, while not the most fertile in town, was arable enough to sustain a living. This community would eventually become integrated, despite the persistence of its older, more offensive name. The cemetery where its inhabitants were buried is now largely obliterated, though some fragments remain. In New Hampshire in Stratham, on the border of neighboring Exeter, is Guinea Road, named after the place of origin in Africa (the Guinea Coast) of formerly enslaved African Americans who once lived in this rocky and hilly strip of land on the outskirts of both towns. In Durham, on the southern shore of the Oyster River, was a spot once designated as "Nigger Point." Here was where Belmont and Venus Barhew, natives of Africa who were enslaved by Deacon Jeremiah Burnham, lived and raised a family, including Caesar, Jubal, Titus, and Peter. Several members of the family were buried on this secluded point of land, but their graves "have since disappeared under the ploughshare" (Thompson, pg. 163). Also in New Hampshire, in the wilds of the Coit Mountain area of Newport, there was a small black settlement, named after Vance Coit, an African American whose life history is unknown. Later residents in this community would include those formerly enslaved in the South who had become runaways. No cemetery or marked burials can be found for this area either.

Maine, too, has its settlements, surprising to many given the state's historically low black population. In Warren, Maine, the historic community of African Americans that once flourished here is today referred to as Peterborough, but was more commonly referred to in its heyday as "Niggertown." This community got its start in the 1790s when Amos and Sarah Peters, both formerly enslaved, settled in the area; it grew to some three hundred individuals at its peak before it faded away by the early 1930s. The Peterborough Cemetery where many of its inhabitants were buried lies in a beautiful and secluded spot; hard to find, it is a gem of African American history. Also in Maine, way up north in Machias, was the black community founded by London Atus and his white wife Eunice; today respectably called Atusville, it was for many years known first as "Nigger-Town" and later, down to more modern times with the coming of the railroad in 1842, as "Nigger-Town Crossing" (LiBrizzi, pg. 41). A somewhat mysterious cemetery still remains in Atusville, though the identity and numbers of its inhabitants remains unknown.

Finally, in Connecticut, among the sites in this state may be mentioned the Glasko Village area in the town of Griswold, where blacksmith Isaac C. Glasko and several other black families lived in an integrated area for many decades, a site now marked by an old mill building, Glasgo Pond, and the cemetery where Glasgo is buried. Another integrated site that was the home to a small community of African Americans is the Little Egypt area of Easton that once encompassed the parts of three Fairfield County towns. The only remnant of this isolated farming community is a small burial site, alternately known as the Den Road or Wheeler-Baldwin Cemetery, where some of its earliest African American residents, Sylvanus and Dinah Baldwin, were buried (Cleary, 21–26).

Finally, despite the many small towns and rural locations listed above, it must be remembered that the majority of free African Americans lived in the larger towns like Boston, Salem, Newport, Hartford, New Haven, New London, Portsmouth, and Portland. Here, African Americans earned a living working as tradesmen, simple laborers, and many were employed as sailors in both the local coasting trade and longer distance mercantile and whaling voyages. Black inhabitants in these towns often lived close to one another either in small neighborhoods in waterfront areas, or in areas on the edge of town, many of which in both instances today have been lost due to a city's growth and development. Many black laborers lived in local boarding houses, such as that operated by Chloe and Cesar Spear in Boston in the first decade of the 19th century, while others lived in modest homes. Most of these small homes were not prominently located on the larger town and city streets, but were instead situated on small streets, lanes, or back alleys; they were not only located very close to one another, but also right on the edge of the road. The black community in Exeter, New Hampshire, was described by Rev. William Bentley during his travels in September 1801 as consisting of "several negro houses and many signs of poverty" (Bentley, vol. 1, pg. 392). Many of Exeter's black citizens, including Revolutionary War veterans Archelaus White and Oxford Tash, are buried in unmarked graves at the back of the Winter Street Cemetery.

One interesting example of a residence for a middle-class black family was that for Pomp and Candace Spring in Portsmouth, New Hampshire. Formerly enslaved, he worked as a baker and had a small home on Church Lane, right in the shadow of North Church, which he purchased in 1799 and subsequently enlarged the following year, making his home and property a total of 32 feet wide and 53 feet in depth (Sammons and Cunningham, pg. 99). Here the couple lived, along with Pomp's elderly mother Phyllis, and operated a bakehouse for seven years before their sudden deaths in 1807 within four months of one another. Pomp and Candace Spring were buried side by side in the North Cemetery.

However, not all African Americans could afford to buy their own land and many who were once enslaved in the larger towns also took up residence on their former masters' grounds and often remained in their employ, as did later generations of black servants. In 1845 in New Haven, Connecticut, though few enslaved individuals are noted in census records, 215 African Americans in that city, a quarter of the black population, lived with their employers and had no home of their own (Warner, pg. 23).

One of the most interesting examples of the living arrangements made between and African Americans and their owner/employers is that for Lucy Foster (known as "Black Lucy") in Andover, Massachusetts. Lucy was formerly enslaved, the servant of Job and Hannah Foster of that town as early as 1771. Even after Job Foster died, Lucy remained with Hannah Foster after her second marriage and the subsequent death of her second husband in 1799. Lucy Foster would remain with her former mistress, though likely free after 1800, until Hannah's death in 1812. Lucy Foster at this time was aged about 55 and a member of the South Church parish, having professed her faith in September 1793. In her will, Hannah bequeathed to Lucy, "The Black girl who lives with me" (Baker, pg. 31), one cow and an acre of land, on which Lucy had built a small house that she paid for in part with money that was left for her by Hannah, as well as donations from others. Here Lucy lived from 1813 until her death in 1845, likely employed as a domestic servant and supported by the town in part (receiving anywhere from $1 to $5 annually) for all the years she lived alone. Lucy Foster was buried in the South Church Cemetery in Andover, but has no stone marking her grave.

Portsmouth, New Hampshire, also offers several similar examples of free blacks living with or near their former master or employer. After the death of their master, General William Whipple, in 1785, Prince and Cuffee Whipple, now free, were offered the use of a small patch of land behind the Whipple house (off High Street) where the two men placed a small, two-story house that they purchased elsewhere and moved. Likewise, Siras Bruce, a free black employed by John Langdon as a domestic servant for many years beginning in 1783, along with his wife Flora, lived in either a small brick house located at the rear of the mansion's grounds, or in small house adjacent to the Langdon mansion. Bruce paid no rent for his housing, as per the specific terms of his employment contract in 1797, but where he may have resided following Langdon's death in 1819 is unknown (Sammons and Cunningham, pgs. 97–98).

Portsmouth was certainly not unusual in these arrangements with former masters and employers, and it is likely that many African Americans employed as domestics in places like Boston and Newport also lived where they worked in some manner or another. In Newport, African American "enclaves" (Youngken, pg. 21) and neighborhoods were established in such locales as Upper Thames Street, Pope Street, and the intersections of Division and School Streets. In Boston the north slope of the Beacon Hill section of town was once home to a thriving African American community that had grown to over 20,000 residents by the start of the Civil War, while at the base of Copp's Hill in the North End there once was a large community of African Americans, formed before the American Revolution, that was known as New Guinea. Many of its residents lie in unmarked graves on the Snow Hill Street side of the Copp's Hill Burying Ground.

One of the most interesting contemporary descriptions of an African neighborhood and its institutions may be found for Salem, Massachusetts, a seafaring town with a large African American population that grew steadily after the American Revolution. The Rev. William Bentley commented a number of times about his town's African American population in his personal diary. In April 1816 he reminisced about the black part of town, stating that he had "Visited in my morning walk the square laying between Mill street, High st., the Pickering Hill burying ground & the Mill pond vulg[arly] called Roast Meat Hill. It was a mere pasture when I came to Salem. There is now a Twine factory & about 100 huts and houses for Blacks from the most decent to the most humble appearance. I found few out at Sunrise & such as I saw were quiet and well clad" (Bentley, vol. 4, pgs. 382–83). This community also had its own black school, as did most of the larger towns in New England. Bentley visited Salem's "African School" many times over the years as a member of the town's school committee and often commented on its high standards and excellent instructor, Chloe Minns, a mulatto woman who later married Abraham Williams. In July 1794 Bentley commented, "Among the writers an African child attracted notice by very decent hand writing. We found blacks in all the writing schools, but no one to be compared to ISAAC AUGUSTUS" (Bentley, vol. 1, pg. 96). Four years later, Bentley commented on the writing skills of Isaac's brother Titus. In August 1809 Bentley recommended new books for some of Salem's schools, particularly the African School, and must have been pleased with the results. In February 1810, Bentley, along with the town treasurer, visited all the schools maintained by the town, commenting, "In south Salem we found 40 children not provided with the best instruction. The African School by Mrs. Minns, 30 blacks, was better kept & several blacks repeated their hymns with great ease and propriety" (Bentley, vol. 3, pg. 500). Several months later, Bentley again comments, "The African School on Mill hill, in good order" (*ibid.*, pg. 528). While many of Salem's earliest African American citizens lie in unmarked graves, the Howard Street Cemetery, established in 1801, is the final resting place for many of the pre–Civil War generations, including Prince Farmer (1788–1852), formerly a mariner well known for his service on board the luxury sailing ship *Cleopatra's Barge*, and later the owner of a well-known oyster house restaurant.

Several other examples of towns also worthy of mention for their African American communities include Hartford, Connecticut. The Lafayette Road area in the Frog Hollow neighborhood, so called for its location next to a large area of swampland, was once the home of the city's large African American population prior to the Civil War. Not far away, just north of the Albany road in Hartford, was a small side-street once called "Nigger Lane." Like Boston, Portsmouth, and Salem, few of Hartford's pre–Civil War dead have marked graves, many of them, at least 300 in number, being buried in the Ancient Burying Ground, including five black governors.

In New Haven, Connecticut, were located the black neighborhoods near the harbor in the eastern part of the town, known as New Guinea and New Liberia. These areas survived for many years, though the "shanties" in New Liberia were mostly torn down by the white establishment in 1867 out of concerns about "vice" (Warner, pg. 29). Another black section of New Haven, situated less than ten blocks north of the other black neighborhoods, was located on "Negro Lane," now State Street, and was an area where many of the domestics who worked for wealthy whites resided. Of New Haven's burial practices for African Americans, one historian has commented, "Even in death they were segregated, for in the official reports, colored dead were separately listed and the corpses buried in a remote corner of the city burying ground, beyond even the 'city square' for the paupers" (Warner, pg. 11).

In Bristol, Rhode Island, the black section of the town, heavily involved in the slave trade, was known as "Goree" or "New Goree," named for Goree Island, a major slave trading center for over two hundred years located off the coast of Senegal in West Africa. This section of town, located between Wood Street to the north and Shaw Lane to the south, began its rise in the late 18th century and thrived for over fifty years, establishing its own African Church, before fading away by the 1870s.

Finally, in Portland, Maine, the free African American population here began to increase by the 1790s, their neighborhood located at the bottom of Munjoy Hill, between the waterfront area, where many African Americans worked as sailors and in the related maritime trades, and the city's oldest burial site, Eastern Cemetery. It was here where the first African American church in Maine, the Abyssinian Meeting House, was built in 1828 and in Eastern Cemetery where many African Americans were buried in unmarked graves.

Citizenship

While many African Americans lived as free men and women in New England, that does not mean that they had the same rights as white citizens and, in fact, this was far from the case. Though blacks could own land, were required to pay taxes, had access to the judicial system to seek redress and were subject to that same system if they themselves committed a crime, there were still many barriers in place that prevented them from being full and equal citizens in New England. African Americans were denied the right to vote both before the American Revolution, when the institution of slavery prevailed, and even afterward when that institution was on the wane. While Connecticut seems to have been the only state to legally restrict African Americans from voting (doing so in their revised state constitution in 1818), by tradition no blacks, free or otherwise, had the vote in the colonial era, and few were able to exercise this option elsewhere in New England until after the Civil War.

Many African Americans no doubt recognized the incongruity of being forced to pay taxes even while at the same time they were denied representation by not having the right to vote, but two black men in Connecticut, Isaac Glasko and Pero Moody of Preston, Connecticut took action by petitioning the state legislature in 1823 for an exemption from paying taxes because they were "excluded by the Constitution of the State, from attaining the high character of Electors" (Connecticut State Archives, Record Group #002, Rejected

Bills, box 6, Folder 12). While the petition of these men was unsuccessful, Glasko at least gained a measure of equality when he was buried in an integrated cemetery in Griswold, Connecticut, upon his death in 1861.

Likewise, the ability to hold office, with rare vexception, was also generally barred to African Americans. However, there were some exceptions. Wentworth Cheswell of Newmarket, New Hampshire, held several public offices during his life, including that of the town coroner, while Alexander Twilight of Brownington, Vermont, became the first African American ever in the country to be elected to a statewide office when he was elected to the Vermont General Assembly in 1836.

In terms of employment, while in rural and isolated areas African Americans could make a living as farmers or common laborers, in the large towns making a living could be equally challenging due to competition with white laborers. During harsh economic times, as happened before and after the American Revolution, African American

NOTICE.

THE people of *colour* throughout the State are respectfully invited to appear at the residence of LONON DAILEY in Exeter, on Wednesday the 13th day of August next at 10 o'clock in the forenoon, for the purpose of forming a society beneficial to said people. The particular objects of the society will be made known at the time and place aforesaid.

Per order of LONON DAILEY.

RUFUS E. CUTLER, *Sec'y*.

N. B. An Oration will be pronounced on said day at 3 o'clock in the afternoon.

Exeter, July 22, 1817

Advertisement, "people of colour" society meeting, 1817, Exeter, New Hampshire. This advertisement documents one of the first organizing attempts by African Americans in the state of New Hampshire. Organizer and meeting-holder Lonon Dailey was a Revolutionary War veteran, while Rufus Cutler was the son of war veteran Tobias Cutler and his wife Dorothy, both of whom are buried in the Winter Street Cemetery (*Exeter Watchman*, August 12, 1817).

laborers in larger cities were often subject to ill treatment and mob violence at the hands of white workers. This was especially true in Boston, where free blacks, including Prince Hall, were targeted, many physically assaulted, for taking jobs away from white workers. As Hall stated in an address to the African Lodge in West Cambridge, "Patience, I say; for were we not possessed of a great measure of it, we could not bear up under the daily insults we meet with in the streets of Boston, much more on public days of recreation. How, at such times, are we shamefully abused, and that to such a degree, that we may truly be said to carry our lives in our hands, and the arrows of death are flying about our heads" (Nell, pg. 63).

Such acts of violence as that experienced by African Americans in Boston were not the only incidents of this kind to occur in New England. In Machias, Maine, in 1795 a young black woman, Nancy Wilkinson, filed a paternity suit against a prominent white man in town. In response to this, nine white men attacked the house where she was residing, armed with clubs and torches, and attacked the house with sticks and stones. Luckily, Nancy Wilkinson was not harmed, and the men involved were brought to court and were fined for their actions.

Another African American who suffered considerable harassment was Jeffrey Brace, born Boyrereau Brinch in West Africa about 1742. In 1758 he was captured and sold into slavery in Connecticut. He served during the Revolution and subsequently gained his freedom by 1783, moving to Poultney, Vermont, in 1784. Here, Brace met and married Susannah Dublin, an African American widow, also formerly enslaved, with two children. Together, they would have three more children. They worked hard in nearby Dorset and Manchester to get the money to improve their farmland in the Ames Hollow part of Poultney. During their stay in Manchester, two children, a son and daughter, were forcibly taken from the Braces and made indentured servants.

Jeffrey and Susannah Brace subsequently moved to their homestead in Poultney, but even here were not safe. The Braces were constantly harassed by a neighbor who turned his cattle loose on their land and ruined their crops, tapped their maple trees, and even tried to force the Brace children into indentured servitude. Tired of this treatment, the Braces subsequently moved northward to Sheldon, and later Georgia, Vermont. As Brace would later state, "I sold my land to the best advantage possible, and was determined to move to some distant part of the country where I might enjoy the evening of life, in a more tranquil and peaceable manner, than I possibly could do in this place. I got about half the value of my land" (Prentiss, pgs. 186–187). Susannah Brace died suddenly in March 1807, while Jeffrey Brace died in 1827. Their burial sites are unknown for certain.

Later incidences of intolerance towards African Americans, especially in regards to education, took place in both large towns and small villages in New England. In 1831 a plan which had been long contemplated by African American leaders and white abolitionist leaders of New Haven, Connecticut, to establish a "Negro College" was put into motion, with funds being raised and trustees appointed. While the founding of such a college was hotly debated among the public and there was much opposition, the situation took an uglier turn when news came of the uprising of Nat Turner and his followers in Virginia. Not only was the local press opposed to the founding of this college, their editorials even incited some instances of mob violence against African Americans in New Haven (Warner, pg. 58). By this time, the issue of establishing a college for African Americans was a dead one.

Just several years later, in 1835 in rural Canaan, New Hampshire, another incident arose. Here, the Noyes Academy, an interracial school, was founded by New England abolitionists, including George Kimball, a lawyer of Canaan, early in the year, with students from as far away as New York attending. However, the town residents were not happy with the school's establishment, whose first class included 17 black and 28 white students, nor were they happy with the increased black presence in town. After just several months of operation, Noyes Academy was attacked by a group of several hundred men from Canaan and surrounding towns. With the help of 90 teams of oxen, the school was torn apart, dragged off its foundations and destroyed over two days' time. During this time, the mob threatened the students and aimed cannons at the house of those sheltering the students. While none of the academy students were harmed, gunshots were fired and the students escaped under the cover of night with the help of George Kimball and others. Among the attendees of Noyes Academy who escaped this assault was Thomas Paul, Jr., who, as a member of the class of 1841, became one of the first black graduates of Dartmouth College. He was the son of New Hampshire native and noted Boston minister and abolitionist Thomas Paul.

In regards to racism in New England, many have argued that it has never gone away completely and exists to this day. While the region was a hotbed of the abolitionist movement in the decades leading up to the Civil War, overt racism persisted in New England, as with many other parts of the country, well into the 20th century. Several incidents which occurred in the first decades of the century may serve to highlight the perceptions against African Americans even at this late date, albeit with contrasting results. In Vermont, when the U.S. Army's all-black 10th Cavalry Regiment was assigned to serve a four year term of duty at Fort Ethan Allen in the summer of 1909, the news of a large influx of black soldiers sent a shock wave through the area, especially the city of Burlington. The passage of Jim Crow laws to keep the black soldiers separate from whites were debated but never passed, and after the initial fury died down, it was soon discovered that these famed Buffalo Soldiers were model citizens. Both Silas Johnson (died 1935) and Willis Hatcher, 10th Cavalry veterans, are buried in the Fort Ethan Allen Cemetery in Colchester, their graves a silent reminder of racism conquered in a small corner of New England.

Such was not the case with Malaga Island off the Maine coast near Phippsburg. This island, whose residents were of mixed African, Native American and white heritage and made a meager living off the sea, was first settled in the 1790s by former slave Benjamin Darling. Though the settlement of families that slowly grew on this island was never large, by 1900 it had gained an undeserved notoriety as a degenerate community of squatters, and by 1905 its residents were made wards of the state. With tourism on Maine's coast growing rapidly, Malaga Island was considered an embarrassment by Maine state officials, with the result that in 1911 some of the islanders were committed to the Maine School for the Feeble-Minded. The island's community was destroyed altogether in the summer of 1912 when Governor Frederick Plaisted issued an order for the remaining islanders to be forcibly evicted and their homes torn down. Some of these residents were committed to the "school," while many others were forced to make a living as best they could. This shameful incident in Maine's past, seen as an example of "ethnic cleansing" by many, has its reminder not just in uninhabited Malaga Island itself, but also in the silent Pinelands Patient's Cemetery in New Gloucester, where over twenty Malaga Islanders were buried in simply marked graves.

Several other aspects of free black life in New England also made for a difficult life at times, these being the attempts to restrict their movements, and the outside efforts to enslave them. Because they often worked as common laborers or domestics and thus went from job to job and town to town, many African Americans were, upon entering a new community, immediately given a warning to depart the town. The custom of "warning out" in New England, established in the earliest days of the colonies, was widespread and had a long tenure, practiced as late as the 1830s in some areas. The "warning out" process, based on old English legal customs and the idea that a group of inhabitants had the right to choose who might join their community, was brought to New England with its early settlers and implemented by the 1650s. It was first meant to exclude those newcomers who could not provide proof of their good behavior and moral standing, and was also used as a method to limit land distribution and the right to use town common land to original settlers. Another use of the "warning out" process, especially in Massachusetts, was to discourage newcomers with opposing religious beliefs.

By the early 1700s the main purpose of "warning out" was to discourage those who were poor and warn them that the town would not support them. By doing so, towns tried to keep those on the lower rung of society's ladder, white and black alike, out of their towns. If the warning went unheeded, as it often did (few individuals are known to have been forcibly removed), then the fact that the town had given notice thereby absolved them from paying for support if a poor person needed assistance, and thereby foisted the costs of such care onto the colonial government. In fact, some towns in New England routinely warned out all newcomers for this very reason, even those who would later become some of their top citizens. On the other hand, for those African Americans who were already often mistreated by society, it was yet another form of legal harassment that could be quite intimidating and added yet another layer of control.

While many towns used the "warning out" practice in hopes of getting rid of their poor black inhabitants, some instances stand out more than others. In February 1787, nineteen African Americans, some of them Revolutionary War veterans, and their families, a significant portion of the African American community, were warned out of Exeter, New Hampshire, while in 1790 the town of Salem, Massachusetts, warned out almost every one of its black inhabitants. In 1792 Chloe Spear and her husband Cesar were among thousands warned out of the city of Boston, while in Stockbridge, Massachusetts, in 1793, Elizabeth "Mum Bett" Freeman and Rose Binney, at one time the slave of the Rev. Jonathan Edwards of Northampton, were both warned out.

While we don't know the thoughts of those who were the subjects of these warnings, the experience of Abigail Oliver and her son Aaron, Jr., in Temple, New Hampshire, in December of 1778 must have been viewed as heaping more misery on a family already in crisis. This warning came just seven months after Abigail's husband Aaron Oliver had died. Oliver, a free black from Malden, Massachusetts, had enlisted for service in the Revolutionary War in April 1775, and while serving in the 3rd New Hampshire Regiment, was taken prisoner at the Battle of Hubbardton in Vermont in July 1777. Held as a prisoner in the British prison ships at Wallabout Bay in New York, Oliver was released from captivity and returned home to Temple in April 1778, but died less than a month later.

Perhaps one of the most difficult aspects of free black life in the 1800s was the ever-present possibility of being kidnapped and sold into slavery in the South. This problem became increasingly commonplace in the larger towns after 1815 as the abolitionist movement to end slavery began to gain momentum and came at a time when new laws were being enacted restricting the importation of enslaved individuals. Further complicating this problem was the increased demand for slave labor in the new states to the west of New England. Due to these circumstances, slave hunters from the South boldly made their way into New England cities to kidnap free blacks, sometimes in collusion with white New Englanders, so that they could then sell down South. Local citizens also took part in these actions, and sometimes even tried to sell indentured black servants into slavery in the south. Because African Americans had no legal standing in the South, those who were kidnapped from northern cities like Boston could not gain any support from local law enforcement and the courts in Southern states. In Boston the kidnappings became so commonplace that free blacks began to arm themselves for protection.

Exemplary of such kidnappings are those that were experienced by the Hall family of New Hampshire. At least two sons, and possibly a third, of Revolutionary War veteran Jude

Hall of Exeter were kidnapped and sold into slavery prior to 1833. James Hall was taken from his father's house while he was absent, in the presence of his own mother, by a local man who stated that he was owed four dollars. James was subsequently taken to Newburyport, Massachusetts, and from thence shipped to New Orleans, though born free, he was jailed as a runaway slave. Here he was beaten and was reportedly taken as a slave to Kentucky. He never saw his family again. Another son, William Hall, served as a seaman on the bark *Hannibal* out of Newburyport, and when the ship made port in the West Indies, he was forcibly sold into captivity. William Hall remained enslaved for ten years until his eventual escape to England, where he subsequently worked as the captain of a vessel operating in the coal trade between Newcastle and London. A third son, Aaron Hall, was also thought to have been kidnapped for a fraudulent debt he was said to have owed. He was captured on the road at Roxbury, Massachusetts, during his journey back home to New Hampshire from Providence, Rhode Island, after arriving from a seagoing voyage in 1807. Likely sold in one of the Southern states or the West Indies, Aaron Hall was also never again seen by his family (Child, pg. 69).

Indeed, because of New England's close shipping ties with the Southern states and active partnership in the cotton trade, the carrying of kidnapped African Americans out of New England was often accomplished quite easily, and for this reason many African Americans moved further north and westward to New Hampshire and Vermont to gain some measure of security.

One of the most interesting of these kidnapping incidents was an unsuccessful attempt that occurred in Amherst, Massachusetts. Here lived a free black girl, Angeline Palmer, who in 1840 was an eleven-year-old orphan. Because of her situation, Angeline had been farmed out for a number of years as a pauper to the Shaw family, which also had a seventeen-year-old black girl working for them as a servant. The Shaws, while originally from the area, were now residents of Georgia, with Susan Shaw returning regularly to visit family and accompanied by her slave. Normally Angeline stayed with another family when the Shaws were down south. When the Shaws' slave girl heard her mistress reading a letter posted from her husband in Georgia detailing a scheme to bring Angeline south and sell her into slavery (her disappearance to be explained by saying that she had run away), she alerted several free blacks in Amherst, including Angeline's half-brother Lewis Frazier, as well as Henry Jackson and William Jennings. These men alerted the Amherst Board of Selectmen, but they were unwilling to believe that Angeline would be sold into slavery. They then planned to hide Angeline in safety to prevent her from being taken to the South and put their plan into action just two days before her scheduled departure in May 1840. With the aid of these three men, as well as her grandmother Margaret "Aunt Peggy" Sash, and several white members of the community, Angeline Palmer remained free in Amherst. All three of the black men were subsequently arrested, as was Henry Frink, a deputy sheriff of the county who had provided transport. At trial, Frink was cleared of any wrongdoing, but the three black men were found guilty. They were each sentenced to 90 days in jail, though offered their freedom if they would tell Angeline's location. All of these African Americans remained in Amherst or the surrounding area for years, with Angeline Palmer marrying Sanford Jackson in 1851 in Amherst, but deceased by 1859 (Smith, pgs. 22–30). Her final resting place in Amherst is unknown, but likely in the rear portion of West Cemetery, where other African Americans, including members of the Frazier, Jackson, and Jennings family, are buried.

Gaining Respect and White Perceptions

While African Americans occupied the lowest rung overall on society's ladder in New England and the majority of individuals lived unrecorded lives (as is true with most people in history no matter what their ethnic background), there are a number of interesting examples of African Americans in many communities who for a variety of reasons, whether it was by force of outstanding character or personality, hard work, past military service, devout religious nature, or their "romanticized" connection to the historic past (and often a combination of several of these factors), were able to rise above the question of race to some measure to become esteemed members of their largely white communities. Examples of such male individuals would include the previously mentioned Amos Fortune of Jaffrey, New Hampshire; Prince Hall of Boston; Venture Smith of East Haddam, Connecticut; Shubael Clark of Hinesburgh, Vermont; London Atus of Machias, Maine; and Newport Gardner of Newport, Rhode Island.

Among the many others worthy of discussion are Agrippa Hull of Stockbridge, Massachusetts. Born a free man, he came to town at a young age and would later serve in the American Revolution. Though best known to history as a favored aide during the Revolution to the Polish patriot General Tadeusz Kosciuszko, Hull was also well known in Stockbridge for his wit and bearing. After attending a sermon by the Rev. Lemuel Haynes, a well-known African American preacher of mixed heritage, he was asked by his white employer, a "haughty and overbearing" man who had also attended, "'Well, how do you like nigger preaching?' 'Sir,' he promptly retorted, 'he was half black and half white; I like *my* half, how did you like *yours*?'" (Jones, pg. 242). This was just one of many quotes that made Hull such a notable, even noble, town citizen, but perhaps his most famous was that in regards to the differences between black and white. Hull argued, "It is not the *cover* of the book, but what the book *contains* is the question. Many a good book has dark covers. Which is the worst, the white black man, or the black white man? to be black outside or to be black inside?" (Jones, pg. 242). Despite his status in town, Hull lies in an unmarked grave in the Stockbridge Cemetery.

Another black man of high standing in his town was Anthony Clark of Warner, New Hampshire. He was also a Revolutionary War veteran, born in Charlestown, Massachusetts, and likely enslaved, though a free man when he served for Massachusetts during the war. By 1798 he had moved to Dunbarton, New Hampshire, where his home was destroyed by fire that same year, and subsequently moved to Warner. Here he married Lucy Moore and had seven children, remaining in this small town the remainder of his life. His life was a simple one, spent tending to his farm, but he was also known for his fiddle playing and dancing skills. Of Anthony Clark, or "Tony" as he was known to all, a local historian states that he "probably did more towards instructing the young people in the arts and graces of politeness and good manners than any other man of his day and generation" (Worthen, pgs. 504–505). Clark, along with his wife, is buried in Pine Hill Cemetery in Warner among his fellow town citizens, with the inscription on his gravestone that he was "A soldier of the Revolution."

A final example among male African Americans that may here be highlighted is Captain Paul Cuffe of Westport, Massachusetts. Born on the island of Cuttyhunk off New Bedford, Massachusetts, in 1759, the son of a former slave from Africa, Cuffe Slocum, and his wife Ruth, a Gayhead Wampanoag. Paul Cuffe (he took his father's name after his death and dropped the slave name his father had been forced to take) quickly took to the sea as his calling when a teenager, serving as a sailor aboard a whaling ship on his first voyage in the 1770s. On his third sailing trip in 1776 his ship was captured by the British and he subsequently spent several months in a prison ship at New York. After his release he moved to Westport, where he worked as a farmer for several years, but soon enough returned to the sea. He and his

Gravestone, Anthony and Lucinda Clark, 1856–1862, Pine Hill Cemetery, Warner, New Hampshire. A Revolutionary War soldier and former slave, "Tony" Clark was renowned in his later years as a model citizen in this small New Hampshire town.

brother John, along with other free blacks in their employ, would soon build or acquire their own fleet of ships and craft a very profitable shipping enterprise as merchants, fishermen, and master mariners. Though successful, Cuffe, a devout Quaker and elder in the church in Westport, was concerned about the status of the enslaved, and also worried about the souls of those in Africa who remained unconverted to Christianity. For this reason, Capt. Paul Cuffe became involved in the "back to Africa" colonizing movement and sailed to Africa himself, stepping ashore on his father's native continent to visit villages and meet with local kings. He saw Sierra Leone as a possibility for blacks from America, and in 1815 transported thirty-eight black immigrants there largely at his own expense. While Cuffe's ideas of colonizing free blacks fell out of favor with other African American leaders even before his death, he nonetheless remains a larger than life figure. Paul Cuffe was not only a black man who achieved incredible success in a white man's world, but also as a man who was genuinely concerned, and acted upon those concerns, with the state of African Americans in our fledgling nation. Not surprisingly, Capt. Paul Cuffe was buried with honors at the Friends Cemetery in Westport upon his death in 1817.

As for the lives of African American women in New England, they received much less attention in the male dominated white society of the times, and for this reason the story of their achievements in New England has for the most part either gone undocumented or has been simply forgotten. Most are recalled simply as the wives or children of better remembered black husbands and fathers; as several historians have put it best, "There is a commemorative stamp in honor of Salem Poor" but no one remembers Mary Poor" (Adams and Pleck, pg. 125). Poor was a hero at the Battle of Bunker Hill in 1775, and the subject of a 10-cent stamp issued by the U.S. Postal Service in 1975, but nothing is known of his second wife Mary.

However, there are a number of African American women whose stories and achievements have been rediscovered and brought to light. I have already mentioned such notable women as Lucy Terry, of Deerfield, Massachusetts, and later Sunderland, Vermont, Elizabeth Freeman, of Stockbridge, Massachusetts; Dinah and Rebecca Whipple, of Portsmouth, New Hampshire; Duchess Quamino of Newport, Rhode Island; Chloe Spear of Boston, and Phebe Ann Jacobs of Brunswick, Maine. Among others worthy of mention are Belinda, a formerly enslaved African of the Royall family in Medford, and later a resident of Boston, and Sarah Harris Fayerweather, a native of Norwich, Connecticut, and later a resident of South Kingstown, Rhode Island.

In 1783 an eloquent petition to the state government was written on Belinda's behalf, possibly by Prince Hall, seeking a yearly pension. In the petition, written as a firsthand account, an aged Belinda (born ca. 1713) details her capture by white slave traders in Africa and a history of her condition of enslavement serving the Royall family. She only gained her freedom in 1776 when the Royalls, supporters of the British cause during the Revolution, were forced to depart Medford after the British evacuated their forces from the town. In need of support, Belinda made her petition for support and it made for such interesting reading that it was not only reprinted in a number of Massachusetts newspapers statewide, but also in Philadelphia. In that year only the state did grant her a limited pension, paid out of the holdings confiscated from the Royall family, but it would not be until 1790 that she received a permanent pension after executors of the Royall estate refused to make any further payments. As some historians have written, "Belinda believed that the Massachusetts legislature had a moral responsibility to her and her daughter. In her view, the Revolution required a reckoning with New England slavery" (Adams and Pleck, pg. 185). After 1790, Belinda fades from view, her final death date unknown, and her burial place, while uncertain, likely in an unmarked site in Copp's Hill Burial Ground in Boston.

Sarah Harris Fayerweather, too, was a pioneer. Born the daughter of a local farmer in 1812, in 1832 she had a desire to enroll in the Canterbury Female Boarding School in nearby Canterbury, Connecticut, operated by Prudence Crandall. Harris's only wish was to further her education so that she could teach African American girls, and Crandall accepted her, making the school the first one to be integrated in America. When white families withdrew their children from the school in protest, Crandall decided to make it a school solely for African American girls, but was forced by Connecticut law to close the school in 1833. Despite these setbacks, Sarah Harris, who married African American blacksmith and Rhode Island native George Fayerweather in 1833, became emboldened and was active in the abolitionist movement for many years before her death in South Kingstown, Rhode Island, in 1878. Among her correspondents in her later years was Prudence Crandall, as well as Helen Garrison, the wife of famed abolitionist William Lloyd Garrison.

Another black woman with an even more fascinating story is Oney Judge Staines. Enslaved from her birth at Mount Vernon in Virginia about 1773, she was for many years the personal servant to Martha Custis Washington, the wife of President George Washington. In 1796 she ran away from Washington's executive mansion in Philadelphia, and no doubt with the help of local free blacks in Philadelphia, was smuggled aboard a small sloop bound for Portsmouth, New Hampshire. After her arrival there, Oney stayed with a free black family in Portsmouth and in 1797 wed a black mariner named John Staines. Despite her escape, Oney was still not safe, as Martha Washington was desirous of getting one of her favorite servants returned to captivity. George Washington himself corresponded with the local customs collector, to no avail, to have her forcibly detained and returned, and there were even efforts to lure Oney Judge into a setting where she could be kidnapped and returned to the Washingtons, again without success. Oney and John Staines had two children, but after John's death in 1803, Oney moved to the home of free blacks Phillis and John Jack in nearby Greenland, and would stay in that town for the remainder of her life, trading a life of elegant captivity with the president of the United States for a simple life of freedom in rural New Hampshire. Late in life she would tell her story to abolitionist magazines. Oney Judge Staines died in 1848, her final resting place in Greenland being unmarked and unknown for certain.

One final example, a later one, is that of Harriet Wilson, a New Hampshire native. She was born free in 1825 as Harriet Adams in Milford, New Hampshire, the daughter of a white woman, Meg Adams Smith, and Joshua Green, a free black who worked as a cooper. Harriet's father would die while she was young, and her mother, poor and unable to take care of her, abandoned Harriet at the farm of Nehemiah Hayward, Jr., of Milford. Subsequently bound out as an indentured servant to the Haywards, here she worked hard, and though not enslaved, she was mentally and physically abused. She gained her freedom at age 18 in 1843 and subsequently worked local jobs as a seamstress and servant to eke out a living. Harriet Adams married Thomas Wilson in 1851, but soon thereafter, while she was pregnant with her first child, he abandoned her. Her first child, George, was born in 1852 while Harriet was staying at the county poor farm in Goffstown, New Hampshire. She later moved to Boston to find work, but life was a struggle.

In order for her to gain money to support her family, she wrote a book titled *Our Nig*, which was published in late 1859 in Boston. This work by Harriet Wilson, which was a fictionalized yet semi-autobiographical account of her years of indentured servitude and abuse, is now considered to be the first published novel in the United States written by an African American. Despite this unique and powerful book, Wilson's only known work, *Our Nig* was not a bestseller among abolitionists, probably because of its northern focus rather than the Southern-based slave narratives that were popular at the time.

After its publication, Harriet Wilson drifted for a time in Massachusetts working to gain a living, but by 1867 was known as a spiritualist. She subsequently gave lectures in the Boston area and as far west as Chicago on spiritualism, but also on such progressive topics as labor reform and children's education. Anecdotal accounts indicate that she was a forceful and entertaining speaker who drew on her own experiences as an indentured servant to make her point.

In late 1870 she met and married a white apothecary from Canada, John G. Robinson, and the couple lived together in Boston for seven years before their apparent divorce. Harriet

Wilson was known for many things during her time in Boston, including her own hair products and her work as a spiritualist healer.

In the later years of her life after her divorce she worked as a housekeeper and boardinghouse manager. She died in the Quincy Hospital in Quincy, Massachusetts, in 1900 and was buried in that town in the Cobb family plot in Mount Wollaston Cemetery. Her book *Our Nig* would not be rediscovered by historians and literary scholars until 1982, when its significance was finally realized. In 2006 a life-sized bronze statue of Harriet Wilson was erected in her hometown of Milford, New Hampshire, the first such honor ever accorded a person of color in New Hampshire.

One final aspect of African American lives, achievement, and the documentation of such in New England, which I mentioned at the very outset, is the fact that much of what we do know comes down to us through the filter of white historians and record-keepers dating back 75, 100, or even 150 years ago or more. Official government records, such as town account books and ledgers, probate and land records, and military records, where they survive, are usually dry and dispassionate, providing names, places of residence, and monetary figures, but little commentary or color. Civil and church records, such as birth, death, marriage, and baptism records that identify African Americans specifically by race (even if sometimes in derogatory terms), are especially valuable in simply identifying persons of color, but are usually lacking in personal detail. Published town histories, however, are even more readily available (every town library has them), and are often an anecdotal rather than document-based source, yet are still invaluable to the student of African American history.

Many supposedly exhaustive town histories, however, fail to mention persons of color or the existence of the institution of slavery at all, even when it was known to have been present. One late example of such a work, and there are many, is W.H. Wilcoxson's *History of Stratford, Connecticut* (1939), an otherwise authoritative and massive work which mentions nothing about the town's large slave population. Works like these are reflective of the sanitizing efforts by New England town historians in general when it came to the uncomfortable subject of slavery, with the result that for many generations some New Englanders came to believe that the institution of slavery never existed in their community to any great degree.

To their credit, some early town historians were frank about the existence of slavery, even if some community members insisted otherwise. C.C. Lord, in writing about a slave held in Hopkinton, New Hampshire, states, "A doubt has been expressed that Caesar Webber was actually a slave, having been possibly only a free *attaché* of the Webber family, but as we have no conclusive evidence in the case, we allow the original assumption to remain" (Lord, pg. 272). For those town histories that do discuss slavery and those slaves held, they must in some cases be approached with a degree of skepticism because of their varied nature.

Some town histories make for dull yet accurate reading, documenting slaves' names as they appeared in legal documents with little added commentary, while some of them highlight African American personalities of the past in vivid and descriptive ways. Town histories of this more descriptive nature may be divided into several different categories. The first of these are those which discuss slavery in a paternalistic and almost beneficial way; often in these accounts individual enslaved or free blacks, if discussed at all, are painted as lowly or worthless persons, while the institution of slavery itself is described in favorable terms. One example of this type of work is Samuel F. Smith's *History of Newton, Massachusetts* (1880), which states that "in families where slaves were found, they were most often treated with the tenderness due to children.... The heart of Massachusetts never harbored the spirit of tyrant towards the black man" (Smith, pg. 537). The historian goes on to discuss just one enslaved African American in Newton, "The last remnant of slavery," a man called Othello (called Tillo), "who was a life-long incumbrance of the estate of General William Hull. ... this slave, as he was known in his old age, seemed to live a very independent life, laboring only so much as was agreeable to him. He was wholly uncultivated intellectually, and it is said could never be taught to read" (Smith, pg. 538). The author here not only paints an easy life of captivity in Massachusetts for the enslaved in general, an ideal that was but a myth, but also criticizes Othello for not working hard enough in his old age, as well as being a "life-long" burden for his master. This raises the question as to why Othello Hull was never manumitted or, for that matter, why he was buried beside his master in the Centre Street Cemetery.

Another work of this kind (and, again, they are not hard to find) is that in New Hampshire by author George Aldrich. In his work *Walpole as It Was and as It Is* (1880), Aldrich, in discussing that town's twelve men who fought at the Battle of Saratoga during the American Revolution, offers the words, without comment, of an older resident, Thomas Bellow, who said of these men that "he never was able to recall the name of the twelfth one" and after some hesitation would say "no matter, twas a black man anyway" (Aldrich, pg. 47). The "twelfth one" here in question, who is never identified in the book, was blacksmith Cato Marcy, formerly enslaved, who had a shop on his farm near where the old meetinghouse stood. He enlisted for service in the 1st New Hampshire Regiment in 1777 and died after May 1778, likely due to disease or wounds sustained at the Battle of Monmouth. Marcy's burial site, like that of so many soldiers, is unknown, but probably lies somewhere in New Jersey or New York.

Finally, in this category there is also Wilfred Munro's interesting *History of Bristol, R.I: The Story of the Mount Hope Lands* (1880). Munro does discuss slavery in general and mentions some individual slaves in his work, but usually with straightforward commentary. However, his description and differentiation of the slave voyages and the conditions under which they were transported, in which the port of Bristol was a significant participant for many years, is clearly an attempt to paint his town in a favorable light. In discussing the passage the slaving ships made between Africa and America, Munro references "the horrors of the Middle Passage" as having taken place only after 1808, when the slave trade was banned, and claims, "With those voyages the name of Bristol should not be connected," believing that prior to this, slaving voyages were "easy-going, and comparatively comfortable" (Munro, pg. 353).

In other town histories that discuss those held in captivity, we see vignettes that depict African Americans in humorous situations (usually at the individual's own expense), or discuss their place in society in a condescending manner. Many of the stories seem colorful and harmless at first blush, but when examined more closely their comic tone is somewhat akin to the minstrel shows that were a popular form of entertainment of the day in which they were written. Oftentimes, these accounts are spiced with exaggerated examples of black vernacular language. For example, in McDuffee's *History of Rochester, New Hampshire* (1892), there is a lengthy account of Caesar Wingate, a slave first of Capt. Jonathan Ham in that town, and later Judge Daniel Wingate, who had previously been enslaved in the South and was also a Revolutionary War veteran. The author discusses Caesar's childlike reaction to seeing his first snowfall, it being stated that he thought the snow was sugar and even tried to gather it up. The author also states that Caesar was very religious and, upon hearing that his master was ill, recited a prayer that was recollected to have been as follows: "O Lord, do sabe Massa Ham, Massa Ham a berry good man, Massa Ham good to make plow, Massa Ham good to make harrow. O Lord don't take Massa Ham. If you must take somebody, take old Bickford, he ain't good for nothin'" (McDuffee, vol. 1, pgs. 550–51). Caesar would remain enslaved even after the war ended and his military service was concluded in 1785, and would continue to work for Judge Wingate and live on his property. He likely died in Rochester but his final death date and burial site are unknown.

In another work, *The History of Norwich Connecticut* (1845) by Miss Frances M. Caulkins we see a rather condescending account of both a black governor in that town, and the process behind his election:

> Whether slaves or freemen, the Africans of Norwich have always been treated with forbearance and lenity. They have been particularly indulged in their annual elections and trainings.... *Sam Hun'ton* was annually elected to this mock dignity for a much greater number of years, than his honorable namesake and master, Samuel Huntington Esq., filled the gubernatorial chair. It was amusing to see this sham dignitary after his election, riding through the town on his master's horses.... The Great Mogul, in a triumphal procession, never assumed an air of more perfect self importance [Caulkins, pg. 185].

This sarcastic account of a black governor seems to have been typical of the white response to black Election Day proceedings. Governor Samuel Huntington is buried in a brick tomb in the Old Norwichtown Cemetery, but where his slave may have been buried is uncertain, though likely in the same cemetery, and possibly even within his master's tomb.

One final example of this type of town history narrative is John Hanson's *History of the Town of Danvers* (1848), an account of this old Massachusetts town which once included the village of Salem. One senses in this work that Hanson is actually quite sympathetic to African Americans and the enslaved, as would be common in the abolitionist state of Massachusetts prior to the Civil War. When discussing Tituba, the enslaved woman who was involved with the incidents right from the start that led to the Salem witch trials in 1692, Hanson states, "Poor Tituba was imprisoned, and when she was found innocent, her sapient accusers did not hang her, they only mildly sold her into hopeless Slavery to pay her jail fees" (Hanson, pg. 292).

However, the author cannot refrain from telling a humorous story about an enslaved man named Cudge and what happened after he threatened his mistress with violence. To be fair, Hanson does preface the story, which came from a biography of General Israel Putnam, by stating that the way in which Cudge was punished for his threatening behavior was "a method more marked with severity than justice" (Hanson, pg. 142). The author goes on to relate the story of how the belligerent Cudge was tricked by his master to accompany a load of potatoes down to the town waterfront where he could earn some money for himself by playing the fiddle for the sailors aboard ship while they loaded their cargo. Cudge did just that and was lured aboard the ship and danced and played the fiddle for some time, as well as being plied with drink. After several hours, when Cudge realized it was time to go home, he was amazed to find that the ship was far out to sea. Cudge subsequently "went to the same market with his potatoes, and was sold for the same account" (Hanson, pg. 144). As has been discussed previously, the sale of New England slaves like Cudge south in the West Indies was tantamount to a death sentence, but here his sendoff is still offered as an entertaining account.

Finally, there are also those town histories that treat African Americans with a large measure of dignity and respect. I have already quoted from Miss Electa Jones's work titled *Stockbridge, Past and Present* (1854), regarding her favorable account of Agrippa Hull. Miss Jones, in discussing the "African Population" of Stockbridge, Massachusetts, states that "the dark cloud of slavery hung for a time over our beautiful valley" and is always respectful in her descriptions of the town's black inhabitants. Joab, a former slave now working as a black-smith, "was a man of good sense and steady, Christian deportment," while his wife, Rose, "stolen from Africa," later joined the church "and ever after adorned her profession" (Jones, pg. 238). In fact, Jones never describes Stockbridge's African American residents as being "black" or "negro," and instead refers to them as individuals and highlights their outstanding character. Enoch Humphrey is "a man of much sound sense and general intelligence," while Jane Darby, formerly enslaved and the wife of Agrippa Hull, was "a woman of excellent character" (Jones, pgs. 241–242). Most of the individuals described by Jones are likely buried in Stockbridge area cemeteries, though their final resting places are not known for certain.

Sarah Loring Bailey does the same for her Massachusetts town in her book *Historical Sketches of Andover* (1880). Bailey not only discusses the fact that slavery was once prevalent in the town, but also offers examples of advertisements for the sale of slaves, emphasizing that both black boys and girls were commonly sold. In describing Cato Phillips (later known as Cato Freeman), Bailey gives the full text of a letter he wrote to his former master on the eve of his departure in 1789, stating, "Many a white man in Andover could not compose so fair an epistle" (Bailey, pg. 42). Cato lived a long life as a free man before his death in about 1852. His final resting place is in North Andover's Second Burying Ground.

III. African American Funeral and Burial Customs

Just as in life, so too did African Americans in New England, whether enslaved or free, after their death also receive different treatment from those who were white. Indeed, it was often the case that people of color after their decease continued to be discriminated against in conformity with the then prevailing standards based simply on skin color and low social standing, and such treatment became standardized and customary within the confines of most New England burial grounds and cemeteries established prior to 1900.

However, before we examine these burial grounds, it will here be appropriate to first take a look at the traditions surrounding African American funeral and burial practices and how these evolved over the years. As will be seen below, in early colonial times, from the 1600s to the 1740s, funeral customs for those who were enslaved, as well as free blacks, included many aspects of their African culture that whites thought were both uncivilized and a public nuisance, and some practices thus became restricted by law. Based on anecdotal evidence, it appears that by 1800 most black funerals in New England had the appearance of conforming to the predominating white funeral customs, and by the 1830s black funerals were probably largely indistinguishable from those of whites. However, despite this appearance of conformity, it would be arrogant for us to think that African traditions simply died out. In fact, some African customs certainly survived, some of them so much so that they have become a part of American culture.

Funerary Traditions

As with most other aspects of early African American history in New England, no firsthand accounts from any person of African descent regarding funeral practices for people of color is known to exist, so the historian must rely on the artifacts discovered at several African American burial sites in the Northeast that have been archaeologically examined, augmented with anecdotal sources like diary accounts penned by white men who were knowledgeable of or had observance of such practices. Period laws governing black funerals that were enacted in some colonies also offer us some clues. These sources, however, tell only part of the story, as the ethnic origin of the enslaved (and their descendants) from Africa must also be taken into account.

It was once thought that the institution of slavery resulted in the "social death" of those slaves forcibly brought to America from Africa, the idea being that their cultural identity and ancestral past was denied to them by their captors by the control they imposed on virtually every aspect of their lives (Jamieson, pg. 39). In fact, this was far from the case, and African American burial practices, though far from being fully understood, would seem to confirm that, whether enslaved or free, some African funerary traditions continued on in the new world. This knowledge was used and passed along by those adult slaves from Africa who had firsthand experiences in their culture's burial customs and traditions, as well as younger slaves who may have witnessed these traditions. These first generation slaves surely passed these traditions down orally to successive generations of enslaved blacks who were born in New England, their accounts perhaps continually bolstered by the later slaves brought from Africa.

After their decease, the ways in which the enslaved were treated varied depending upon the community in which they had lived. Those who had been singularly held as the only enslaved black, say in a rural or early frontier New England towns, likely received a very quick burial with little, if any, accompanying ceremony or religious observance. They were not only buried in unmarked graves (as most of the enslaved were), but may not have even been afforded a coffin, as this would have just been seen as an added expense. However, even in larger towns, a proper burial was not always given. In one Massachusetts town, a slave owner did not bury his servant, but instead had the body stripped down to its bare skeleton, this being saved as a curiosity and displayed by its owner to give a scare to local children. In Waterbury, Connecticut, a similar occurrence took place. When Fortune, the slave of Dr. Preserved Porter, died due to an accidental drowning in 1798, his body was not buried, but instead was reduced to its skeleton and preserved by his doctor-master as an anatomical specimen to be used for study. While doctors in Waterbury and the surrounding area apparently used Fortune's remains for study for some years, the skeleton remained in the Porter family until 1933, when it was donated to a local museum. Fortune's remains would not be given a proper burial until September 12, 2013, when he was finally laid to rest in Waterbury's Riverside Cemetery.

In locales where there was an African American community, whether free, enslaved, or a combination of both, as in the larger New England towns like Newport, Hartford, or Boston, then matters were different. In fact, New England slave owners seem to have given the enslaved some measure of latitude and freedom in their burial practices. In these communities, the deceased's body was properly attended to by family and friends; it would have been washed and prepared for burial probably by a family member or other individual with special training (as was the case in African society) and watched over at night prior to its burial within a day or two. Simple coffins made of pine, crafted in the hexagonal shape that was used in colonial times (and later the more box-like coffins) were commonly used for the enslaved and most other people, white and black alike. These coffins were cheap and easy to make by a local carpenter and did not have the elaborate handles, hinges, and nameplates used by the more well-to-do whites. The coffins used by African Americans were made by white carpenters, but likely also by black craftsmen themselves in some locales like Newport, Rhode Island.

One coffin unearthed in New York's African Burial Ground, that for burial #101, had a heart-shaped outline delineated with tacks, along with the year of decease and possibly the deceased's initials, on the coffin lid. While this tantalizing heart-shaped design is often described as a representation of the Sankofa, a heart-shaped symbol from the Akan-Asante people of West Africa that signifies one's connections to the past and the importance of ancestral remembrance, recent scholarship suggests that this New York burial pre-dates the emergence of the Sankofa symbol in Africa by about a century (Seeman, pgs. 112–13). In fact, many white New Englanders also decorated the coffin lids of deceased loved ones by using tacks to create a heart-shaped motif, so several possibilities present themselves. Either African Americans adopted white burial traditions entirely in regards to coffin décor, or perhaps they ascribed different, non–Christian, meanings in their use of the heart-shaped symbol. Which situation may have prevailed in this case, of course, is unknown.

While most African cultural traditions and practices were in fact denied or prohibited to the enslaved because of their perceived heathenism, or non–Christian appearance, African culture could not be completely denied, and it was in the burial ground, where those of African descent, whether free or enslaved, had a larger degree of autonomy than elsewhere in white society, that such cultural traditions were clearly maintained to some degree.

In addition to procuring a coffin, arrangements also had to be made for digging the grave itself. Until the advent of modern undertaker and funeral home business services by the time of the Civil War, some graves were dug by the sexton, a town or church official responsible for maintaining the public burial ground. However, in many towns it was the family of the deceased themselves who either dug the grave, or had to pay someone else to perform this backbreaking work. Economic status was likely the primary motivator here, with the less well-to-do digging graves for their own family and friends, whether white or black. Though undocumented, it is highly likely that in places like Newport, Boston, and Portsmouth that had large free black populations, men within that community did the work of grave-digging for their fellow citizens, while for those in bondage it was the master who either hired out such work to be done, or had other slaves they held do the grave-digging.

One slave employed as a gravedigger was Prince Barnard of Deerfield, Massachusetts, previously the slave of Dr. Thomas Wells in the 1740s and later sold to Joseph Barnard. Prince was hired out by his new master for hard manual labor on a number of different jobs, including clearing land, sowing and reaping, mending fences, and helping to build a bridge. However, on at least five occasions he was hired out as a gravedigger, including one day in March 1744 for his old master, Dr. Wells (Romer, pgs. 69–71). When Prince Barnard died in 1752, his master paid a local carpenter to make him a coffin, but Prince's final resting place, and who may have been employed to dig *his* grave, are unknown (Romer, pg. 75).

Another such man so employed was Pero Moody of Preston, Connecticut. In December 1788 he cared for a poor woman from nearby Groton who fell ill while on a visit for six weeks, and after her death paid for the costs of a burial shroud, provided the coffin (whether he made it himself or not is unknown), and dug her grave, being paid just over five pounds for his work (New London County Court African Americans and People of Color Collection, Records Group 003, *Crary vs. Gallup*, Box 3, Folder 37). A final example of a man employed as a gravedigger was London Atus of Machias, Maine. In September 1797, after he had gained his freedom, the town paid him $1.50 to dig the grave for "black Nancy's child" (Drisko, pg. 270). The child that London Atus helped bury was likely the six-year-old child of former slave Nancy Wilkinson.

As to the clothing worn by the deceased, artifacts such as shroud pins and buttons recovered from African American burial sites in New York, as well as Portsmouth and Amherst, New Hampshire, that have been the subject of archaeological study indicate that many individuals were clothed in some fashion, often a burial shroud or perhaps their regular clothing. Shrouds, often called winding sheets, were commonly used, being a simple piece of fabric wrapped around the body, with pins used to keep it in place and to keep the face exposed for final viewing prior to burial. Shoes were not usually buried with the deceased for the practical reason that they were expensive and, as was also the practice of many white families, were passed on for others, friends or relatives, to use. In some cases the deceased's jaw was secured shut with a cloth wrapped about the head. Also included in the coffin, as was also the tradition with white burials, was a ceramic plate placed on the stomach. While this plate may have had some personal or cultural significance (as did other personal objects), it is likely that it was filled with salt so as to act as a temporary preservative (this being in the days before the embalming process was used) to delay the bloating and decay of the corpse prior to burial.

Personal items were often included in African American burials, and though direct evidence for this is lacking in New England, the custom of collecting small items has been documented among the enslaved in the American south and the West Indies. In Massachusetts there is one anecdotal account that suggests that the inclusion of small personal items that had been collected by the deceased for their final journey was also practiced in New England. In Deerfield, Massachusetts, there is the town historian's account of Jenny (1722–1808), the enslaved woman of Jonathan Ashley. She was a native of Africa and of her it was said that she "fully expected at death, or before, to be transported back to Guinea; and all her long life she was gathering, as treasures to take back to her motherland, all kinds of odds and ends, colored rags, bits of finery, peculiar shaped stones, buttons, beads, *anything* she could string." Her son Cato, who died in 1825, also "gathered trinkets to provide for his translation, his most valued possessions being brass or copper buttons" (Sheldon, vol. 2, 897–98).

Of the other items possibly found in African American burial sites in New England, we are forced to rely on the findings from New York's African Burial Ground (*New York African Burial Ground*, pgs. 85–90), as the most recently discovered site in New England, the African Burial Ground in Portsmouth, New Hampshire, was heavily disturbed prior to its excavation. One of the most common items discovered, in addition to coffin nails (from decayed coffins) and the previously mentioned shroud pins, were coins, usually two, often found at the head of the grave and likely placed over the eyes of the deceased. This was done for the practical purpose of keeping the eyes closed, but was also a European tradition dating back to the mythology of ancient Greece, where the coins served to provide the deceased with a means to pay the ferryman who carried the dead across the River Styx. This custom seems to have been adopted by African Americans early on in America.

Even more interesting are the other, seemingly disposable, objects that African Americans were sometimes buried with, including such items as clay pipes, glass beads, jewelry, and shards of shiny glass, ceramic ware, or rocks such as quartz or mica. The clay pipes, found for both men and women (pipe smoking was a common habit among both sexes prior to the Civil War), may have been the personal items of the deceased, or may have been placed with the body for ceremonial purposes, as was done with the enslaved in the West Indies. Glass beads were the most common type of personal item found in New York, some of them of European, some of West African origin. Some were worn as part of a necklace, while others, those for a woman and a child, were worn around the hips and waist.

Jewelry, too, has been found in African American burials, albeit in small numbers. Cuff links have been found in both female and male graves, some of them broken, some intact. These, like the many metal buttons also found, may have been part of the clothing the deceased was wearing, but were also regarded as valued treasures in and of themselves. Women and children were sometimes buried with rings, often made of a copper, or neck pendants, and sometimes earrings. Adornments of this type, beads and metal jewelry, were certainly prized possessions and are entirely in keeping with African traditions. The beads, usually a light or translucent color, or opaque black may also have been buried with the deceased for ceremonial purposes; their reflective surfaces were perhaps symbolic of water, through which medium, according to many African beliefs, the deceased had to travel to make it from the land of the living to that where the spirits of the dead resided. Similar in nature to the glass beads were the small pieces of shiny or reflective glass, broken ceramic shards, or even pieces of rock such as mica, calcite, or quartz. These ceremonial items were called "flashes" and, like transparent beads, were symbolic of water and the deceased's journey in the afterlife. Sometimes these "flashes" were, like shells (also symbolic of water), placed on top of the coffin, but they also have been found within the coffin (*New York African Burial Ground*, pg. 100).

Finally, wildflowers, based on pollen evidence found at excavated sites, may also have been placed within the graves of early African Americans, either on top of the coffin or inside the coffin itself prior to burial. This would be entirely in keeping with many African religious beliefs and their relationship with earth elements, but would not become a New England custom until the coming of the Victorian Age in the 19th century, primarily as a way to mask the odor of decomposition. The embalming process, though used by ancient Egyptians, was not used widely in America until the coming of the Civil War.

African American funerals in early New England were very different from those practiced by whites. The typical New England funeral and the customs surrounding them for white members of society was largely a very somber and subdued affair. The day prior to burial, a wake was held for the deceased, at which copious amounts of liquor were served, but it was here that any celebration for the life of the deceased ended, at least in public. On the day of burial, mourners at the funeral, the number of whom varied based on one's standing within the community, dressed in black clothing, quietly followed the coffin to the burying ground, with the church bell tolling in the background. In later days a horse-drawn hearse was utilized, but during colonial times the deceased was carried to the grave by his or her fellow townsmen. One set of men, usually the younger and the stronger among them, bore the coffin to the gravesite, while older and more distinguished men were the "pallbearers," their job to carry the black cloth (or "pall") above the coffin on its final journey. The procession to the burial site was ordered in nature, with both societal status and one's relationship to the deceased dictating one's position. Leading the procession was the town minister, accompanied by the widow or widower and their children, thence followed by other family members, friends, and fellow townsmen.

At the gravesite, customs varied over the years. In the 17th century, no prayers were said according to Puritan tradition, and instead the mourners stood in silence as the grave was filled. However, by the eighteenth century, customs had changed and a sermon was given by the minister, perhaps lasting as long as an hour or so, that usually touched on points of doctrine, extolled the Christian virtues of the deceased in calm and reasoned fashion, and offered a few personal words about the deceased's character and standing in town. Following this, the coffin was silently lowered into the ground, with loved ones perhaps tossing a handful of dirt on top before the grave was filled.

Both free and enslaved African Americans, as members of the community at large, also participated in these ceremonies, but sometimes broke white protocol; in speaking about Primus Fowle of Portsmouth, New Hampshire, the enslaved pressman for the *New Hampshire Gazette* publisher Daniel Fowle, one historian relates:

> He mourned the loss of his mistress and called her an old fool for dying. At funerals it was the custom for the negroes of the family to walk at the left hand of each white survivor, among the chief mourners. At the funeral of Mrs. Fowle, Prime should have gone on the left of his master, but he went on the right. His master whispered, "Go the other side." Prime did not move. His master touched him and whispered again, "Go the other side." This was too much. The old peppery negro sputtered out, as loud as he could, "Go tudder side ye self, ye mean jade" [Brewster, pgs. 210–11].

This was probably not just an example of an irascible slave, but rather more likely a measure of Primus's grief; he had likely known and served his mistress, Lydia Fowle, since she was young and was probably owned by her family prior to her marriage to Daniel Fowle.

In direct contrast to white funerals, African American funeral rites from early colonial times to the early years of the 19th century were both celebratory and mournful and were much more animated in practice. These life celebrations for the deceased in some ways were much more akin, at least in spirit, to modern American funerals where the deceased is given a celebratory sendoff and mourning takes on a secondary aspect. For the enslaved and free alike in early New England, a proper African funeral service was considered important so that the deceased could live properly after death, a failure to do so meaning that the deceased might become a wandering ghost that could haunt or harm those still living.

In the larger black communities like Newport, there were "undertakers" (as there were in larger white communities); these men were different from today's undertakers and funeral home directors, their job being, quite literally, to undertake the task of organizing the funeral proceedings and all the details thereof, rather than simply tending to the body of the deceased. In many cases the undertaker was aided by the church sexton, whose job, among others, was to dig a proper grave, and, if one was provided, help to set the gravestone. One of the main tasks of the undertaker was to ensure that members of the black community turned out in full force to give the deceased a proper sendoff.

We know nothing about most of the early African American undertakers and sextons in New England, including their names, except for Scipio Burt and Caesar Walker, both of Bristol, Rhode Island, and Mintus Brenton of Newport, Rhode Island. Burt was the slave of the Rev. John Burt and his wife and was both the sexton (graveyard caretaker and gravedigger) of the Congregational church and undertaker. Among the many people he buried over the years were seven of his own children. Caesar Walker, who was probably older than Burt and possibly the slave of William Walker, was the sexton of the town's Episcopal church, St. Michael's, at the time when the British invaded Bristol during the American Revolution and burned the church down. He was said to have been devastated by the loss of his church, wondering how the British could have burned it when he held the keys (Thompson, pgs. 158–59).

Better known is Mintus Brenton of Newport; of him, one local historian states:

> There was but one colored undertaker, and he had charge of all the funerals of his race. The last one to fill this office bore the euphonious name of Mintus. He was tall, spare, and angular, with grizzly locks, full on the sides of his head but wanting on the scalp. But this last defect was not observed when he was on the street, conducting a funeral, for then he wore a bell-crowned hat that seemed older than himself. A stiff stock threw his head well back, and the erect collar of his shirt crowded up hard under his ears.... He wore on state occasions—albeit a funeral was a state occasion—a long, blue, swallow-tail coat, with brass buttons; and when he stepped, in long strides, the coat-tails nearly touched the ground.... Gloves he never wore, and with scarfs and flowers he was not familiar. It took Mintus some time to organize a funeral; but when everything was ready, he gave the signal to move, by walking ahead of the hearse in the middle of the street, one hand under his coat-tail, and taking long strides which carried him some distance ahead of his charge; then he turned his head, and, jerking his thumb over his shoulder, exclaimed in a hoarse whisper, "Come along with that corpse!" This was repeated from time to time till they reached the grave, where Mintus sought to do everything "decently and in order"; which meant with him as much pomp and ceremony as he could muster. But he too, in time, was gathered to his fathers, and a white man bore him to his grave; for there was no one to fill the vacancy caused by his death [Mason, pgs 106–07].

Funerals in Newport especially were likely well-attended and all-encompassing affairs because of the size of the African American population there. In his diary for May 20, 1770, the Rev. Ezra Stiles describes a black funeral, likely for Quash Dunbar, stating "A Negro Burying, the Chh. [church] bell toll'd (all our Bells sometimes toll for Negroes), a procession of Two Hundred Men, & one hund[red]. & thirty Wom[en]. Negroes" (Stiles, pg. 52).

Early on, African American processions to the burial ground were viewed by whites as riotous and heathen affairs, accompanied as they were by music, singing and chanting, as well as mourners who keened loudly for the deceased, a long-standing African custom that was totally at odds with the Puritan tradition of muted mourning. Bells, too, were tolled for the black deceased during the procession, but evidently to a much greater extent than was practiced by whites, as laws were passed in Boston in 1723 regulating funerals for the enslaved, including banning funerals on the Sabbath altogether and limiting the amount of the bell-ringing for black and Indian funerals to just one toll of the bells. The vigorous bell-ringing which was banned in Boston may have harked back to the African custom of the beating of the drums to notify the villagers that a death had occurred.

Not only was the procession to the gravesite very animated, it was also a long and

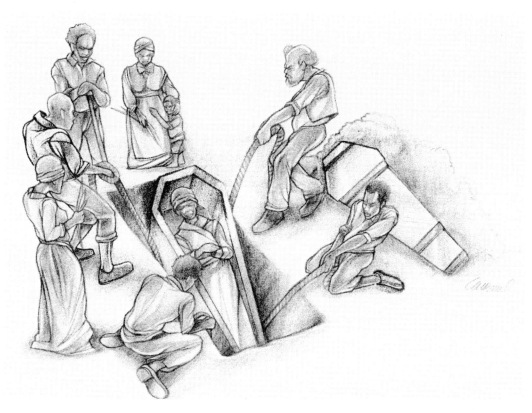

Artist's rendition of an African-American interment, by Michael Colbert, 2004. Most African American burials were conducted by members of their own community, combining both customs from their native land and those adopted while serving in captivity in America (*The New York African Burial Ground*, page 83).

winding affair, taking a seemingly haphazard (to whites) journey among the neighborhood. Once again, this was an old tradition, based on "an African belief that most deaths were caused by evil forces, and that persons who were killed through sorcery could be discovered by a mysterious tipping and shaking of the coffin as it passed the malefactor's house" (Piersen, pg. 152). This winding path to the gravesite may also have been taken so that, according to African beliefs, the dead cannot remember the way back to the living. Not surprisingly, Boston officials banned these winding processions in 1741.

Finally, the colorful garments of African American mourners, as in everyday life, were anything but somber, and, yet again, in direct contrast to Puritan dress for such an occasion. At the gravesite, prayers were offered and loud demonstrations of grief continued. After the coffin was lowered into the ground, personal items were often placed on top of the coffin, and possibly flowers as well, adding some measure of color to a normally unadorned burying ground.

While exact descriptions of funerals for African Americans are lacking, the diarist Rev. William Bentley of Salem, Massachusetts, records several of them between the years 1793 and 1814. Vestiges of the old African ways were certainly present in the 1790s, but Bentley's comments make it clear that by 1800, at least in Salem (and likely most of the larger towns in New England), African Americans had largely adopted the customs of typical white funerals. Here are some of his observations:

> July 26, 1793: "Poor Roger," the slave of Capt. Allen who died by drowning the previous day, "was buried this afternoon, in due form, & the negroes appeared in all order, & well clad. The procession returned without confusion to the house" [Bentley, vol. 1. pg. 36].
>
> August 27, 1797: "We had this day, the funeral of a young Black, born of African Parents, according to the rites of the Church of England. The appearance was pleasing to humanity. Tho' the number of men was not great yet that of the women was so. All of them were clean & they were dressed from common life up to the highest fashions. We saw the plain homespun & the rich Indian muslins & trail, so that they completely aped the manners of the whites & in happiness seemed to surpass them. They did not express so much sorrow at the funeral, as real gratification at appearing so well, a greater sympathy with the living happily than the bereaved" [Bentley, vol. 1, pg. 235].
>
> June 24, 1806: "This day was buried our old Servant Mingo, known by the name of Robert Freeman. He belonged to the African Society. Was a large, well proportioned man & of great note among his colour. Capt. Jacob C[rowninshield] brought him into America & held him his servant till the revolution. This is the first funeral in which members of the African Society appeared with their music. The procession was long & everything well conducted" [Bentley, vol. 3, pg. 237].
>
> June 1, 1809: "I saw the funeral procession of young Rose, wife of Said (Derby), both lately servants of E.H. Derby, deceased. It was an honor to Salem to see such a length of procession of decently clad & orderly blacks. 80 blacks capable of dressing themselves in good fashion & of conducting with great solemnity, without the ignorant state & the awkward manner of a new situation, is favourable to the hopes of civil society" [Bentley, vol. 3, pg. 437].
>
> May 23, 1814: "funeral at Guardship for Robert Roberts, Blackman, age 25.... The body was borne to the new ground by six blacks, decently clad, belonging to the ship & the procession was formed from the families of blacks belonging to the town. The coffin was covered by an American ensign" [Bentley, vol. 4, pg. 256].

The Reverend Bentley, in the accounts above, is both condescending and complimentary in his comments; clearly, dress and an orderly procession were important to this white Congregationalist minister, as it would have been to other white ministers throughout New England. Note the lack of "confusion" for Roger's return procession back to the church, as opposed to the boisterous and indirect wanderings of the African funerals of old. Bentley's comments about the funeral for the "young Black" is complimentary at first, but soon turns a bit sour when he notes in derogatory verbiage that the mourners have adopted white customs (which is what whites *wanted*). This account is also interesting because it clearly shows that African traditions, even if somewhat muted, were still being observed. The "rich" clothing of the mourners, which would have been different from the plain clothing of white mourners, is indicative of colorful African dress, while the lack of sorrow among the mourners demonstrates that this funeral was also a celebration of the life of the deceased, another African tradition. Even in Africa today, funeral rites are not simply one day affairs, but celebrations that can last up to seven days. The subsequent funerals in 1806 and 1809 described by Bentley are notable and pleasing to him for the introduction of music; of what kind is unknown, but probably not the drumming used in traditional African services, into the funeral services and the fact that the African Society was conducting the services, as well as the overall good conduct and solemn appearance. The last funeral described by Bentley is interesting in that it describes a military funeral which takes place during the War of 1812 for a young naval sailor who was not from Salem, but was nonetheless honored for his service by the town's African American community.

Salem was not the only town with an African Society or like organization that was established directly by black citizens (as opposed to those groups established by whites to promote black education, etc.) involved in local African American funerals and other affairs. Boston, Newport, and Exeter, New Hampshire, also had such groups, while black churches in many other towns were also heavily involved. Perhaps the most interesting of these groups when it came to African American funerary practices was the African Union Society in Newport, Rhode Island. This society, established in 1780, was the second such for African Americans to be established in America, following Prince Hall's African Lodge in Boston in 1775. The African Union in Newport also established a subsidiary group, called the Palls and Biers Society, which handled the rental of items used for black funerals. The group rented out the bier, the stand on which the casket was placed while being carried to the burying place, and the pall cloth used in funerals, with the proceeds from the profits earned being distributed among the proprietors. While this was a largely male-dominated organization, Dutchess Quamino was sold a one-sixth share in the business in 1792, likely because of her high standing and connections within the black community, thus making her "the first black woman invited to join a black male organization in New England" (Adams and Pleck, pg. 179).

In addition to the above details, there are several other burial practices worthy of mention, some of which may shed some light on the survival of African customs and traditions. The first of these involve orientation of the deceased's burial as a whole. In most cases, whether of African descent or white, the body was buried on an east-west axis, with the head to the west and feet pointing eastward, where the sun rises. This was a tradition among both western Christians and non–Christians in Africa alike, the rising sun and its relationship to the afterlife being a nearly universal symbol. However, there are a few known deviations from this practice, including one found in New England. In Portsmouth, New Hampshire, the excavations of the African Burial Ground in 2003 revealed that burial site #3 contained an individual (sex undetermined) who was buried with the head facing to the east and the feet to the west. This could be an indicator that the deceased was a practicing Muslim, as was a common tradition in parts of Africa. In addition, two

Gravestone, Violet Quamino, 1792, Common Burying Ground, Newport, Rhode Island. The Quamino family was one of the most notable and prosperous in Newport's African American community. This detailed gravestone is indicative of their success and standing.

women in New York's African Burial Ground were buried with their heads pointing southward for reasons unknown. The positioning of the body within the coffin, as far as is known, was the same as that for whites, with the body positioned lying on the back, face up (supine). However, there were some indications in both New York and Portsmouth that some burials may have been stacked upon one another, a sign of a family connection. Stacked burials are common in West African culture, but were not a western tradition. Finally, the excavations at New York also revealed that multiple burials in the same coffin, and in one case a coffin for an infant within an adult coffin, were also practiced. Once again, this was a common practice in both western and African culture. As there are many gravesites in New England for white women buried with their infant children, we can be certain that burials of this type also occurred among women of African descent.

Finally, we might wonder about early African American mourning customs that took place in the post-funeral period. In white households it was customary for a widow to dress in black for a period after the funeral, while in the home of the deceased black crepe fabric was often hung around doorways, mirrors, and, if one existed, the portrait of the deceased. Americans of African descent may have acted in a similar fashion. Though anecdotal evidence in this regard for black New Englanders is lacking, African customs even today dictate that mirrors in the home of the deceased be turned so that the corpse cannot be reflected, while the windows of the home are also blackened. In addition, it is an African tradition for women in mourning to wear either black clothes, or to wear a black cloth attached to their everyday clothing. Since these African customs are not greatly different from those of New England, it may be that they were not noticed, if seen at all, as seldom did whites in New England have opportunity to visit black households to make such observations.

Public Notices and Legal Aspects

Notifying members of the community that a death had occurred was also a part of everyday life in New England for both whites and African Americans. While the methods of such notification have evolved over the years, many of the methods employed in colonial times to let fellow townsmen know that a death had occurred are still employed even today. Perhaps the most immediate source was the local church and the town minister. Not only were the church bells tolled when it became known that a death had occurred (a custom that has since largely died out), but the minister also announced these deaths on the Sabbath day to the deceased's fellow parishioners. African Americans who belonged to these congregations, probably even those enslaved members who had been baptized, were also announced upon their decease.

As with all such matters, when multiple deaths occurred within a short time from one another, it was usually the case that the most distinguished and highest standing members of the church (and, by extension, local society) were given first mention. This was not the case, however, in one New Hampshire town: when Revolutionary War veteran Cato Fisk (born ca. 1759), formerly enslaved, and Revolutionary War officer Michael McClary both died in Epsom within several days of each other in March 1824, the Rev. Jonathan Curtis subsequently gave his weekly sermon in which he eulogized both men. Local tradition states, however, that some members of the parish were offended because Cato's name was mentioned first by the reverend! This controversy is Cato Fisk's only remaining legacy in town; while McClary received a prominent burial in the McClary-Epsom Center Cemetery, Fisk's final resting place is unknown. Since he likely died a pauper (he had been previously listed as such in surrounding towns in the years 1797–1801), Fisk may have been buried in an unmarked grave in the Poor Farm Cemetery located on Black Hall Road.

Another manner in which deaths were made public, one that is still in use today, is through mention in local and state newspapers. While not all towns had local newspapers, each state had at least one newspaper that had a large distribution. Prior to the Civil War, most of these newspaper death notices were brief, consisting of but a sentence or two about the deceased, his or her age, and place and cause of death if known. Only if the deceased, whether white or black, was a prominent individual was there anything more substantial written. Notices for African American deaths prior to 1800 are relatively rare and such notices concerning the enslaved when the institution of slavery was in full swing prior to the Revolution even more so. In many cases, the specific names of African Americans were not even mentioned; the April 18 edition of the *New Hampshire Gazette* in 1760 published an entry for "A negro woman" who died at an age estimated to be 110.

In this same newspaper the names of those individuals who had died during a yellow fever epidemic in Portsmouth, New Hampshire, in August–September of 1798 were listed by the town's health committee; all the white victims were identified by name, as were those individuals who died of other causes, and 41 individuals who survived. The only adults who were unnamed were "A black man," "A black woman," and "Silas Bruce's wife" (*New Hampshire Gazette*, Oct. 9, 1798, pg. 3). Siras (not Silas) Bruce was formerly enslaved and after gaining his freedom became the servant of John Langdon, a senator and later governor of New Hampshire. Siras Bruce married Flora Stoodley, also formerly enslaved, in May 1785. Though Flora Bruce's final resting place is unmarked and unknown for certain, it could be at the back of North Cemetery, where many victims of the yellow fever are said to have been buried, or in the old African Burial Ground.

One of the most unusual pre–1800 death notices for an enslaved individual is that for Primus Fowle of Portsmouth, New Hampshire. He was the slave of printer Daniel Fowle and was employed as a

Epitaph on the Death of PRIMUS

UNDER thefe clods, old *Primus* lies
  At reft and free from noife,
No longer feen by mortal eyes
  Or griev'd by roguifh boys ;
The cheerful *dram* he lov'd 'tis true
  Which haftened on his end,
But *fome* in *paved-*ftreet well knew
  He was a *hearty* friend,
And did poffefs a grateful mind
  Though oft borne down with pain.
Yet where he found a neighbour kind
  He furely went again ;
Too often did the mirth of fome
  His innocence betray,
By giving larger draughts of rum
  Than he could *fwill* away,
But now he's dead, we fure may fay
  Of him, as of all men,
That while in filent graves they lay
  They'l not be *plagu'd* 'agen.

Primus Fowle Epitaph, Portsmouth, New Hampshire, 1791. Few African Americans, whether slave or free, garnered extensive notice at the time of their deaths. However, Primus's master was the publisher of the newspaper in which this poetic and slightly derogatory epistle appeared. Primus for years was the pressman for this newspaper, so the placement of such an epitaph was certainly in recognition of his years of news service (*New Hampshire Gazette*, May 26, 1791).

pressman in the production of Fowle's newspaper, the well-known *New Hampshire Gazette*. Certainly because of Primus's connection to the paper, a poetic epitaph was published in his honor in the *Gazette* in May 1791. His burial site, while uncertain, is likely in the recently rediscovered Portsmouth African Burying Ground.

Death notices for African Americans, mostly free individuals but not always, are more common after 1800. Of greatest interest to newspaper editors, in regards to African Americans and whites alike, were those who died at a great age, as well as Revolutionary War veterans, but even plain entries with little information are also found. African Americans were almost always identified by race in these notices, a practice that continued consistently up to the 1840s; it lessened thereafter, but nonetheless remained in use well into the 20th century. A sampling of early New England African American death notices include the following individuals whose burial sites are unknown;

- "A negro woman of Mr. Shapleys" [*New Hampshire Gazette*, June 25, 1789].
- "Dinah, a black woman, at the house of Thomas Brattle, Esq, Cambridge, Mass, aged 100 years" [*Providence Gazette*, January 13, 1798].
- "Betsey, A worthy black woman, at Rehoboth, aged 92 years" [*Providence Gazette*, December 22, 1810].
- "Cato Overing, colored, supposed to be 110 years old, at Newport" [*Providence Journal*, October 5, 1821].
- "Primas Slocum, colored, aged 71 years, a Revolutionary Soldier, at Seekonk" [*Providence Journal*, November 13, 1826].
- "Old Fortune, an African, Georgetown, age 110" [*New London Gazette*, February 18, 1829].
- "Violet, colored woman, Bridgeport, age 104 years or more, February 25th" [*Bridgeport Spirit of the Times*, March 7, 1832].
- "Cato Treadwell, Trumbull, a soldier of the Revolution, March 5, aged 96" [*Bridgeport Republican Standard*, March 13, 1849].
- "Dinah Freeman, Fairfield, January 26th, age 92" [*Hartford Courant*, February 3, 1859].

Finally, we may also take a look at the legal proceedings that were set in motion when a death occurred in New England. Just as is the case today, many individuals of varied economic backgrounds had wills drawn up in New England from early colonial days. While it is true that the enslaved could and did hold property in rare instances, I've found no wills or probate records for such individuals. However, many free blacks in New England from the 1740s onward, and probably even earlier, did have such legal documents drafted when occasion warranted. These wills, whether for white or black, were usually made up by a local lawyer, witnessed by two or more friends or respected townsmen (usually men, but sometimes women), and specified how an individual desired his or her estate to be divided, any special bequeathals that were to be made, whether in currency or prized possessions, to an individual, groups of individuals, or an organization, as well as any other specific directions that involved providing for a surviving spouse or children.

One of the traditional requests in these wills, especially for African Americans, was the desire to receive a proper burial and, in some cases, appropriate gravestones to mark their final resting place. Given the fact that most African Americans were buried in unmarked graves in isolated areas, such requests by those with the financial means to ensure a "proper" burial are not surprising. In his will, Pomp Spring of Portsmouth in 1807 asked that "my body after my decease to be decently interred" (Rockingham County, NH Probate, reel 18, #7780). Similarly, the will for Cuffee Dole (1743–1816) of Rowley West Parish, Massachusetts (now Georgetown), in the first provision requests "that my body shall be decently buried" (Comiskey, pg. 19). Both men were provided with gravestones to mark their final resting places, which can still be seen today.

For every will, an administrator or executor was also designated, usually someone close to the deceased, perhaps a family member or friend, to make sure that its provisions were carried out. The previously mentioned Cuffee Dole appointed the Rev. Isaac Braman, the pastor of the church to which he belonged, to be his sole executor, and, as will later be detailed, the good reverend faithfully served his congregant and friend. In Portsmouth, New Hampshire, in late 1807 the estate of Candace Spring, the widow of Pomp Spring, was administered by a family friend, the formerly enslaved Caesar Whidden. He was a truckman who lived near the old African Burial Ground (by this time likely abandoned) and was married to Pomp Spring's sister. As was the legal requirement, he placed an advertisement declaring, "All persons indebted to the estate ... are desired to call on the subscriber and make immediate payment; and those who have demands against said estate are requested to call on the subscriber and receive their dues" (*New Hampshire Gazette*, Nov. 17, 1807, pg. 3).

While the procedures varied from state to state, in general after an individual died, his estate was inventoried and a list of all of his or her assets, including personal possessions, livestock and landholdings, and any notes (IOUs) for debts, were carefully listed in detail and valued. The local probate courts subsequently examined the proceedings and made a final determination of the estate's disposition to make sure it was done in accordance with the law, ensuring that any debts the deceased may have owed, including, as was often the case, the final doctor's bill, were paid in full, as well as ensuring that funds were distributed in accordance with the provisions of the will. If an individual with property died without having a will drafted (otherwise known as being "intestate"), the probate court would handle the final disposition of the estate, including its valuation and deciding who would be the beneficiary (usually the spouse or the deceased's children if there were any) according to law.

When Cuff Smith, the son of Venture Smith and a Revolutionary War veteran, died in Haddam, Connecticut, in 1822, he had little in material pos-

ALL perfons indebted to the eftate of CANDICE SPRING, late of Portfmouth, deceafed, and widow of the late Mr. Pomp Spring——are defired to call on the fubfcriber and make immediate payment ; and thofe who have demands againft faid eftate are requefted to call on the fubfcriber and receive their dues. CÆSAR WHIDDEN, *Adminiftrator,* Portfmouth, Nov. 17, 1807.

Candace Spring estate notice, 1807, Portsmouth, New Hampshire. While many free African American families struggled to make a living, Pomp and Candace Spring built a successful life after gaining their freedom and by the time of their deaths had acquired a modest estate (*New Hampshire Gazette*, November 17, 1807).

sessions. A pauper in town by 1818, Smith owned less than $15 in personal possessions and had no house or land at the time of his decease. The largest part of his meager estate was the $34.40 due on his monthly veteran's pension, but in the end Cuff Smith's estate was insolvent, as he had debts for his final illness and funeral expenses totaling $67.09 (White, David, pgs. 42–43). Cuff Smith's final resting place is unknown, perhaps a pauper's grave somewhere in Haddam or an unmarked spot in the First Church Cemetery next to other members of the family.

In contrast, the inventory of Chloe Spear's estate was substantial considering the fact that she had once been enslaved. Owned by the Bradford family of Andover, Chloe Spear (1750–1815) learned to read in secret, even after being beaten and warned by her master for doing so, by purchasing a psalm book and arranging secret lessons. Given her freedom sometime in the 1780s, Chloe subsequently was baptized in the Second Baptist Church of Boston and married Caesar Spear. The couple for many years owned and operated a successful boarding house for laborers and mariners and lived a simple, yet financially secure life. After her husband died, Chloe Spear opened her home to host worship groups for people of all colors from her church. At her death, she was highly respected for both her business acumen and her religious devotion. In her will she leaves money not only to her son, but also to six other black women who were members of the church. An inventory of her estate shows that her belongings included part of a house located on White Bread Alley in Boston valued at $700, as well as household goods valued at $103, including a brass fire set, five pictures, brass candlesticks, two small looking glasses (mirrors), a desk, a pine table, seven chairs, and various kitchen implements and personal items (Minardi, pg. 1).

While there are found in the probate records of all the New England states wills and estate accounts for African Americans, these numbers are still relatively small. Again, it must be remembered that many blacks had no such wills drawn up for the simple reason that they possessed no substantial holdings in personal belongings, other than the clothes upon their backs, and no land holdings. Thus it is that probate records are often lacking for those who were on the lowest rung of the economic ladder, no matter what their color. This group usually included African Americans who worked as simple laborers and moved from job to job, and often town to town, as well as those employed on the high seas as sailors and those working as domestic servants and living with their employers. Because of these circumstances, black citizens such as these often lived lives that went largely unrecorded, making the job of today's African American historians and genealogists a challenging one.

While African Americans often lived on the economic and social fringes of a predominantly white New England society, that does not mean that they were not actively involved in that society. One of the most interesting of the wills drafted by African Americans is that for Amos Fortune (1710–1801) of Jaffrey, New Hampshire. The first, third, and fourth provisions all concern "Vilot, my beloved wife" and her financial support; the second provision is a standard one directing that all demands against his estate be satisfied, while the fifth provision contains details for supporting "Ceylandia Fortune, my adopted daughter ... while she remains single" (Lambert, pgs. 49–50). The sixth provision is interesting in that Fortune ordered "my executor after my decease and after the decease of said Vilot my beloved wife that handsome grave stones be erected to each of us if there is any estate left for that purpose" (*ibid.*). The Fortune estate did indeed have the funds to make this provision a reality, and these gravestones can still be seen today in the Old Burial Ground located behind the Jaffrey meetinghouse. The seventh and final provision of Amos Fortune's will is even more interesting and indicative of his character and community standing; it directs that the remainder of his estate, if any, after the decease of his wife Vilot, who died in 1802, be used to "give a handsome present ... to the Church of Christ in this town, and the remaining part ... be give as a present for the support of the school in school house No. eight in this town" (*ibid.*). As a result of this provision, in 1805 funds in the amount of $100 were given to the church, which was used to buy a pewter communion set. This set was eventually sold by the church in 1878, but now is part of the collection of the Brooklyn Museum in New York. The final $233 from Fortune's estate went to the school system in Jaffrey (schoolhouse #8 was closed by 1809), and in 1928 the remaining funds were used to fund prizes for public speaking contests in the schools. After these contests were discontinued, the money remained idle until it was eventually transferred to the Jaffrey Public Library, the funds later used to develop educational materials about the man who had donated them.

IV. Together Yet Separate; Characteristics of African American Burial Sites

African Americans, as with all other New Englanders, were buried in several types of cemeteries; these include burials in plots on privately owned land, in public burial grounds, in pauper's cemeteries or like sites reserved for the indigent, and those in neighborhood cemeteries. In addition, the enslaved in New England were first buried in slave cemeteries that were typically located on the land owned by their masters. All of these different types of burial sites are discussed below. While there is a general chronology regarding the use of different types of burying places (burials were usually were first located on private land until formal public burying grounds were laid out), over time the use of these different types of burial sites overlapped one another. There is, in most cases, no distinct time frame when one type of site was used and another fell out of favor. While I have used the terms "burying ground," "burial yard," "graveyard," and "cemetery" interchangeably, it should be understood that the last term, "cemetery" (from the Greek language, meaning "sleeping chamber"), which is common terminology today, did not come into use until the 1830s.

As to records which may have been kept regarding where a person was buried in any given town, and where his or her burial plot is located within a particular cemetery, these records vary from town to town, but are almost entirely lacking for the time period with which this work is concerned. Indeed, prior to the 1900s, it was the minister of the church who typically kept the vital records of those in town who had been born, married, or died, and some ministers were more thorough than others. These ministerial records were often given to town selectmen for recording in the town records, but they were not all inclusive and many of those outside the church or otherwise on the fringe of society, including African Americans, Native Americans, itinerant laborers and, later on, many immigrants, did not have their life events recorded. Formal burial records are almost nonexistent prior to the 1870s, so in many cases the answer to the question as to where a person may have been buried depends on the time period and some guesswork if there is no identifying gravestone.

Slave and Family Burials on Private Land

From the earliest days when the first colonists settled New England, it was first the practice to bury the dead in private plots on their own land, and the same held true for the enslaved as well. In the Puritan mindset, these burial grounds, burying yards, or graveyards, as they were typically called, were not consecrated or sacred ground as we think of them today, but merely places to bury the earthly remains of the deceased. As such, there was no religious or even social requirement that the dead be buried in an established churchyard or meetinghouse burying ground. While it is true that one of the first public structures built in any early New England settlement was usually the meetinghouse, with a public burying ground laid out right adjacent, this was not always the case. Providence, Rhode Island, was first settled by Roger Williams and his followers in 1636, but the North Burial Ground, the city's first public cemetery, was not established until 1700. In fact, burials on private land remained a common practice in many New England towns, even when there was a public burying place, well into the 20th century.

As a result of these customs, it was usually the case that the enslaved were buried on their master's land. Many of the earliest of these graves prior to 1700, whether for white or black, were unmarked, though some were marked with simple rocks or fieldstones obtained locally in the rocky New England soil. It is unknown for certain whether the graves for the enslaved were segregated from those of the white families they served early on, but it soon became the practice to bury the enslaved in separate plots or enclosures so designated for "slaves." Thus it is that many towns throughout New England that have areas that, though devoid of any burial markers or other such evidence, are anecdotally referred to as "slave" cemeteries. While some of these sites may be mere legends or tall tales, others may indeed have been burial sites for the enslaved.

In Berwick, Maine, the cemetery records for that town indicate that there were two separate burial places on the land once owned by Joseph Ricker, one for white Ricker family members, and another designated "negro interments; slaves of Joseph Ricker" (Spender, pg. 49). Rhode Island records are also very particular in this regard, noting the many slave burial grounds and cemeteries that are now lost. These include the Potter family slave lot in Cranston, four Gardner family slave or servant lots, the Morey family slave lot, and the "colored" lot on the Schartner farm, all in Exeter; the Sambo lot, the Phillips slave lot, the Willett-Carpenter slave lot, and three other designated slave/servant/black lots in North Kingstown; the Babcock slave lot, the Dockray slave lot, and two general slave lots in South Kingstown; the Spink slave cemetery, the Waterman family slave lot, and the Peter Greene slave lot in Warwick; and the Thompson family slave lot in Westerly. Most of these sites have been lost, due to development, deliberate destruction, or simple neglect, the Willet-Carpenter lot in North Kingstown being perhaps typical of this. The family lot for the Rev. James Carpenter was walled and well kept and is still in existence today, but the burial yard for the enslaved members of the family was located on a knoll to the southwest on the opposite side of the road and contained ten graves in an open, unprotected space that was located extremely close to plowed farmland. By 1989 all traces of this cemetery were lost. Likewise, the remains of two children of mixed African and Native American descent, ages 11 and

13, that were examined by archaeologists at Beattie Point in Tiverton, Rhode Island, in 1946, indicated a likely slave burial ground that was located on marshy land on the east shore of the Sakonnet River once owned by slave holder Nathaniel Briggs from 1785 to 1801 (Bullen and Bullen, pg. 5).

Despite the loss of most slave cemeteries located on private land, there are some that have survived. In Portsmouth, New Hampshire, may be found the burial ground for the enslaved members of the prominent Langdon family, while in Kingstown, Rhode Island, is the Niles Farmstead Cemetery, which may have been the final resting place for both the enslaved who worked the 350-acre farm between 1730 and 1783, as well as members of the Niles family. Likewise, in nearby North Kingstown, Rhode Island, off Stony Fort Road, there can be found in an overgrown area with no fence or boundary marker of any kind what is likely one of the largest private slave cemeteries in all of New England. This plot is for the slaves of the Gardiner and Stanton families and contains about 80 graves marked by simple fieldstones.

Perhaps the most unusual of the slave cemeteries to be found in all of New England are those burials found at the site of the New Salem Plantation in Salem, Connecticut. This site, which is privately owned, was once a 13,000-acre plantation owned by Colonel Samuel Browne of Salem, Massachusetts. On its former grounds are one traditional cemetery, which may be the final resting place for nine slaves of the Browne family, who operated the large farm with as many as sixty slaves, from 1718 to 1780, but also found nearby are many small cairns, piles of rocks decorated with pottery shards, that may indicate the burial site of many more slaves who held onto their West African customs.

With the eventual dying out of the institution of slavery on a widespread basis and the corresponding growth of a free black population, burial places on private lands, whether their own or those for whom they worked, continued throughout New England. In the town of Dracut, Massachusetts, there is buried Silas Royal, who was once enslaved by the Varnum family in that town and who first went by the name Royal Varnum. He served in the American Revolution and saw action at the redoubt during the Battle of Bunker Hill. He was eventually freed after his military service and remained close to the Varnum family. General James Varnum included a clause in his will specifying that Royal be taken care of "and honorably buried after death" (Quintal, Jr., pg. 189). At his death in 1826, as per his request, Silas Royal was buried in the Varnum Cemetery in Dracut.

Many such sites for free African Americans have gone undocumented. For example, while the final resting place for most of the black residents of the Walden Pond community in Lincoln and Concord are unknown, they were almost certainly buried on the land on which they lived. Because most of these sites were not conspicuously marked and were located on the geographical edges of an otherwise white society, many have been lost to history, or nearly so.

Among the private burial lots for African Americans that have been lost over time, many of them are in Rhode Island, including the Caesar Onion lot in Exeter and the Joe Sambo lot in Cranston. There are many other examples of sites that are close to being lost, as well as some that were once lost and have been recently rediscovered. The John Jack homestead in Greenland, New Hampshire, where John and Phyllis Jack lived, along with their children and later Martha Washington's runaway slave, Ona Judge Staines, was once a cleared homestead with a small family cemetery but was abandoned by the 1840s with the death of its residents. By the 1990s the Jack site had reverted to wilderness; only a few gravestone fragments and a portion of a stone wall remained to show that anyone had ever lived there. Another private burial site is the endangered, but still intact, small cemetery located on the Prince Walker homestead site in Barre, Massachusetts. Several stones remain here, most unmarked fieldstones except that for Prince himself. The Parting Ways community in Plymouth, Massachusetts, is also one that has a cemetery that was nearly lost, but has now been recovered.

Another example of such a cemetery, one located in a more urban area, is that for the members of the African Masonic Lodge, founded in Boston in 1775 by Prince Hall. The land for this cemetery, located on Gardner Street in Arlington, was purchased in 1856 and was designated the Prince Hall Cemetery. It remained in use for members of the lodge until about 1897, after which it was no longer used for unknown reasons and was subsequently abandoned, only to be rediscovered in modern times.

Yet another site that has been recently rediscovered is the Hall Cemetery located in Madbury, New Hampshire. This site, consisting of five unmarked field stones, lies at the back right portion of the farmland located on Nute Road across the street from the former residence of farmer John Ricker, a two-story Georgian-style home. This site, located near the confluence of two stone walls, is referred to in one local deed dating from 1885 as a "Negro grave," but little else is known for certain. Research by local residents Carolyn and Tom Ramsbotham, who live in Ricker's home, indicates that these are probably the graves for the children of George and Mary Hall, George, Jr. and Elizabeth, and possibly Mrs. Hall herself. George Hall was a free black laborer and farmhand, a next-door neighbor to John Ricker, who traveled wherever there was work to be found. George Hall was possibly a descendant of Jude Hall of Exeter, or perhaps a descendant of those who were enslaved by the Hall family of Madbury or nearby Dover. This small cemetery was probably established out of necessity in the fall of 1868 when an illness struck the neighborhood in late September, taking the lives of John Ricker, several children of the Small family, almost certainly the Hall children, and possibly Mary Hall. Town records make no mention of the death of any the Halls, but given the fact that the family lived a transient life this is not surprising. In contrast to the Halls, John Ricker and the Small children were buried in a plot, nicely fenced in, and located directly behind the Ricker house, their graves marked with professionally carved stones.

Surprisingly, northern New England has a number of private burial sites for African Americans which are in some cases the best indicator of a historical black presence in an otherwise white region. The Cheswell family cemetery in Newmarket, New Hampshire, is the final resting place of Revolutionary War soldier Wentworth Cheswell (1746–1817), a free black who was of mixed heritage and one of the most prominent members of town. His cemetery, with its elaborate wrought-iron gate, has been restored in recent years and is designated with a New Hampshire state historical marker. Also in New Hampshire, in the town of Andover, is the family plot for Richard Potter (1783–1835) and his wife Sally (1787–1839). Potter, who was once either enslaved or an indentured servant, was of mixed ancestry and became a famed magician and performer who brought his show to many theatres throughout New England and as far south as Baltimore. He later moved to New Hampshire and built a mansion which is no longer standing in an area of town near the old railroad station that is still known as Potter Place.

In Maine, too, there are a number of African American family cemeteries. One of the most interesting is the Heuston Cemetery in Brunswick; this cemetery (not open to the public), is located on family land near the bank of the Androscoggin River. It was restored and documented by 2003 and is the final resting place for Francis Heuston (1764–1858) and his descendants. Heuston, formerly enslaved and employed as a mariner, first arrived in Brunswick about 1800 and soon became a leading light in the town's small African American community. After his first wife Mehitable (1781–1851) died, he married a runaway slave named Clara "Mary" Battease and had many children. One son, Francis Eben Heuston, served as a steward aboard the steamship *Portland* and was one of the crewmen lost when she went down in a gale off Cape Cod in November 1898 with the loss of all 193 crew and passengers, one of New England's most famous shipwrecks (Price and Talbot, pgs. 61–64).

Other black family cemeteries that are known to exist in Maine include the Ruby Cemetery in Durham, located on a knoll deep in the woods and enclosed by a rock wall, is the final resting place of nine members of this well-known black family from Portland, including Samuel Ruby (1790–1837); the Avery Cemetery in Waterboro, named after a farming family, including patriarch and Maine native James Avery (1790–1865), locally renowned for their skill in building stone walls (Price and Talbot, pg. 346); and the Seco-Sewall Cemetery and the Talbot Cemetery, both in China. The Talbot Cemetery is located in the Yorktown section of town near a rock wall and a small stream and has two marked graves, those for Eliza Talbot (1790–1872), a New Hampshire native and wife of farmer Ezekiel Talbot, and their daughter, Sarah Freeman (1828–1895). The Seco-Sewall Cemetery lies at the end of a dirt road in a small wooded clearing and contains five marked graves, including that for farmer William Seco (1793–1866), who in later years was blind, and Ambrose Sewall (1787–1851), of mixed descent, also a farmer, with sizeable holdings that were larger than those of most of his white neighbors.

Public Burying Grounds and Cemeteries

The second type of burial site to be established in New England, the most common for African Americans, was the town or public burying ground, usually located either adjacent to or nearby the town meetinghouse, though as towns expanded and additional cemeteries were established this was less and less the case. The use of these public burying spaces was convenient, especially for those who lived within the confines of a town or village, thus eliminating the need to set aside a part of their own land for family burials. In addition, the town burying ground, and the graves of those contained within, was an indicator of one's status and social standing. Here was where large gravestones or, later on, monuments could be placed, for all to view, to remind fellow townsfolk of the deceased's status and importance. Early on, this status, based on old English customs, was also indicated by one's burial spot within the yard itself. Those buried closest to the church, whether it be the town minister, a judge, local militia leader, or town founder, were the most prominent in social standing. Indeed, just as in Westminster Abbey in London, where prominent church members and the elite are buried inside the church, so too did this happen in New England, albeit to a lesser degree. The Rev. William Shurtleff, pastor of the South Church in Portsmouth, New Hampshire, was so revered and respected he was buried under the church pulpit, while one prominent church member in Newington, New Hampshire, was buried at the foundation of the church, near the entrance to his private pew.

Just as these burial sites were indicative of the status of whites, so too was the status of African Americans, whether enslaved or free, indicated by their burial positions *within* the public burying ground. In most instances, blacks were buried in the far back of the burying ground, away from the graves of even the lesser white members of society, an indicator of the lowest position they occupied on both the economic and social ladders of society. Sometimes these graves were marked, but often times they were not, and sometimes sections of these burying places were clearly designated in town records as the "slave," "negro" or "colored" sections and were often first utilized for enslaved burials, and later free black burials.

This practice of segregating African Americans in New England burial grounds by relegating them to the back edges and far-flung corners remained in practice into the 20th century. However, this segregating practice has remained a bit of a secret in some cases, mainly because, as time has gone forward and town cemeteries have filled up over the years, black burial sites within some public cemeteries that once were on the fringe are now surrounded by later burials as cemeteries grew and expanded, thus giving the appearance of an integrated burial ground. A closer examination of the dates of nearby gravestones often reveals the true isolation of some of these sites, with sometimes two or three decades passing before an adjacent grave for whites was established.

While segregation within New England graveyards was based on both color and race, it was also based on social standing and the "otherness" of African Americans in general. Though purchased and forcibly transported to New England towns at their owners' will and desire, the enslaved were also viewed as strangers and outsiders to these tight-knit communities. So too were paupers, transient laborers and farm workers, and mariners, all of whom (whether white or black) often moved from town to town to make a living and seldom set down permanent roots. Is it any wonder, then, that many communities set off these farthest ends of their burying grounds and designated them as "stranger's grounds," where those from outside the community were buried?

Yet another possible indicator of their lesser status in the public burying ground may also be found in the orientation of African American burial sites. As I've discussed earlier, most grave sites in New England until well into the 1800s were oriented on an east-west axis with the head of the deceased facing west, a longstanding tradition among Christians and non–Christians alike involving the concept of the deceased facing the rising sun to the east, a metaphor for the dawn of the Resurrection. However, there are a few African American grave sites, including some in the African Burying Ground in New York and in the North Cemetery in Providence, Rhode Island, that are not oriented in this fashion, but the reasons for this are unclear and the numbers are small. Perhaps these burials reflected a different belief system (some African slaves were Muslims), or were the subtle result of prejudice by the sexton or whoever had dug the grave. On the other hand, burials of this type (both for black and white) are so rare that there may be no hidden meaning behind their different orientation.

One supposed case of prejudice that is similar in this regard may be found on the island of Martha's Vineyard. Here is where Captain William Martin (1830–1907), an African American whaling captain, is buried on Chappaquiddick in a large cemetery with relatively few stones. Martin, like other African Americans on the island, lived on Chappaquiddick Plantation, a part of the island that was owned by Native Americans. He made a living as a sailor, eventually rising up through the ranks to gain command of the *Golden City* in 1878, and later on the *Emma Jane* in 1883 and the *Eunice H. Adams* in 1887. Captain William Martin was Martha Vineyard's first and perhaps only black whaling captain. He and his wife Sarah (Brown) were married after a nearly four-year-long whaling voyage ended in 1857. Despite William's color (Sarah may have been of mixed ancestry) the couple would become respectable members of the Edgartown community.

The large granite marker for the Martins, placed after the death of Sarah in 1911, was erected in the cemetery with the inscribed front facing away from the sea, the bodies of the captain and his wife oriented in the typical east-west fashion. While Captain Martin almost certainly experienced his share of prejudice while alive, he was well respected in his community and at his death was buried as any white member of the society would have been. However, by the early 2000s some in Martha Vineyard's African American community came to believe that the orientation of the Martin stone, facing away from the sea upon which he had sailed many a voyage, reflected a prejudice against the sea captain that persisted even after his death. As a result, these well-meaning individuals, unversed in New England burial practices, turned the Martin stone around so that it faced the sea. Eventually the error was pointed out by others in the know and, once the facts were known, plans were made to return the stone to its original orientation by 2013.

Monument, Captain William Martin and Sarah Martin, 1907–1911, Hilltop Cemetery (a.k.a. Indian Burial Ground or Jeffer's Lane Cemetery), Chappaquiddick Island, Martha's Vineyard, Massachusetts. The Martins' sizeable monument is indicative of the captain's success as the island's only black whaling captain.

The largest number of African American burials, not surprisingly, are found in the public burial grounds of the largest towns that were also once the home of a considerable enslaved population. In Hartford, Connecticut, over 300 African Americans, and likely many more, are documented as having been buried in the Ancient Burying Ground, including five black governors, though none have contemporary grave markers. In the Old North Cemetery there are buried over two dozen African American soldiers who served in several black regiments in the Civil War, including the 29th Connecticut. In the Grove Street Cemetery in New Haven, Connecticut, are buried six of the former African slaves who captured the slave ship *La Amistad*, on which they were being transported in 1839. In the rear portion of the Old Norwichtown Cemetery in Norwich, Connecticut, there are an unknown numbers of graves, all but one unmarked, for African Americans, the most notable being that for black governor Boston Trowtrow, whose grave is marked. In Newport, Rhode Island, there is the God's Little Acre portion of the Common Burying Ground, which is the resting place for hundreds of that town's black residents, including many who were enslaved, and is the most significant African American burial site in New England. In Providence, Rhode Island, there is the North Burial Ground, where many of that city's African Americans are buried, including the freed slave turned restaurateur Emanuel Bernon, whose grave marker "is as substantial a memorial as those of most of the wealthier white men of his day" (Johnston, pg. 33); Patience "Sterry" Borden, remembered for her charitable giving; and the lovely floral-themed gravestone for Bristol Bernon (1762–1781), the son of Hannah, "servant to Mr. Gideon Crawford." And in the Copp's Hill Burial Ground in Boston are buried thousands of that city's African American residents, including Prince Hall, most with no grave markers.

Despite all these locations, and many others in surrounding locales where lesser numbers of African Americans are buried, there are several towns where some unusual practices were established. In Newport, Rhode Island, the God's Little Acre portion of the Common Burying Ground is unique and unprecedented in that, of the unknown number of African Americans buried there, there were professionally carved gravestones for hundreds of these burials, of which nearly two hundred have survived to this day. While the gravestones in this cemetery will be discussed in detail later on, it should be noted that the sheer number of headstones found here for the enslaved is much greater than all of the others known to exist in the rest of New England *combined*.

Another town which had a significant enslaved population was New London, Connecticut. Here, in the Antientist Burial Ground, the town's oldest public burying place located on a hillside overlooking the Thames River, is the grave for Florio (1689–1749), the wife of Hercules, one of Connecticut's black governors, as well as those for Sappho Clancy and her daughter Morocco, Florah Hurlbut, and a number of other African Americans. The number of marked graves for African Americans at this site makes New London the most important town in this regard in Connecticut, and only Providence and Newport in Rhode Island have more marked graves for African Americans dating prior to 1800 in all of New England.

The city of Boston is also interesting in that it limited black burials beginning in 1723 to the closest burying ground to the home of the deceased, but only if that place would accept them. This was probably an attempt to prevent the long and winding funeral processions that so annoyed and offended white residents, but it is unclear where such a burial might take place if they were not accepted. By the 1740s Boston officials even asked that there be designated spots within their burial grounds for African Americans, leading one to believe that burial spots within these places may not have been strictly regulated prior to that time. Also in Boston, there is the well-known Granary Burying Ground; here were buried in 1770 in a common grave the five victims of the Boston Massacre, a seminal event leading up to the American Revolution. Among the dead was Crispus Attucks, a man formerly enslaved in Framingham, of mixed African and Native American descent, who later gained his freedom and worked as a mariner. The first to die in the massacre, Attucks almost instantly became a martyr of the Revolution, which fact trumped his skin color when it came to his final resting place alongside the other white victims.

Portsmouth, New Hampshire, is also interesting in that it was one of the few slaveholding towns known to have formally designated a wholly separate public burying space,

```
                    CONGRESS      STREET.

  15  Prison Lane.  14  13  12  |  11  10  9  8  |  M. H.
                    16  17  18  |  19  20  21  22 |  1
       Fetter  Lane.   (now Warren st.)  Pond  Lane.
            (now Chest-  23  24  25  |  26  27  28  29  |  Church  2
        51                 Fleet                              3
                        30  31  32  |  33  34  35  36         4
                  Broad st.      (now State st.)
            nut st )   37  38  39  |  40  41  42  43  |  street.  5  6
       Negro                  street.                            7
       Burying Ground.  44  45  46  |  47  48  49  50
            Jaffrey st.      (now Court st.)

                                              Parsonage.
```

PLEASANT STREET.

Glebe Land Map, Portsmouth, New Hampshire. This map shows the location of the so-called "Negro Burying Ground" (bottom left) in this port city as detailed in 1709 town documents. This segregated burying space was used for 100 years until it was eventually abandoned and obliterated by the town's growth (Brewster's *Rambles About Portsmouth*, page 45).

the so-called "Negro Burial Ground" according to 19th century records, early on in its history, far away from the public burial ground reserved for whites. This early African American cemetery, which was rediscovered in 2003 and is now designated the African Burying Ground, was established by 1705, possibly earlier, and was located on what was then the farthest edge of the town, near where the jail and poorhouse would also be built. However, while there are few details about this burial site that offer any insights as to why a wholly separate spot was chosen by Portsmouth officials, it seems clear that they wanted black burials to be formally segregated in a space that was to be all their own, this likely becoming an increasing issue for whites as the enslaved population increased dramatically after 1700. Prior to this, most of the enslaved were likely buried on their owner's land, there being no evidence, anecdotal or otherwise, suggesting that the enslaved of Portsmouth were ever buried in the town's oldest public burial place, Point of Graves.

Perhaps one of the first black interments in what would soon be a segregated burial ground in Portsmouth was that for the unnamed "Negro woman" who was "consumed in the Flames" (*Boston News-Letter*, November 6, 1704) when the home of the Rev. Nathaniel Rogers caught fire and burned to the ground on the morning of October 30, 1704. This was the first newspaper account of a house fire in American history. While the graves for the two other victims of this fire, Rogers's mother-in-law and his daughter Elizabeth, can be seen in Point of Graves, there is no marked grave for the enslaved woman who died a tragic death while serving them.

One other type of burial for the enslaved, as well as those once enslaved, that took place in the public burial grounds in the larger New England towns, may also explain, at least in part, why marked graves for African Americans are often lacking prior to 1790. Many of the wealthiest members in society, including those who were slave holders, in New England were not interred in single gravesites, but in larger family burial vaults, crypts, or tombs, as they are variably called. Some of these were located below ground, some above ground, the latter often set into the side of a small hill or mound, all within the confines of the public burial grounds. These burial sites contained the remains of many generations of family members and sometimes included the enslaved who served them. Those located above ground usually have a brick or granite facing, with a hinged iron door that allowed access to the interior. Inside, shelves were built along the sides and back wall which held the coffins of the deceased, which, in order to identify their occupants, usually had an engraved brass plaque. Whether African Americans interred in such vaults also had their coffins marked with their identity is unknown.

The interment of the enslaved within these family vaults was likely done out of a combination of factors that may be speculated upon. The enslaved were almost certainly in some cases viewed as extended family members for whom some affection must have been held, and thus it does not seem incongruous for such a burial. Other slave owners may have done so out of economy, it being cheaper for such an interment rather than paying for a separate grave to be dug and a suitable grave marker provided. While a combination of both of these factors may have been at play, one telling anecdote for a man enslaved in Connecticut also reveals that such a burial site may have been offered as a "reward," dubious in the eyes of the subject of this sketch to be sure, for the enslaved individual's years of forced servitude: "An old gentleman, at the point of death, called a faithful Negro to him, telling him that he would do him honor before he died.... 'I intend, Cato,' said the master, 'to allow you to be buried in the family vault.' 'Ah! Massa,' returns Cato, 'me no like dat. Ten pounds would be better to Cato. Me no care where me be buried; besides, Massa, suppose we be buried together, and de devil come looking for Massa, in de dark, he might take away poor Negro man in mistake'" (Fowler, pg. 130–131).

Though the burial of enslaved and free blacks who were serving wealthy families is largely undocumented and would seem to hark back to the days, at least in spirit, of the Egyptian pharaohs who had their servants buried with them so that they could continue to serve them in the afterlife, there can be little doubt that burials of this type certainly took place in towns like Boston, Hartford, Norwich, Portsmouth, and likely many more. One interesting example is the burial of Chloe Spear; when she died a free woman in Boston in 1815, she was buried in the Bradford vault in the Granary Burying Ground with the family that had once held her slave.

The tradition of family vaults eventually faded away, replaced by the early 1830s with the advent of the rural cemetery movement, by family plots that were out in the open for all to see. Not only were these modern cemeteries landscaped with ornamental trees and shrubs and winding pathways, in sharp contrast to the plain burial grounds of Puritan New England, but separate family plots became the new standard, often having a central monument or obelisk, with family memorials surrounding them. In addition, this family space was physically defined, often enclosed with elaborate wrought iron fences and gates or granite curbing.

Even in these burial spaces, we see examples of African Americans women (I've found no examples for men) being buried here due to their close relationship with the family, both the formerly enslaved as well as those women who worked for these families. In Brunswick, Maine, in Pine Grove Cemetery there is buried Phebe Ann Jacobs, who was born into slavery in New Jersey and eventually came to be owned by the Wheelock family of Pittsfield, Massachusetts. When Maria Wheelock married William Allen, Phebe went with her to serve in the Allen household, and when William Allen moved to Brunswick to become the president of Bowdoin College, Phebe also came to Maine, and was freed by 1839 when William Allen left Bowdoin. She is buried in the Allen family plot, right near the front of the cemetery. In contrast, Isaiah and Louisa Freeman, an African American father and daughter, are buried at the rear of the cemetery as was traditional with most African Americans.

In another example, Elizabeth "Mum Bett" Freeman (ca. 1742–1829) is buried in the Sedgwick family plot in the Stockbridge Cemetery in Stockbridge, Massachusetts. Formerly enslaved, she gained her freedom via a court case litigated by a young attorney, Theodore Sedgwick. After gaining her freedom, Elizabeth Freeman went to work as a servant and midwife for the Sedgwick family, helping to birth one child of Theodore and Pamela Sedgwick and several of their grandchildren. In this case, the mutual love and respect that existed between the Sedgwicks and Elizabeth Freeman makes it clear that she was considered one of the family.

Finally, in Quincy, Massachusetts, Harriet Wilson, the former indentured servant from New Hampshire who wrote *Our Nig*, the first novel written by an African American, was buried in the Cobb family plot in Mount Wollaston Cemetery after dying in a Quincy hospital in 1900. It is unknown for certain what Wilson's connection to this family may have been, but perhaps she worked for them as a housekeeper or had befriended them through the spiritualist community in which she had been a leading figure.

Though I have discussed the larger towns and cities and their public burying spaces, there are numerous other such sites located in smaller towns and villages in every New England state, and in most cases the layout is the same, with black burials relegated to the rear or far side of the cemetery. Many of the marked burials in these cemeteries, as will be discussed further on, are for men who were veterans of the American Revolution or the Civil War, and while marked graves for the enslaved and women of color are smaller in number, there are some surviving examples to be found.

One of the most interesting of the small-town public burying grounds in which African Americans were interred is the Meetinghouse Cemetery in Princeton, Massachusetts. Here are buried three enslaved individuals, two men and a woman, all the slaves of Moses Gill, Esq., a prominent landholder who owned a 3,000 acre estate with a fine mansion on land first held by his father-in-law, the Rev. Thomas Prince of Boston. As a government official of Massachusetts and a judge in Worcester County, Moses Gill split his time between Boston and his country estate, and at his death in 1800 was buried in Boston. Three of the enslaved individuals (there were at least five in all) employed on Gill's estate—Flova, Thomas, and Nero—not only had their graves marked with finely carved gravestones, but were also buried near the center of the burial ground, rather than at the back as was usually the case for African Americans. Their prominent burial location within Meetinghouse Cemetery is likely a reflection of the Gill family's status and the respect he, and all associated with him, commanded in Princeton. Their final resting place may also be indicative of the affection that Gill's second wife, Rebecca Boylston Gill, had for these individuals, as Flova, and another enslaved man named Jack (whose burial site is unknown), had previously been enslaved by the Boylston family in Boston and were later willed to her in 1771 prior to her marriage to Moses Gill.

A few other examples of these small-town public burial sites include the following. The Wethersfield Village Cemetery in Wethersfield, Connecticut, has four marked burials, including one of the oldest marked African American graves in all of New England, and Quash Gomer (1731–1799), who was a native of Angola enslaved at the age of seventeen. The Brick Cemetery in Colrain, Massachusetts, is where may be found the final resting place for members of the Greene family, including Peter Greene, Sr. (1750-ca. 1836), a Revolutionary War veteran who served in the 2nd New York Regiment. Old Burial Hill in Marblehead, Massachusetts, is the resting place of many African Americans, including Joseph "Old Joe" Brown (1750–1834), whose patriotic gravestone denotes his service as a Revolutionary War soldier. Also buried here, though her gravestone is now lost, was Agnis, a "Negro servant" to Samuel Russell, who died in 1718. Eastern Cemetery (formerly called the "New Yard") in Gorham, Maine, is the final resting place of at least three enslaved individuals: Prince McLellan (ca. 1729–1829), a sailor during the Revolutionary War, and his wives Dinah (died 1800) and Chloe (died 1827), all formerly enslaved and all memorialized on the same gravestone. Nearby, in the older Village Cemetery in Gorham, lies Neptune

Stephenson (1780–1824), "a pious man." In the Grafton Village Cemetery in Grafton, Vermont, are buried Alexander (1845–1923) and Sally (1855–1933) Turner, who were formerly enslaved in the South before Alexander Turner escaped from captivity during the Civil War and, after serving with a New Jersey regiment, moved northward to New England. In the West Brattleboro Cemetery in Brattleboro, Vermont, was buried Jacob Cartledge, formerly enslaved and a native of Georgia. He fought in a black regiment from Pennsylvania during the Civil War after escaping from his master and moved to Vermont about 1880, largely employed as a farmhand and laborer. In the Bennington Village Cemetery in Bennington, Vermont, is the small and weathered gravestone at the back for Margaret (Smith) Greenleaf (ca. 1791–1858). She was the wife of Nimrod Greenleaf (1780–ca. 1865), both of them likely former slaves in Connecticut who arrived in Vermont by 1810, and the mother of Sarah, Sylvia, and Harriet Greenleaf. In the Palisado Cemetery in Windsor, Connecticut, is the grave for Nancy Toney (1775–1857), formerly enslaved by the Bradley and Loomis families. In Milford, New Hampshire, is the burial plot for the Blanchard family in the Elm Street Cemetery, including patriarch George Blanchard, a signer of the Association Test during the American Revolution and a veterinarian. In Barrington, Rhode Island, the Allin Burial Ground is the final resting place for Revolutionary War veteran Scipio Freeman (ca. 1746–1816), whose grave is marked, as well as Adam and Becky Allin, formerly enslaved by the Allin family, and Henrietta "Ritty" Allin, Adam's sister, whose graves are all unmarked.

Finally, it is of interest to note that while most public burial grounds in New England are assumed to have been, and probably were, established with the intent that they would be for white burials, with the result that whites were the first individuals to be interred (a fact often noted on their gravestone), there is one possible example of a public burial ground in New Hampshire that may have established on ground first used for black or Native American burials. The historic East Lempster Cemetery was established in 1773 in Lempster, New Hampshire, a town in the southwestern part of the state first settled by men and women from Connecticut in the 1760s. This cemetery was the burial site of Rufus Beekman (killed by the fall of a tree); he was, as church deacon Reuben Roundy noted in 1856, "the first white person interred on the spot and it has been used by the town (excepting a few families) ever since" (Lawrence, pg. 460). Some of the families that settled in Lempster from Connecticut very likely included slaves in their households, and at least

Monument, Alexander and Sally Turner, 1923–1933, Village Cemetery, Grafton, Vermont. The Turners came to Vermont after the Civil War, becoming the town of Grafton's first black family and well respected citizens for over a hundred years.

one free black, Isaac Tatten, came here from East Haddam, Connecticut, on behalf of his former master Joseph Spencer. Though unrecorded and unmarked, the statement about this site's first white burial implies that at least one black individual who came to Lempster may have died prior to 1773 and was buried on the rocky and hilly land next to Dodge Pond that is now within the confines of the East Lempster Cemetery.

Pauper/Indigent Burial Sites

In addition to the regular public burial grounds and cemeteries found in every New England town, big or small, there was also one other type of public burial space that is often found; these were variably known as pauper or almshouse cemeteries, or sometimes poor-farm cemeteries. These burying places were segregated, but not by race, and included whites, blacks, Native Americans, and others. Instead, pauper cemeteries were segregated by an individual's economic status, being specifically designated for the

Gravestone, Scipio Freeman, 1816, Allin Cemetery, Barrington, Rhode Island. Freeman and his family were amongst this town's small African American population, some of whom are buried here without grave markers, in the decades after the end of the Revolutionary War (courtesy Julie Nathanson).

more unfortunate members of society who, due to age, monetary circumstances (and often a combination of both), or infectious medical conditions, had became public charges. Upon the death of these individuals, they were often buried at public expense because there was no family member to claim the body. These cemeteries were sometimes established adjacent to the public burial grounds, but in other cases were either established away from the center of town, near the almshouse or the town or county poor farm if one was established. The "Negro Burial Ground" (now designated the African Burying Ground) in Portsmouth, New Hampshire, was located on what was then the far edge of town in 1705, near where the jail and almshouse were also built; it is likely that this cemetery was also used as the final resting place for the poor and perhaps even criminals, no matter what their race.

Because pauper cemeteries were most often the final resting place for the poor and/or aged, as well as those who died from communicable diseases (such as tuberculosis), documentation for those who may have been buried in them is often lacking. A man known only as "Jack the sailor" (ca. 1784–1858), who may have been African American, was buried in the West Rutland, Vermont, Poor Farm Cemetery, located just off Rte. 133 on North Lane, but nothing is known of this individual. At some sites, even less is known, as many paupers have no gravestones with their name and many burials simply went unmarked. Interestingly, graves in some of these cemeteries are marked with a just a simple stone with only a number carved on them and no name, the idea being that the deceased could be identified through records kept by the town corresponding to the deceased's assigned number. One of the largest such sites in New England may be found in Providence, Rhode Island, in historic North Burial Ground.

In fact, in many cemeteries like these, countless numbers of African Americans found their last resting place. In Uxbridge, Massachusetts, the Almshouse Cemetery, which was moved from its original location due to highway construction, had at least thirty known burials, but only one, that for Mrs. Nancy Adams, was marked; her stone calls her "A respectable colored woman" and gives her place of birth as Louisiana, though records from the 1850 federal census indicate she was born in Maryland.

Similar in nature to these almshouse or poor farm cemeteries are those that are affiliated with other town, regional, and state institutions, like prisons and asylums; here also are buried those individuals who were living on the edge and were deemed unfit to be a part of society. They, too, seldom have properly marked or documented burial sites. Buried on the grounds of the old Wethersfield State Prison was a slave from Africa named Prince Mortimer (1724–1834). He was convicted in 1811, at the age of 87, of trying to poison his master after a promise to give him his freedom was later ignored, and he was given a life sentence at Connecticut's infamous Newgate Prison. He died in 1834 at the new state prison in Wethersfield and, like all other inmates whose bodies went unclaimed, was buried in an unmarked

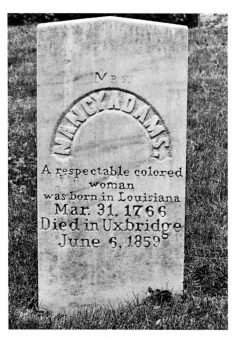

Gravestone, Nancy Adams, 1859, Almshouse Cemetery, Uxbridge, Massachusetts. There are 31 known burials at this site, which was moved to its current location in 1985, but the grave (a modern replacement) for Adams, who is listed as a slave (runaway?) in death records, is the only one that is inscribed.

grave in the prison cemetery located on a cove, now called Cove Park, on the Connecticut River (Caron, pg. 150). Here, as with many cemeteries of this kind, are found no individual markers and no records were kept by the prison of who exactly was buried here. The site, which went out of use after the prison closed in 1963, is now marked with a simple plaque.

The burial of Prince Mortimer in Connecticut was at least a civilized one, but this was not always the case for criminals who died either at the hands of the state or under state care in New England. The white victims who were hanged as witches during the Salem witch trials in Massachusetts in 1692 had their bodies thrown into a ravine or interred in unmarked graves because they were considered un–Christian, though several families did recover them after night had fallen. But Thomas Powers, a black man executed for the crime of rape in Haverhill, New Hampshire, in 1796, was not even buried. Powers is said to have sold his body prior to his death for dissection to two New Hampshire doctors; his skin said to have been flayed from his body after he was hanged, and subsequently tanned and made into a fine pair of boots for one of the doctors.

Then there is the Pinelands Patients Cemetery in New Gloucester, Maine. This burial spot, which was utilized beginning in 1907 after the Maine School for the Feeble-Minded was established, is located behind the Webber Cemetery, the two separated by a line of trees. Among the many burials at this institutional site, where the quack science of eugenics reigned supreme (as elsewhere in the nation) for over four decades, are the family members of those who lived on Malaga Island, just off the coast of Maine near Phippsburg. These African American and mixed ancestry families were forcibly removed from their homes on the island by Maine authorities, some of them committed to the Maine School for the Feeble-Minded, in an incident that has been cited as the state's worst case of racial intolerance. No matter where these cemeteries are located, their undocumented burials, isolated locations, and often poor upkeep makes them somewhat more forlorn places than most cemeteries, a sad reflection of their inhabitants' low standing in society.

Neighborhood Burial Sites

The final type of cemetery found in New England comprises the smaller, more localized neighborhood cemeteries that are usually found in outlying areas of a given town. These cemeteries are semi-public in nature, established to serve a small cluster of residents within a part of the town. Such cemeteries may have started out as private family plots, later expanded to include other burials for those in the immediate vicinity, or were established to serve several related families and later grew to include others living in the area. Such cemeteries were established not only out of reasons of kinship and community, but also out of sheer convenience if the public burying ground was located some distance (i.e., several miles or more) from the center of town. This makes perfect sense when we consider the fact that the dead, long before the days of professional undertakers and hearse transports, were conveyed from their home to their final resting place by relatives walking on foot.

As I've previously discussed, many African Americans, especially after 1800, were buried in these neighborhood cemeteries. More often than not, these cemeteries were integrated, serving areas where blacks and whites lived in proximity to one another, even if white townsfolk outnumbered their fellow black citizens. While burial locations for African Americans within public cemeteries, even as late as the early 1900s, were located at isolated spots at the back or far edges of a cemetery, this seems to have been less often the case in neighborhood cemeteries. Though speculative, we can easily infer that this was because the families that lived in these areas knew each other and lived in similar circumstances as land owners and farmers. It may also be the case that in these neighborhood burying places, for the reasons just stated, demonstrating one's social status within the confines of the cemetery was less of a concern. Thus it is, for example, that in the town of Lowell, Massachusetts, today (in an area once part of the neighboring town of Dracut), we see Jeffrey Hartwell, formerly enslaved, and members of his family buried in the Hamblett Cemetery close by prominent members of the Varnum family. Hartwell (who also went by the name Jesse Freeman), was once a slave in Bedford, Massachusetts, and his wife Maria was a former slave in Boston; both gained their freedom after the American Revolution and had a farm. The couple had six children, all of whom are likely buried in this same cemetery.

In Connecticut, there is the small Canoe Hill Cemetery in New Canaan. Here may be found, at the rear of the cemetery, the grave of Onesimus Comstock (1761–1867), who was born into slavery in New Canaan. He is said to have been a Revolutionary War veteran (though this is undocumented) and the last slave in Connecticut, enumerated in the 1850 Federal Census as a "voluntary slave." Another such site in Connecticut is the Old Kinne Burial Ground in Griswold. While this cemetery, as its name implies, was first used by the white Kinne family, it evolved into a neighborhood cemetery whose burials included that of a black man, Isaac Glasko, and his wife.

Another interesting site, among the hundreds that may be found throughout New England, is the Daily-Ceasar Cemetery in Johnston, Rhode Island; located on Borden Avenue, this cemetery is named after two black families, both natives of Rhode Island. William Daily (born ca. 1806) and his wife Maria (born ca. 1805) both worked as common laborers, while Henry Ceasar and his wife Rhoda were also laborers in Johnston and surrounding towns. Among the burials in this cemetery is that for their daughter Harriet, who died in 1849. While there are many other burials at this site, it is uncertain if this was an integrated cemetery. Likewise, in South Kingstown, Rhode Island, may be found the Old Fernwood Cemetery, where members of the Fayerweather family of blacksmiths are buried.

Finally, in Reading, Vermont, in the Baileys Mills Cemetery, there are the burials for Revolutionary War veteran Silas Burdoo (1748–1837), a free black formerly of Lexington, Massachusetts, and his wives Betsey (died 1816), Rosanna (died 1836). The Burdoo family moved to New Hampshire after the war, and soon thereafter to Reading, Vermont, perhaps because Vermont's constitution prohibited slavery, or maybe to escape the risk of being kidnapped and sold into slavery. In any event, they became well-respected citizens of Reading, as is evidenced both by their fine gravestones and central location in the cemetery, as well as Silas Burdoo's active involvement in town affairs regarding road construction and land allotments (Quintal, Jr., pg. 72).

While all-black neighborhood cemeteries are a relative rarity in New England, or at least few surviving examples are known to exist, the presence of several such sites in the state of Maine may come as a surprise to many. The most intriguing is the cemetery site in the Atusville section of Machias, named after the former slave London Atus. He and his descendants, as well as other African American families, lived here for many generations, with Atusville hitting its peak in the 1850s but in decline by the 1870s as the community gradually faded away. No visible remnants of this cemetery remain, though local lore surrounding its existence abounds. In contrast to the Atusville site is the beautiful and tidy Peterborough Cemetery in Warren, Maine. This African American cemetery is the only distinctly identifiable remnant of a vibrant black community that once existed in town. The Peterborough community, as it came to be known, was named after Amos and Sarah Peters, with Amos, said to be formerly enslaved, a Revolutionary War soldier from Plymouth, Massachusetts, and his wife a slave from Africa who was brought to Warren in 1782. The community grew apace and at its peak had some 300 residents before its gradual decline after the 1920s.

V. African American Grave Markers

The most interesting aspect of any cemetery for most observers are the various types of grave markers. As I have discussed in the previous chapters, by studying the location of a cemetery in general, and the burial patterns within it, we can learn a great deal about our ancestors, no matter what their color. However, we can learn a great deal more when burial markers are present; some of what may be discovered by studying these artifacts is obvious, including the deceased's name, date of death, age at time of death, a spouse's name, and perhaps their occupation, military service, or even social affiliations. Less obvious in what they may reveal about the deceased are the design aspects found on these markers. Taken as a whole, all of these factors can often tell us something about an individual, or a group of individuals, information that may be absent from official records and the town history books.

First and foremost, when it comes to the number of known, identifiable (those with at least a name) African American burial markers dated prior to 1800, the actual numbers in New England are very low, fewer than 300. Most of these, approximately 225, may be found in Newport, Rhode Island's Common Burying Ground, all but a handful located in the God's Little Acre section specifically set aside for people of color, which will be discussed at length shortly. In addition, there are a small number of other examples, fewer than fifty, to be found in the rest of Rhode Island, most in Providence's North Burial Ground. The remainder of these known sites are scattered throughout New England, about evenly divided between Connecticut and Massachusetts, while New Hampshire has only one example (that for Caesar Wood, "Negro," dated 1785 in Stratham); Maine and Vermont have no such sites. While it is certainly possible that there are other sites that I have overlooked, the fact remains that the numbers are startling low, especially when it is remembered that New England was the home to tens of thousands of African Americans between the 1630s and 1800 (the exact total is uncertain), many enslaved, some free.

Why, then, we may ask, are the graves of the vast majority of these individuals, less than one percent of the entire black population, not marked today? Were they once marked and later lost? Or were there cultural considerations that have led to this loss of identity for African Americans in New England's burial grounds? The answer to both of these questions, to be discussed further on in detail, is a qualified "yes."

One reason advanced for the small number of personally identifiable African American gravesites that I have both read in print and heard voiced is the idea that few people in general in "the old days," including most whites, could afford such grave markers. While this is true to a limited extent, in that indeed not everyone could afford professionally crafted grave markers, this explanation does not suffice, as many whites of ordinary standing, farmers and common laborers, not just wealthy lawyers and ministers, could and did purchase such grave markers prior to 1800 in disproportionately higher numbers than blacks. The reason for the lack of African American grave markers in most cases is a simple one: for most of those who were enslaved, their masters seldom saw fit to purchase such a luxury item, while for free blacks such a purchase, or lack thereof, was often dictated by their income level, but perhaps also by cultural considerations. Each of these factors will be discussed below.

No matter what a person's skin color, it must be remembered that personal grave markers, like clothes and household décor, were an indicator of one's standing within the community. Most importantly, in addition to a prominent location within the burial ground, the size and elaborate design of a grave marker really mattered and was a last show of wealth for, and sometimes designated by, the deceased, hopefully one that would last for the ages. Go into any New England burial ground established before 1800 (and this applies to many, perhaps most, later cemeteries as well) and look for the largest grave stone or monument. Chances are, upon closer inspection, you will find that it marks the grave of a town minister, a lawyer or judge, perhaps a militia captain, or maybe a member of one of the town's elite or founding families, all persons of standing and wealth. Since African Americans occupied, with rare exception, none of these positions, and given their oft-segregated space within the burial ground, it should not come as a surprise that their graves usually went unmarked.

Gravestone, Caesar "Negro," 1785, Stratham, New Hampshire. This stone, now housed in the collection of the Stratham Historical Society, once stood on private land in nearby Greenland, where Caesar Brackett, the slave of Thomas Brackett, was employed. In the 1980s, when the land on which Caesar was buried was sold, his marker was removed and sold to an antiques dealer before it was eventually recovered.

This would only change after 1800, as free African Americans, while always in the minority, became increasingly visible and participatory members of the communities in New England in which they lived, establishing churches and schools and becoming what many well-intending whites considered to be "respectable" people of color.

Before taking a look at the characteristics of African American grave markers, it will be here instructive to discuss the several types of grave markers that were in common use by all in New England from the earliest days down to the 1880s. The first grave markers in New England's early settlements, from the 1620s to the 1640s, were generally impermanent in nature. Archaeological evidence suggests that early markers were made of wood, consisting of a wooden post at either end of the grave to mark its outlines, perhaps connected by a cross-piece, the whole resembling a section of a wooden fence, or perhaps a simple upright wooden marker crudely cut in a square or bed-head form, the later imitative in form of the professionally carved gravestones of the British Isles. Interestingly, despite what may be seen in book illustrations or the movies regarding these old New England burial grounds, no wooden crosses were used, their very form being abhorrent and the antithesis of the early Puritan ideals that predominated in colonial New England. Whatever wood grave markers may have been used, none have survived to this day.

While wood markers were initially in use, this practice was quickly ended for the simple reason that they were impermanent and that rocks and fieldstones abounded everywhere in New England. The first gravestones were roughly fashioned, upright pieces of stone used to mark a burial sites. Some were crudely carved with the deceased's name or initials and sometimes a death date and age, while most were unlettered in any fashion, whether for white or black. The use of fieldstone markers was first done out of necessity, as there were no professional gravestone carvers in the colonies, but even after such craftsmen arrived to practice their trade, fieldstones remained in use for many years; such stones were easy to procure, and importantly for those who could not afford a real gravestone, cost nothing. For free African Americans who had little money to spare for the luxury of a carved gravestone, fieldstones continued to be used well into the 1800s. There is one other consideration to take into account regarding the use of fieldstone markers, this being the fact that fledgling communities, whether those established by the first settlers, or in later settled areas, were composed of a relatively small number of individuals, all of whom were well-acquainted with one another. These individuals likely knew all too well who was buried under which headstone and there was no thought given to preserving that information for later generations.

Professionally carved gravestones began to appear in the colonies by the 1640s, and by the early 1700s a number of important craftsmen, the major suppliers in New England and beyond operated out of shops in Boston, Charlestown, Dorchester, and Haverhill (to name just a few) in Massachusetts, with others soon to follow in Connecticut and Newport, Rhode Island. In northern New England, Maine and New Hampshire imported their gravestones from carvers in Massachusetts and beyond for over a hundred years; stonecutters (or "sculptors," as they often called themselves) did not set up shop in New Hampshire until the 1740s, with Vermont carvers appearing a few decades later, and Maine had no professional carvers of note until after 1800. These professionally cut stones were first commonly made of slate (colored black, blue, or gray), procured at a number of locations in New England, with a brown sandstone (more rough in appearance than the smooth slate stones) also in use, particularly in Connecticut and the Merrimac River valley area of northeastern Massachusetts. Marble gravestones came into common use by the late 1700s, especially in the upper Connecticut River valley. By the 1830s limestone gravestones were very common and replaced slate as the primary material in New England, while marble remained a popular material. Granite as a material for gravestones and monuments did not come into widespread use until after the 1850s, by which time machine-cut gravestones had replaced hand-carved stones.

Up until the mid–1800s gravestones always came in pairs, with a larger headstone to mark the head of the grave, and a smaller footstone to mark the other end, with the deceased buried in between. The footstones are important to remember as, today, many people who are unfamiliar with gravestone traditions mistake these smaller footstones for children's gravestones or burial sites for the poor as they are usually undecorated and simply have the initials of the deceased (the key information, of course, being on the headstone). This final "resting place" configuration, with a headstone and footstone is, of course, reminiscent of a bed; in colonial times up to 1800 (there is no exact end date), headstones had rounded tops with shoulders, resembling a headboard, but in all periods there can be found some unusually shaped gravestones, some with pyramidal tops, others with square tops, and so on. However, rectangular-shaped headstones did not come into common use until after 1800 and would remain a standard, though rounded top gravestones (without shoulders), and Gothic-arch shapes would also become popular during the Victorian era and the advent of the rural cemetery movement beginning in the 1830s.

Monumental stones are another type of grave marker that came into use by the early 1800s, coming in many different sizes. Among the most recognizable types are the tall obelisks resembling the Washington Monument, ranging anywhere from six to ten feet tall, inscribed on all sides and commemorating not just one deceased individual, but a whole family. These and similar elaborate monuments came into popular use by the wealthy and were usually the centerpiece in the elaborate family plots that became a hallmark of the new types of park-like cemeteries and monumental gardens which were typical of the rural cemetery movement. One characteristic of these monuments is that fact that in many cases they memorialize an individual who is not buried at the spot in which it has been placed, often for an individual whose final resting place is either unknown, or far away from home. This is especially true for sailors lost at sea and soldiers who were killed in battle and buried on the battlefield, but also for others who simply died in other towns while traveling. Monumental stones are characterized, too, by the fact that they are often erected many years later, sometimes decades or even a century or more, long after the individual they are commemorating has passed away. One of the most common types of monument stones, particularly important to our subject, are those erected for specific military veterans.

Finally, in this description of the types of burial markers that were in common use in New England, we should not forget the burial markers left behind by non–Europeans. Here the historian is challenged by an almost complete lack of documentation. The Native Americans who had occupied the land that became known as New England for thousands of years left behind burial mounds and other burying grounds that have all been largely obliterated. The slaves that were forcibly brought here from Africa, as well as their descendants, also utilized their own cultural burial markers that have been all but lost. Just what kinds of varied African traditions were followed in this area is uncertain, but their possible use may offer yet another explanation as to why so few African American grave sites in early New England have been identified.

Slave Grave Markers

The grave markers for the enslaved are, in many ways, the most interesting, and certainly the most visible artifacts that document the institution of slavery in New England.

The earliest grave markers for slaves were unmarked fieldstones, such as those found for the Langdon family slaves in Portsmouth, New Hampshire, with seventeen marked burials packed close together in a small lot. Throughout New England, simple stones like these remained the standard for most slaves during the time when slavery existed, with professionally carved stones being an unusual exception. The small number of professionally carved stones found for the enslaved, as previously discussed, makes this painfully clear, as is the fact that the lack of such markers was almost certainly an economic decision on the part of a slave's master.

In Portsmouth, New Hampshire, the African Burying Ground offers, perhaps, a typical example. There is no evidence, anecdotal or archaeological, that any of the burials in this large site were marked by professionally carved stones. In contrast, the vast majority of gravestones for white individuals buried in the town's other cemeteries prior to 1800, just when the African Burying Ground fell into disuse, were imported from Massachusetts carvers. Such stones were purchased during the regular trading voyages that Portsmouth's merchant families conducted with Boston on a regular basis and carried back to town as part of their cargo. Portsmouth traders were certainly willing to allow the use of such cargo space for their own family markers, but when it came to gravestones for their slaves, they were apparently unwilling to pay for such stones and the expenses incurred in their transport. Even in Boston, where there were many gravestone carvers operating in proximity, there was no tradition of marking the graves of the enslaved. Once again, this was almost certainly due to economic factors; once a slave had quit paying out, so to speak, for his master, there was no reason to invest in a stone that memorialized him. This frugality in the graveyard is interesting when we ponder the fact that many slaves served their masters for many years and were considered to be almost a part of the family, and that some of these slaves were baptized church members.

Despite the fact that most African American burial sites went unmarked prior to 1800, there is one significant site, the Common Burying Ground on Farewell Street in Newport, Rhode Island, where the graves of slaves were sometimes marked. This burying ground was established in 1640 and was gradually expanded over the years. In the northern part of the yard is the segregated portion that was eventually established first for slave burials. Today, this part of the burying ground is known as God's Little Acre, and it is the resting place for an untold number of African Americans. This alone does not make the Common Burying Ground a notable site, for Boston, Hartford, Norwich, and New London, to name just a few, also had public burial grounds with segregated sections. However, it is the fact that many of the deceased slaves had gravestones erected in their memory that makes this site historically important as the largest collection of colonial African American gravesites in the country. Of the approximately 500 marked graves in this section of Common Burying Ground dating from 1720 to the late 1960s, about 225 are for enslaved individuals or free blacks (it is not always clear which was the case) dated prior to 1800. The open spaces within God's Little Acre suggests that most black burials went unmarked, but the number of marked graves is still remarkable given the traditions predominant in the rest of New England. For this reason, Newport must serve as our statistical basis when discussing slave gravestone characteristics and tendencies.

The reasons as to why Newport was different in regard to the number of marked slave burials are speculative at best, but are nonetheless worth exploring. Newport's most active stone-carving family, the Stevenses, were located very close to the burying ground on Thames Street, and members of this family, including John Stevens, his sons William and John Stevens II, as well as the younger John Stevens's son, John Stevens III, are all documented as having carved stones for African Americans. Since there was some degree of autonomy within Newport's large enslaved African American community, it may be speculated that some of these gravestones were purchased by the family of the deceased in a tradition that became unique to Newport. Some of these stones may have been bought with extra money that the enslaved had earned in their spare time, including, perhaps, those stones for Lucey and Bell (both died 1756), the daughters of Rhode Island and Phyllis. In the account books of carver John Stevens II, which rarely mentions African Americans, there is an entry dated September 17, 1748, showing that he provided "a pair for Mingo Tate's child" (Luti, pg. 298), but it is unclear who exactly made the purchase. In some instances it was almost certainly the case that such stones were financed by a slave's master in order to provide a proper marker. This may have been done out of a master's genuine

Gravestone, Phillis and Prince Lyndon/Stevens, 1773, Common Burying Ground, Newport, Rhode Island. Phillis was the ""faithful servant" of Josias Lyndon, as well as the wife of Zingo Stevens. She likely died from the effects of childbirth, followed to the grave by her infant son (depicted in her arms at the top of the stone) just thirteen days later. Note also the pairs of arrows at the top, symbolizing the darts of death that called away both mother and son. This gravestone is one of the most historically significant for an African American in all of New England (courtesy Barb Austin).

feelings of love and respect for his slave and maybe even a sense of responsibility, but such a marker was also indicative of the master's status in the community, a clear demonstration of both his benevolence and his financial resources. Such motives would be in the same vein as those masters who helped finance their slaves' efforts to be elected as king or governor in the black community for the added prestige holding such an office would impart to them.

As to who may have paid for these gravestones, we can speculate that in some cases these stones were paid for by their masters, as about 24 percent of them mention the deceased's status as "servants" or specifically note the deceased's race, in most cases using the term "negro." Significantly, I have found only two extant African American gravestones in New England dated prior to 1800, those for John Jack (died 1773) in Concord, Massachusetts, and Caesar Maxcy (died 1780) in North Attleboro, Massachusetts, which identifies a slave specifically as a "slave." While this term was frequently used in advertisements, legal documents, and other records, it is telling that the more gen-

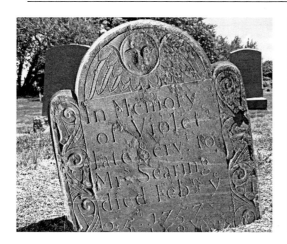

Left: Gravestone, Violet Searing, 1757, Common Burying Ground, Newport, Rhode Island. This gravestone noting Violet's female master is a rarity, as most slave gravestones list only their male masters. Violet is one of three slave owned by the widow of the Rev. James Searing who are buried here. *Right:* Gravestone, Edward Collins, 1738/39, Common Burying Ground, Newport, Rhode Island. This stone is notable for specifically identifying a slave's race, as well as the fact that Edward "was faithfull and well Beloved of his master," both sure signs that this stone was ordered and purchased by his master.

teel term "servant" was often preferred on the gravestones marking their final resting place. A person's status and title were important in white society and such titles indicating military rank or position (say as a lawyer, judge, or minister) were always noted on male gravestones where appropriate. Even for women, their status as wives, mothers, and even widows is often noted. It is thus not surprising that a master would also identify his "servant" on the gravestones he provided. For gravestones such as these, it is possible to conclude that they were probably made on the order of their masters.

Interestingly, only four gravestones in New England, all in Newport, specifically identify the slave's owners as women. Three of them—Peggy (died 1770), Cesar (died 1763), and Violate (died 1757)—were the slaves of "Mrs. Searing," i.e., Mary Searing, the widow of the Rev. James Searing. The fourth, the oldest extant stone in God's Little Acre, is for Hector Butcher, "Negro, late Servant to Ms. Ann Butcher of Barbadoes," who died at the age of 37 in 1720. While it is possible that some of the enslaved may have self-identified as "servants" to a certain master, it is unlikely that most African Americans would have chosen such descriptions, including the term "negro," for their

Gravestone, Cambridge Bull, 1769, Common Burying Ground, Newport, Rhode Island. Though many of the gravestones for African Americans here do not have outright race designations, individuals with place-names like "Cambridge" are sure signs of slave burials, in this case for members of the Bull Family, which included Newport gravestone carver John Bull.

family members. Conversely, it is interesting to note that about 76 percent of these early African American gravestones in Newport have no servant or race identity terms, their racial identity belied only by the location of their burial site and their names, such as Quammine Brown (died 1756) and Cambridge Bull (died 1769), and often backed up by church records. That some, perhaps most, of these individuals died while still enslaved is certain, yet the fact that this is not highlighted on their gravestones is possibly indicative of a conscious choice made by their family and friends.

As to the motifs, for which New England gravestones are justly famed, those carved for the gravestones of the enslaved are largely identical to those found for whites. In the earliest days of Puritan New England, the winged skull (or "death's head") was the predominant motif carved in the upper portion of the gravestone (called the "tympanum") that was the stonecutter's canvas. These grinning skulls, unique to each carver, were often accompanied with crossed bones, the implements of the grave digger (the pick-axe and shovel), as well as the hourglass signifying man's short time on this earth. These grim images were usually surrounded by more appealing floral and fruit images, making the whole stone creation a conveyor of a dual message. The skull was an indicator of man's mortality and that death, ultimately, was the fate of all, while the other natural elements and swirling designs were indicative of the possible rewards that awaited them in heaven if such an assent was so ordained. These gravestones were visual aides, so to speak, that augmented the fire and brimstone sermons preached on the Sabbath. Not everyone in colonial days could read the Bible, but all could understand the images readily visible in the public burial ground.

Gravestone, Lonnon and Hagar Phillips, 1726–1727, Newport, Rhode Island. This dual gravestone was once located in the private slave lot of Christopher Phillips in North Kingstown, Rhode Island, but is now in storage at the John Stevens Shop in Newport. This early stone likely sported a death's head motif and is unusual in that it identifies two slaves serving the same master who were also brother and sister (courtesy Letty Champion).

The earliest remaining gravestone for an enslaved individual in New England to carry such a motif, and perhaps the oldest extant stone of any type for an African American in all of New England, is the small stone, dated November 1699, for a three-year-old "sarvant" girl named Mary found in Marblehead, Massachusetts, in historic Old Burial Hill. Another stone that likely bore this motif is the dual stone for Lonnon and his sister Hagar, dated 1726–27, the slaves of Christopher Phillips of North Kingstown, Rhode Island. This stone was once placed in a slave burial ground, now gone, that also held 15 other graves marked by simple fieldstones, located on Phillips land on what is now Tower Hill Road. Though the death's-head motif is broken and mostly lost, the floral borders on one side are still intact.

Another slave gravestone that is interesting for what is not present is the previously mentioned gravestone for Hector Butcher (died 1720). The tympanum and borders of this stone, carved by the first John Stevens, have no motif at all and have been left blank, while the lettering is well done. This gives us pause and leaves modern historians to speculate as to why this was the case. Perhaps it was simply for reasons of economy, as a simple undecorated stone was less costly than one that was carved. However, might this blank stone also be indicative of the carver's thoughts regarding Hector and his religious state? Did Stevens perhaps consider Butcher a mere heathen, a black from the West Indies, someone unworthy of the religious symbols and messages usually carved for whites? The answer to this question, of course, is unknowable, but intriguing nonetheless.

A much later stone, that for Adam (died 1792, age 12), the "servant" of Elizabeth Miller, is also carved without any motif and could be indicative of the same train of thought, but this stone was produced at a time late in the 18th century when such plain stones, more secular in nature, were becoming more common as the old religious symbolism found on New England gravestones was gradually fading away. The "death's head" motif itself gradually, by the 1740s, had become an overused and rather tired motif, its power to serve as a symbol for repentance largely vanished. One of the latest examples of the use of this motif to be found for African Americans is that for the gravestone of Ann, the daughter of Mimbo (died 1743, aged 2), the slave of Robert Oliver, found in God's Little Acre.

While the "death's head" motif would never entirely disappear, it was eclipsed by a brighter, more hopeful symbol beginning in the 1740s, that of the so-called soul effigy, figures that have variously been described as cherubs or angels. This class of motifs came in many configurations, limited only by the carver's imagination, some with wings, some with-

Left: **Gravestone, Hector Butcher, 1720, Common Burying Ground, Newport, Rhode Island. This stone is notable not only for its early date and the fact that it identifies a slave from the West Indies, but also for its lack of any religious motif. What meaning such a blank slate may have been implied by the stone carver, if any, is uncertain.** *Right:* **Gravestone, Ann Oliver, 1743, Common Burying Ground, Newport, Rhode Island. This stone is for the two-year-old daughter of "Negro" Mimbo Oliver, its death's head motif a late example of this style of the stonecutter's art before more pleasant symbolism on gravestones became the norm by the mid–1740s.**

out, some with happy, smiling faces, some with frowning or foreboding looks, some with round heads, some with pear-shaped or square heads, some male in appearance, others female, some rather ambiguous. As with the old-style "death's head," these figures were often accompanied by floral and fruit carvings and other swirling, geometric, or other types of unique designs. The use of these "soul effigies," gentler images, thought to be a representation of the soul of the departed in semi-human form, became popular when the Great Awakening hit New England, a religious revival of mass proportions that arose in the colonies all up and down the Atlantic seaboard from Maine to Georgia. This "new" religion, pitting the "old light" ministers who still favored the hellfire and brimstone approach and the Puritan doctrine of the preordained destination of one's soul versus the "new light" ministers who favored a more joyful theology that preached that all could be saved and experience heaven if properly adhering to the faith, affected everything from gravestone carvings to church services. Not only were the church services now more joyful and spiritual, especially with the introduction of music, but gravestones, too, offered more pleasant images of the afterlife to contemplate.

These "soul effigy" figures are common for both whites and African Americans, with numerous examples to be found in God's Little Acre in Newport and elsewhere. Some of the most charming are those for the Gill slaves in Princeton, Massachusetts. While many of these "soul effigy" figures are uniform in appearance, there are some gravestones in Newport, most carved between 1771 and 1775, that are unique in that their figures clearly exhibit

African American facial features, including a flat broad nose, full lips, and curly hair. The most striking of these is the gravestone for Phillis (died 1773), the wife of Zingo Stevens, and her newborn son, Prince (born and died in 1773). While

Left: **Gravestone detail, Phillis and Prince Lyndon/Stevens, 1773, Common Burying Ground, Newport, Rhode Island. The African American features on the small child depicted in this portrait-style gravestone are unmistakable, while Phyllis's portrait, though not as well defined in this regard, depicts a bandanna wrap on her head and covering her hair, indicative of the style in which slave women wore their hair.** *Right:* **Gravestone detail, Dinah Wigneron/Wanton, 1772, Common Burying Ground, Newport, Rhode Island. This gravestone for the slave wife of Cesar Wanton, who was only 19 years old when she died, offers more subtle details of the African features carved by John Stevens III.**

the mother holding the child depicted on the gravestone carving is not fully African American in appearance (though her hair appears to be wrapped in a turban), the child that she is holding clearly is. While not all observers and experts are in agreement as to which stones exhibit these African American characteristics, the other stones in God's Little Acre that appear to have some of these same features are the following; Margaret Rivera (1771), Jack Cranston (1772), Violet Hammond (1772), Dinah Wigneron (1772), Pompey Brenton (1772), Rose Flagg (1773), Judith Rivera (1773), Pompey Rogers (1773), Mintus Brenton (1774), and Tower Brinley (1775). All of these stones were carved by John Stevens III and while many of their features are quite similar to his other works, these few stones are different. Why this is the case is unknown. Perhaps John Stevens, influenced by the ideals of the American Revolution that were then taking full shape, was inspired to take a more egalitarian approach, albeit a subtle one, when it came to the images on the stones he carved for his clients of color.

It is at this point that we may address the question as to whether any of the gravestones in Newport and elsewhere in New England, especially those for the enslaved, were carved by African Americans. In fact, almost every known gravestone for African Americans was carved by white stonecutters. However, in Newport there are two gravestones in God's Little Acre that were carved by an enslaved African American, those for Pom-

Top: Gravestone, Judith Rod Rivera, 1773, Common Burying Ground, Newport, Rhode Island. The closely coiffed hair, full lips and broad nose on this carved soul effigy are indicative of African American traits. *Middle:* Gravestone, Violet Hammond, 1772, Common Burying Ground, Newport, Rhode Island. The facial features on this soul effigy, especially the nose and hair, are illustrative of some of the African features carved by stonecutter John Stevens III in the early 1770s. This stone's African associations are also shown in the name of Violet's husband, "Cape Coast" James, Cape Coast being a slave-trading locale in Africa. *Bottom:* Gravestone detail, Pompey Brenton, 1772, Common Burying Ground, Newport, Rhode Island. The broad and flattened nose and curly hair depicted in this soul effigy for Pompey (aged 55 at his death) are typical of some of the works carved for African Americans by John Stevens III during this time period in Newport.

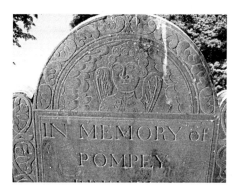

pey Lyndon (died 1765) and Cuffe Gibbs (died 1768). The first stone has the notation "cut by P.S." in the inscription area, while the second states in bold lettering, starting at the top, "This Stone was cut by Pompe Stevens In Memory of his Brother Cuffe Gibbs." Based on this later work it is reasonable to assume that the first stone for Lyndon, signed "P.S.," was also cut by Pompe Stevens.

These two stones, for many years now, have led to some wild speculations about Pompe Stevens and where he may have worked. First and foremost, there is no evidence that Pompe Stevens was an independent stonecutter working out of his own shop, whether in land records, newspaper advertisements, or even anecdotal accounts. Indeed, had he worked on his own, it is likely that historian George Mason, in his 1884 informal history of Newport, would have mentioned Stevens, just as he does the black undertaker Mintus (Brenton), but such is not the case. Of course, by his last name, we can assume that Pompe Stevens likely worked for one of the members of the Stevens family of stonecutters. The stylistic elements on the stones signed by Pompe makes it clear that he worked for William Stevens, who was the most prolific of the Stevens family in the 1760s.

While the story still persists after many years that Pompe Stevens worked for John Stevens II, and later changed his name to Zingo Stevens to return to his African roots, this is clearly not the case. The primary expert on the subject of Newport gravestone carvers, Vincent Luti, has amply demonstrated that while John Stevens II did have a slave named Zingo, he was not the same man as Pompe Stevens, and there was thus no name change (Luti, 297–300). While Zingo Stevens, and several other slaves, including an Indian man and woman, Sypeo and Prince (died 1749) worked for John Stevens II, there is no evidence that they

Top: **Gravestone, Pompey Lyndon, 1765, Common Burying Ground, Newport, Rhode Island. This historic stone is one of only two such stones known to have been carved by an African American stonecutter in all of New England. Note the wording at the bottom, "Cut by P.S.," an indication of Pompe Stevens's work.** *Bottom:* **Gravestone detail, Cuffee Gibbs, 1768, Common Burying Ground, Newport, Rhode Island. The epitaph on this gravestone, starting off with the declaration that it was "cut by Pompe Stevens in Memory of his Brother," makes it one of the most historically significant works of its type in all of New England. It is also another indicator that there were few jobs, skilled and unskilled, in which captive blacks were not employed while slavery existed in New England.**

did any actual gravestone carving. However, they may have possibly helped prepare the slate stone for carving, as Sypeo, according to the Stevens account books, was employed for one day in July 1727 rubbing stones (Luti, pg. 298). As to Pompe Stevens, because his carving style is identical to those from the William Stevens shop, it is highly likely that this same man was his master. William Stevens did, in fact, have four slaves as late as 1774, but their names are unknown.

In regards to Pompe Stevens's carving career, nothing in the way of solid documentation has yet been found. Since Pompe's style matches that of his master, it is difficult to know whether any other stones in Newport can be attributed to him. However, given his two signed works, it seems unreasonable to assume that he carved no other gravestones on his own. Could Pompe Stevens, for example, have been assigned by his master to carve all the stones for his black customers, many of whom have gravestones carved in the style of William Stevens? This is certainly a possibility, but one for which no evidence has been found.

Interestingly, there are a small number of stylistically variant gravestones, none of which feature any African American characteristics like those previously discussed, that may be attributable to slaves, perhaps Pompe himself, working in the William Stevens shop, including that for Geney Newton (died 1777, the wife of Caesar), Prince Green (a stone that has been missing since 1996), Frankey and Judey Baner (both died 1732), Juber Tillinghast (died 1773), and Cudjo and Flora Ekeley (died 1772 and 1771, respectively). Another stone, that for Cambridge Bull (died 1769), may have been cut by an enslaved individual working for the carver John Bull, or possibly one working for William Stevens, with whom John Bull served an apprenticeship (Sterling, Austin, and Champion, pgs. 182, 192, 194, 198–199). All of these suppositions are largely based on inferior lettering techniques and subtle design variants exhibited on the stones in question. Despite these tantalizing prospects, until further evidence is found, the output of Pompe Stevens, or any other black apprentice, will remain a mystery. However, it does seem quite fitting and appropriate that there *was* at one time an African American gravestone carver working, if even in a subordinate role, in Newport to mark the burial sites of his fellow slaves, thereby helping to preserve their names for future generations.

Finally, another piece of important information to consider on gravestones for those who were enslaved is the epitaph itself. What is found in these words, and sometimes what is not found, can also speak volumes. Most immediately noticeable is the lack of an exact age at the time of death for

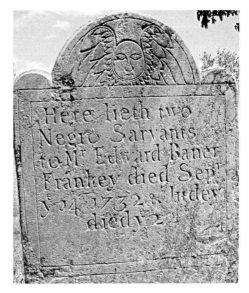

Gravestone, Frankey and Judey Baner, 1732, Common Burying Ground, Newport, Rhode Island. This early dual gravestone for two slaves, ages unknown, who died within eights days of each other, has subtle design variants that may be attributable to an unknown slave stonecutting apprentice.

adult African Americans; most slave gravestones in Newport, and those found elsewhere, use the term "aged about" when giving the deceased's age. Tobe Brightman of Newport died in 1721 (buried not in the segregated section, but in a largely white section not far from his master), "aged About 40 years," while John Jack in Concord, Massachusetts, died in 1773 "aged about 60 years." Of course, the exact age of most slaves brought to New England from Africa was unknown. In contrast, gravestones for whites of all ages often meticulously recorded the age of the deceased, not just in terms of years, but also in months and days. This same detailed age recording, however, is often found for black children born into captivity, as their birthdates, unlike that of their slave parents, were usually recorded by their owners. Thus, we see that Cuffe, the son of Jack and Vilut Carr of Newport, who died on February 19, 1745, was "Aged 7 Years & 5Mo."

Another common feature in the inscription area of the gravestone are such introductory phrases as "In Memory of," "Here Lyeth the Body of," or some like phrase, followed by the name of the deceased. These are almost always used on the gravestones for white individuals, but for those African American gravestones dated prior to 1800, about a quarter are lacking such a phrase, their gravestones instead just giving the bare facts, such as the epitaph in Newport for "Domine, son of Domine Dyre & Philis Bull, died November ye 12th 1740, aged 4 Years & 5 Mo." The reason for this lack of an introductory memorial phrase is unknown, though again perhaps the decision to omit one was made out of sheer economy (fewer carved letters meant a lower-cost stone), but this could also signify a lack of emotion on the part of owners when it came to the death of a slave. That some owners *did* have some emotional attachment to the death of their slaves is also sometimes evident on slave gravestones. For a small number, about six percent, of the gravestones for those who either died as slaves, or were once slaves, we see some key words or phrases that give us some insight into how a master viewed his slave. The most common of these is the word "faithful," while the terms "good," "beloved," "worthy," and "best" are also found. In Newport, Caesar Serring (died 1763) was a "Good & Faithful Servant" to Mrs. Serring, Hercules Brown (died 1762) was "faithful & well beloved of his master" Capt. John Brown, while in the Newman Cemetery in East Providence, Rhode Island, Sherrey (1682–1762) is described as "that true & Faithfull Negro Servant (of Mr. John Hunt)."

Gravestone, Sherrey Hunt, 1762, Newman Cemetery, East Providence, Rhode Island. This simple stone details a slave who was considered a "true & Faithfull Negro Servant." Though uncertain, her epitaph indicates that Sherrey, who was born ca. 1688, had likely been a slave for many years or even decades prior to her death (courtesy Julie Nathanson).

Finally, the only known slave gravestone in northern New Hampshire, that for Silva Marcy Kimball (1786–1800) in the Webster Place Cemetery in Franklin, describes this "faithful black servant" girl as having "lived esteemed and died lamented."

To end this section, it will also be of interest to note that on a few slave gravestones there are some references, both direct and indirect, to their African heritage. Some names of the enslaved, such as Quammine, Cudjo, and Cuffe, are traditional African names, as previously discussed, that were commonly used, but other, less common African names are also found on gravestones. When found etched in stone they serve as a concrete and powerful example of the slaves' attempts to retain their African heritage. In Newport may be seen the graves for Prince (1774–1778), the son of Prince and Bynah Amy; Adam (1747–1748) and Kedindo Pero (born and died in 1749), the son of Kedindo and Minne; and Solomon Nuba Tikey (died 1785, age 5), the son of Arthur Tikey (also known as Arthur Flagg) and his wife Flora. It is interesting to note that the burials for the Pero and Tikey families are next to one another. Might these families have been from the same immediate area in Africa, perhaps the same village, or did they simply share a common bond in their attempts to retain an African identity? Related and interrelated white family members were often buried close to one another in New England burial grounds, so it would not be unreasonable to suppose that the enslaved also followed this tradition.

Gravestone, Adam and Kedindo Pero, 1748–49, Common Burying Ground, Newport, Rhode Island. This weathered stone is significant for the African names it depicts for a slave man and his son. Kedindo Pero and his wife Minne were the parents of two short-lived sons, Adam (died 1748, age 7 months) and Kedindo (born and died in 1749). The name "Kedindo" is an African one, with the father likely passing his name on to his son in hopes of keeping his African roots alive.

The Tikey-Flagg family story is an interesting one in Newport's African American history; Arthur Flagg was enslaved by a merchant family and learned the trade of a ropemaker. He seems to have gained his freedom in the 1780s, during which time he changed his name to Arthur Tikey, perhaps the name he had been born with in Africa, and named his son in a like manner. Arthur, who may have later reverted to his old enslaved name of Flagg, also was a prominent member of the African Union Society and owned several plots of land in town (Youngken, pg. 49). His gravestone will be discussed later on.

Other references to African heritage that appear on slave gravestones include those for Violet Hammond of Newport; Francois ("born in Africa") and Quash Gomer ("a Native of Angola in Africa") of Wethersfield, Connecticut; Yarrow, "An African," of Providence, Rhode Island; and Caesar Maxcy of North Attleboro, Massachusetts. While Violet Hammond's place of birth is unknown (she may have been born free in Africa, or enslaved in America), her epitaph states that she was the wife of "Cape Coast James," a clear reference to her husband's place of origin or purchase, Cape Coast being an important trading town located on the Gulf of Guinea in modern day Ghana. While the Hammond stone offers only a brief epitaph, that for Quash Gomer is the only African American gravestone in existence in New England that denotes the specific place in Africa from where he were born.

The gravestone for Caesar is perhaps one of the most interesting to be found in New England, its epitaph ranking right up there with those found on the gravestones of whites for the transformational story it tells. His epitaph states in poetical fashion:

Here lies the best of slaves
Now turning into dust;
Caesar the Ethiopian craves
A place among the just.
His faithful soul has fled
To realms of heavenly light,
And by the blood that Jesus shed
Is changed from Black to White.
Jan. 15. he quitted the stage
In the 77th year of his age.
1780.

That Caesar came from Africa is certain, but whether Ethiopia was really his homeland may be questioned, as Ethiopia (an ancient Greek term meaning "burnt" or black "face") is often referred to in a biblical context, the name appearing a number of times in the Old Testament to describe the land, and its black inhabitants, south of Egypt. Few if any enslaved African Americans came from this part of the continent. Of course, what is most telling in Caesar's epitaph is the ideal that by his apparent conversion to Christianity (he was a member of the Baptist church), he had changed in body and spirit from a black man to a redeemed white man.

A much later stone, that in the Old North Burial Ground in Providence, Rhode Island, for Lucey Haskell (1780–1812), also expresses a like notion, with the words "complexion" and "white" carved in bold font in the epitaph found at the bottom of her stone. It states that Lucey was:

Left: Gravestone, Francois, 1816, Ancient Burying Ground, Wethersfield, Connecticut. Little is known of this man "*who was born in Africa*"; such references to a specific birth in Africa are uncommon. *Right:* Gravestone detail, Lucy Haskell, 1812, North Burial Ground, Providence, Rhode Island. Themes of African American transformation from black to white after death were part of the common religious doctrine that was preached in early New England, here emphasized on this gravestone. Note that the words "complexion" and "white" are carved in bold relief (courtesy Julie Nathanson).

A professed disciple of Jesus Christ;
She lived in the practice of his precepts,
    And died in hope
of reaping the rewards of grace in his kingdom,
where every **complexion** will unite
in praising Him who has washed their robes
and made them **white** in his own
    Blood.

Free Black Grave Marker Characteristics

The grave markers for free African Americans usually follow the same traditions as those of white New Englanders. Whether they mark the graves of those individuals who were born as free men or free women or those who had formerly been enslaved, they utilize the same materials and motifs current at the time of their decease that were in use for whites. Gravestones that exhibit any unique African themes or motifs are nonexistent. In order to procure these stones African Americans, just like whites, patronized local or regional stonecutters who were almost exclusively white to obtain markers for their loved ones. In many cases, we find that the first African Americans to gain their freedom often had burial sites that were either unmarked or marked with simple fieldstones with no identifiers. This is certainly the case in the Peterborough Cemetery in Warren, Maine, where its earliest settlers have simple fieldstone grave markers, likely for reasons of economy. This is somewhat similar to the first generations of white settlers in New England, most of whom also did not have personally identifiable markers, first because there were no stonecutters in the settlements, and later often because of the distance and costs associated with procuring gravestones. With later generations, when settlements became more established, we see the number of gravestones increasing. This same is true for African Americans, especially for those who had accumulated the economic resources to make such purchases possible, even though they were still handicapped by the issue of segregation within the burial ground.

Because of these factors, most gravestones for African Americans that can be found in New England, especially after 1830, are indistinguishable from those of whites in almost every way. The family plot for the Cheswell family in Newmarket, New Hampshire, is one of many examples of this, serving as an indicator of Wentworth Cheswell's success and prominence within his community, but without any racial identifiers. The same is true for James Mars (1790–1880) and Andrew Mero (1826–

Gravestone, Andrew Mero, 1870, River Street Cemetery, Woodstock, Vermont. Late 19th century headstones like this often give no indication of race, except, in this case, the fact that Mero was "A member of Co. B, 54th Regt. Mass. Vols."

1870). Mars was born into slavery in Connecticut and gained his freedom at the age of twenty-one, later telling the story of his life in one of the few published autobiographies by African Americans to be found in New England. His gravestone in Center Cemetery in Norfolk, Connecticut, is a typical example of the gravestones used in this era with no distinguishing features.

Mero was born free in Vermont and was later a soldier in the Civil War; his gravestone in the River Street Cemetery in Woodstock is nearly identical to that of other soldiers found buried here. Only the fact stated on his stone detailing his service as "A member of Co. B, 54th Regt., Mass. Vols.," an all-black regiment, belies his status as an African American. All the other white veterans buried here, of course, served in homegrown Vermont regiments, but for Andrew Mero this was not an option, as his state, like Maine and New Hampshire, did not have enough of an African American population to raise their own black regiments. A final example is provided by the gravestones for Pomp and Candace Spring in Portsmouth, New Hampshire; though formerly enslaved, their hard work and financial success enabled the executor of their will, also a former slave, to purchase gravestones upon their death in 1808 that made no mention of their former status and were identical in size and style to those for working-class white individuals.

However, there are some interesting gravestones for those who were formerly enslaved that exhibit some unique characteristics. These gravestones, generally dating from the early 1800s to the 1850s (with but a few earlier examples to be found), not only often mention the deceased's former status as a "slave," but also his race or place of origin, as well as his outstanding qualities or religious nature. The oldest of these gravestones is that found in Wethersfield, Connecticut, for Primus, a "free Negro" who died in 1731. Some, perhaps most, of these stones have epitaphs that were written by prominent whites who lived in the same community and were closely associated with the African Americans whom they memorialize.

One of the earliest of these unusual stones is that for John Jack (1713–1773) of Concord, Massachusetts. His stone in the Old Hill Burial Ground, with a death date of 1773, states in no uncertain terms that he was "A native of Africa.... Tho born in a land of slavery, He was born free. Tho' he lived in a land of liberty, He lived a slave. Till by his honest, tho' stolen, labors, He acquired the source of slavery, Which gave him his freedom; Tho' not long before Death, the grand tyrant, Gave him his final emancipation." This descriptive epitaph was written by Daniel Bliss, a Harvard-educated lawyer, who was the son of the Rev. Daniel Bliss and the brother-in-law of the Rev. William Emerson (the grandfather of transcendentalist Ralph Waldo Emerson). Bliss was also a Tory during the American Revolution (who later left his hometown, never to return), with some of his skepticism about the Patriot cause expressed in John Jack's epitaph which points out the clear contradiction (or perhaps hypocrisy) of his life as a "slave" in the "land of liberty." Even Bliss's take on John Jack's homeland is an interesting one that is based solely on the white point of view, it being highly unlikely that Jack himself actually considered Africa "a land of slavery."

Yet another interesting set of stones are those for Amos and Violate Fortune in Jaffrey, New Hampshire. These stones, as has been previously discussed, were purchased based on the wishes expressed by Amos Fortune in his last will and testament, but it is almost certain that their epitaphs were not dictated by Fortune, but by the executor of his will, Eleazor

Spofford, a local church deacon. Amos Fortune's gravestone states matter-of-factly that he was "born free in Africa, a slave in America, he purchased liberty, professed Christianity, lived reputably, died hopefully." However, the stone for Violate Fortune has a slightly different white perspective, stating that she was "by sale the slave of Amos Fortune, by marriage his wife, by her fidelity his friend and solace." While it is true that Amos Fortune did purchase his wife, never did he likely consider her to be his "slave," but rather his "beloved wife" (Lambert, pg. 50), according to his will. Indeed, though Amos Fortune purchased Violate's freedom in 1779, it was only so that she could be free to marry him, while from the white perspective, her very sale (and presumably the fact that Amos never formally manumitted Violate) meant that she was indeed his "slave," as well as his wife. While such phraseology may be a matter of splitting hairs when considered by modern historians, one can't help but wonder whether Amos Fortune would have approved of the epitaph crafted for his wife.

Another African American gravestone which features an epitaph written by a white man is that for Cuffee Dole in Georgetown, Massachusetts. The story of his gravestone is one of the hidden stories of racism in New England and a valiant attempt to overcome such attitudes. Dole's gravestone, dated 1816, states at the top that he was "A respectable man of color. Died rejoicing in the Lord." However, it is the on the lower portion of this stone, often obscured by overgrown grass, where the real interest lies, for here it is written: "White man, turn not away in Disgust, Thou art my brother, Like me akin to earth and worms." This blunt message of equality was crafted, not by Dole's family, but by the Rev. Isaac Braman, and is a tangible remnant of a dispute which arose after Dole's death. The issue at hand was whether or not Cuffee Dole, because of his color, would be buried in the public burial ground. "One good deacon said that a man was a man whatever his color and that his soul was as white as anybody's, while another old deacon, equally good, said that a black person was no more than a beast and as such should not be buried in the same cemetery with white people" (Comiskey, pg. 2). While it is not clear where exactly Cuffee Dole was buried in 1816 in terms of the cemetery boundaries (he was either buried at the back of the cemetery as it was then laid out, or on a neighboring parcel of land abutting the cemetery that in later years became a part of the cemetery), the Reverend Braman made sure that his feelings on the subject, as Dole's pastor, friend, and executor, were carved in stone.

Who may have written the epitaph for Venture Smith (1729–1805) in East Haddam, Connecticut, is unknown, but it is remarkable for its concise account of his life, stating that he was "an African, tho the son of a King he was kidnapped & sold as a slave but by his industry he acquired Money to purchase his Freedom." Perhaps this narrative was

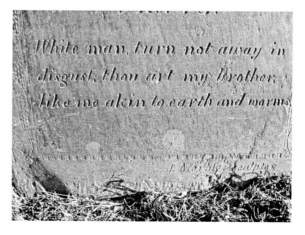

Detail, gravestone for Cuffee Dole, 1816, Union Cemetery, Georgetown, Massachusetts. The lower inscription on this former slave's gravestone is indicative that some in New England, like Dole's friend the Rev. Isaac Braman, believed in some form of racial equality.

written by his son Solomon or even his wife Margaret (known as "Meg"), both of whom are also buried in the First Church Cemetery, but it could also have been written by Elisha Niles, a school teacher who edited Smith's autobiography, which was published in 1798. Interestingly, Margaret (or "Marget," as it is misspelled on her gravestone) Smith (1730–1809) also has a fine gravestone, the same as that for white women of the same time period in the same circumstance, denoting her status as "the Relict," or widow, of Venture, with no mention of her nativity or former status as a slave.

A final stone worthy of mention is that for Arthur Flagg in Newport. Once enslaved, when he became free he took the name of Arthur Tikey. When his son Solomon Nuba Tikey died in 1785, Arthur "Tikey" was listed as his father. However, when Flora his wife died in 1802, she was noted as being the wife of Arthur Flagg, and the same is true when Arthur died in 1810, he being buried under a headstone bearing the name of Arthur Flagg. What may have occurred in this case is uncertain and may never be able to be ascertained. Did Arthur Tikey at some point late in life revert to his old enslaved name? Or did the white stonecutter who carved the later gravestones for Arthur and his wife refuse to recognize the native name that Arthur had chosen as a legitimate one, even if, presumably (at least for his wife Flora), Arthur paid him for the gravestones? It may even be that Arthur used both names, preferring to use "Tikey" in personal and black community contexts, but used his old enslaved name of "Flagg" in his dealings with the white community.

African American women, too, were memorialized on this type of gravestones; in Newport, Rhode Island, Dutchess Quamino (1739–1804) was celebrated as being "A free Black of most distinguished excellence: Intelligent, industrious. Affectionate, honest, and of Exemplary Piety." Her epitaph is said to have been written by Newport native William Ellery Channing, a celebrated Unitarian theologian who was the pastor of Boston's Federal Street Church for nearly 40 years beginning in 1803. In Brunswick, Maine, the gravestone in Pine Grove Cemetery for Phebe Ann Jacobs (1786–1850) is also of note. It reads: "Born a Slave. For about 40 years a faithful friend in the families of Pres. Wheelock and Pres. Allen. An eminent Christian. Beloved and honored." Who may have composed her epitaph is uncertain; perhaps, since she was buried in the Allen family plot, it was one of the Allen daughters or William Allen himself, formerly president of Dartmouth and Bowdoin colleges. At her funeral it was said, "Those following nearest her remains were President Allen and daughters who, informed by telegraph, had come nearly two hundred miles to testify their respect and affection for the deceased" (Upham, pg. 8). Another possibility is Mrs. Phebe Upham, a prominent citizen in town known for championing antislavery and women's rights causes, who also wrote a small pamphlet entitled *Narrative of Phebe Ann Jacobs* shortly after Jacobs's death. A final candidate might be the Reverend Dr. Adams, the pastor of the First Parish Church where Phebe Ann Jacobs was known as one of its most devout members. Jacobs's biographer states that not only did she look in on the pastor's sick wife just hours before her own death, but that afterwards her fellow congregants were distressed: "'Who now will pray for us?' said one; 'Phebe is gone.' 'We have lost Phebe's prayers,' said another" (Upham. Pg. 7). No matter who wrote Jacobs's epitaph, it is clear that despite her simple life in freedom working as a washerwoman for the students of Bowdoin College, she had a wealth of friends and admirers in a community that was predominantly white.

Our final gravestone in this category worthy of discussion, though others can be found, is that for Elizabeth "Mum Bett" Freeman (1742–1829) in Stockbridge, Massachusetts. Her gravestone found in the Sedgwick family plot in the Stockbridge Cemetery is unusual both in that its epitaph was likely written by a white woman, and also because it does not focus on Freeman's religious nature (as was common with black women), but rather on the personal traits that, in essence, helped her to gain her freedom. This epitaph, thought to have been written by Catharine Sedgwick, a short-story writer and novelist, the daughter of Theodore Sedgwick, the man who helped Freeman gain her freedom, states: "She was born a slave and remained a slave for nearly thirty years. She could neither read nor write yet in her own sphere she had no superior nor equal. In every situation of domestic trial, she was the most efficient helper, and the tenderest friend. Good Mother, farewell." The last lines in this epitaph reflect Elizabeth Freeman's significant role in the Sedgwick family as their chief domestic servant and the trusted midwife who delivered many of their children. Given these roles, is it any wonder that the Sedgwick women, particularly Catharine after her mother Pamela's death in 1807, viewed Elizabeth Freeman as both a friend and a mother-figure?

Gravestone, Sylva Church, 1822, Bridge Street Cemetery, Northampton, Massachusetts. Church, who may have been born in New York, was the slave of watch and clock maker Nathan Storrs "for many years." While relatively few enslaved African American women have gravestones to mark their final resting places, those who do are often extolled for their virtues. As Sylva's gravestone attests, "Very few possessed more good qualities than she did."

Cultural Burial Marker Possibilities

In addition to those burial markers just discussed for African Americans that correspond to white, European practices and traditions, we must also consider the possibility of marked graves that followed more closely African traditions. While it is very evident that remnants of such sites are now almost nonexistent in New England, it should also be clear that the idea that those of African heritage entirely abandoned their unique cultural practices (including funerary customs) and entirely adopted white customs would be rather presumptuous at best, and perhaps an example of Eurocentric arrogance at worst. I believe that, for at least a small percentage of African Americans, one reason that their burial sites are unknown or have become lost is due to the fact that they did indeed follow their own cultural practices. Below are discussed several of these practices that may have been cultural survivals from Africa.

In discussing these African traditions, while I do make speculations and suppositions for which there is but little evidence, we must not forget that African Americans in the time period under discussion here never, even while living in the brutally controlling conditions that were the very essence of the institution of slavery, gave up their religious cultural identity, though they were often forced to practice their beliefs in secrecy. For instance, it is known that some African Americans in both New England and the American South, after being forced into servitude, continued to fashion small idols out of clay or stone and prayed or conversed with them when their masters weren't around, and many carried amulets or charms of widely varying types to ward off evil spirits (Piersen, pgs. 79–80). Perhaps the best publicized of these practices, what New Englanders called "witchcraft," involved Tituba, the slave woman (whether of Native American, African, or Caribbean ethnicity is uncertain) of the Rev. Samuel Parris of Danvers, Massachusetts, and the conjuring games that she taught Parris's daughter and friends that played a small part in the Salem witch trial events in 1692.

One possible type of African-influenced grave markers that may have been used in New England that have now vanished are those that were crafted out of wood. White Europeans, too, used wooden grave markers early on, but generally only until trained stonecutters arrived in the colonies. However, in some parts of Africa, wooden mortuary posts or grave markers were commonly used. These were elaborately carved, thin, upright posts that often had circular tops that represented a face, some of them nearly six feet high. While the best known examples of these posts, called *kikangu*, were crafted by the Giryama people from East Africa in modern-day Kenya, this was an area from which few, if any, of the enslaved Africans transported to North America originated. However, given the many different ethnic peoples in Africa, it may be that other peoples that were enslaved and transported to America also utilized similar grave markers made of wood. Those for the Giryama are particularly interesting in that these were portable monuments, used to mark the grave of a loved one, but when the village moved, the mortuary posts were taken down and carried to the new location. Whatever shape these wooden markers may have taken if so used in America, whether in the African tradition or copies of the European styled gravestones, they would have had but a short life in the harsh New England climate. While the African-carved mortuary posts were very distinctive, any such item crafted in New England by the enslaved or those who had gained their freedom was likely very simplistic and smaller in nature so as not to attract the negative attention of white masters or ministers.

Stone-marked burials are also a strong possibility for vanished African American graves, by which I mean natural boulders and rocks rather than the European tradition of finely finished gravestones or even their predecessors, simply cut fieldstones that were set in place. Once again, even early New England settlers used larger rocks or boulders to mark freshly dug graves; these were often called "wolf stones" for the simple reason that by placing these large, unadorned rocks upon the graves of the recently deceased, they protected them from being desecrated by wild animals. Large rocks and boulders, indeed, were (and still are) not hard to come by when working the New England soil, so it is entirely possible that early African American landholders, especially those trying to carve out a farm on undesirable (to whites) land located in usually remote areas of town, may have used such rocks as grave markers. As many of these lands where African Americans once lived were later sold or even abandoned, burial sites marked in this fashion would be indistinguishable from the rest of the rocky New England landscape. Likewise, the use of African-influenced stone cairn burials, such as those found in Salem, Connecticut, would also remain largely unrecognizable as burial sites, as they closely resemble the many ruined stone fences that also dot the New England landscape. While these stone markers may have been used out of mere convenience due to their easy availability, stone-marked burials were also a custom in West Africa (where most of the enslaved in New England came from) dating as far back as the third century B.C. At such places as Wassu and Kerbach in modern-day Gambia and Sine Ngayene and Wanar in Senegal are to be found the so-called Senegambian stone circles and megaliths that resemble those found in England at Stonehenge. While no such elaborate stone burial sites as these, of course, would have been possible in New England, it is not unreasonable to assume that miniature versions, either singly or in stacked cairn form, could have had the same cultural meaning.

While wooden or large stone-marked burials may have been used, probably the most common marked burial practices used by African Americans that have now been lost were those that involving marking the border or outline of the otherwise flat or slightly mounded burial site with small stones, rocks, or, in coastal areas, shells. This was not only a very common practice in many parts of Africa, but also among Native Americans as well. The common belief in this practice for many ethnic groups is a simple one: the enclosed area was meant to keep the spirit of the deceased from wandering out among the living. Once again, as with so many other burial customs, these marked grave outlines were also used by white Americans; in Victorian times in many New England cemeteries oval-shaped grave borders were crafted out of wrought iron to delineate the outline of a loved one's burial site. However, for African Americans, either buried on their own land in remote locations, or even those buried in the far-distant corners of the public burial ground, this simple type of grave delineation was subject to the ravages of time and the New England weather, as well as a lack of any family to maintain the site, and could be easily disturbed or lost within a decade or less.

However, at the Parting Ways site in Plymouth, Massachusetts, there is some evidence of a similar type of site. Across the road from the original settlement is an area paved with natural cobblestones and measuring twenty-five by forty-five feet. In two distinct areas, which may represent burial sites, thousands of artifacts, mostly in the form of pottery fragments and glass shards, were discovered. Significantly, these are determined to have been intentionally broken on the spot before the 1840s, at a time when the site was occupied by its original African American inhabitants. Since no other debris or trash-related items were found at the site, and the stones were clearly not building-related, it was determined by archaeologists to closely resemble not only similarly marked, known graves for African Americans in the American South, but also the "ritual compounds" of the Akan people in Ghana (Deetz, pgs. 207–208). In both areas, as well as likely at Parting Ways, this broken pottery and glass, which to the white eye might have appeared to be nothing more than a trash heap, served as grave offerings and ornamentation meant to help the deceased in their transition from the land of the living to the land of the dead, based on old African customs and beliefs. How many other such sites may once have existed in New England can, of course, never be known, but it is doubtful that Parting Ways was the only one of its kind.

A final type of site to be considered, one easily lost over the years, is that type known as the house-yard burial. This practice, that of burying the dead close by the homes where they lived and worked, is well documented among the Africans enslaved in the Caribbean in the 17th century, including at the Seville plantation site on Jamaica's north coast, and reflects the African idea of the dead being buried close to their family and loved ones so that they could "watch" over them and their descendants (Piersen, pg. 76). Even in New England, there is a suggestion that burials like this may have occurred. In Middleboro, Massachusetts, Aaron, an aged enslaved man serving the widow Morton, was a "devout" Christian and church member, but also "had all the superstition of the negro" (Weston, pg. 104); he expressed a desire to be buried near his mistress's house so that he could hear the voices of the children as they played. Whether Aaron or any of his fellow slaves in the Morton family, including Shurper, also a devout worshiper, or a neighbor free black woman, Elsie (formerly owned by Cyrus Wood), who "lived until her death" in a small cottage on land in back of the Morton house, were buried close to their homes is unknown, but a possibility (Weston, pg. 103). Given the African beliefs surrounding such house-yard burials, it may also be the case that those formerly enslaved individuals who became free and could later afford to purchase their own land and homestead were also buried close to their homes. Many of these homesites for free African Americans, of course, have been lost over the years, due to either development in now urbanized areas or subsequent abandonment due to their fringe locations on marginal land and/or subsequent family generations leaving the area.

A similar example for this type of close-to-home burial is that for an enslaved woman named Phillis living in Suffield, Connecticut. Prior to her death she requested that she be buried "near a great beech tree" so that lightning could not get her, surely a reflection both of the hell-fire and brimstone sermons preached by Puritan ministers since the founding of New England, and of African religious beliefs that had their own gods of thunder and retribution (Piersen, pg. 79).

VI. Preservation Challenges and Recovery and Remembrance Initiatives

Cemeteries and old burial grounds or gravesites within them, become lost for two reasons: some are abandoned by the communities that once used them and fall into disrepair and subsequently become lost altogether, others are lost because they are destroyed—sometimes deliberately, sometimes inadvertently—for reasons usually involving changing land use patterns. Today there are laws in place in every state that not only prevent the destruction of an existing cemetery for any reason (though there are provisions for moving a cemetery to another locale), but also limit or halt construction altogether if lost cemeteries or burial places are discovered during the course of a project.

However, these laws are relatively recent ones enacted in the mid–20th century or even later. Prior to this, the desecration of a cemetery for development purposes was commonplace in New England for all burying places, not just those associated with people of color. This is not really surprising, as in early New England common citizens and the clergy alike did not consider burial places to be sacrosanct, but merely utilitarian places where the dead were buried. Indeed, if a family left town and their family graves in the public burial ground became overgrown or damaged, so be it. It was even the practice in some cases for older gravestones to be removed for other purposes. One of the oldest known gravestones in Boston was found being used as a well cover, while in other cases gravestones are known to have been re-carved (usually on the back) and re-used for a later individual, no doubt an extreme example of Yankee frugality.

As to lost African American burial sites, I have already mentioned many of these. One significant example is the segregated "Negro" Burial Ground in Portsmouth, New Hampshire. This site, established by 1705, fell out of use after 1800, and by 1850 was largely gone as the city expanded into this once outlying area. It seems clear in this case that this burial site was taken over in the overall interest of expansion, and may be seen as an early example of a type of eminent domain, but without the legal proceedings that usually accompany such a move. Though Portsmouth had a thriving black population, there is no evidence that they were consulted about such a move for the simple reason that they were in the minority, and had no voting privileges. Had this been a case where a white cemetery was going to be built over or removed, there would indeed have been town meetings held on the subject (the outcome may have been the same), but since it was a black cemetery, no debate was necessary.

However, it should be pointed out that public burial grounds for whites were also sometimes destroyed in the interest of town expansion. In Waterbury, Connecticut, the Grand Street Cemetery, which had a segregated section for non-whites, had become almost abandoned by the 1880s. When a public library was proposed for the site, it was eventually decided to lay all the remaining gravestones in the main cemetery flat and bury them. In 1893 construction of the Silas Bronson Library was begun at the site, though the segregated portion was apparently left untouched. A successor library was later built on the site and the black section of the old cemetery is located near the sidewalk in what is now the front of the current library. Likewise, the old Congregational church burial ground in Exeter, New Hampshire, laid many of its gravestones flat on the ground in the early 1800s for unknown reasons and by 1920 these gravestones were deliberately buried so that the adjacent Front Street could be widened for increasing auto traffic. How many African Americans, if any, may have been buried at this site is unknown.

Relocated "Free Ground" burials section, North Burial Ground, Providence, Rhode Island. The stones in this section date back to 1730s and include some of the earliest African American grave markers found here, including Cesar Whipple (died 1730), two-year-old Primus Tillinhast (died 1750), and former slave Eve Cushing (died 1780). These stones were relocated within the cemetery in 1964 due to highway construction. Lying face-up and exposed to the weather, many are illegible and will soon be lost altogether.

As has been previously discussed, many African American graves were located in rural areas, whether in small family or neighborhood cemeteries or separate slave cemeteries. Many of these sites were lost also due to changing land uses; in Rhode Island many slave cemeteries were lost because they were unenclosed and/or had no grave markers. After slavery became a thing of the past, many of these sites were developed over or were turned into farmland. Elsewhere in New England, cemeteries where African Americans were buried—in places like Barre, Massachusetts; Greenland, New Hampshire; South Kingstown, Rhode Island; and Hinesburgh, Vermont—have now reverted to wilderness, with only a few remnants left to show they once existed.

The question as to whether any of African American burial sites were destroyed or lost due to any malicious intent based on racial considerations is an interesting one. While the answer to this question appears to be in the negative, it would be naïve to think that racial considerations played no part in these losses. Because of African Americans' social status, some of these sites were lost or otherwise redeveloped due to, at best, a reflexive attitude of casual indifference among white town officers and decision-makers, and at worst a blatant disregard for the black community. In some cases of land development that would result in the loss of a cemetery, white graves were often moved to a newer cemetery. However, instances of such an occurrence for African Americans are rare, one example being that involving the grave of Revolutionary War veteran Jeffrey Hemenway (1737–1819) in Worcester. He was buried in the Mechanic Street Cemetery with a standard slate headstone, but when that cemetery's stones were relocated to the newer Hope Cemetery due to development issues, his stone was among those moved, although it was still placed separate from the removals for whites. However, had Hemenway been buried without a grave marker, it is unlikely his remains would have been removed and reburied at all.

Gravestone Preservation

While cemetery losses remain a concern in some cases, the biggest concern today is the preservation of known gravesites within a cemetery and, specifically, the preservation of gravestones for all individuals, African Americans included. This is a problem that is prevalent not just in rural areas, but urban areas as well. In some cases the problem is cemetery vandalism in general, which has been a chronic problem in many locales for the last two decades or more. This type of damage and resulting loss is due to random acts that seldom have any meaning behind them, let alone a racial motivation. In the God's Little Acre section of the Common Burying Ground in Newport, Rhode Island, at least 66 gravestones have gone missing since 1903, many of them for African Americans, including Primus Scott, Hartford Brown, and Peg Brinley, while the famed stone for Mintus Brenton has been severely damaged, its upper portion depicting an African American soul effigy now entirely gone. Some of these stones were likely damaged beyond repair and discarded by cemetery maintenance workers in an era before their historical nature was appreciated, while others may have been stolen. Indeed, the theft of colonial-era gravestones, prized for their unique carvings and made into tables or used as doorstops and other decorative pieces, was once a common problem in the early 20th century. Antique dealers used to sell these items willingly but now there are laws in most states preventing the sale of such stolen items.

In Stratham, New Hampshire, there may be found a broken gravestone for Caesar "Negro, 42, 1785." This stone is likely that for Caesar Brackett, though this is disputed by others who believe it to be the stone for Revolutionary War veteran Caesar Wood. This gravestone was originally placed in the "negro graveyard" (where three graves have been documented) on land once owned by the Brackett family located at 7 Tidewater Farm Road in neighboring Greenland. The family's private cemetery was located a short distance away. The black cemetery, with its one lettered headstone, was recorded in 1937, but by 1972 Caesar's stone was in pieces and leaning up against the old farmhouse. In the 1980s the old Brackett farmstead was sold for residential development and Caesar's stone was sold to an antiques dealer. A member of the Stratham Historical Society eventually tracked it down and purchased the gravestone, and it now resides in their collection. Perhaps because of this stone's wandering past, as well as the fact that it is the oldest identifiable gravestone for an African American in New Hampshire, the society has refused requests to return the

stone to its original location that is well off the beaten path.

While vandalism and theft have been problematic over the years, it is the New England weather that has caused the greatest damage and losses. This is particularly true in the state of Connecticut, where most of the colonial-era gravestones were carved out of a red or brown sandstone that is particu-

Left: Gravestone, Sarah Huso, 1879, Winter Street Cemetery, Exeter, New Hampshire. Preservation and restoration efforts in New England cemeteries, especially in earlier years, were often under-funded or ignored altogether, resulting in many broken or lost gravestones over the years. This broken stone for an African American woman whose ties to the local area dated back to Revolutionary War times may now be lost entirely; photographed in 2002, the stone was missing by 2014. *Right:* Gravestone detail, Eve Cushing, 1780, North Burial Ground, Providence, Rhode Island. Eve (born ca. 1731) was the wife of Prince Cushing and, as her worn gravestone states, "was a native of Africa, as a servant was faithful and as a free woman an example of industry and economy." Her headstone, which features a winged hourglass motif carved by local stonecutter Stephen Hartshorn, is indicative of the respect she had earned in the community at large during her lifetime.

larly susceptible to both weathering and water retention, resulting in gravestones that are heavily pitted or flaked. Some of these stones, such as those for Florio Hercules (1689–1749), Phillis (1722–1777), Sawney Miller (1716–1761), and Juno Anderson (1757–1797) in New London are now so weathered that their original lettering is largely gone, and were it not for historians and antiquarians of an earlier day who documented each stone's epitaph and, indeed, its very existence, they would be meaningless to us now. While the slate gravestones elsewhere in New England, particularly in Newport, Rhode Island, have fared better, they too are suffering these same problems.

Gravestone, Florio Hercules, 1749, Ye Ancientist Burial Ground, New London, Connecticut. The years have not been kind to the red and brown sandstone gravestones carved by early Connecticut stonecutters. This historic stone, for a black woman who was the wife of one of Connecticut's known black governors, Hercules, has flaked and peeled over the years, causing the loss of most of its inscription area. In a few short years this stone's wording will be entirely lost.

This situation has led many historians, scholars, and gravestone enthusiasts to recommend that the most significant of these stones be brought out of the weather and placed in local museums, replaced with an exact replica on the original site. While this is an option that has previously been used for some notable gravestones for prominent white settlers in New England, including some in Massachusetts and New Hampshire, this solution also presents some unique problems. One of these is the fact that by removing a gravestone from its original location, the item is also taken out of its original contextual setting. Further, removing an original stone, even if it is replaced with a replica, also changes the character of the cemetery itself, taking away from its original and historical nature. Yet another concern is the fact that by placing a gravestone in a museum setting, the opportunity for viewing these artifacts is also limited.

Finally, gravestones can be difficult items to care for and display and, if improperly cataloged or stored, can be misplaced or even lost. In 1975–1976 a number of gravestones and fragments of gravestones were removed from the historic Common Burying Ground in Newport, Rhode Island, with the intent to document and restore them. These stones subsequently remained in storage for twenty years until most were finally reset in 1996. Of the forty stones removed, 29 returned to their original home, including those for African Americans Pero Overing and Judith Rivera, but the remainder, deemed too fragile to be returned, were subsequently lost, likely thrown away by accident, including the stones for African Americans Prince Green and Charles Stevens (Sterling, Austin, Champion, and Bamberg, pgs. 419–420).

Despite such problems, there are a number of African American gravestones that, due to their historical nature and/or fragile condition, are prime candidates for removal to a protected historical setting, including those for Cuffe Gibbs and Pompey Lyndon (both carved by Pompe Stevens), Adam and Kedindo Pero, and that for Phillis Stevens and her infant son Prince, all in Newport; the stones for Florio Hercules and Morocco Clancy in New London, Connecticut; the stone for Prince McLelland and his wives Chloe and Dinah in Gorham, Maine; and the stones for Quash Gomer and Primus in Wethersfield, Connecticut.

Cemetery Maintenance

Another preservation issue that is a constant factor is the overall processes regarding cemetery maintenance. Every town or city is responsible for maintenance and upkeep of their historic public burying places and many perform this work to excellent standards. However, problems can arise in any locale when finance and taxation issues arise, and when times are tight services and resulting expenditures in a community sometimes have to be prioritized. Often cemetery maintenance and repairs fall low on this list, especially when competing with other more pressing problems like road repairs. Such decisions, though, can have consequences. Allowing a cemetery to become overgrown and fall into disrepair often gives it an air of abandonment, making it a perfect hideout for the homeless, and for underage drinking parties and similar activities, which often can lead to further damage from vandalism. In contrast, a well-maintained and repaired cemetery tends to discourage such activities. In cities such as Newport, Rhode Island, and New London, Connecticut, cemeteries that were once sadly overgrown and in a disheveled condition several decades ago are now in good condition and well maintained and their African American sections are a source of community pride.

While many communities have seen a revival in their old cemeteries, sometimes with special emphasis on the historic graves of African Americans, this is not always the case. The Second Burying Ground in North Andover, Massachusetts, is a curious example of a cemetery whose African American section has been rather ignored. The black section of the town's second-oldest public burying place, where members of the Freeman and Lew families have marked graves in the far back right corner, has become a dumping ground for cut brush and old tree stumps, and at most times of the year is inaccessible due to its overgrown condition. The rest of the cemetery is fairly well-maintained, so it is a mystery as to why the town, which takes pride in its historic appearance by all accounts, has not included

Second Burying Ground, North Andover, Massachusetts. Cut brush and old logs litter the historic black section of this old cemetery, while the rest of the cemetery is well maintained. Treated as second class citizens in life, the town's early black residents have been, in death, treated much the same way.

this section in its maintenance plan. In fact, the monetary expense to keep this area clear and perhaps seed it with grass would not be great, yet year after year nothing changes and it may take some community activism to fix this easily correctable blemish on the town's historic landscape.

Such community activism was indeed the solution for the Claypit Cemetery (also known as the Pierce-Coburn Cemetery or the Old Burying Ground) in nearby Lowell, Massachusetts. This site, ironically, is one that also is the resting place for at least one member of the Lew family, and quite possibly several others, including patriarch and Revolutionary War veteran Barzillai Lew and his wife Dinah, who lived in the area and were local church members. This old burial site, located off Varnum Avenue in the Pawtucketville section of town, is of the neighborhood variety and includes burials for white individuals as well. The land which encompasses this cemetery was originally a part of the neighboring

Portrait of Barzillai Lew (1743–1822), attributed to Gilbert Stuart. A Revolutionary War veteran and noted musician, Lew is likely buried in the recently restored Claypit Cemetery in Lowell, Massachusetts, where at least one member of his family is known to be buried (courtesy U.S. Department of State, Washington, D.C.).

town of Dracut (which still holds title to the cemetery), but was annexed by Lowell in 1874. By 1880 this cemetery was nearly abandoned and some prominent white individuals were disinterred and buried elsewhere. Over the years the cemetery continued to deteriorate, though interest in the cemetery, the oldest burial site in Dracut, cropped up from time to time. By 2007 only eleven headstones were remaining, with those for the Lew family gone entirely.

Here we have a case where a city's indifference and jurisdiction issues nearly caused a site to be lost. Even today, though the site is located within the city of Lowell, the city's official website makes it clear that it does not maintain this cemetery. While Dracut retained title to the cemetery, because it was outside their own city boundaries, it seems clear that town officials lost interest in the site, despite its historical nature. I visited this site in the mid–1990s and found it nearly impenetrable due to heavy brush and junk strewn throughout the site. Searching for evidence of the Lew family documented as having been buried there, I could find nothing. It was not until 2007 that the site was yet again discovered, this time by a local middle-school teacher in Dracut named Rebecca Duda. This award-winning teacher saw a chance not only to preserve history, but also to offer her students a unique opportunity to help in documenting and recovering this site. This they have done, and though the long-term challenge of maintaining Claypit Cemetery remains, there is now hope that that challenge will be met.

A final problem with African American burial sites in New England, particularly in those areas where there is today little ethnic diversity, may be a lack of knowledge and sometimes simple apathy regarding the black individuals who once lived there. For some towns this is far from the case. Wentworth Cheswell in Newmarket, New Hampshire, and Prince Whipple in Portsmouth, New Hampshire, are well celebrated in New Hampshire, while the same is true in Massachusetts of Prince and Quok Walker of Barre and Prince Hall of Boston. In Connecticut, Nero Hawley, buried in Trumbull's Riverside Cemetery, is quite well known as a Revolutionary War soldier, while in Rhode Island the local African American community, including some individuals whose roots here date back to colonial times, take great pride in the God's Little Acre site. However, not all towns have embraced this history. Though unspoken and unwritten, one gets the sense when visiting some sites that a town has no interest in highlighting a part of its past, specifically the issue that slavery once existed there, that may be perceived as embarrassing or otherwise casts some shadow over the town's reputation.

While there are a number of towns throughout New England that may fall into this category, one of the most surprising in this regard is Amherst, New Hampshire, a town that boasts the largest historic district in the state of New Hampshire and takes great overall pride in its history. When a town hall construction project in 2003 resulted in the discovery of likely African Americans remains, including a young woman and an infant (possibly her daughter), the town showed no interest in making any investigations into what this find might reveal and eventually re-interred the remains with little fanfare and marked them on the site as simple unknowns.

Recovery and Remembrance Efforts

The process of identifying, maintaining, and preserving African American gravesites and cemeteries in historic New England, at first glance, often seems like an insurmountable challenge and one that is of but recent occurrence. Sometimes these challenges are due to a simple lack of knowledge about such sites, and sometimes due to a lack of interest, especially in those towns where there is no descendant population. Additionally, the resources (i.e., money) needed to achieve these goals is often lacking. Despite all these obstacles, efforts to preserve this unique aspect of history, even if it has highlighted the region's shameful participation in the institution of slavery, began earlier than many might think.

Perhaps the earliest example of such recovery efforts took place in Concord, Massachusetts, a bit ironic when we consider that not only was it in Massachusetts where slavery in the region got its start, but also in Concord where one of the opening battles for American independence was fought in 1775. As you will recall, in Concord's Old Hill Burying Ground may be found the gravestone for John Jack, who died in 1773. As one author has stated, "John Jack's epitaph has made him immortal" (Tolman, pg. 6), so famous was the wording on this stone. One British officer, while the British occupied Concord for a brief time in April 1775 (using the hill as an observation post), even copied the inscription and included it in a letter he sent home; it was later published in a London newspaper. However, by the 1820s Jack's gravestone had been toppled over and broken into several pieces. In 1830 a native of Concord, Rufus Hosmer, a lawyer living in Stow, took notice of its condition and solicited donations from members of the Middlesex County bar in order that a new stone might be set up as a replacement. Hosmer was successful in his efforts, the new gravestone said to be "as nearly as possible a *facsimile* of the original." "For many years during the anti-slavery times ... this grave, almost alone of all the graves in

Top: Gravestone, John Jack, 1773, Old Hill Burial Ground, Concord, Massachusetts. The lengthy epitaph on this slave's stone is indicative in part of the uncomfortable hypocrisy of slavery's existence in America at a time that the colonists were fighting to be free from British tyranny, something that was ultimately achieved with the help of many African Americans, both enslaved and free. *Bottom:* John Jack Homestead, Greenland, New Hampshire. This site in the Bayside area of town was the home of Revolutionary War veteran John Jack, his wife Phillis, and their children Nancy, Phillis, and Tomas, and even the runaway slave of George Washington, Oney Judge Staines, for a span of nearly 50 years. After the property was sold in 1845, the area gradually reverted to wilderness. By 2000, the only remnants of this homestead were the remains of a stone wall (visible here at far left) and a few gravestone fragments for daughter Phillis Jack (Hall's *Rambles About Greenland in Rhyme* [1900]).

the Hill Burying Ground, was carefully tended and looked after; lilies were planted upon it, the clinging lichens were not permitted to gather upon the stone, and the long rank grass that might have hidden it was kept shorn and trimmed to a decorous smoothness" (Tolman, pg. 8).

The first known monument to a freed African American erected by an African American community itself may be found in Boston in the Copp's Hill Burial Ground. It was here where the formerly enslaved Prince Hall, a prominent black leader in Boston from the time he was freed on the eve of the American Revolution until his death in 1807, was buried. His original grave marker, one of the few found for African American in Boston, was a simple slate stone that still stands today. However, beside it was built in June of 1835 an impressive granite monument that stands about ten feet high, sponsored by the Grand Masonic Lodge that he founded in 1784, the first black Masonic Lodge in America.

In the more recent past, monuments have been erected at a number of other cemeteries where African Americans have been interred, particularly in Massachusetts and Connecticut. In Westport, Massachusetts, in June 1913, Horatio Howard, the great-grandson of Captain Paul Cuffee, erected a monument to his ancestor, described as "A Notable Character," adjacent to the Friends Central Cemetery. While the original gravestones for Cuffee and his wife Alice still remain, they are small and very weather-worn. In the years following World War II, a group of citizens banded together in Marblehead, Massachusetts, to place a patriotic stone in the historic Old Burial Hill yard memorializing Revolutionary war soldier and tavern-keeper Joseph "Black Joe" Brown. Similarly, at the Parting Ways Cemetery site in Plymouth, Massachusetts, where only a few broken and unidentified gravestone remnants are left, a monument was erected in the 1980s denoting the place as the burial site for Revolutionary War veterans Quamany, Prince, Cato, and Plato. Finally, in Great Barrington's Mahaiwe Cemetery, the Great Barrington Historical Society in 1994 erected a bronze plaque highlighting the burial sites of W.E.B. DuBois's son Burghardt (died in 1899) and first wife Nina Gomer DuBois (1871–1950).

In Connecticut, among the significant sites recently memorialized that are worthy of mention are those located in Hartford, New Haven, and Farmington. In Hartford's Ancient Burial Ground, where no marked graves for the over 300 African Americans buried here are to be found, an impressive memorial stone was erected in 1998. In New Haven's historic Grove Street Cemetery there is a monument, erected in 2001, for six Mende Africans from Sierra Leone who were among the slaves on the slave ship *La Amistad*. Interestingly, one former *La Amistad* slave, a man named Foone, would later live in Farmington, Connecticut, where he died due to accidental drowning in August 1841, just months after the slave's court case was decided. His limestone marker, now well-worn, may be seen in Riverside Cemetery, accompanied by a recently placed bronze plaque which tells his story.

In the remaining states in New England which, with the exception of Rhode Island, had small African American populations, a few monuments, memorials, or historic marker plaques exist to highlight the presence of African American burial sites. In Vermont there is a state historical marker at the bottom of Lincoln Hill in Hinesburg, erected in 2009, which celebrates the African American farming community established here in 1795 by Shubael and Violet Clark and members of the Peters family; it also mentions the old cemetery that is but a short distance away.

Monument, Parting Ways Cemetery, Plymouth, Massachusetts. While no inscribed gravestones remain today to mark the burials of the four black men who founded the Parting Ways community, this site is one of the best documented early free-black settlements in New England.

Also to be found in Vermont is the Brownington Village Historic District in the town of Brownington. While this district highlights a number of buildings, the most important and impressive are the Alexander Twilight house (built 1830) and the Old Stone House (also known as Athenian Hall, built in 1836). Also within this district is the Village Cemetery, where Alexander Twilight (1795–1857) is buried. Twilight, the son of Revolutionary War veteran Ichabod Twilight, was born free in Corinth, Vermont, and was the first African American college graduate in America, graduating from Middlebury College in 1823. During his career Twilight served as a minister and educator in Orleans County, where he built the Old Stone House to serve as a dormitory for the county grammar school. Twilight is also significant as the first African American to be elected to public office, this happening in 1836 when he became a Vermont state legislator.

In New Hampshire there is one state historical marker (#209) in Newmarket paying homage to Wentworth Cheswell, located adjacent to the historic Cheswell family cemetery. The most significant site in New Hampshire is the African Burying Ground in Portsmouth. This site was recovered in 2003 after roadwork uncovered some remains. After many years of community discussion, debate, and fundraising, an on-site memorial was completed in 2015. Though the closing of a local street may pose some challenges to Portsmouth's historic downtown area, the city's officials and residents alike have been supportive in getting this site properly memorialized. Particularly notable in this case was the involvement of the African American community and the mutual cooperation between them and city officials in developing a memorial plan.

As for Maine, there are two historic burying sites with monuments worthy of mention: up in Machias, at the site of the Atusville Cemetery, a granite monument was erected in 2005, while in the large and ancient Eastern Cemetery in Portland several plaques and memorial stones have been erected in remembrance of some of the city's earliest black residents.

War Service Recognition

Not surprisingly, many towns and cities throughout New England have also erected monuments and memorial stones to African Americans who served for their community in the Revolutionary War and the Civil War. In many ways these markers, and in some cases actual gravestones, represent the first historic recognition these men have been given outside the town history books. Previously, any such monuments and memorials that were erected focused on white military men of stature, generals and colonels of state militia and Continental or Union regiments, but seldom the common, everyday soldier. While such recognition began as early as the 1880s, they became more common with the Bicentennial celebrations of 1976.

The first African American soldier to be recognized in a New England community with a memorial stone is unknown, but one likely candidate is Peter Salem (?–1816), who is buried in the Old Burying Ground Cemetery in Framingham, Massachusetts. Salem was born enslaved in Framingham but gained his freedom prior to the war. He served as a minuteman during the Lexington Alarm in April 1775 and subsequently enlisted in Col. John Nixon's regiment. Salem fought valiantly in the redoubt during the Battle of Bunker Hill in June 1775 and is said to have been the soldier who fired the shot that killed British officer Major John Pitcairn, who had called on the Americans to surrender. After this action, Salem continued his service during the war, taking part in significant action in the New York campaign, as well as at the Battles of Saratoga, Monmouth, and Stony Point. After the war, he married and lived in Framingham for a time before moving to Leicester. Shortly before his death he returned to his home town, where he was cared for until his death. So well-known was Salem for his service that his musket was for many years a feature in the Bunker Hill museum until it went missing in the 1970s, and his supposed image from a painting by artist John Trumbull was depicted on a U.S. postage stamp issued in 1968. Peter Salem, for all the accolades he received for his military service, was treated no better than most black soldiers after his death, being buried at an unmarked spot in the cemetery in low-lying ground. However, in 1882 the town of Framingham spent $150 to grade his burial site and erect a suitable monument stone that may still be seen today. This stone, which was quite weather-worn after enduring 118 New England winters, was restored by the local DAR (Daughters of the American Revolution) in 2000.

Other more recent examples of such soldier memorials in New England cemeteries include the gravestone in North Canaan, Connecticut's Hillside Cemetery, erected in 1996 for Milo Freeland. A native of Sheffield, Massachusetts, Freeland was among the first African Americans from New England to enlist in the Civil War when he joined Company A of the 54th Massachusetts Regiment. In Groton, Connecticut, there are two bronze plaques at historic Fort Griswold commemorating the actions of African American soldiers Lambert Latham and Jordan Freeman in defending the fort before it fell to the British on September 6, 1781. Both men played prominent parts in the battle and the aftermath, when the British massacred American soldiers after the surrender. Both men died at Fort Griswold but their burial sites are unknown for certain. Jordan Freeman may be buried in the nearby Colonel Ledyard Cemetery, as one historian asserts, while Lambert Latham's burial place is unknown.

These bronze plaques, though they do not mark an actual burial site, are nevertheless important as the only tangible memorials to these heroic black soldiers.

In New Hampshire, in the Winter Street Cemetery in Exeter, a monument was erected to Revolutionary War soldier Jude Hall in 2000. While Hall, perhaps the state's most famous black veteran after Prince Whipple, was buried somewhere near the back of the cemetery where this monument may be found, his exact burial site here is unknown. In Massachusetts, in the Olde Burial Grounds in Bedford, there is a bronze plaque mounted on a boulder in the northeastern corner of the cemetery giving the names of three "Negro Slaves, Soldiers in the Revolution"—Cambridge Moore (born 1752), Caesar Prescott, and Caesar Jones—who are buried here in otherwise unmarked graves. In the Old Burying Ground

Monument, Old Burial Ground, Bedford, Massachusetts. Because the graves of African Americans veterans were seldom marked early on, many towns have honored their black veterans by erecting plaques and monuments such as this within the cemetery grounds. Efforts at such recognition became heightened during the run-up to our nation's Bicentennial in 1976 and have continued to this day.

in Cambridge a plaque mounted on the cemetery fence identifies "Black Soldiers of the Continental Army" Cato Stedman and Neptune Frost as being "Buried In This Ground," also in unmarked graves. Finally, in the back of the Old Center Cemetery in Winchendon, Massachusetts, may be seen the gravestone for Eden London (1744–1810) which was erected in modern times and denotes the fact that he was enslaved when he served in the Revolutionary War, and was "Disch[arged] Yet A Slave 1779."

Military Headstone Programs in the Post–Civil War Era

While many individual towns have recognized their black servicemen by commissioning their own monuments, one of the best methods, in place now for over 140 years, to memorialize African American men who have served in America's armed forces has been through the use of the U.S. government's military headstone program. Formerly administered by the Quartermaster General's office and now operated by the Veterans Administration, this program got its start in the first year of the Civil War, when the government began to provide wooden markers for those killed in battle. In 1873, when it became clear that such wooden markers would only last for a short period, the government moved to replace these with stone monuments that were uniform in size and more durable, but this effort only applied to immediate war casualties and those buried in battlefield cemeteries.

In 1879 the headstone program was expanded, by the influence of the powerful Civil War veteran's group GAR (Grand Army of the Republic), to include those buried in private and city or village cemeteries anywhere in the country, and a few years later was further expanded to include the veterans of all wars. Most importantly, the headstone program was egalitarian in nature, not only supplying a monument to anyone who applied and had documentation of service, but doing so at no charge to the veteran's family. This is an important program that has continued to this day and is used by not only many military families, but also veterans and historical groups in many communities large and small to pay homage to deceased veterans that might otherwise be forgotten.

The design of these first military headstones, found in countless towns throughout New England, offer some clues as to when a veteran died, while the applications for these headstones (first made by family members or GAR) can also be valuable sources of genealogical data. The earliest of these monuments were flat-topped and forty-two inches high (with 12 inches showing above ground), featuring a shield that displayed the veteran's name, rank, and home state. No date of death or military unit was displayed.

After World War I, the design was changed, the stone's height and width were increased and the top more rounded, with the individual's military unit and date of death also added within the shield device. The only possible racial identifier can be found on the headstones for those enlisted men who had served in the Civil War holding the rank of sergeant, private, or corporal in a federally (as opposed to state) organized and segregated regiment, which displays the number of the regiment followed by the initials U.S.C.T. (United States Colored

Troop). Also at this time a religious symbol option was also added if desired, the two options being a Latin cross for those of the Christian faith and the Star of David for those of the Jewish faith. (Though outside the scope of this work, an additional 56 emblems of belief have become available to veterans since the 1950s, as was the Medal of Honor insignia. Flat headstones were authorized by the early 1940s to accommodate those cemeteries that prohibit upright markers.)

Gravestones for veterans prior to the establishment of this headstone program had to be purchased by the family from a local or regional monument company, but this could be a financial burden for some. However, with this new program in place, families of deceased service veterans could now obtain a proper headstone and often did so with the assistance of local veterans' chapters, friends, and even town

Gravestone, Abram Peters, Peterborough Cemetery, Warren, Maine. Early military headstones like this one were simple in design, featuring a man's name, rank, and branch of service, all inset within a shield device. As the government's military headstone program evolved over the years, additional information was added.

officials knowledgeable about the application process.

Several early New England examples of these military headstones include those for Alexander Garrison (1838–1880) and Abel Prince (1828–1891) in Vermont, members of the 54th Massachusetts Regiment, and both buried in St. Albans, Vermont, at Old

Greenwood Cemetery; George Hazard (1825–1891), who served in the 3rd U.S. Colored Infantry Regiment (organized in Philadelphia) and is buried in the Hills Farm Cemetery in Hudson, New Hampshire; Francis Olney (his name misspelled on his gravestone as "Oney"), a member of the 43rd U.S. Colored Infantry Regiment who later lived in Warren, Maine, and is buried in the Peterborough Cemetery; and George W. Easton (1832–ca. 1885), a member of the all-black 14th Rhode Island Heavy Artillery during the Civil War; and Robert Scott (1883–1906), a 3rd Class Mess Attendant (a rating largely restricted to African Americans) in the U.S. Navy. Both Easton and Scott are buried in Newport, Rhode Island's Common Burying Ground, God's Little Acre section.

Interestingly, while most states participated in this national headstone program, the state of Connecticut acted independently for a period of time. Because there were problems with the new national program for the first few years in regards to the material the military headstones would be crafted from and problems with suppliers providing substandard stones, in 1882 the Connecticut General Assembly appropriated money to provide headstones for their Civil War veterans, a program that lasted for many years. Because of this, the military headstones in this state's cemeteries are distinctly different from those designed for the federal program. These stones were simple in design, standing two and a half feet above ground and with a rounded top. The standard stone had no shield device, merely the designation "Civil War" at the top, followed by the name of the deceased, the military unit he served in, and the date of death, though there were some variances in the information presented. In most cases, those who served in Connecticut's black volunteer regiments had no outright racial identifiers on their stones; the stone for Sgt. Daniel Oliver, who is identified as having served in the "Colored Conn. Vols" is an unusual exception. These stones are found throughout the state, with the greatest concentration found in Hartford's Old North Cemetery, where at least 50 African American Civil War veterans, about half of whom served in the all-black 29th Connecticut Regiment, are buried, including Sgt. Daniel Oliver (1841–1919), Sgt. Thomas Paull (1820–1889), and Pvt. William Thompson (1831–1877), who was wounded in action at Richmond, Virginia.

Gravestone, Sergeant Alfred Powers, 1907, Washington Street Cemetery, Middletown, Connecticut. Powers (born 1844) is among several black soldiers of the 29th Connecticut who are buried in a separate section in this cemetery. He and his wife Emily lived in Middletown and nearby Cromwell over the years, with Alfred earning a living after the war as a cook. His stone is typical of the many Connecticut-issued military headstones.

It is interesting to note that even after the Civil War, segregated burial practices for African Americans continued in New England, a fact amply demonstrated in Connecticut's capitol city and elsewhere. Black veterans were buried in segregated sections in both the Old North Cemetery and Spring Grove Cemetery in Hartford, as well as at the Washington Street Cemetery in Middletown, where the graves for 29th Connecticut veterans Christian Gordon (died 1865) and Sgt. Alfred Powers

(1845–1907), as well as several other black soldiers, may be found at one end of the cemetery. Likewise, Hope Cemetery in Worcester, Massachusetts, has several large Civil War veterans' sections, including one that was largely reserved for African Americans. Many of them having served in the famed 54th Massachusetts Regiment, including Pvt. Emery Phelps, First Sgt. Augustus Hemmenway, and Pvt. James Cinque Quow.

However, such segregation was not always the case. In the Zion Hill Cemetery in Hartford, two sections were reserved for GAR members where black and white soldiers are buried together, among them George Washington (d. 1883), a veteran of the 31st Regiment of U.S. Colored Troops, a unit organized in New York that saw action at the Siege of Petersburg, Virginia, in 1864–65. The politically powerful GAR veterans' group actively supported its African American members, advocating not only for voting rights on the political front, but also by refusing to segregate their members in the local cemetery.

While the military headstone program was first mainly used for Civil War veterans, after about 1920 these stones began to be requested, albeit in small numbers, for black Revolutionary War veterans whose graves were previously unmarked. The stones for Peter Pomp (1747–1778) in Epsom, New Hampshire, who died (and was buried) at Valley Forge, Pennsylvania, and Prince Estabrook (1740–1830) of Lexington, Massachusetts (and, in the last years of his life, Ashby, Massachusetts), the first African American to be wounded in battle during the American Revolution, were requested in 1929 and 1930, respectively, for previously unmarked graves. Pomp's stone was erected in the McClary Cemetery in Epsom, while Estabrook's stone may be found in Ashby's Old Burial Yard. Similarly, there is a military headstone, ordered in 1934, in the Dead River Cemetery in Leeds, Maine, for Cuff Chambers (1738–1818), a veteran who served in a Massachusetts company at the Battle of Bunker Hill. However, government-issued headstones for two African American Revolutionary war veterans from New Hampshire were likely requested even earlier: those for Sampson Battis (1752–ca. 1834), also known as Sampson Moore, of Canterbury, buried in a back corner of the Center Cemetery in that town, and the famed Prince Whipple (1756–1796) of Portsmouth, buried in the historic North Cemetery. These stones were likely erected sometime between 1909 and 1923.

What is interesting about the ordering of these headstones for earlier veterans now long deceased, a true act of remembrance and respect, is the fact that many were ordered by white citizens, both men and women, many likely affiliated with local veterans' groups or lineage and historical societies, but without any personal connections to these soldiers. Prince Estabrook's stone may be an exception, as it was ordered by Henry Estabrook, according to federal census records a white pharmacist from Fitchburg, Massachusetts. He was a chairman of the Brig. General James Reed Chapter of the Sons of the American Revolution and likely a descendant of the family that owned Prince.

Indeed, because of New England's close association with the historic period of the American Revolution, with many African American soldiers whose graves would likely not otherwise be given any thought, the military headstone program has proven pivotal in keeping the region's African American history alive. The program's importance today is highlighted in the Eastern Cemetery in Portland, Maine, the city's oldest public burial place. In the African American section of this cemetery there is only one contemporary marker, that for Revolutionary War soldier Lewis Sheppard (1751–1833), who has a fine slate stone marking his burial site. However, other African American veterans are known to have been buried here. Their markers may have been lost, or perhaps they were never accorded one in the first place. Due to the efforts of the local black community, military headstones have been recently placed here for Revolutionary War veterans Cato Shattuck, James Bowes (1764–1800), and Plato McLellan. In 2012 another stone was placed here for War of 1812 veteran Richard Hill (1792–1861; his stone mistakenly states his death year as 1881), who led an interesting and tragic life.

Gravestone, Cato Shattuck, Eastern Cemetery, Portland, Maine. This stone is an example of a modern-day government-issued headstone. Because little is known about Shattuck's life, including his birth and death dates and religious affiliation, this stone offers few details except the war and the unit in which he served.

The West Street Cemetery in Rutland, Vermont, is also an example where a community has made an effort to mark the graves of their Revolutionary War heroes. While most of these graves are for white soldiers, there is one notable exception, that being the stone for Pearson Freeman (1761–1847). Freeman served in the Massachusetts Continental Line and after the war moved to Rutland, where he became one of the city's most noted African American citizens and the patriarch of a distinguished family. In fact, it is in the state of Vermont, more than any other in New England, that these military headstones are important reminders of early African American residents. Unlike elsewhere in New England, gravestones of any kind for Vermont African Americans dating before the 1860s are a relative rarity; while some early burial sites have certainly been lost, it also appears from the scarcity of grave markers that few black citizens prior to the Civil War could afford the luxury of a professionally carved gravestone. However, for veterans and their descendants after the 1860s, this all changed with the advent of the military headstone program, and now even the poorest black citizens, aided by the government or a local GAR post, could have the graves of their veteran husbands, fathers, and sons properly marked.

Heritage Trail Recognition of African American Burial Sites

While there are many people, enthusiasts and historians alike, who seek out old burial grounds, many historic cemeteries are still underappreciated sites. In fact, for many more this unique and, perhaps to some, morbid aspect of New England history seldom comes to mind at all when it comes to visiting historical sites in the region, with old meetinghouses, town greens, taverns, Colonial-era homes, and museums given more precedence. However, these cemeteries, often referred to as "open-air museums," have been highlighted more and more in recent years with the advent in many locales of marked heritage trail sites specifically relating to African American history. These trails consist of a series of sites that are usually marked with historic plaques or signs, the visitor or tourist guided by an informative trail map that can be found online or in brochure form available at local historical societies, museums, or visitor centers. Most of these tours are self-guided, giving individuals time to explore at their own leisure, while some heritage trails offer guided or audio tours that are more structured, but also offer in-depth information and color commentary, as well as the chance for those taking the tour to ask questions. No matter how these heritage trails are structured, their establishment has been yet another factor in increasing the awareness of New England's black history. Not surprisingly, almost all these heritage trails feature at least one cemetery where African Americans are buried, while many also feature the burial sites, places of worship, and homes of prominent African Americans and/or white abolitionists. In some cases, the inclusion of cemeteries in such heritage trails has given these burial places not only a higher profile, but also contributed to their upkeep and maintenance.

The earliest of this type of historical attraction to be organized was the Boston Freedom Trail (www.thefreedomtrail.org), which was established in 1951 and has served as the general model for all subsequent freedom and heritage trails. The Freedom Trail, while it is not focused on African American history, does include such sites as the Copp's Hill Burying Ground, where many, perhaps thousands, of Boston's black population were buried in unmarked graves, and the Granary Burying Ground, where there is a memorial stone for Crispus Attucks and the other victims of the 1770 Boston Massacre, as well as the grave for John Wheatley, the slave owner of famed poet Phyllis Wheatley (whose final resting place is unknown). Another historic trail closely linked to the Freedom Trail is the recently developed Black Heritage Trail (www.afroammuseum.org), the two known collectively since 2012 as "Boston's Trails to Freedom." This heritage trail does not feature any cemeteries on its stops, but its keystone site is the 1806-built African Meeting House located on Joy Street, the oldest black church still standing in America today. The first pastor of this church was the Rev. Thomas Paul, a native of Exeter, New Hampshire, while the man who raised a significant amount of the money required to build this church was African native Cato Gardner, whose final resting place is unknown.

The state of Massachusetts, not surprisingly, has the largest number of heritage trail sites in New England. In addition to operating the Black Heritage Trail in Boston, the Museum of African American History also operates the Black Heritage Trail on Nantucket Island (www.afroammuseum.org/bhtn). This trail has two sections: the downtown area, and the "New Guinea" section of town where African Americans lived. This section of the trail features the African Meeting House on York Street, but also the so-called "Colored" Cemetery off Prospect Street. Among the many burials in this cemetery, which was once quite neglected and overgrown but is now well-kept, are those for early black ministers Arthur Cooper (a runaway slave from Virginia) and James Crawford.

More modern burials include that for Eunice Ross (1824–1895), who as a young woman was denied entrance into Nantucket High School in 1840, setting up a long and contentious debate on the island. The school finally became integrated in 1843, but when the island school board tried to force the removal of black children, African American families, and some white families also, boycotted the school system by removing their children altogether in the 1844–1845 school year. The protestors sent a number of petitions, including one signed by Ms. Ross, to the Massachusetts State House in Boston. As a result, in 1845 the state passed a law ensuring equal access to schools for all children regardless of color, but even then Nantucket school officials ignored the new law. It would not be until 1846 that integration was finally achieved when the old school board members were voted out of office and the new members complied with the new law. At the age of 24, Eunice Ross was finally admitted to the school, and is said to have "excelled in French" (White, Barbara, pg. 62).

Another Massachusetts island with an interesting African American past is Martha's Vineyard. Here may be found the African American Heritage Trail of Martha's Vineyard (www.mvafricanamericanheritagetrail.org). Among the sites on this trail is the Eastville Cemetery. Located in Oak Bluffs, off Shirley Avenue near Lagoon Pond, this was an integrated burial place largely reserved for African Americans, strangers, and others low on the socio-economic ladder, and was originally on the grounds of the island's first marine hospital. There are only several marked burials here today. As for other black heritage trail sites in Massachusetts, central Massachusetts has none, though in 2014 one was proposed for the city of Worcester and the surrounding area, and may be developed in the near future.

In the western part of the state there is one site, the outstanding Upper Housatonic African American Heritage Trail (www.africanamericantrail.org), which encompasses 29 Massachusetts and Connecticut towns located on or near the Housatonic River. This trail offers several self-guided themed tours within the region, one of the most interesting being the 54th Massachusetts Volunteer Infantry Regiment Trail. On this route are featured six cemeteries in five Massachusetts towns which are the final resting for members of this pioneer regiment, including the Center Cemetery in Dalton, the West Stockbridge and Stockbridge cemeteries in Stockbridge, the Cemetery at the Church on the Hill in New Lenox (which is the resting place of four 54th veterans, as well as Anna Shaw, the widow of 54th regimental leader Colonel Robert Gould Shaw), the Pittsfield Cemetery in Pittsfield, and the Mahaiwe Cemetery in Great Barrington. Three members of the 54th are buried in the "negro plot" in the back of Maihawe Cemetery, as well as members of the family of W.E.B. DuBois, the father of the American Civil Rights movement and a Great Barrington native.

In Connecticut there is a statewide heritage trail network, the web-based Connecticut Freedom Trail (www.ctfreedomtrail.org), which is very comprehensive and encompasses numerous sites in all areas of the state, including twenty-five cemeteries and burial sites. While I have previously discussed many of these sites, others of note include the gravesite of Bristol, a former slave, in West Hartford's Old Center Burying Yard, and the Green Farms Colonial Burying Ground in Westport, whose back portion was reserved for blacks and includes the burials of Lyzette Munroe (1778–1836) and Dorcas Hyde, both formerly enslaved. The website for this trail is excellent and the information found here is important for the visitor, as most of the sites themselves have no historical markers to identify their significance. The only other such site in Connecticut is the Hartford African American Heritage Trail, established about 2010, but it contains no cemetery listings, likely because most of these are already included in the Connecticut Freedom Trail.

In several of the remaining New England states there are also found other black heritage trail sites. The best-known and most established of these is the Portsmouth Black Heritage Trail (www.portsmouthhistory.org/portsmouth-black-heritage-trail/) in Portsmouth, New Hampshire. Founded in 1996, it features several cemeteries, including the African Burying Ground on Chestnut Street and, as part of its extended tour, the Langdon slave cemetery located on Lafayette Road, next to Christ Episcopal Church. This popular trail saw enhanced interest once the African Burying Ground Memorial was completed in the spring of 2015. In Portland, Maine, there is the Portland Freedom Trail (www.portlandfreedomtrail. org), established in 2006, which features sixteen sites related to this maritime city's African American history. These include the 1829-built Abyssinian Meeting House, the first black church in Maine, located on Newbury Street; and Eastern Cemetery, where many of this town's African American residents living in the adjacent Munjoy Hill neighborhood were buried. In Vermont, there is the Vermont African American Heritage Trail (www.historic sites.vermont.gov/vt_history/african_americans), which was established by the state in 2012. It highlights nineteen sites statewide, the only state other than Connecticut that features a statewide web-based heritage trail. As of this writing, the Vermont trail has no exclusive website and its online pre-sence is rather underdeveloped, but this may change as time goes on. Only one burial site, the River Street Cemetery (to be discussed at length later on) in Woodstock, is featured, but there is also a historical marker on Lincoln Hill in Hinesburg, not far from the cemetery that served the community here. The town of Grafton, the residence of the notable Turner family (also to be discussed), is also highlighted, and the burial places of Alexander and Sally Turner and grand-daughter Daisy Mae Turner can be found nearby.

In regards to heritage trail sites in Rhode Island, the state has lagged in this area, and though it has many heritage trails within its borders, there are none that are African American–themed. There is the Providence Heritage Trail, established in the capital in 2011. This trail offers a walking tour of the downtown area and among the sites included within the area of this trail (though not specifically highlighted as of this writing) is the historic North Burial Ground located on Branch Avenue, where many of that city's black residents, both enslaved and free, are buried. As of 2014, this trail has no dedicated website and has seen little development. On the Newport Military History Trail there is a monument in Portsmouth dedicated to the black Revolutionary War soldiers of the 1st Rhode Island Regiment. However, the city of Newport itself, quite surprisingly, has no black heritage trail or related site, which seems like a lost opportunity given the city's close connection to the slave trade. This city is quite well-known for its Cliff Walk along the ocean, which highlights the many historic mansions found here, and the Newport Historical Society does offer a number of tours that briefly discuss some aspects of black history, but nothing dedicated solely to the topic. The closest is perhaps their Souls & Stones Tour of the Common Burying Ground, which discusses the God's Little Acre section as part of the presentation.

Part Two: Significant African American Burial Sites

In this section I will highlight some of the most important and interesting of the African American burial sites located throughout New England. While this selection is subjective in nature, I have striven to include not only those sites that are illustrative of the various types of cemeteries discussed, but have also tried to represent the geographic regions within each state. Nearly all these sites were chosen because they are accessible to the public. I have also chosen sites where the details regarding the lives of individuals, most of whom are not famous, are known. For each site I have provided, when known, information about the cemetery itself and, if one exists, a credible website. Unfortunately, most towns have no cemetery specific websites. Those that do often vary widely, some providing a great amount of information, both helpful and historic, while others provide so little information that they are of little use to the visitor and historian alike. Of course, there are many other non-official online sites dedicated to cemeteries and related topics that the interested explorer can find with little effort. One of the most useful of these sites is findagrave.com, always a good starting point for those new to the field of cemetery research and exploration, and one that usually offers accurate mapping and location information. While many contributors on this site provide excellent pictures and solid historical data to the entries they create, the reader is cautioned that, as with any website of this contributory type, errors are not uncommon and firsthand research to verify the historical data presented is recommended.

If the reader is inspired to visit these sites in person, which is one of the main purposes of this book, here are some helpful hints that will make your visit more enjoyable. First of all, plan ahead by finding out when the cemetery is open. Most city cemeteries are open from dawn to dusk, but there are some sites that have more restricted hours. Also, while most cemeteries are easily accessible, some of them are locked at all times (most notably the West Street Cemetery in Rutland, Vermont; Eastern Burial Ground in Bristol, Rhode Island; and the older cemeteries in Middletown, Connecticut) and require a visit to the town hall, local firehouse, or some other arrangements beforehand.

Please use common personal safety sense when visiting. If possible, bring along a companion, as some cemeteries are in isolated areas. While I have generally had few problems in this regard, cemeteries in populated places should be visited in full daylight hours, never the early morning or after dusk (unless on a guided nighttime tour) due to safety reasons.

In regards to illustrative souvenirs from your visit, please note that while photography is always permitted, by law most New England cemeteries prohibit gravestone rubbings. In some locales they are prohibited outright, and that fact is so stated on the cemetery gate; in other locales no such mention is made. If you want to practice this unique art form, the best practice is to inquire in advance by calling the town hall, cemetery maintenance department, or the cemetery office to see if rubbing is permitted. As to the art of gravestone rubbing itself, this should always be practiced with only those gravestones that are in good condition that have no cracks or breaks in the stone. When applying pressure to a stone in the rubbing process, you don't want to be the one to break a stone in half or otherwise cause further damage. And be sure not to mark the stone with whatever medium you have chosen and leave no tape residue. Of course, protecting and respecting the ancient gravestones is every visitor's responsibility. Do not lean upon or sit on any stone, especially those in a deteriorated condition, and supervision of children in this regard is always a must.

If you want to photograph a favorite stone, by all means do so. You may want to use a handheld flash attachment if you have one to illuminate stones that are in shady portions of the cemetery, a quite common occurrence. If you have someone accompanying you, one of the best and least expensive ways to illuminate a stone is by using a large mirror; usually an inexpensive door mirror standing about four feet tall will do. This can be used to reflect sunlight on a gravestone that is otherwise in the shadows from up to 50 feet away, and sometimes even further. This can be tricky, but is easy to get the hang of, and I have used this method for many of my published gravestone photographs. You will better your chances of having the perfect light for photographic and viewing purposes by visiting New England cemeteries on a sunny day between the hours of approximately noon and 2 p.m. in the spring and summer, and 11 a.m. and 1 p.m. in the fall. In many cases, during these timeframes no further illumination will be needed. With a little prep work, you'll be surprised at how good your pictures will turn out.

Finally, as with any outdoor trip, some basic precautions are in order. Some cemeteries can be overgrown, so wear good footwear, socks and, if possible, long pants to avoid catching poison ivy and, in some locales, bring some insect and tick repellant to minimize mosquito bites. Be sure also to look where you're walking. Some cemeteries can have broken gravestone fragments or even slight depressions in the ground that pose tripping hazards. By following these simple steps, your visits are sure to be successful.

I. Connecticut

All of the sites listed here, except those denoted with an *, are on the Connecticut Freedom Trail and can be viewed online at www.ctfreedomtrail.org.

*Onesimus Comstock Burial Site
Canoe Hill Cemetery
Laurel Road, near intersection of Canoe Hill Road
New Canaan

This cemetery, established in 1760, is one of the oldest in the area. Here is buried Onesimus Comstock, who may have been the last male slave held in the state of Connecticut. Onesimus was born into captivity about 1761 in neighboring Norwalk, possibly the son of an enslaved woman named Candace. His first owner was Jonathan Husted, but he was sold while still a young boy on November 1, 1772, to Sarah and Phoebe Comstock, the daughters of Moses Comstock, for the sum of 39 pounds. Because Husted was a Tory, he was forced to leave the town and was living at Brookhaven, New York, on Long Island when he sold Onesimus, perhaps in need of cash. What may have become of Candace is unknown, but Onesimus spent the remainder of his life with the Comstock women, first with the two sisters on their family farm, later with their niece, a second Phoebe Comstock, to whom he was willed in 1810 and who was about the same age as Onesimus. She died three years before he did in 1854, his later care subsequently attended to by Darius Ferris (Comstock, pg. 15).

Onesimus Comstock served for a brief time during the Revolutionary War in July of 1779 during the British invasion of Norwalk. The chaplain of the American Continental forces was quartered in the home of Phoebe Comstock, and when his waiter died, Onesimus took his place and was enrolled in the army. After the burning of Norwalk, Onesimus continued in the service of the Comstocks. One day, when gathering hay in the Comstock meadows, he spied several British soldiers lurking about and, with Phoebe Comstock's help, alerted the local militia, resulting in the capture of two prisoners. This seems to have been the end of Onesimus's wartime service.

After the war, local lore suggests that Onesimus's freedom was discussed by the family but that he was content to remain in their service. Onesimus also became a devout member of the Norwalk Congregational Church when it was rebuilt in 1779–80, having been witness to the burning of the town, including its church, during the British invasion. He would

Gravestone, Onesimus Comstock, Canoe Hill Cemetery, New Canaan, Connecticut (courtesy JoAnn Rice).

remain a faithful church member for over seventy years and attended church regularly no matter what the weather, usually accompanying Phoebe Comstock every Sunday on horseback. In the 1850 federal census, Onesimus is listed as still living with Phoebe Comstock and was denoted as a "voluntary slave." Local lore also states that Onesimus was Phoebe Comstock's constant companion for many years and was the one who took care of her in her final years.

After Phoebe Comstock died in 1854, Onesimus was given some land and a small house to live in, located in New Canaan. Though uncertain, that house may be the 1735-built house still in existence located on nearby Ferris Hill Road. Upon his death, Comstock was buried in the nearby Canoe Hill Cemetery at the back left corner close by his former mistress and friend, Phoebe Comstock, as well as several other Comstock family members.

African American Section
Green Farms Lower Cemetery—Colonial Burying Ground
Intersection of Green Farms Road and Sherwood Island Connector
Westport

This old cemetery, filled with many exquisitely carved stones from the Colonial era, was established in the early 1720s. As with many other burying places of the time, it has a section at the far back corner that was reserved for African Americans. In this black section of the cemetery may be found several surviving stones, including those for the Munroe, Hyde (also spelled "Hide"), and Gregory families. The Munroe and Gregory families, at least in later years, were interrelated and lived together. This section of the cemetery is the primary indicator of the large black presence in the town (formerly part of Fairfield until its incorporation in 1835) throughout the 19th century.

One of the earliest free African Americans in the Green Farms section of what would later become Westport was Henry Munroe (also spelled "Monroe," died 1821) and his wife, Lyzette Hyde Munroe (1778–1836). Henry Munroe, who came here from the Greenfield section of Fairfield, bought eight acres of land here from John Burwell in 1802, and by 1806 had built his own house, which still stands today (a private residence located at 108 Cross Highway). After his death, Henry Munroe was possibly buried in this cemetery (but may have also been buried on his own land). His wife, Lyzette Munroe, was likely a former slave of the Hyde family of Fairfield. Her stone, a typical one for the time, may still be seen today. The Munroes had at least one child, a son named Henry, who was born about 1798, and operated the family farm for many years after his father's death. The stones for Dorcas Hyde and Maria Gregory can also be found here. Dorcas Hyde, who was born sometime between 1790 and 1798 (the dates of census records and that on her gravestone are conflicting), was likely born enslaved, perhaps even a daughter of Peter Hyde, but nothing is known for certain. In her later years she earned a living by working as a domestic servant in the home of Dr. George Blackman, who perhaps tended to her medical care and may have provided her with a suitable headstone, one of the few in this section of the cemetery for African Americans.

Maria Gregory (ca. 1804–1878), whose gravestone as of this writing was broken, was of mixed ancestry and made a good living for a time as a shirt-maker in Westport, along with her companion (possibly a sister), Amelia Gregory. According to the 1860 federal census, Maria Gregory had holdings valued at $600, a

Gravestone, Doras Hyde, 1876, Green Farms Lower Cemetery, Westport, Connecticut.

tidy sum for the time. By 1870, however, Maria Gregory was living with Henry Munroe and his wife Phebe. Also living in the Munroe household was Amelia (Gregory) Munroe, all the women employed as housekeepers. Her relationship to Henry Munroe is uncertain, but possibly she was married to a brother or one of his cousins (there are many black Munroes in this area of the state), all of which are good indicators of the close-knit aspect of the African American community in Westport.

Nero Hawley Burial Site
Riverside Cemetery
Daniel's Farm Road
Trumbull
http://www.trumbullhistory.org/freedomtrail/

Several of the New England states have at least one African American Revolutionary War veteran who epitomizes the black contribution to the fight for freedom, and in Connecticut that man seems to be Nero Hawley. He was born into captivity in North Stratford (now Trumbull) in 1742; his owner was Daniel Hawley, who operated a sawmill. Like many of the enslaved, Nero Hawley was married, his wife being Peg, the slave of the Rev. James Beebe, with whom the couple lived, along with their five children. By early 1777, Peg was expecting her sixth child.

It was likely the promise of both gaining his freedom and a signing bonus that Nero Hawley enlisted for service in the Revolutionary War, joining the company of Captain Samuel Granger in the 2nd Connecticut Regiment on April 20, 1777. As a member of this regiment, serving alongside his fellow white soldiers, Hawley saw a great deal of action and hardship, fighting during the Philadelphia campaign at Whitemarsh in 1777, enduring the brutal winter of 1777-78 at Valley Forge, taking part in the Battle of Monmouth in 1778, and, most notably, in July 1779 was among the handpicked men chosen to serve in the light infantry assault forces that defeated the British in the Battle of Stony Point on the Hudson River in New York.

Hawley was subsequently discharged from service in April of 1781 and was emancipated by his master on November 4, 1782. At least two of his children, all of whom were owned by the Reverend Beebe due to his ownership of Peg, were listed in the reverend's estate after his death in 1785, and were not formally emancipated until 1801. After gaining his freedom, Nero Hawley and his wife purchased over forty acres of land, much of it wooded. Nero made a living by selling timber from his woodlands, as well as manufacturing bricks from the clay found on his land.

Though life was often hard for many black war veterans, Nero Hawley did better than most. He was involved in community affairs as a church member in North Stratford, and in 1791 was among those who withdrew from that church to join the Episcopal church in nearby Ripton (now Huntington). Later in life, by the early 1800s, Nero Hawley was disabled, and by October 1815 was receiving a disability pension for his wartime service. He was deemed an invalid, no doubt worn down by his years of hard physical labor, a combined result of his years as a slave, his wartime service, and the years of hard work on his own land.

Hawley died on January 30, 1817, survived by his wife Peg, who was a member of the Church of Christ in Trumbull and lived in town until her death at the age of 90 on July 26, 1833. Two of the Hawley grandchildren, Grant and Peter Hawley, were active churchmen, trustees of the Zion Colored Methodist Episcopal Church in Bridgeport, Connecticut, at its founding in 1835, now the Walter's Memorial African Methodist Episcopal Zion Church.

Nero Hawley's current grave marker is not contemporary; it was likely erected sometime after 1900, and it is unknown if his final resting place was originally marked. In front of his gravesite there are set in stone several bricks fired from the same kiln that Hawley used, with a bronze plaque giving the details. Interestingly, the home of Daniel Hawley, where Nero once lived as a slave, is still standing today at 49 Daniel's Farm Road, not far from Nero's burial site, and is a private residence. This home is said to be inhabited by the friendly ghost of Nero Hawley, who in 1968 appeared to a resident wearing his soldier's uniform, and has appeared at other times since. Nero Hawley's story is told in full in the 1975 book *From Valley Forge to Freedom: A Story of a Black Patriot*, written by E. Merrill Beach.

*Jeffrey Liberty Burial Site
Old Judea Cemetery
Judea Cemetery Rd., off Rte. 47 (Woodbury Rd.)
Washington

This hillside cemetery was established when the Judea Parish area was part of the town of Woodbury until the town of Washington was incorporated as a separate entity in 1779. Located at the far back of the cemetery, center left in front of a large tree, is an area that is largely devoid of marked graves and was likely the section of the cemetery that was reserved for African Americans. While there are no gravestones here to mark the final resting place of any African America per se, one can view here instead an old cast iron marker, probably erected in the early 20th century, that denotes this area presumably as the burial site of "Jeff Liberty And His Colored Patriots." Sadly, little is known about Jeff Liberty or any of his fellow black Revolutionary War soldiers who may have been buried nearby. Given his name of "Liberty," we may be certain that Jeffrey, as he is referred to in military records, was once enslaved, and perhaps gained his freedom as a result of his military service in the years 1781–82 for the newfound town of Washington.

Cast iron marker, Jeff Liberty, Old Judea Cemetery, Washington, Connecticut.

Jeffrey Liberty enlisted on June 27, 1781, in the newly consolidated Connecticut Regiment and served for five months when the regiment was performing garrison duty somewhere along the Hudson River in New York until his service ended in October 1781. Liberty served in a largely black company that also included Sharp Liberty, Pomp Liberty, Cuff Liberty, and Congo Zado. Jeffrey Liberty was not related to any of these men, as the surname was one commonly taken by newly freed slaves. However, another man, James Liberty, did serve from the town of Woodbury from 1777 to 1780 and is more likely tied to Jeffrey in some way. Another black man serving with Jeffrey Liberty was Simon Rose, who enlisted in neighboring Woodbury on June 16 of the same year.

Other "Colored Patriots," almost certainly former slaves, who served in the war from Woodbury and may be buried in the Old Judea Cemetery include Cummy, Galloway, Jem, and Tony, all of whom served in the war in 1778; Peter (no years given); and in 1777–1779, Robin and Tite (White, David, pgs. 59–63). After the war, Jeffrey Liberty was counted as a citizen of the town of Washington in the 1790 federal census, one of only two free black households in the town, but disappears from history afterward, perhaps deceased before 1800. His cast iron marker is a simple yet elegant reminder of the role Connecticut's black soldiers played in winning America's independence.

Hillside Cemetery
U.S. Rte 44 (East Canaan Rd.) between Casey Hill and Canaan Valley roads
East Canaan

In this bucolic and well-groomed cemetery, in the rear portion in Lot B8, is the final resting place for Civil War soldier Milo Freeland. The stone that marks his grave was erected in 1996 to commemorate his service as a soldier in the 54th Massachusetts Regiment, the first all-black regiment to be raised in the North. Freeland was a native of Massachusetts and a resident of nearby Sheffield, Massachusetts, when the war broke out. At the time of his enlistment on February 16, 1863, he was a farm laborer and married to his wife, Sophronia Way Freeland (born ca. 1845). She was a resident of Lee, Massachusetts, in 1855, possibly an orphan, living with Marhatiah and Emeline Jones, an older African American couple, according to the Massachusetts state census.

Like most of the early enlistees in the 54th Massachusetts, Freeland only received $50 of the promised state bounty, while later recruits received as much as $325. Freeland likely joined the service at the enlistment station established in Pittsfield, Massachusetts. Though his modern-carved gravestone states that he was the first black soldier to enlist in the Civil War in the North, this claim is unfortunately inaccurate, as there were other men in Company A from Boston, where the first recruits were signed, who enlisted for service as much as five days earlier. However, Freeland was one of the first African American soldiers in the entire regiment to enlist and serve from outside the Boston area, the first to serve in the regiment from western Massachusetts, and may have had the distinction (and thus the error on his gravestone) of being the first in the regiment to report for duty at Camp Meigs in Readville, Massachusetts where the men would receive their military training before heading off to war. Whatever the case may have been, Milo Freeland would be a participant in almost every battle the regiment fought in, including the famed assault on Fort Wagner, South Carolina, in July 1863 and the Battle of Olustee in Florida.

After his service ended in April 1865, Milo Freeland returned home to his wife Sophronia in Sheffield. The couple would subsequently have five children, including their first, daughter Jessie (born 1870); Eugene (born 1875); Harry (born 1877); Sarah (born 1878); and Benjamin (born May 1880), all detailed in the 1880 federal census. Milo Freeman worked as a farmer until his death in East Canaan, Connecticut, on April 16, 1883, at the young age of 43. While Sheffield and East Canaan are relatively close to one another, the circumstances surrounding Freeland's death and how he came to be in East Canaan are unknown.

As for the Freeland children, several would have long and productive lives. Jessie Julia Freeland moved to Somerville, Massachusetts, as a young woman and worked as a domestic servant. In July 1895 she married Mahlon Ward in Boston, and by 1920 was living in New Haven, Connecticut, with her husband and daughters Mabelle and Alice. By 1940 Jessie Ward was a widow and was living in New York City with her daughter Alice Ward. Milo Freeland's son Benjamin was later a resident of Springfield, Massachusetts, and was still alive to register for the draft during World War I, while his son Harry Freeland was a resident of New Haven, Connecticut, in 1930 and the owner of a battery factory.

Mars, Freedom, and Freeman Family Burial Sites
Center Cemetery
Old Colony Rd., off North St.
Norfolk

Here in this quiet corner of Connecticut in one cemetery may be found the gravesites for several African American families. The most famed of these are for a most remarkable man, James Mars, and that of his father, the celestially named Jupiter Mars. In 1864, James Mars wrote and had published a brief account of his early life titled *Life of James Mars, A Slave born and sold in Connecticut*, an eminently readable autobiography that is one of the few such works by an enslaved African American in New England.

From his sometimes blistering account, we learn that his father, Jupiter Mars (1751–1818), was born enslaved in New York and served in the American Revolution as a personal servant to Robert Van Rensellaer, first the colonel of the Albany County militia, and later brigadier general of a unit composed of the Albany and Tryon County militias. Jupiter was subsequently owned by a series of masters in New York and Salisbury, Connecticut, before becoming the property of the Reverend Thompson of North Canaan, Connecticut. Jupiter was well known in Norfolk for his fiddle-playing prowess and was well respected.

James Mars's mother was Fanny Mars; she was born enslaved in Virginia and about 1789 came to Connecticut with her mistress, who married the Reverend Thompson and subsequently lived in Canaan. However, apparently the newly married Mrs. Thompson had no intention of staying in the North and persuaded her husband to move to Virginia, leaving Jupiter Mars behind with his family, including James (born 1790) and three children who died while infants, to work the Thompson farm.

In 1798 the Reverend Thompson sold his farm with the intention of moving south and taking his slaves with him, but this Jupiter Mars would never allow, stating that "he would never go alive" (Bontemps, pg. 39). Fearing for his family's safety, when the time was right Jupiter Mars sent James and his other son John away to prevent them from being taken south. With the help of a number of whites in Norfolk, they remained hidden, and finally Thompson was forced to negotiate with Jupiter, offering him and his wife their freedom if he could take their two boys. This they would not allow, and after much negotiation it was decided that the reverend would sell the boys so that they could stay in Connecticut. James was sold to a Mr. Munger in Norfolk, while his brother John was sold to a master in nearby Salisbury. As Mars would later write, "we two boys were sold for one hundred pounds a head, lawful money, yes, sold by a man, a minister of the gospel in Connecticut, the land of steady habits" (Bontemps, pg. 46).

In 1811, at the age of 21, James Mars would finally gain his freedom. He was married to his wife Clarissa, and lived in Norfolk before later moving to Hartford, where he became a deacon in the Talcott Street Church. He was noted for his civil rights activities in trying to gain the state's black citizens the right to vote and advocating for the abolishment of slavery. He would later reside in Pittsfield, Massachusetts, for many years before returning to Norfolk, where he was noted by many in town for his fine preaching abilities.

Mars was compelled to write his story not only to raise some money to support himself in his old and infirm condition. But he also meant to expose the myths about slavery in the state, writing near the end of his book: "What I have written of my own history, seems to satisfy the minds of those that read it, that the so-called favored state, the land of good morals and steady habits, was ever a slave state, and that slaves were driven through the streets tied or fastened together for market. This seems to surprise some that I meet, but it was true. I have it from reliable authority. Yes, this was done in Connecticut. I think the time is not far distant when the colored man will have his rights in Connecticut" (Bontemps, pgs. 57–58).

The Marses had several sons and daughters, including Georgeanna, Dewitt, Minor, and Geraldine. Georgeanna would move to Liberia, Africa, in 1859 to become a teacher, following in the footsteps of her aunt, Charlotte Mars, who was born free. Charlotte also went to Africa and later encouraged James Mars to write his life story. Minor Mars served in the U.S. Navy during the Civil War, while another son enlisted in an artillery regiment and died during the course of his service.

Also buried in this cemetery are Peter Freedom and his wives Clorony and Bilhah, and daughters Jane (by his first wife) and Amanda (by his second wife). Peter and Clorony Free-

dom were likely born enslaved and may have gained their freedom after the American Revolution. The Freedom family was well known in Norfolk, where Peter worked at a grist mill and was considered "a very respectable man" (Eldridge and Crissey, pg. 371). Little is known of his first wife, but his second wife, Bilhah Freedom, was born in Litchfield, Connecticut, in January 1783, probably also enslaved. She was said to have been "Of African and Princely Descent. Of Queenly yet Deferential Demeanor. Grateful and Happy in Her Humble Lot, Tender and True" (Eldridge and Crissy, pg. 372). Bilhah Freedom would later become known as Aunt Bilhah and was famed for her cooking skills, including her tasty gingerbread, and made a living after her husband died by preparing her famed meals for hire at local weddings and at Thanksgiving time.

Yet another African American family with members buried here is that of the Freeman family. Both Alanson Freeman (1844–1913) and William Freeman (1843–1919), likely brothers, saw service in the Civil War, serving in Company A of the all-black 29th Connecticut Regiment. Alanson Freeman's origin is uncertain, as census records for June of 1870, when he was in prison in Litchfield, Connecticut, indicate he was a New York native, while the 1910 federal census lists him as a Connecticut native, earning a living as a farmer.

Top: Gravestone, Peter Freedom, 1837, Center Cemetery, Norfolk, Connecticut (courtesy Janis L. Franco). *Bottom:* Bilhah Freedom, 1871, Center Cemetery, Norfolk, Connecticut (courtesy Janis L. Franco).

Nancy Toney Burial Site
Palisado Cemetery
Junction of Palisado Ave. (Rte. 159) and Pierson Ln.
Windsor

In the far back left corner of this large cemetery, where there are few stones to be found, is the final resting place for Nancy Toney. While she has been erroneously referred to as the last slave to be held in the state of Connecticut, Nancy certainly is representative of that small group who remained enslaved in the state well after the institution of slavery had died out elsewhere in New England. Nancy (first called Anna) was born enslaved in 1774; her mother was Nanny, a slave of the Rev. Andrew Elliot in Fairfield, and her father was Toney, the slave of Jeremiah Sherwood. She was baptized at Christ's Church (now the

Portrait of Nancy Toney (oil on canvas), ca. 1863. This painting, attributed to Osbert Loomis of Windsor, was created within less than ten years after Nancy Toney's death and is a rare artistic portrayal of a black woman from this time period (collection of the Loomis Chaffee School Archives, Loomis Chaffee School, Windsor, Connecticut).

First Congregational Church) on November 27, 1774, and remained in the family before being sold to Hezekiah Bradley.

In September 1785, Bradley gave Nancy to his daughter Charlotte Bradley Chaffee as a wedding present. Nancy subsequently went with Charlotte to her new home in Windsor, where the newly married couple built a substantial home near the Palisado Green. Here it was that Nancy Toney would spend the rest of her life, largely performing domestic work and child-care services. While Charlotte's father in law, Dr. Hezekiah Chaffee Sr., who lived next door to his son, also held slaves, they were manumitted by 1810, leaving Nancy as the sole slave held in the town of Windsor.

In 1821, Nancy became the slave of Abigail Chaffee Loomis and her husband James Loomis after the death of Dr. Hezekiah Chaffee, Jr., as per his 1818 will, a common practice in earlier times, but unusual for this time period. While no formal manumission documents have been found, Nancy was apparently freed by 1830, being listed in the 1830 federal census as a free black woman. Despite her freedom, Nancy remained with the Loomis family for the rest of her life, likely performing the same duties as she had all along, though hopefully with a lessened burden as she grew older. Nancy Toney (though her death record gives her name as Nancy Joyce) died on December 19, 1857, due to the effects of tuberculosis, and she was buried in the Palisado Cemetery, a fine stone erected by the Loomis family in honor of her faithful service. This weathered stone was replaced in 2004 with a replica stone.

How many other African Americans may be buried nearby to Nancy Toney in this section of the cemetery is unknown for certain, the only other marked grave for an African American being that for Virgil Simmons (1842–1864). He was a native of Windsor and likely knew Nancy Toney in some capacity due to her long residence in town. Simmons was employed as a waiter and as a stable hand in Hartford in 1863. He enlisted in the 29th Connecticut Regiment of black volunteers on November 31, 1863, at Hartford, but died due to disease on June 28, 1864, at New Haven, likely becoming ill before the regiment left the state. Whether his body was brought back to Windsor by family, perhaps his father Henry Simmons, or George Simmons (possibly his brother), is unknown, but Virgil Simmons's short life may be seen as yet another link in Connecticut's African American past, connected to Nancy Toney in death by proximity and residence, as well as to his fellow black soldiers who fought in the war that forever put an end to slavery in America.

Civil War Soldiers Burial Site
Old North Cemetery
Intersection of North Main and Mather streets
Hartford
http://hartford.omaxfield.com/cems/oldnorth.html

This cemetery was established in 1807 and is the final resting place of many of the city's most prominent white citizens. However, off the beaten path in this cemetery, away from the elaborate monuments for the white Colt, Wadsworth, Trumbull, and Olmsted families, there may also be found nearly thirty stones for African American veterans of the Civil War. These stones are in the center of the cemetery and can be found by following

Black Veterans' Section, Old North Cemetery, Hartford, Connecticut (courtesy Cathy Rimcoski).

the driveway into the cemetery off North Main to a path. In the section between this path and another path located to the right is the section that was reserved for African Americans. Nearly fifty black veterans of the Civil War are buried here, perhaps more, though not all of these headstones, most of the standard Connecticut-issued military type, have survived.

Indeed, this cemetery for many years was badly neglected and many monuments were lost due to vandalism and a lack of maintenance. My first visit to this cemetery in the late 1990s showed the place badly overgrown and largely ignored, but since 2011 things have improved greatly. The city is now in the midst of a ten-year restoration initiative, committing over a million dollars to the effort. With such a large concentration of black veterans in one burying place, Old North Cemetery is truly indicative of the state's African American contribution to the Union cause. Many of these men served in the 29th Connecticut Volunteer Infantry Regiment, a unit manned by black noncommissioned officers and enlisted men and commanded by white commissioned officers, so it is here appropriate to give a brief history of that unit.

The state of Connecticut was a bit slow in following its neighbor to the north, Massachusetts, in forming a regiment of black soldiers, but when the war continued to grind on and more and more men were required to fill Union regiments, Governor William Buckingham, an ardent supporter of President Lincoln, finally persuaded the state legislature in

November 1863 to authorize the raising of a black fighting unit. When news of this pending authorization became public knowledge, recruiting efforts began in August and were in full stride by October. The 29th Connecticut was fully manned by January of 1864, but with so many black men willing to serve, another regiment, the 30th Connecticut, was subsequently authorized. In all, about 1,600 black men enlisted for the Union cause (McCain, pg. 12) for the state; the 29th Connecticut always maintained its state identity, while the 30th Connecticut was eventually merged into the 31st Regiment of U.S. Colored Troops.

As with the 54th Massachusetts, equal pay and enlistment bounty problems became an issue, and most black soldiers never received all of the pay they were promised, but no matter; like their white counterparts, these black soldiers were patriotically compelled to serve to protect the Union, with the additional added incentive of being actively involved in the fight to end slavery once and for all and gain more rights for themselves and their fellow black citizens.

After the regiment was mustered in at Fair Haven, training exercises were conducted, following which the regiment moved to New Haven. It was from this city that the men of the 29th Connecticut departed for the war zone in March 1864 and were first stationed in South Carolina, seeing no action. Things changed in August 1864 when the 29th had its baptism under fire during the Siege of Petersburg at Malvern Hill. The regiment also saw significant action in the Battle of New Market Heights (also known as the Battle of Chapin's Farm), where many African American soldiers were in action and some of them (none from Connecticut) were awarded the Medal of Honor. The 29th suffered its greatest casualties in the fighting near Fair Oaks, Virginia, in late October 1864. Following this, the 29th Connecticut was assigned to construction duties around Richmond, and elements of the regiment were the first Union soldiers to enter the Confederacy's capital city after Richmond fell on April 3, 1865. After the war ended, the 29th Connecticut was employed guarding prisoners in Maryland, and was subsequently sent to Texas for garrison duty before being released from duty in October 1865, arriving back in Connecticut in November.

Among those soldiers who served in the 29th Connecticut that are buried in the Old North Cemetery are the following men; William C. Dewey (1845–1893), a native of Baton Rouge, Louisiana, who was living in Hartford and working as a farmer when he enlisted in December 1863. In January–February 1864 he was employed as a hospital attendant helping to take care of his fellow soldiers who were sick in addition to being trained to fight. David Branch (1834–1896), was a native of Connecticut, living in North Stonington when he enlisted in December 1863; promoted to corporal in February 1865, after the war he lived in Hartford with his wife Maria, and made a living as a laborer. Chauncey Douglass (1833–1912), a native of Norwich, living in Hartford and employed as a coachman when he enlisted for service in December 1863, was wounded in action at Kell House, Virginia, on October 27, 1864. Mustered out of the service in October 1865, he continued to live in Hartford with his first wife Susan and their children Susan and Daniel, later married to Clara.

In addition to the men of the 29th Connecticut who are buried here in Old North are a number of other men who served in all-black regiments, including some raised outside the state, including Sgt. Thomas Freeman (1840–1890), a native of New Jersey living in

Bridgeport who enlisted in December 1863 and was wounded in action at Petersburg, Virginia, during the Battle of the Crater on July 30, 1864, while serving in the 30th Connecticut Regiment. Theodore Pompey Brindley (1842–1897), a native of Freehold, New Jersey, who first enlisted in the U.S. Navy at New York in May 1863 as a landsman. He later served as a soldier, enlisting under the name Pompey Brindley in the 127th U.S.C.T. regiment in September 1864 at Camp William Penn, just outside of Philadelphia. Brindley fought in the regiment's only wartime action at Deep Bottom, Virginia. He was a resident of Hartford by 1870 working as a cook. Francis Demory (1828–1884) of New Bedford, Massachusetts, enlisted in Co. C of the 54th Massachusetts, serving under the later Medal of Honor recipient Sgt. William Carney (also from New Bedford). He was wounded in action while on foraging duty near Salkehatchie, South Carolina, in February 1865. Geraldo DeMars, possibly a native of Hartford, enlisted in the 14th Rhode Island Heavy Artillery Regiment, the state's only black regiment (manned by men from Rhode Island and Connecticut) at Providence in September 1863. He died in November 1864, likely at Port Hudson, Louisiana, due to disease while serving garrison duty.

African American Section
Ancient Burying Ground and Village Cemetery
250 Main Street, behind the First Church of Christ
Wethersfield
http://www.wethhist.org/services/burying_ground/

This site, established in the 1630s, is considered to be one of the most historic cemeteries in all of Connecticut, and a walk through the cemetery quickly demonstrates why. The closely packed graves and exquisite carvings in this compact village setting truly give off an air of the ancient colonial past. In the back corner of this cemetery, near the children's playground and close by the parking lot, is a section where four men, all of African or possibly mixed African and Native American descent, are buried, their graves all lined neatly in a row, dating from 1731 to 1816. Though uncertain, I believe these gravestones were likely relocated at some point, perhaps to allow for church expansion, as their positioning in such a neat and orderly row over an eighty-five year time span is inconsistent with the scattered burial patterns that were often the norm in colonial-era burying grounds. Despite this, the survival of these stones is impressive and one of the best indicators of the practice of slavery in New England.

How many other slave or free blacks may be buried in this cemetery is unknown, but Wethersfield, like many other Connecticut towns, had a long connection with the institution of slavery. Like many so-called seaport towns on the Connecticut River in colonial times, Wethersfield had a large maritime trade and was active in the slave trade. One of the town's first slave holders was Leonard Chester, who at his death in 1648 had recorded as part of his estate a "Neager maide" (Adams, pg. 700) valued at 25 pounds.

Of the African Americans buried here, we know few details, but their stones are unusual. Two of them, that for Francois (1766–1816) and Quash Gomer, detail their African origin, while Gomer's stone is the only one I've found in all of New England that identifies

African section, Ancient Burying Ground, Wethersfield, Connecticut.

his specific place of origin, in this case Angola, in Africa. Like many slaves, Quash almost certainly took as his new surname one that was indicative of his African roots after gaining his freedom. The oldest of the stones here, that for a free black named Primus, is one of the earliest professionally carved and identifiable gravestones remaining for someone of African descent in New England, and the oldest outside of Rhode Island. Primus's stone could also be the oldest stone extant for a free black in the entire region.

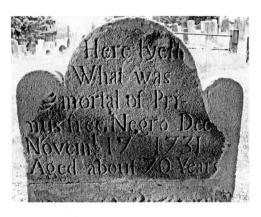

Gravestone, Primus, 1731, Ancient Burying Ground, Wethersfield, Connecticut.

African descent in New England, and the oldest outside of Rhode Island. Primus's stone could also be the oldest stone extant for a free black in the entire region.

Quash Gomer is the only one of these men about whom anything is known. Formerly the slave of John Smith, he purchased his freedom in 1766 for 25 pounds. How he may have earned this money, or afterwards earned money to support the six-person household listed in the 1790 federal census, presumably including a wife and four children (names unknown) for the 33 years he lived as a free man is unknown, but that he desired a proper burial with a fine headstone is undeniable. His children may have remained in the area, as members of a Gomer family are recorded in the church records of nearby Middletown, including Catharine Gomer, a free black woman who married Ichabod Blackstone, also a free black, on March 12, 1794; Mesdora Gomer, who died in late 1802 shortly before her daughter Emilyne was baptized in January 1803 at the age of 15 months; and Mordove Gomer, who married Sally Binks, "a negro," of Hartford in January 1803 (Connecticut Church Record Abstracts, vol. 70, Part I, pg. 239).

Francois, designated as a "negro servant" (Connecticut Church Record Abstracts, vol. 126, pg. 277), was working for Justus Riley at his death in 1816. The fact that he has no surname listed on his gravestone makes it probable that he died while still enslaved. Little is known for certain of Tenor Abro, but it is possible that he was the son of Barsheba and Dolphen (Ely) Abro, both "negroes" (Connecticut Church Record Abstracts, vol. 22, pg. 1) from nearby Cromwell, Connecticut, who were married in the congregational church in that town on October 28, 1762. Tenor was the "negro servant" (Connecticut Church Record Abstracts, vol. 126, pg. 258) of Samuel Williams of Wethersfield, but it is interesting that his gravestone depicts his original surname Abro. Perhaps Tenor's stone was provided by a kindly master, but it is also possible that it was purchased by a family member or friend.

Top: Gravestone, Tenor Abro, 1793, Ancient Burying Ground, Wethersfield, Connecticut. *Bottom:* Gravestone, Quash Gomer, 1799, Ancient Burying Ground, Wethersfield, Connecticut.

Sambo and Fillis Burial Site
Riverside Cemetery (also known as MacDonough Cemetery)
Corner of Main Street and on-ramp to Rte 9
Middletown

This historic cemetery, located in a more urban location and the oldest burial ground in Middletown, is not an easy one to find, nor is it easy to gain access as its gate is usually locked. The easiest way to find this cemetery is to park on Main Street near the famed O'Rourke's Diner, and around the corner from there on the hillside is the cemetery. Keys to open the gate are easily available at the Main Street firehouse.

Once you get inside, it's like stepping back in time. The cemetery is small, but filled with colonial-era sandstone gravestones. Though the earliest extant gravestones date to the 1680s, the site has been in use since at least 1658 and was also where the first religious services in town were held. Like many of its neighbors located on the Connecticut River, Middletown was at one time a thriving maritime city that was also active in the buying and selling of slaves. The first slaves here probably arrived by the 1660s, and within a hundred years there were some 200 slaves in Middletown.

Indicative of this presence are the graves, found in the back corner, for Sambo and Fillis. Sambo (1706–1776) was the longtime slave of local blacksmith Thomas Hulbert and was likely a native of Africa. Of Fillis, we know from her gravestone that she was the wife of Cuff. Whether Fillis or Cuff were free blacks is unknown, but unlikely given the fact that Fillis has no surname on her gravestone. Fillis (or Phyllis) was possibly the wife of the Cuffe that was the slave of Joseph Write and who became a church member in Middletown

in August 1747. The couple likely had at least one child, a son named Cuffe who was baptized on March 29, 1752 (Connecticut Church Record Abstracts, vol. 70, Part II, pg. 655). Beyond these suppositions, nothing more is known.

Gravestone, Sambo Hulbert (1776) and Fillis (1760), Riverside Cemetery, Middletown, Connecticut (courtesy Middlesex County Historical Society).

La Amistad Slaves Burial Site
Grove Street Cemetery
Grove Street
New Haven
http://www.grovestreetcemetery.org/

This beautiful cemetery was established in September 1796 after the old public burying ground, located behind the Center Church on the Green, was filled up due to an outbreak of yellow fever in 1794–95. It is notable as one of the earliest examples of the rural or garden-style cemetery in the world, predating the Mount Auburn Cemetery in Cambridge, Massachusetts, by over three decades, and distinguished by its decorative plantings and the many pathways that lead through the cemetery. Though this is a private cemetery, the proprietors were civic-minded, and, as was typical for the time, one portion of the cemetery was reserved for people of color (lot 1 of the sixth tier), while another was set aside for the city's poor (lots 3, 5, and 7 in the fifth tier). The tiers of the cemetery were laid out and numbered from east to west, while the lots within ran from Grove Street in a northerly section. An additional lot in the northeast corner was designated as a potter's field.

A number of African Americans are buried here, including some Civil War veterans, and Mary Goodman (1804–1872), "a woman of African descent" who earned a living as a domestic worker. She was a devout member of the College Street Church, and who donated her entire holdings upon her death, totaling nearly $5,000, to the Yale Divinity School to help in the education of African American clergymen.

Just inside the entrance to the cemetery to the left of the chapel there is a monument, erected in 2001, to six Mende slaves buried here in unmarked graves. These men were taken by force from their home in Sierra Leone in 1839 and were subsequently transported to Cuban waters on the slaving vessel *La Amistad*. The travails of these slaves, including forty-three other men and four children, is not only one of the great stories in New Haven and Connecticut history, but also one that gained national attention and was even the subject of a 1997 Hollywood movie directed by Steven Spielberg.

Schooners like *La Amistad* made hundreds of voyages every year to and from Cuban waters prior to the Civil War, and had done so for years without much note or incident, but the voyage of the *La Amistad* would be very different. On June 28, 1839, Spanish slave dealers Jose Ruiz and Pedro Montez loaded their 53 slaves aboard the ship, captained by Ramon Ferrer, for a short voyage from Havana to Puerto Principe. Because slave trading was outlawed in many countries, including the U.S. and England, the slaves, who had been sold to Ruiz for $450 apiece, were given false Spanish passports in case the vessel was intercepted by English or American naval ships that patrolled international waters around Cuba.

When the ship's cook made a joke stating that the Mende slaves would be killed and eaten by the crew, the men, under the leadership of Sengbe Pieh (soon to be known as Joseph Cinque), revolted on the third day of the voyage, killing the ship's cook and captain and releasing two other crewmen who leaped overboard but never made it ashore. The former slaves held Ruiz and Montes and ordered them to navigate the ship back to Africa by setting course toward the rising sun. This Montes did, but at night he reversed course so that the ship might be picked up in American waters. *La Amistad* continued its haphazard voyaging, during which time ten of the Africans died. Short on provisions, Cinque finally ordered the Spaniards to put in at the next land they encountered, which proved to be Long Island, New York. The schooner was quickly seized by the U.S. Navy brig *Washington* and Ruiz and Montes were arrested for piracy and murder, but were soon released.

Interestingly, the schooner was soon towed to New London, Connecticut, by order of the *Washington*'s commanding officer, possibly so that he could claim both the vessel (valued at $15,000) and the slaves (valued at $25,000) as salvage and sell them for a tidy profit. In New York, where slavery was abolished, the slaves would have immediately become free and thus could not be sold, but this was not the case in Connecticut, where slavery was still legal. However, a U.S. District Court judge quickly dispelled the notion that the slaves would be treated as salvage, though the *Washington*'s commander and crew eventually received one-third of the value of the ship and its other cargo. The *Amistad* slaves were subsequently transported to New Haven and held in jail until their fate could be decided by the courts.

At first it was hard to communicate with the Africans, but soon enough the lawyers representing them located several black sailors in New York City, including a Mende native named James Covey, who had been captured and sold into slavery as a child, but was later rescued by the British Navy and lived in Freetown, Sierra Leone. The six slaves memorialized in the Grove Street Cemetery died from the effects of the long voyage or disease in the days and months after the ship landed in New Haven. The Mende slaves, while many court proceedings took place, were treated reasonably well, being given both English language and religious instruction while in jail, as well as having legal counsel to help argue their case for freedom. However, to offset the costs of their upkeep, the slaves were put on public display at the viewing price of 12 cents, and "the Black Prince, as Cinque was often called in the newspapers, cheerfully consented to perform native dances and turn somersaults on the lawn" (Wepman, pg. 288). Indeed, Cinque and his fight for the freedom of his people would become a powerful symbol to African Americans, and many an infant black boy born in 1839 and thereafter was given the name Cinque in his honor.

Eventually the remaining slaves were ruled to be free men and women by the U.S. Circuit Court, a decision that did not sit well with President Martin Van Buren, who was ready to send the slaves back to Cuba due to Spanish government protests. The Federal District Court upheld the decision in 1840, with the result that the case was appealed to the U.S. Supreme Court in February 1841. Thanks to the arguments of defense co-counsel, and former president John Quincy Adams, the *Amistad* slaves were subsequently deemed to be free men once and for all and were thus allowed to return to Africa. While the U.S. government refused to pay any of the costs for their return back to Sierra Leone, the former slaves, aided by a citizens' group called the *Amistad* Committee, organized speaking tours for the abolitionist cause and soon, buoyed by the eloquence of Cinque's speaking abilities (in the Mende language, no less!), raised enough money to return home. In January 1842 the thirty-five surviving former *Amistad* slaves, Cinque included, returned home to Sierra Leone, thus ending Connecticut's role in the only successful slave rebellion in American history.

While the case of *La Amistad* would ultimately have little or no direct effect on ending slavery in America, New Haven has in recent years firmly embraced its role in the *Amistad* affair, as is evidenced by the *Amistad* Memorial, a fine relief sculpture erected at 165 Church Street in 1992, and the building of a replica of the schooner *Amistad*. This replica, which was launched in 2000, retraced the original voyage of the ship back to Sierra Leone in 2007, and today is a traveling museum ship home-ported out of New Haven. It is also Connecticut's official state flagship.

Venture Smith Family Burial Plot
First Church Cemetery
Rte 151 (Town Street)
East Haddam

The small community of East Haddam is well-known for many things, including its status as a resort town for much of the 20th century. It is home to the 1913-built East Haddam Bridge across the Connecticut River, at 899 feet long, said to be the longest swing bridge in the world. In addition, the bell hanging in St. Stephen's Episcopal Church, originally cast in 815 A.D. in Spain and brought to the U.S. in 1834, is the oldest church bell in the New World. A less spectacular attraction, but one equally interesting, is the burial plot for Venture Smith and his family in the public cemetery, established about 1794 and located adjacent to the old Congregational church.

Here in this quiet spot is the final resting place for one of the town's most interesting citizens. Even more important, most of what we do know about Venture Smith's life comes not from anecdotal accounts penned long after his death, nor from simple town records, but from an account of his life that he himself narrated seven years before his death. This work, titled *A Narrative of the Life and Adventures of Venture, A Native of Africa, But Resident Above Sixty Years in the United States of America*, was first published in 1798 (with reprints appearing in 1835, 1896, and 1897), and is one of the few African American autobiographies published prior to 1800. The first African American autobiography, that for Briton Hammon of Massachusetts, appeared in 1760 and is just fourteen pages in length, while Smith's narrative is twenty-six pages long, filled with details of his early life and capture, as well as his life both as a slave and as a free man.

Originally named Broteer Furro, born the son of a prince in Dukandarra, Guinea, in about 1729, Smith was sold into slavery by a neighboring tribe that invaded his father's territory in 1735, and was subsequently among a group of 260 slaves sold to a Rhode Island ship captain. While on board the ship, the young Broteer was purchased by the ship's steward

Venture Smith Family Plot, First Church Cemetery, East Hadddam, Connecticut.

Robertson Mumford for the price of four gallons of rum and a piece of calico cloth. He was renamed Venture, representative of his new owner's newfound business venture.

Venture arrived in America in 1739 and lived with his master's family on Fisher's Island, not far off the coasts of both Connecticut and Rhode Island. Due to his age, Venture was first employed in household work, but later was employed in more strenuous outdoor work. Venture married his wife Meg (Margaret) in 1754, who was also a slave of the same family and about his same age. Venture was later sold to owners in Stonington, Connecticut, and separated from his wife and daughter. However, he had earned extra money by cleaning shoes, catching muskrats and minks and selling their fur, as well as other odd jobs, and he gave these earnings to his master for the purposes of purchasing his wife and daughter to bring them to the same household. Unfortunately, after this master's wife abused Meg over a small incident and Venture came to her defense, the master sold Venture to yet another man, who in turn pawned him to yet another master. Venture worked hard, working for both his masters and his own account on the side, being especially adept at cutting firewood in large amounts on Long Island, so much so that he has been referred to in modern times as the black Paul Bunyan.

Finally, in 1765, Venture was able to purchase his freedom at the price of 71 pounds, and would subsequently work to raise the money to purchase the freedom of his family, including his wife Meg and sons Solomon and Cuff. In about 1769 he was able to purchase the freedom of his sons, earning the money by cutting wood on Long Island. By 1773, Venture was able to purchase the freedom of his wife, but this came at a high price; the Smiths' eldest son Solomon was hired out by Venture to make a whaling voyage to help earn money,

Gravestone, Venture Smith, 1805, First Church Cemetery, East Haddam, Connecticut.

but died of scurvy on the voyage. Venture and Meg would later have another son, named Solomon in honor of their first son. In 1775 Venture was finally able to purchase the freedom of his daughter Hannah, thus completing his goal of liberating his family.

Venture Smith also purchased three other men, like him black slaves, but his motives here are less clear. The first man was probably purchased in order to work with Venture to help earn the money to buy his family, but he ran away in a short time. Of the two other slaves Venture Smith purchased, one soon returned to his former master, while the other left him for unknown reasons.

By 1777, Smith had sold his property on Long Island and moved to East Haddam, where he would live the remainder of his life. Here he made a living as a farmer, fisherman, shipper, and entrepreneur, owning at least twenty vessels, including canoes and sailing ships. The Smiths lived at several locales within East Haddam over the years, the last on land overlooking a cove on the west bank of the Salmon River. For over a hundred years after his move to the town, Venture Smith, who was over six feet in height, was well-remembered for his prodigious strength and ability to harvest a field or cut great amounts of cordwood in a short time like few others could. While he expressed some disappointment in his sons and their character, since they apparently did not work as diligently as Venture would have liked, Cuff and Solomon by all white accounts were respectable and hard-working men in the town.

The Smith family was indeed a large one, and even today descendants of the family live in the area. In 2006 these descendants gave permission for scientists to exhume Venture's body in the hopes of gaining DNA samples that might give more specific clues to his origin in Africa, as well as to possibly reveal details about his diet and living conditions. While this testing was opposed by some activists outside the Smith family, the courts sided with Venture's relatives and allowed the body to be exhumed. Unfortunately, due to their age and the nature of the cemetery soil, the remains were too degraded to recover any DNA, and Venture Smith's remains were subsequently given a second burial, complete with ceremonies, in August 2006. Smith may be the only such individual, a former black slave, deliberately exhumed from a marked burial site for scientific purposes in all of New England.

While today the burial site of Venture and his family appears to be well integrated within the cemetery, in actuality he was buried apart from the rest of the town's citizens in a segregated site, with surrounding burials only being made many decades later. However, the finely carved sandstone markers for Venture and Meg Smith, as well as the storytelling epitaph carved on Venture's stone, are certainly indicative both of Venture's character and his acceptance within the community of East Haddam as a citizen in good standing.

African American Section
Ye Ancientest Burial Ground
Between Hempstead and Huntington streets
New London
http://www.rootsandroutes.net/body.htm?http&&&www.rootsandroutes.net/nlburial.htm

This old burial ground, located in an urban setting, is one of the most significant in all of New England in terms of marked African American burials from the colonial era. While most of these stones have either been lost or are now badly degraded, the information about them has been preserved. Indeed, twenty-five years ago the poor condition of this cemetery, neglected and nearly abandoned for years (although always a site to visit for old gravestone enthusiasts and genealogists), was a cause for concern and much history seemed on the verge of being lost. Today, this is no longer the case, and the site is a historic showcase for all New Londoners, including the town's significant African American population.

On a recent visit to this burial ground in the late spring of 2014, I was particularly moved by the mementos, consisting of several pieces of jewelry, placed in front of the gravestone for Florah Hurlbut (1720–1764), the "servant" of Captain Titus Hurbut. How long these personal items had been there is unknown, perhaps several months, maybe a year or even longer. Were they placed there, perhaps, on the anniversary of Florah's death in

December, or perhaps even on Mother's Day? No matter what the case may be, these offerings are representative of how these burial places provide both a physical and emotional connection for many to New England's African American past.

This burial place is one of the oldest public cemeteries in New England, and the oldest in the area, the land being set aside as a burial space in 1645 and the first interment recorded in 1652. Located on an eminence formerly known as Meeting House Hill and overlooking the Thames River, the site was once rather open in nature, but is now fenced in. The African American section can be easily found in the back right corner of the cemetery when entering from the main gate, in a space largely devoid of gravestones. Local preservation efforts include the placement of plaques made of durable plastic which have the epitaphs that were once visible on the degraded gravestones themselves. Some of these plaques have been placed directly in front of the gravestones themselves, while others are placed where a gravestone was presumably once located. This is a nice solution to the problem of vanishing gravestones and one that I've not seen extensively used elsewhere.

Information about the African Americans buried here is only scant, despite the fact that New London has long had a black presence. The port of New London was a major one from which slave trading voyages emanated, as well as a locale where slaves were landed, both from Africa directly and from the West Indies, and subsequently put up for sale. By the 1750s there were over 300 blacks (how many were free is uncertain) living in New London, and by 1774 the number had grown to 522 individuals, nearly ten percent of the overall population (Greene, pg. 345). New London, too, was an important town in the plantation economy of southeastern New England, and the institution of slavery here lasted well into the first decades of the 19th century, even as the black population of the town fluctuated. The 1810 federal census enumerated only 147 free blacks and 13 slaves, while in 1820 over 1,600 free blacks were recorded, many likely employed in maritime related trades, and six slaves.

How many African Americans may have been buried in this old colonial burying ground is unknown due to a lack of records, but the number is probably substantial. Perhaps the most significant stone remaining is that for Florio (1689–1749), the wife of Hercules, one of Connecticut's earliest black governors. Given the classical surname carved on her stone, it is almost certain that both she and her husband were slaves, and her gravestone seems to be the only evidence we have of Hercules's position of leadership within the community.

The most poignant stones, however, may be those for the wife and daughter of Samuel Clancy. Sappho, his wife, died in 1789 at the age of 47, while Morocco, their daughter, died three years later in 1792 at the age of twelve. Whether the Clancy family was free or not is unknown, but likely. The name "Morocco" for their young daughter is an unusual one, and may perhaps point to Samuel or Sappho's specific African origins.

Yet another interesting stone is that for a young man known only as Neco (1760–1791). Without a surname on his stone, it is likely that he was a slave, but possibly one with mixed Native American and African heritage as was common in this area. The name of Neco may be an indicator of his link to the Mohegan people, who were led by their great sachem Uncas (died about 1683 in nearby Norwich) and were allies of the English during the Pequot

Plaques denoting African American burial sites, Ye Ancientest Burial Ground, New London, Connecticut.

War and King Philip's War. His father and son were named Owaneco, sometimes simply spelled W'Neco by whites.

Of the other black individuals known to be buried here, Juno Anderson (1757–1797) was the wife of Scipio, and both may have been free at the time of her death. Later on, in January 1803, the widower Scipio Anderson would marry Jane Smith in New London and they would have several children (Connecticut Church Record Abstracts, vol. 79, pg. 7). Sawney (1716–1761), "Servant of Esqr. Miller," was possibly owned by Jeremiah Miller, a 1709 Yale graduate who moved to New London in 1711 and was prominent in local affairs for many years. Of "Negro" Samuel Williams (1748–1781), we know little, but there were many Williams families in New London, many of whom owned anywhere from one to six slaves, according to the 1790 federal census.

Finally, the oldest dated burial in this section of the cemetery is that for Augustine Paviddo (died 1745, age unknown), the son of Francis and Elizabeth Paviddo. Nothing is

Gravestone, Morocco Clancy, 1792, Ye Ancientest Burial Ground, New London, Connecticut.

known about this family, including whether or not they were black. Their surname gives some indicator that the family may have been of Spanish or Portuguese heritage, perhaps coming to New London on a merchant voyage. If this is the case, then the Paviddo grave here is an indicator that this section of the burial ground, like others in colonial New England, was also used to bury strangers and others from outside the local community.

*Isaac Glasko Burial Site
Old Kinne Burying Ground
Jarvis Rd. and junction of Rte. 201
Griswold
http://pdfhost.focus.nps.gov/docs/NRHP/Text/01000351.pdf

This rural cemetery started out as a family burial ground for the Kinne family, with burials here dating as early as 1713, but evolved over time into a neighborhood cemetery where many local families interred their dead, including many children whose graves are marked with simple fieldstones. Among the later burials here are those for a black man of

Old Kinne Burying Ground, Griswold, Connecticut. The large gravestone for Isaac Glasko and his wife Lucy is at left front.

mixed Native American and African heritage, Isaac C. Glasko (1776–1861), and his wife, Lucy (Brayton) Glasko (1777–1849), as well as that for family friend, also black, named Martha Moody (1799–1834).

Though little is known of Glasko's life, what we do know of him and his activities in this small corner of Connecticut reveals that Isaac Glasko was a remarkable man. He was born, probably free, in Rhode Island to Jacob and Martha Glasko (likely former slaves), and by 1790 the family, including Isaac's brother George, was living in North Uxbridge, Massachusetts. By the late 1790s Isaac Glasko may have moved back to Rhode Island for a time, as he was married to Lucy Brayton of Smithfield, Rhode Island, in December 1800. By the early 1800s Isaac moved to Connecticut and would here spend the rest of his life. Jacob Glasko remained in Massachusetts until at least 1807, but after his wife Martha died in 1815, Jacob would subsequently marry Elizabeth Dayley (Dailey) of Putnam in September 1818. He later moved to Griswold, where he died in December 1824. Though uncertain, he may also be buried in this cemetery.

Isaac and Lucy Glasko, along with his brother George Glasko (employed as a shoemaker in partnership with William Kinne), arrived in town in 1806. Isaac purchased from Alexander Stewart (also a member of the Kinne family) three-quarters of an acre of land and a house, along with the rights to water-power access from the dam where Stewart had a gristmill. That same year, Jacob Glasko (still of Massachusetts) purchased fifty acres of land and a house along the Pachaug River and by the edge of a pond (now Glasgo Pond) for $1,250, a third of which holdings he sold to each of his sons in 1807.

For much of the next decade the Glaskos were active buyers and sellers of land in the area, with Isaac increasing his holdings substantially. He also built up a large blacksmith business, and was apparently quite active in making implements, probably harpoons and lances, for the whaling trade. These tools are said to have been sold in many New England ports, and Isaac may have gained several patents (none of which could be located in U.S. patent records) for some of them, according to local tradition. By 1841, when Isaac was now in his declining years and had to sell off land to satisfy his debts, he owned at least 54 acres of land with four dwelling houses, a sawmill, a gristmill, two barns, a coal house, and a number of other small outbuildings, where at one time he employed as many as ten men in his blacksmith business.

Isaac and Lucy had three children, including Azubah (born 1810), Isaac Moody (born 1814, named in part after Isaac's friend Pero Moody), and Miranda (born 1819). Nothing is known of Azubah Glasko and it is possible he died young. Isaac, Jr. would learn the blacksmith trade from his father and continued in this line of work, living next to his father, for many years. Of Miranda Glasko, little is known, though in 1850 she was living with her father, along with a young black girl (age 12) named Mary James.

Isaac Glasko, however, was more than just an accomplished landowner and businessman. He also recognized the inequality between white and black in his state and in his town. Accordingly, he, along with his friend Pero Moody (1750–1830) in 1823, filed an unsuccessful petition to the Connecticut General Assembly for exemption from being taxed on the grounds that they could not vote. In part, this petition stated that they were "descendants of African Citizens brought to this Country against their will" and that "in the midst of most mortifying discouragements have acquired some property" (Rejected Bills, Connecticut State Legislature, Records Group 002, Box 2, Folder 3).

This petition gives some indication as to the reaction of Glasko's white neighbors for at least the first seventeen years of their residence. While Isaac and his wife were buried in the Old Kinne Burial Ground, and by the time of their deaths had therefore gained a measure of acceptance and respect in the community, this was certainly not the case early on. Even their burial site within the cemetery, located at the far back left corner, is an indicator of their lesser status.

Whether or not Pero Moody is buried in this cemetery is unknown, but possible, as Martha Moody (likely his daughter) is also buried here. Moody, a former slave of William Mattison of Preston, was freed in 1777, apparently along with his brother Tidal Moody. He took action against the town of Lisbon in 1819, one year after the state constitution had been passed which prohibited African Americans from voting, by refusing to pay taxes because he did not have the right to vote. Interestingly, Pero Moody won his case in August 1822 when a local justice of the peace ruled in his favor, but later lost when it was appealed to the county court level. It was this case that served as the basis for the 1823 petition by Moody and Glasko to the General Assembly.

The Old Kinne Burying Ground was for many years a sad and neglected place after the last interment in 1912, despite the fact that at least seven early Connecticut gravestone carvers' works are represented here. However, with the addition of Glasgo Village to the Connecticut Freedom Trail in 1995 (the cemetery itself is not specifically designated), efforts to clean up this remote cemetery were put into motion. Spurred on by members of the Connecticut Gravestone Network, a group dedicated to preserving the state's old cemeteries and gravestones, by 1999 restoration efforts in the cemetery were largely complete. Many gravestones were reset and repaired, including that for Isaac and Lucy Glasgko, which is a typical marble gravestone of the time. In 2001 the cemetery was placed on the National Register of Historic Places due to both its notable gravestone carvings and its connection to Isaac Glasko.

On the pathway that leads to this cemetery are located the ruins of a mill building and other structures that were likely once part of the Glasko's blacksmith operations. The location of his house can also still be seen in Glasgo Village (though only the original foundation remains, above which a later house was built). Access to this cemetery is difficult: visitors must park at the end of Jarvis Road, and the pathway that leads to the cemetery begins in the back yard of the last home located here. Because of this, it is advised that visitors pay a courtesy call to the homeowners before proceeding toward this path that leads toward the cemetery.

II. Rhode Island

In addition to town specific sites, the Rhode Island Historical Cemetery Commission website (http://www.rihistoriccemeteries.org/webdatabase.aspx) has an excellent database for many Rhode Island cemeteries, including those listed below.

African American Section–God's Little Acre
Common Burying Ground
Farewell Street, at junction of America's Cup Avenue
Newport
http://www.colonialcemetery.com/burial-markers/

This historic cemetery is located just a short distance north from the center of historic Newport and is one of the most important colonial-era cemeteries in all of New England. It should not be confused with the Island Cemetery (a historic cemetery in its own right), which is located adjacent to the Common Burying Ground (the two are separated by a fence) and is the first cemetery to be encountered when entering Newport on Farewell Street. Many tourist maps, in fact, lump the two cemeteries together and label them incorrectly as Island Cemetery.

Despite this understandable confusion, it is the Common Burying Ground that is the oldest public burying place in Newport, having been laid out in 1665 on land once granted to Dr. John Clarke. The oldest gravestone remaining that was originally erected here dates from 1666 (two older gravestones were relocated here over a hundred years later), and about fifty other stones remain that were erected in the 1600s. Nearly 2,700 other gravestones may also be found here dating from the 1700s, including some that are considered to be the finest examples of the gravestone carver's art in all of New England.

These features alone make the Common Burying Ground a must-see site, but its historical importance is even greater because of its segregated African American section known as God's Little Acre. This part of the Common Burying Ground is found at the northernmost end of the cemetery, located to the left of Dyre Avenue, the first entrance road into the cemetery when coming into Newport on Farewell Street. The section used to have its own sign (which went down in a storm about 2009 and, as of 2014, has yet to be replaced), leading many to believe, incorrectly, that it is a separate entity altogether from Common Burying Ground. This section of the cemetery was largely vacant of marked graves until the early 1700s, when Newport's role in the slave trade was on the rise, with the town's black population as a result increasing at a quick rate.

Common Burying Ground, on one hand, is a typical New England public burial ground in that its black or slave section was located on the fringe of the cemetery on land farthest away from town. However, what makes this burying place unique is the fact that many of the graves for African Americans, most of them slaves, some free, are marked with professionally carved gravestones. As previously discussed at length, this is a phenomenon not seen elsewhere in New England, where unmarked graves were the norm for blacks. Thus, in this one place may be seen the elaborate gravestones (similar to those carved for whites) for about 250 people of color who died before 1800, more than anywhere else in the region combined. While nearly 600 individuals are documented as being buried in this section of Common Burying Ground, about 80 gravestones once known to have existed are now gone, and there are probably many others missing that have never been documented. Indeed, when Common Burying Ground first began to be documented and catalogued in 1874, this section was only partially recorded, and when further efforts were made to document the cemetery in 1895, the God's Little Acre section was ignored altogether.

Taking a stroll through the God's Little Acre section of the Common Burying Ground is like stepping back in time. One encounters many unusual and significant stones for African Americans; of most of these individuals, but little is known, while for others some infor-

Gravestones, God's Little Acre Section, Common Burying Ground, Newport, Rhode Island.

Top left: Catharine Almy, wife of Hurricane Dunbar, 1743. *Top right*: Caesar, son of Cato Cranston, 1753. *Bottom left:* Newport Ryder, 1760. *Bottom right:* Bell, daughter of Rhode Island and Phillis, 1756.

mation has been preserved. At the far northern end of the cemetery in the front row, look for the stones for Dutchess Quamino, one of the best-known and most highly respected black women in Newport during the late 1700s, and her daughters Violet and Cynthia. Toward the front center, several rows back, may be seen the oldest dated stone here, that for Hector Butcher (1683–1720). In the far back center, close by the fence separating this cemetery from Island Cemetery, is a dual portrait-style gravestone that must be seen, that for Phyllis Stevens and her infant son Prince, whose African American facial features are unmistakable. Not far from here, in the upper right area, several rows behind a large decorative bush among a large grouping of stones, are two stones close to one another, those for Cuffe Gibbs and Pompey Lyndon, both carved by black stonecutter Pompe Stevens. Finally, several rows in front of and to the left of the large decorative bush in this section is a row of stones marking the burials for the well-known Arthur Tikey Flagg and his family, and those for Adam and Kedindo Perro. The latter has a large bullet hole through it which likely dates back to the days of the American Revolution, when the British occupied Newport and may have used stones in the cemetery for target practice. These are just a few of the many notable colonial-era stones in God's Little Acre.

Left: Mille (1765) and Katharine (1766), Servants to Henry Bull, Esq. *Right:* Primus Gibbs, 1775.

Like most cemeteries, the Common Burying Ground evolved over time; by the time of the Civil War, this section was not just reserved for African Americans. Some sailors, both white and black, who died while serving at the Newport Naval Station are buried here, as are some white Marine and Navy veterans, making this section of the cemetery one that evolved into a sort of "strangers' ground" for those outsiders who died far from home. These burials include Makiajiro Omura (died 1897), a man of Japanese heritage serving in the U.S. Navy as a steward. This section also likely became the place where at least some individuals of little or no means were also buried, both white and black.

Among the later African American burials here are a number of individuals who moved here no doubt seeking work and perhaps a more safe and secure life away from the Jim Crow laws of the South. These include Sarah Carter (1843–1898), a native of South Carolina who was in Newport by 1885 working as a seamstress; America Clarke (1864–1898), the wife of John Clarke, a Virginia native who later made a living as a farmer in Bristol, Rhode Island, after his wife's death; and John Ancrum (1882–1912), a native of South Carolina making a living as a day laborer in Orangeburg, who moved to Newport after 1900. While these more modern gravestones are not as interesting, visually speaking, as those for colonial-era blacks, their presence is nonetheless indicative of the stories that remain to be told of Newport's latter-day

Left: Jubbaaford, daughter of Harford Green and Jane Hart, 1755. *Right:* Quash Dunbar, 1770.

black citizens and their struggles for economic freedom and equality. Burials in this section continued into the 1970s.

While the vast majority of African Americans are buried in God's Little Acre, there are black burials in other sections of the Common Burying Ground. At the south end of the cemetery, behind the houses on Warner Street, in one section toward

Left: Cato, former servant of Job Almy, lately a servant to Silas Cook, 1753. *Right:* Jem Howard, a twin brother of Quash and son of Philis, 1771.

the center may be found a close grouping of gravestones for several enslaved individuals. These include Tobe Brightman (1681–1721), the slave of Capt. William Brightman; Harry Easton (1706–1729), the son of Dick and Giffe Easton; and Muirear Easton (1702–1733), the wife of Caesar and "servant" to Peter Easton. Why these individuals were buried outside the previously established segregated section of Common Burying Ground is unknown. Most of the white Easton family members, including Peter Easton, are buried in other cemeteries in Newport, so proximity to the families they served, in the Easton case, was not the overriding concern. Still, some Brightman family members are buried in this section, meaning that perhaps Tobe Brightman was viewed as one of the family. This is no doubt the case with Jeanette, a "black girl" (Sterling, Austin, Champion, and Bamberg, pg. 172), who died after 1818 and "was a good and faithful servant in the Phillips family over 50

Left: Gravestone, Tobe Brightman, 1721, Common Burying Ground, Newport, Rhode Island. *Right:* Pero Overing, 1770.

years, she died respected and lamented by all who knew her." She is buried in a southwest part of the cemetery amidst many of the family members she served for most of her life. Curiously, her plain gravestone offers no birth or death date information and is void of any iconography, not unlike that of the stone for Hector Butcher. Finally, Lymas Keith (1731–1796), a former slave, is buried in a section adjacent to God's Little Acre in the northeast section of the cemetery, near to where William Ellery, a signer of the Declaration of Independence, is also buried. Lymas himself was a prominent member of Newport's black community, being an officer in the Free African Union Society.

Footstone, Sippeo Rodman, 1759.

The Common Burying Ground, including the God's Little Acre section, is currently in very good condition and is well maintained with many stones having been repaired. This is a welcome change from the early 1990s, when Common Burying Ground was overgrown and neglected and many gravestones were knocked down or broken. While some of the damage from this time was irreparable and thus still visible, today this is a cemetery whose historical nature makes it an alluring place to anyone interested in our colonial past. Visitors who wish to drive to this cemetery should note that while one can drive into the Common Burying Ground, the narrow drives are deeply worn and thus not suitable for many cars, though SUVs should have no problem. On-street parking is frequently available nearby, and Common Burying Ground is within easy walking distance of downtown Newport.

Gardiner-Stanton Slave Lot
Between Congdon-Gardner Way and Stony Fort Rd., off Mooresfield Rd.
North Kingstown

This cemetery is likely one of the largest slave cemeteries in all of New England, and like the subject of slavery in New England, it is not for the faint of heart when it comes to finding and viewing the site. In fact, it is the only cemetery described in this portion of the book that is not open to the public, as it is located on private land in a densely wooded area that has no direct right of way access. However, its size makes it an important site worthy of inclusion here with the hope that someday it may be better marked and maintained as a historic site, with some access to the public provided. Currently, local residents are wary of disclosing the site of this and other old rural cemeteries in the area due to recent acts of vandalism. Though uncertain, it would appear that part of this cemetery, due to its expanse, actually lies in South Kingstown, though it is typically attributed to North Kingstown. This lot is severely overgrown, has no enclosure of any kind, and since all the stones, said to be about 80 in number, are simple unmarked fieldstones, it is a challenge to view in its entirety.

Many in the local community refer to this as an Indian burial ground, which is probably true to some extent as many Native Americans were also held as slaves along with those who were black.

The Gardiners (now typically spelled "Gardner") were one of the oldest families to settle Rhode Island, arriving here in the 1630s, and were prominent landowners in Kingstown (divided into North and South Kingstown in 1722). When William Gardiner died in 1738, he divided up nearly 1,300 acres of land among his male heirs, including 300 acres to his grandson Amos Gardiner and a 500 acre homestead to his son John. Like most prominent Narragansett farming families, most of the Gardiners held slaves to work their land and in their homes, doing so at least from the 1730s to after 1790. When Nicholas Gardiner (1674–1746) died, his will mentions ten slaves, including Jeffrey, Scipio, Phillis, Patience, Silver, Thankful, Dellee, Jemima, and Frederick (Robinson, pg. 15). Through marriage connections, the Gardiners were also related to many other families, including the Stantons, the Watsons, the Robinsons, the Shermans, the Potters, and the Northrups, almost all of them also slave holders, to name just a few. While this cemetery is known as the Gardiner-Stanton slave lot, the Stantons were not as heavily invested in slaves as the Gardiners. No matter what the case may be, any or all of the slaves of the Gardiners, including those named above, may be buried in this cemetery, though, of course, none of the identities of those buried here will ever be known for certain.

Indeed, this cemetery in many ways, overgrown and all but lost, is typical of the African American presence in early New England that remains hidden from view. When this slave cemetery was established is unknown, probably early in the 1700s, and the large number of stones here indicates it may have been in use as late as the first decades of the 19th century. It was possibly the burial place for even former slaves that were given their freedom in the years after the American Revolution ended and for a subsequent generation of free blacks that lived in the area.

The 1790 federal census for North and South Kingstown are interesting in this regard; in North Kingstown in 1790 Ezekiel Gardiner still held five slaves, while several other branches of the family had living in their homes at least twelve free blacks. Among the black heads of household for the town in this census were Bristol Gardiner (head of a 3-member household), Phillip Gardiner (7), Pero Gardiner (4 or 5, counted twice), Samson Gardiner (5), Sarah Stanton (head of a black household of 3) and Joseph Stanton (also 3). In neighboring South Kingstown, the 1790 federal census numbers are even higher; though there was only one free black family, that for Dick Gardiner (with nine black family members), that carried the Gardiner name. Among the white Gardiner families there enumerated, there were still held more than 40 slaves, including Col. John Gardiner and Caleb Gardiner with seven each, and Henry Gardiner with nine, as well as 25 free blacks working in ten different Gardiner families overall, as well as two employed by Joseph Stanton.

The black descendants of the Gardiner family slaves would remain in the area for many years. In 1830 Amos Gardiner lived near the widow Hannah Stanton, while Candesaw Gardiner was also counted among the African Americans living in North Kingstown; in the 1850 census Cato (born ca. 1770) and Jane (born ca. 1760) Gardiner were an African American couple, almost certainly aged former slaves, living in neighboring Exeter, Rhode

Island (formerly the western part of North Kingstown until it became a separate town in 1742). And in 1900 Frank Gardiner (born ca. 1881 in Rhode Island) was a young farmhand living in South Kingstown. While the white Gardiner family is renowned for their connection to the town of North Kingstown and the name is still a prominent one in town to this day, the black, slave "side" of the family and their descendants are but little known.

Fayerweather Family burials
Old Fernwood Cemetery
Young Family burials
New Fernwood Cemetery
Kingston Road (Rte 138)
South Kingstown

The Old Fernwood Cemetery was established about 1813 and is an integrated one, with blacks and whites buried together in this tidy and well-maintained space that is surrounded by a stone wall and owned by the Kingston Congregational Church. Though their color is not mentioned on their gravestones, one of the most important and interesting families that has burials here is that of the Fayerweathers, who resided in the Mooresfield Road area in South Kingstown for many years. In fact, at 1859 Mooresfield Road may be seen the 1820-built house where former slave George Fayerweather (1774–1841) lived and practiced the trade of a blacksmith. His grandson Solomon Fayerweather (1820–1901) had a house at 18 Mooresfield Road, built in 1852, which was where he and his father George II (1802–1869) practiced the blacksmith trade for a combined 80 years. All of these men are buried in the Old Fernwood Cemetery, as are their wives, including George's wife Nancy Fayerweather (1785–1865), and fourteen other family members.

Due to their long presence in the area, there is much that is known of the Fayerweather family. George was the slave of the Rev. Samuel Fayerweather, the minister of St. Paul's Episcopal Church, the oldest such church in the Narragansett region. He was likely freed by the mid–1790s and by 1800 is listed in the federal census as a free black living in Newport, the head of a household of two. He is also listed as a resident of Newport in the 1810 census, after which time, by 1820, he moved to South Kingstown. His wife was Nancy Rodman, also a former slave (probably in Newport) who was of Native American heritage and said to be a descendant of the Narragansett sachem Ninigret. The couple had twelve children, with George, Jr. and Solomon serving in succession as the village blacksmith. Solomon Fayerweather is also notable as being the sexton of the Kingston church and was said to very skilled at ringing the church bell on Sunday mornings. His holdings in 1860, valued at $1,800, were sizeable one for the day, greater than that of some of his white neighbors, and speak to his success as a blacksmith and businessman. Descendants of the family lived in the original Fayerweather house until 1962; it is now a National Historic Site owned by the Kingston Improvement Association and used as an arts and crafts center.

George Fayerweather, Jr. left Rhode Island as a young man and migrated to Connecticut, where he married Sarah Harris Fayerweather (1812–1878), a native of Norwich, Connecticut. She was the first black woman to attend Prudence Crandall's Canterbury Female

Boarding School in Canterbury, Connecticut, in 1832. When the whites in town withdrew their children from the school in protest, Crandall began to teach only African American girls, but this ended when Connecticut's notorious Black Law, passed in 1833, forced the closure of the school. George and Sarah were married in 1833 and later lived in New London, Connecticut, where they were both active in the abolitionist movement, while

Gravestone, George Fayerweather, 1869, Old Fernwood Cemetery, South Kingstown, Rhode Island.

George also practiced the family trade of blacksmithing. In 1855 the couple moved to Rhode Island and lived near the Fayerweather homestead for the remainder of their lives, still active in the abolitionist movement.

Fayerweather Hall at the nearby University of Rhode Island (URI) is named in honor of Sarah Harris Fayerweather and her achievements. It is also at URI where the Fayerweather family papers are housed, which includes correspondence between Sarah Fayerweather and Prudence Crandall Philleo (her later married name) and Helen Benson Garrison, the wife of prominent abolitionist William Lloyd Garrison, as well as letters sent to Mary and Isabella Fayerweather, George and Sarah's daughters, by Prudence Crandall Philleo.

In addition to Old Fernwood, there is a newer cemetery located right next to Old Fernwood, an extension (now called Section B) of the New Fernwood Cemetery, which is directly across the street. Though New Fernwood was established about 1931, this portion of New Fernwood was, according to local lore, established earlier, about 1920, when the white landowner gave permission for the local black and Native American population to use the land for burials with the promise that they would maintain the site. This site, along with other cemeteries in town, was maintained for many years by Charles H. Young (1877–1948), born in Rhode Island, a black farm laborer of South Kingstown who first came to town by 1910, and later, by the 1940 federal census, is listed as a cemetery worker. His wife was Josephine Reels Young (1877–1941); both they and some of their children, including Charles, Jr. and Leonard, are buried in the main portion of New Fernwood Cemetery.

Old Section and Free Ground
North Burial Ground
5 Branch Avenue
Providence
https://www.providenceri.com/parks-and-rec/north-burial-ground

This cemetery, located in the gritty, working-class city that is the state's capital, may be one of New England's best kept secrets when it comes to historical cemeteries. In fact, it is not even the most visited cemetery in Providence, since the later Swan Point Cemetery, a beautiful and historic local example of a garden-style cemetery where literary notable H.P. Lovecraft is buried, has more visitors. The burial ground in question, often referred to as the Old North Burial Ground, was not established until 1700 and was the first public cemetery in Providence. It was slow in gaining acceptance, as the first burial here did not take place until 1711. Prior to this, burials in the area were made in private, family owned lots for the simple reason that Providence Plantation founder Roger Williams and his followers believed in a true separation of church and state, with the result that the typical New England tradition of building a meetinghouse and laying out an adjacent town burying ground was not the norm in Rhode Island.

Eventually, however, as Providence grew in size from a humble farming and fishing town to a true maritime commercial center (fueled in large part by the slave trade), this cemetery was established on the northern edge of the town, part of a parcel of land set aside for public use, including a militia training ground. The cemetery has expanded from its original ten acres over the years and now covers 109 acres of land and contains about 35,000 gravestones and monuments. This cemetery is an active one to this day, with several hundred burials a year taking place. Originally laid out in typical New England fashion, in the middle of the 19th century the city hired a landscape architect (the same one who designed Swan Point Cemetery) to change it into a modern cemetery, adding many ornamental plantings, pathways, and sculptures. The southern area of this cemetery, the so-called "old section," is where the earliest graves are to be found, while in the northwestern area of the cemetery near the highway there is an area, usually referred to as the "free ground," where the poor and those of all colors low on the socio-economic ladder are buried. Overall, about 200 African Americans are documented as being buried in North Burial Ground, according to historian John Sterling.

Like many New England public burial grounds, North has gone through many changes. There were several segregated "free" grounds for both blacks and whites established in the old section in the early 1800s that were moved to the free ground established in the northwest part of North in the early 1870s. As was typical for the poor, only a small number of these graves were marked. These surviving stones, 112 in number, including several slave burials, were moved to their current location between River Avenue and the highway in 1964 when I-95 was built and took over a corner of the cemetery. These stones have been laid flat on the ground and are often covered by grass and dirt and can be difficult to read. Here may be found some of the earliest African American gravestones in North, including that for Cesar Whipple (1712–1730), Eve Cushing (1731–1780), and Primus Tillinghast (1748–1750). Adjacent to these stones is the latter-day potter's field, where the graves are marked by simple stones that have no name, but a number only. This free ground section of North Burial Ground (located to the far north, accessible by a small bridge off River Avenue which crosses the Blackstone Canal and is still in use today), is a striking example of how wealth, or a lack thereof, is often a prime factor in determining one's final resting place and how it is marked.

As with many public burial grounds, early records of the burials that took place, other than the gravestones themselves, do not exist, with records only being kept since 1848.

While the cemetery today is famed as being the final resting place of notable Rhode Island political and Revolutionary War leaders, as well as many members of the Brown family, major participants in the Rhode Island slave trade and founders of Brown University, the number of early marked African American graves, some free, some enslaved, found here make this a significant site. Indeed, outside of Newport, Rhode Island, there are more early marked African American burial sites here than in any other site in New England. For this reason, it seems quite appropriate that the first burial recorded when records began to be kept was for a black man named William Dixson, who died in 1848 at the age of 36.

Early on there seems to have been no segregated section set aside for people of color in the North Burial Ground, a possible reflection of the liberal ideas espoused by early Rhode Islanders. As a result, African Americans like slaves Primas Borden (1731–1768), the father of Patience "Sterry" Borden, whose stone is now gone, and Seasor Olny (1732–1747), as well as free blacks like Charles Haskell, are laid to rest near members of rich and prominent merchant families. In fact, one of the most prominent gravestones that used to be found here (it is now apparently lost) was that for Emmanuel Bernon, a former slave who became a successful restaurant owner after gaining his freedom. At his death he had a gravestone erected in his honor that was said to be larger and more elaborate than those of many white men of higher standing.

However, the earliest African American burials here, about twenty in all, that are still extant date from the colonial era and are located in the section designated as AG, located on Central Avenue (the fourth section on the right), right off Main Avenue and close to the main entrance to the cemetery. Most of the African American burials in this section are oriented on the traditional east-west axis configuration, but there is a row of stones for African Americans in the corner of this section that are oriented on a north-south axis. What this may mean, if anything, is unknown, but due to the many changes and moves made within North Burial Ground after 1850 (the roads and avenues found here today were not present in colonial times), it is likely that these stones were relocated from their original location.

The stone for Bristol Bernon (1762–1781), the son of Hannah, a "servant" to Gideon Crawford, is interesting for its intricate floral motif, while those for Ceasar (1778–1782), the son of Pomp and Flora Bower, and for Vilet Burden (1716–1786), the wife of Prime Burden (Borden) and likely the mother of Sterry Borden, are more plainly carved. The dual stone for Pegy Gardner (1764–1791, wife of Cato) and her child Mannawill (1785–1792) is also an interesting one that has a floral motif, while that for Revolutionary War veteran Caesar Wheaton (1733–1780) is notable for its elaborate main floral motif and side decorations depicting architectural columns with an inlaid heart decoration. Yet another interesting stone is that for Amanuel Bernew (1723–1769),

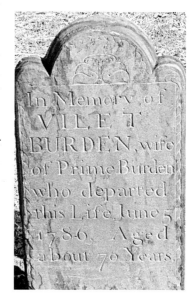

Gravestone, Vilet Burden, 1786, North Burial Ground, Providence, Rhode Island. This woman may be the mother of "Sterry" Borden.

the son of Pegga Bernew, "Negro," both likely enslaved by the Bernon family of Huguenot settlers. This man may have been the son of Emmanuel Bernon, and it may even be his stone that has been mistaken for that of his older namesake. After 1800 many free blacks, including former slaves who migrated here from the South, like Robert Mallett (1783–1823) of North Carolina, were also buried in the old section.

Among the most notable burials in North Burial Ground are those for Patience "Sterry" Borden, Charles and Lucy Haskell, and Christiana and Edward Bannister. Little is known about Sterry Borden (1758–1811), except that she was probably born a slave (the daughter of Primas and Vilet Borden) and after becoming free became a devout member of the First Baptist Church. Additionally, as her gravestone notes, Borden was a significant contributor to a relief fund for poor blacks in Providence. Borden's stone has the initials J.J.F. within an oval at the bottom, an indicator that the stone was likely carved by a young stonecutter named Joseph J. French of nearby Pawtucket, and later Quincy, Massachusetts, and Providence. The stone is a nicely carved one typical of the times and was likely paid for by the First Baptist Church in recognition of Borden's good character and charitable deeds. Given the prominent initials of the carver, it may also be that this was one of French's earliest commissions, and that he may even have donated his work, gaining in return perhaps some local recognition and cemetery advertising.

Charles Haskell (1760–1833) was a native of Massachusetts, town origin unknown, who may have been enslaved prior to the American Revolution. In the fall of 1780 he enlisted in the 1st Massachusetts Regiment, commanded by Col. Elijah Vose, at Boston for a three-year term of service. He subsequently served in Captain Jeremiah Miller's "company of colored men" (as indicated by Haskell himself) while the regiment was stationed in the Hudson Highlands in New York performing garrison duty at the end of the war. Haskell was honorably discharged from service, having been "a good and faithful soldier," as personally attested

Left: Gravestone, Caesar Bower, 1782, North Burial Ground, Providence, Rhode Island (courtesy Julie Nathanson). *Right:* Gravestone, Ahmanuel Bernew, 1769, North Burial Ground, Providence, Rhode Island (courtesy Julie Nathanson).

to by Col. Vose. Haskell later moved to Providence, where he married Lucy Brown, the daughter of Pero and Phyllis Brown, both former slaves of Moses Brown. Pero Brown was freed by his master in 1773 at the age of eighteen, so Lucy Brown always knew freedom. Lucy Brown Haskell (1780–1812), sadly, died at a young age and, as her epitaph states, was a devout church member. Her epitaph, previously discussed at length, is notable for the claim that "the rewards of grace in his kingdom" would result in changing her complexion from black to white "in his own blood."

Charles Haskell worked as a servant for Seth Wheaton, a merchant sea-captain of Providence. Even in his old age, when he became deaf and infirm, he lived the remainder of his life with Wheaton and was supported by the family. By 1818 Haskell was supported, at least in part, by his Revolutionary War pension, his service attested to in writing by his former regimental commander and other white soldiers in his reg-

Gravestone, Charles Haskell, 1833, North Burial Ground, Providence, Rhode Island (courtesy Julie Nathanson).

iment. Charles Haskell's finely carved gravestone, signed at the bottom by Samuel Tingley and an expensive one for the times, was likely commissioned by the Wheaton family and notes both Haskell's color and his war service. The nearly identical stone for his wife Lucy Haskell, though unsigned, suggests that it too was carved by the Tingley family of stonecutters. Lucy's stone was likely erected after Charles's death, with her grave having perhaps been either previously unmarked, or marked in a simpler fashion.

Among the later African American burials in North Burial Ground is that for Edward Bannister (1828–1901) and his wife, Christiana (Babcock) Carteaux Bannister (1819–1902). Christiana Bannister was a remarkable woman, born in North Kingstown, Rhode Island, her parents of mixed African American and Native American ancestry, descended from slaves employed on the large plantations in southern Rhode Island. As a young woman, Christiana moved to Boston where she worked as a hairdresser and wigmaker. She married a clothier named Desilene Carteaux, possibly a native of the West Indies, but the marriage didn't last long. Madame Carteaux, as she was professionally known, became a successful salon owner and wigmaker, selling her own hair products at the salons she operated in Boston for nearly 25 years until moving to Providence with her husband in 1871. During her time in Boston, Christiana was an active participant in the Boston Underground Railroad prior to the Civil War, as well as working during the war to gain equal pay for black Union soldiers.

It was also in Boston that Christiana met her future second husband, a native of Canada, when he applied for a job as a barber in one of her salons. The two were subsequently

Home for Aged Colored Women lot, North Burial Ground, Providence, Rhode Island. While almost all of the burials here are unmarked, there are several that are, including that for Hancy Willis (died 1828), a native of New Bern, North Carolina, and Amanda Robinson "of Narragansett Tribe."

married in 1857. Edward Bannister, with Christiana's support and financial resources, later became a noted and award-winning landscape artist. He won a bronze medal for one of his paintings exhibited at the Centennial Exposition in Philadelphia in 1876, only to have the directors unsuccessfully attempt to take it back (Bannister's fellow white artists supported him) when they discovered he was black. Bannister was also on the board of directors of the Rhode Island School of Design and founded the Providence Art Club, but after his death his work remained forgotten until the 1970s. Now his work is found in many major museums, including the Smithsonian.

As for Christiana Bannister, in addition to operating her Providence salon, in 1890 she worked to establish the Home for Aged Colored Women to provide help and support to aged domestic workers who could no longer earn a living, raising food, clothing, and cash contributions from both the African American community and white society. Now known as the Bannister House, this nursing home is still in operation to this day. Not only is there a monument in North Burial Ground for Edward Bannister, but there is also one designated for the women from this home in the western part of the cemetery (section GG, close by the highway, marked simply "Shelter").

Tragically, after Edward Bannister died of a heart attack, Christiana, due to her age, was unable to care for herself and was later deemed to be insane. She spent a short time in September 1902 in the Home for Aged Colored Women, which she had helped to establish, before being sent to the State Hospital for the Insane in Cranston, where she died after several months in December 1902. While Christina Bannister was buried in North Burial Ground in January 1903, there is nothing in the cemetery records to confirm this, and her resting place beside her husband is unmarked. This is an indicator of how low the Bannisters' finances had sunk in their old age, with Edward Bannister's grave only being marked because of efforts by his fellow artists who were white, while his wife Christina apparently had no one left to erect a suitable memorial.

The North Burial Ground, like many older New England burial grounds, was once in terrible shape, but has improved considerably in the last twenty years and its grounds are now well maintained. To visit this cemetery in search of a single person requires some planning. The cemetery office is manned during regular business hours (8 a.m.–4 p.m.) during the week and the staff is knowledgeable and helpful. However, if you are planning a visit on the weekend, then you're on your own, as the cemetery office is not open. Because African Americans were not regularly segregated here, their later burials are more difficult to find unless historical sources are consulted. Those planning a visit are advised to do some research in advance, the best single source being John Sterling's authoritative *North Burial Ground, Providence, Rhode Island, Old Section: 1700–1848* (published in 2000).

Burt and Haskell burial sites
East Burial Ground
Corner of Wood Street and Mount Hope Avenue
Bristol
http://bristolri.us/NBG/east.php

The town of Bristol's connection with the slave trade was a substantial one and this fact makes its cemeteries important sites that provide a tangible link to the tens of thousands of African slaves who were brought here directly from Africa, as well as via Cuba and the West Indies. There are some traces of the slave trade still to be found in Bristol's historic setting, including several old buildings on Thames Street that housed the counting house of the DeWolf family, and later the Bank of Bristol, where the profits of the slave trade

East Burial Ground, Bristol, Rhode Island.

were tallied. The 1818-built structure that served as the DeWolf warehouse where slaves and other merchant goods were brought upon landing, also still stands.

While Newport and Providence had much larger African American populations by the time of the Revolution, this deep-sea port was a place where large numbers of slaves were landed and quickly sold to fulfill the demand for slaves in the rest of New England and beyond. Illustrative of this trade is the fact that "Bristol" became one of the most common of the non-classical names bestowed by whites on their newly purchased slaves, in keeping with the tradition of naming slaves for the geographical locations at which they were bought or sold. The most prominent Bristol merchants involved in the slave trade were various members of the DeWolf family, including Mark Anthony DeWolf, who began the family involvement in the trade beginning about 1769, and his son James DeWolf. This family will be discussed in greater detail in the next entry. As to the number of African Americans, both slave and free, living in Bristol, the numbers fluctuated over the years and were fairly small until after 1810: 128 (most slaves) were counted in 1749 (Greene, pg. 344), 73 in 1785 (Munro, pg. 244), and in the 1790 federal census, 108 individuals, most of whom were enslaved.

Despite the numbers of slaves who were sold in Bristol, marked African American burial sites are low in number here, the town being similar in this regard to the rest of New England, unlike the traditions that developed elsewhere in Rhode Island in Newport and

Providence. For example, it is unknown where Primas Greenhill (died ca. 1755) is buried, nor are the final resting places for the few other African Americans mentioned in Bristol church records known, including Quashee Babbitt (died ca. 1816), Dido Woodson (died ca. 1768), Sylvia Usher (died ca. 1821), and Violet Smith (died 1840). Some, all, or none of these individuals may be buried here, but nothing can be known for certain at this late date.

The East Burial Ground, the town's most prominent early burying place, was established in 1739 in the southeast part of the town common and was extended in 1811, taking over land once allotted for the grazing of livestock. In 1817 some older graves dating from the late 1600s were relocated here when a new courthouse on the common was being built. East Burial Ground once had about 1,000 marked burials, but today fewer than 700 of these gravestones have survived. Fenced in and located just a short distance from the ocean, this burial ground is well-maintained and is a historic gem that highlights many works by early Rhode Island stonecutters, though the lettering on many stones has been worn away by the effects of the salt air. One of the most significant and poignant stones to be found here is that for the seven children of Scipio and Sukey Burt, Prince, Scipio, Cato, Abraham, Sarah, Judith, and Welcome, who all died between the years 1792 and 1805, their ages ranging from seven days to three years. This stone is located directly in front of the cemetery entrance gate on Wood Street, about fifty feet away, and is the only stone in the immediate area.

Scipio Burt (1760–June 20, 1821) was a slave of the Rev. James Burt and his wife Anna and was born in Rhode Island. He is best known as being an undertaker, employed in arranging local funerals (presumably for blacks), as well as being the sexton of the Congregational church (Thompson, pg. 210), though it is unclear if these were jobs he performed while enslaved or after he became free. Either way, Burt is one of the few black sextons and under-

Gravestone, the children of Scipio and Sukey Burt, 1792–1805, East Burial Ground, Bristol, Rhode Island (courtesy Julie Nathanson).

takers in New England whose name is known, one of the others being Caesar Walker, the black sexton of the town's Episcopal church. Interestingly, it is likely through his work as a sexton that Scipio Burt became acquainted with the man, William Throop II, who carved his children's gravestone. One of the jobs of a sexton was not only to dig graves, but also to help set the gravestones in place, including those that came from Throop's shop in Bristol. Since this professionally carved stone, which was first carved about 1798–99 (with Judith and Welcome's names added about 1805), is a rarity for slave children, it may have been purchased by Anna Burt, but it also may be speculated (there is no documentary evidence) that Scipio may have worked enough on the side to save money to purchase the stone himself from Throop.

Scipio Burt's wife Sukey was a slave of the DeWolf family, the two being married in Bristol on March 21, 1782, according to local church records. Scipio Burt remained in his master's charge until the Reverend Burt's death in October 1775 during the British invasion of the town, after which time he was the slave of the reverend's widow, Anna Burt. When a new minister, the Rev. Henry Wight, settled in Bristol in 1787, Scipio was sent to help plant the reverend's garden on several occasions, and was likely hired out by Anna Burt to perform similar tasks at various times of the year. Since he is not listed in the 1790 or 1800 federal census as a separate head of household, Scipio, as well as his wife Sukey, likely remained slaves until after Anna Burt died in June of 1806. Despite the deaths of their children early on, including twins Abraham and Sarah in 1792 (aged just seven days) and the much expected but short-lived Welcome (1805), the family would eventually grow in size from a household of three individuals in 1810 to a household of six in 1820. One of their

later children was Susan Burt, a member of the Congregational Church in 1820, who left the church in 1832 (possibly because she moved away from Bristol). It is unknown when Sukey Burt died, nor is it known where both Scipio and Sukey are buried, but likely in an unmarked grave in this cemetery, perhaps not far from their infant children.

The other notable burial in this cemetery is for Mary (her name also given as Maria, Morea, or Murea) Haskell (1773–1840), the wife of Song Haskell. Her stone may be found in the grouping of stones directly to the left of the entrance gate on Wood Street. Maria and Song were at one time the slaves of the widow Haskell in Bristol, who named the boy Song for his fine singing voice. In later years Song Haskell, who was employed cutting wood and drawing water, was known as "Uncle Song," and both he and his wife were said to be "of pure African blood" (Thompson, pg. 210). The entire family, Song, his wife, and children Hannah (1800–1812), Lucy, and John, joined the Episcopal

Gravestone, Mary Haskill, 1840, East Burial Ground, Bristol, Rhode Island.

church and were baptized in November 1807. The couple are also known to have had at least two other children, including Benjamin (1803–1811) and Song, Jr. (1805–1812). Benjamin's grave is also marked, and it seems likely his siblings are also buried here in unmarked graves. After gaining their freedom, the couple lived in the black section of Bristol that was called "Goree," or "New Goree." The house in which they resided in this neighborhood on the corner of Ministerial Lane and Wood Street, built by Song in 1808, is said to be the same one that is now located at 100 Franklin Street. Song Haskell survived his wife by six years, dying on April 24, 1846, and though his grave is unmarked, he, too, is likely buried in East Burial Ground.

The East Burial Ground is a picturesque site that is well-maintained; visitors to this cemetery should make plans in advance, as it is locked and can only be accessed by obtaining the keys at the town clerk's office located on nearby Court Street.

DeWolf family slaves
DeWolf Lot
Opposite 107 Woodlawn Avenue
Bristol

This private cemetery was established about 1824 for Bristol's most prominent merchant family of the 18th and 19th centuries. It is notable for being the burial site not only of James DeWolf, a Rhode Island merchant who was one of the largest dealers in the slave trade and one of the nation's richest men as a result, but also several individuals, including Adjua and Pauledore DeWolf, who were enslaved and served the DeWolfs personally for most of their lives. It is perhaps ironic that while slaves and master were buried close to one another here in this scenic wooded lot, their origins and status in life could not have been further apart. Thus it is that this location, this one quiet place, in one of New England's largest slave-trading ports, is where all of the elements of the slave trade can be symbolically found.

James DeWolf (1764–1837) was one of fifteen children of Mark Anthony and Abigail DeWolf. Mark Anthony and his brother-in-law Simeon Potter began the slave trade in Bristol beginning in the late 1760s, establishing a family business in which they and later generations of the family would be involved with for over fifty years. James DeWolf, known as "Captain Jim," was a true mariner, serving on privateers at a young age during the American Revolution, and was twice captured by the British. After the war he served on a number of ships, including those owned by the Brown family that participated in the slave trade, and rose to command a number of slave voyages. By 1790 DeWolf had earned enough income through the purchase of shares of the cargo to buy his own vessel, and from this time forward, up to 1807, he made a vast fortune in the slave trade, and was responsible for transporting some 11,000 slaves to America altogether.

While James DeWolf was considered a fine and upstanding citizen of Bristol and the state of Rhode Island by many, the slave trade brought out his dark side; during one slave voyage in 1789 he murdered a female slave on the *Polly* who was sick with smallpox. The woman was tied to a chair and lowered off the ship and drowned. DeWolf was later indicted for murder by a grand jury in Newport for this action and left Bristol for a voyage to the Gold Coast of Africa to avoid prosecution. Later on, in 1794, while living in St. Thomas in the West Indies, DeWolf was again indicted on the charge of murder; witnesses stated that DeWolf's action was necessary to save the whole ship from being infected, and the judge subsequently ruled in his favor.

When Congress in 1794 passed a law prohibiting Americans from participating in the foreign slave trade between Africa and Cuba or into states forbidding the importation of slaves, James DeWolf sidestepped these laws by transporting slaves to Georgia, the only state allowing the importation of slaves, and from here sold them to Cuban interests, as well as smuggling many slaves into New England via Bristol. He was able to do this because, by his influence, the customs inspector at Bristol was his own brother-in-law, who was also active in the slave trade.

DeWolf's holdings were not just located in Bristol, where he owned rum distilling operations, maintained a large warehouse made of stones imported from Africa as ballast in the holds of his ships, and operated an insurance company that profited by insuring slave voyages. He also owned several coffee and sugar cane plantations in Cuba where slaves were both worked and held until their later sale could be made at optimum profit. The DeWolf family themselves also had personal slaves serving them in Bristol, the most well-known being Adjua and Pauledore, who were brought to Bristol in 1803 as a Christmas present for DeWolf's wife Nancy while they were children.

When Congress banned the slave trade altogether in the U.S. in 1807, James DeWolf turned to other pursuits, including heavy investment in New England textile mills, and during the War of 1812 added substantially to his wealth by financing privateering voyages to capture British merchant ships. By 1815 DeWolf was said to be the second richest man in the U.S. Due to his wealth and influence, DeWolf later went into politics, serving as a Rhode Island senator from 1821 to 1825. When he died in 1837 in New York, his body was brought back to Bristol for burial in the family cemetery, and it is here where his crypt, a rather unremarkable example for one so rich, may be found. Within a few short years after his burial, DeWolf's tomb was raided by a local man who believed that DeWolf had been buried with a large amount of gold; all he was able to find were the gold fillings in DeWolf's teeth.

Interestingly, the DeWolf family's involvement with the slave trade did not end in 1807, but continued into the 1820s. At that time it was carried on by George DeWolf, James's nephew, a man considered to be a true scoundrel and James's rival. George DeWolf continued to import slaves by making false sales of his ships to Spanish interests in Cuba and reaping the profits from the voyages they made, including those ships cleared at Bristol while the customs inspector looked the other way. Oftentimes these ships were fitted out in Bristol before voyaging to Africa, and most of the Bristol ships that were later captured and condemned as slave ships by American and British naval forces off Africa and Cuba were owned by George DeWolf. As a whole, the activities of the DeWolf family from the 1760s to the 1820s resulted in the importation of nearly 30,000 slaves from Africa to America and made them the largest slave dealers in all of New England, and one of the largest in the entire U.S.

James DeWolf's tomb may still be seen today in this woodland cemetery, located at the back of the lot on a wooded hillside which can be reached by following a short trail that begins at the back of the main cemetery. Other than the iron door on the crypt, this eerie site, which has even been featured in a ghost-hunting video posted online at YouTube, is not marked.

Less famous and mostly overlooked are several graves for slaves of the DeWolf family, located on the far left of the main cemetery near the wooded border. The most prominent is that for Adjua D'Wolf (1794–1868), the woman who was brought to Bristol directly from Africa as a Christmas present in 1803. Interestingly, Adjua was allowed to retain her African given name (for those girls born on a Monday). The other half on this Christmas gift to Nancy DeWolf was a young boy, Pauledore, who later became Adjua's husband. His burial site in this cemetery is unmarked. Both were said to be favorites of the DeWolf family, and in their later years they lived in a separate cabin on the DeWolf estate and were pleasant to the many visitors who passed by.

Gravestone, Adjua D'Wolf, 1868, DeWolf Lot, Bristol, Rhode Island.

The presence of Adjua and Pauledore in the DeWolf household was a large one, since they not only worked for the family, but at a young age may have served as playmates to the DeWolf children. As they grew older, these favorite slaves worked on the estate, cared for their children and were even the subject of a tune or nursery rhyme that has remained in the family lore for over two hundred years. It goes as follows:

> Adjua and Pauledore
> Sitting on the cellar door
> Pauledore and Adjua
> Sitting in the cellar way
> Down fell the cellar door
> Bump went Pauledore
> Up flew the cellar way
> Off blew Adjua!

This nursery rhyme is detailed in the 2008 PBS film *Traces of the Trade: A Story from the Deep North*, documenting the journeys that several DeWolf family descendants, one of whom remembered this tune being sung to her by her grandmother, made to Africa and Cuba to come to terms with their family's slave-trading past. During this sobering experience, one of the women photographed in Ghana by the family during visits to historical slave trading sites turned out to be named Adjua. It is interesting to note that while numerous DeWolf family descendants, many of whom are well-connected, were invited to participate in the making of this film, most declined, either concerned with putting the family name in a negative spotlight or worried about possibly being asked to pay reparations for the family's involvement in the slave trade.

In regards to Pauledore and Adjua, white anecdotal accounts suggest that they were happy with their lives. When the abolitionist movement gained ground in Bristol, the DeWolf family is said to have discussed the possibility of returning Adjua and Pauledore to Liberia in Africa, but that they were unwilling to go. Whether or not Adjua and Pauledore had any children is uncertain, but Alexander DeWolf (born ca. 1818 in Rhode Island), a black seaman living in Bristol in 1850, may have been their son, while Ruth DeWolf (born ca. 1825 in Rhode Island), a black servant working in Bristol in 1870, is of sufficient age to have been their daughter. As was the case with many latter-day slaves in New England who had aged while in their masters' employ, Adjua and Pauledore's duties likely lessened in their older years and they were supported by the DeWolf family until they died. When Pauledore D'Wolf died, and whether or not his grave was originally provided with a marker, is unknown; that for his wife Adjua is broken in two and lying on the ground. The only other stone for an African American here is that for Judith Honeyman (died 1831), who is listed as a "faithful servant," but whether or not she worked for the DeWolf family is unknown, and efforts to track down her life details have been unsuccessful.

III. Massachusetts

Elizabeth Freeman Burial Site
Stockbridge Cemetery
Intersection Main and Church streets
Stockbridge

This, the main public burial space in town, is a classic New England cemetery that is well-maintained and still in use. The older sections are laid out in traditional fashion, while the newer parts of the cemetery were developed with the pathways and ornamental plantings characteristic of the rural cemetery movement. One of the most historic and visited sections here is the plot for the Sedgwick family, which is located in a small glade behind and to the right of the chapel that sits at the end of the main entrance road into Stockbridge Cemetery.

At first glance from afar, this plot and its monuments appear to be pretty typical, but as you get closer to the center, the unusual layout becomes more apparent and striking. Here you will find the central monuments for Theodore Sedgwick (1746–1813) and his wife Pamela (1752–1807), sitting on a raised circular stone platform, usually referred to as the "Sedgwick Pie," with the graves of other members of the Sedgwick family oriented around this pie and facing inward. While much has been written about this burial arrangement, especially the fact that the graves are not oriented on the typical east-west axis found in most New England cemeteries, this is not as unusual at the later date in which most of these burials took place. Clearly the intent here was to pay homage to the patriarch and matriarch of this branch of the family in Stockbridge, both of whom were born in Connecticut. Theodore Sedgwick began his law career in 1766 at nearby Great Barrington after graduating from Yale University. Among the gravestones surrounding the pie is that for Elizabeth "Mumbet" Freeman (1742–1829), a black woman born enslaved who gained her freedom with the help of Theodore Sedgwick, which may be easily found at the back left portion of the pie.

Elizabeth Freeman (1742–1829), first known as "Bett," was born into slavery in Claverack, New York, a town close to the Massachusetts border. She was owned by Pieter Hogeboom and served his family until sometime in the 1750s. Though most accounts of her life state that "Mumbet" was given as a wedding present to Hogeboom's daughter Hannah, who married John Ashley of Sheffield, Massachusetts, in 1735, this is incorrect, as she

191

Sedgwick "Pie," Stockbridge Cemetery, Stockbridge, Massachusetts.

was not yet born when this marriage took place. The Ashleys instead purchased Bett while she was a teenager and brought her to Sheffield to serve in the Ashley household, where she perhaps was the playmate of the two youngest Ashley children, Hannah and Mary. By 1771, Bett was one of five slaves serving the Ashley family.

Her life in captivity serving the family was no easy task; though Col. Ashley was a kind master, his wife Hannah was often quite cruel and was "the most despotic of mistresses" (Sedgwick, pg. 418). Around 1780, Hannah Ashley tried to strike a fellow slave of Bett's, a frail girl named Lizzy (some believe that it was Bett's daughter Betsy) about the year 1780 with a heated shovel for making a wheat cake from the leftover scraps of dough prepared for the family's bread. Bett shielded her from the blow and received a severe arm wound which she would carry with her for the remainder of her life. Bett would later tell the story that she deliberately refused to cover this wound when she went out with her mistress in public. When people questioned her about it, she told them to ask her mistress, raising the question: "Which was the slave and which was the real mistress?" (Sedgwick, pg. 418). While enslaved, Bett was married and had four children, one of whom, Betsy, may have married Jack Burghardt, the great-grandfather of black historian, author, and civil rights activist W.E.B. DuBois; her husband (name unknown) served in the Revolutionary War but never returned home afterward.

Given her age and strong character, Bett was undoubtedly a protector and mother figure to her fellow slaves who were younger than she. Bett was also intelligent and listened to what was going on around her during the war years. Since Colonel Ashley was a great supporter of the American cause and heavily involved in the politics of the day, many important issues regarding American rights were discussed at his home and in Bett's presence. (Interestingly, the Ashley home where Bett was employed is still standing today, a historic site located at the corner of Rannapo and Cooper Hill roads in Sheffield.) In 1780, matters came to a head when Bett overheard in the Ashley home a reading of the Massachusetts State Constitution and its Article One, which stated in part "that all men are born free and equal, and have certain natural, essential, and unalienable rights; among which may be reckoned the right of enjoying and defending their lives and liberties." This, perhaps combined with her mistress's harsh treatment, spurred on Bett

Gravestone, Elizabeth Freeman ("Mumbet"), 1829, Stockbridge Cemetery, Stockbridge, Massachusetts.

to gain her own freedom. This she did by consulting with a young lawyer in town, Theodore Sedgwick, who agreed to take on her case and that of her fellow slave, a man named Brom. The case was heard in the County Court in Great Barrington in August 1781, with Sedgwick and his co-counsel arguing that Article One in the Massachusetts State Constitution effectively abolished slavery in the state once and for all. In the end, the jury ruled in Brom and Bett's favor, awarding them not only their freedom, but also damages in compensation for their labor. Despite this, three male slaves remained in the Ashley home, aging along with their master and serving Col. Ashley until his death in 1802. Hannah Ashley died in 1790.

After winning her case, Bett took the name Elizabeth Freeman, and was subsequently known affectionately as "Mum Bett." Though Col. Ashley asked Freeman to stay in his employ for wages, she refused and instead went to live and work for the Sedgwick family, where she was employed as a senior servant (also in the Sedgwicks' employ was black Revolutionary War veteran Agrippa Hull). She helped care for many of the Sedgwick children, on whom her kindness, strength, and intelligence made a lifelong impression. Freeman was also well known in the town of Stockbridge at large as an excellent midwife and delivered an unknown number of children over the years. After working for the Sedgwick family for 27 years, their children now all grown, Freeman left their employ in 1808 and lived in Stockbridge in a small home she shared with her daughter. Not surprisingly, at her death she was buried in a place of honor in the Sedgwick family plot, a fitting final resting place if ever there was one. Her gravestone was purchased by the family, and its inscription, which ends with the exhortation "Good mother, farewell," was almost certainly composed by Catharine

Sedgwick, a noted female author and daughter of Theodore who was raised by "Mum Bett" Freeman.

Interestingly, unlike most of the other gravestones in this section, Freeman's gravestone is distinguished by the small stones, pebbles, coins, and flowers that have been placed on top by visitors who have come here to see her final resting place. While this custom is common in Jewish cemeteries, for which this area of Massachusetts is also known (and many of the visitors here are likely Jewish), it is similar to the African American tradition of loved ones decorating the grave of the departed with personal items and mementos. From this we may conclude, perhaps, that even over 180 years after her death, Freeman, by her courageous action and strong character, continues to serve as a figure who can span the divide between black and white in America.

W.E.B. DuBois Family Burial Site
Mahaiwe Cemetery
Silver Street, just off Rte 7 (S. Main St.)
Great Barrington

This cemetery, also known as South Cemetery, is the largest in Great Barrington and is a typical burying place of the times. While prominent local white politicians and town residents, including Civil War Medal of Honor recipient Frederick Deland, predominate here, the cemetery also has direct connections to one of America's foremost civil rights pioneers, the renowned black author and historian William Edward Burghardt DuBois (1868–1963). It is here in Great Barrington that DuBois was born, raised, and gained an education, and where he also buried his infant son, Burghardt Dubois (ca. 1897–1899), as well as his first wife, Nina Dubois (1871–1950). Also buried here is the Duboises' daughter Nina Yolande Cullen Williams (died 1961) and other members of the Burghardt family. For many years these graves went unnoticed, while Burghardt Dubois's grave was unmarked altogether until recently. In 1994 the Great Barrington Historical Society erected a bronze plaque to denote the presence of these DuBois family members in Mahaiwe Cemetery. The placement of this plaque was in fact one of the earliest physical efforts by the town, a liberal bastion in western Massachusetts, to recognize the importance and historical significance of their hometown son, and marked a sort of a beginning in coming to terms with some of the more controversial aspects of his life.

While the full details of W.E.B. Dubois's remarkable career have been covered in many authoritative works, a brief account of his life will here be appropriate to underscore his importance in Great Barrington. Growing up in Great Barrington was a relatively happy time for DuBois; while he and his family, part of a small group of African American residents in the town, experienced a mild form of racism, he always fondly remembered the Berkshire Hills in which he grew to manhood. DuBois attended an integrated school, and after graduation in 1885, when he decided he wanted to further his education. The church he attended, the First Congregational Church, helped raise the money so he could attend Fisk University, a black college in Tennessee. It was during this, his first time visiting the South, that he first experienced racism in its worst form, defined by Jim Crow era laws and the lynchings that he would later, as a historian and activist, document and write about. Upon graduating from Fisk, DuBois attended Harvard University, graduating with a degree in history in 1890, and in 1895 graduated from there with a Ph.D. in sociology, the first African American to earn a doctorate from Harvard.

In 1896, Dubois married Nina Gomer, a student of his while he was teaching at Wilberforce University in Ohio. In 1897 Dubois and his family moved to Atlanta, Georgia, where he taught at Atlanta University. It was during his time here that Dubois rose to prominence and became one of the most renowned black leaders of the day. However, unlike Frederick Douglass and Booker T. Washington, who believed in integrating into and accommodating with white society, DuBois believed that African Americans should embrace their unique heritage and actively fight for equal rights.

In 1903 was published Dubois's seminal work, *The Souls of Black Folk*, now considered to be one of the most important books by and about African Americans. In this collection of essays, one of the most poignant is titled "Of the Passing of the First-Born"; this essay describes, in hauntingly beautiful prose, the birth and death of W.E.B. DuBois's son Burghardt, who "died at eventide, when the sun lay like a brooding sorrow above the western hills, veiling its face" (DuBois, pg. 129). Though his son died in Atlanta in May of 1899 due to a diphtheria outbreak, DuBois "could not lay him in the ground there in Georgia, for the earth there is strangely red; so we bore him away to the northward, with his flowers and his little folded hands" (DuBois, pg. 130). On the day of his funeral in Great Barrington, DuBois writes: "Blithe was the morning of his burial, with bird and song and sweet smelling flowers. The trees whispered to the grass, but the children sat with hushed faces. And yet it seemed a ghostly unreal day,—the wraith of Life. We seemed to rumble down an unknown street behind a little white bundle of posies, with the shadow of a song in our ears. The busy city dinned about us; they did not say much, those pale-faced hurrying men and women; they did not say much,—they only glanced and said, "'Niggers!'" (DuBois, pg. 130). It is unknown why DuBois did not mark the final resting place of his son, as he certainly had the financial resources to do so. Perhaps this is due to the fact that, though he was raised in the Congregational church, as an adult DuBois had little use for religion and is generally regarded as having been an agnostic or possibly even an atheist. However, in his work *The Souls of Black Folk*, DuBois, speaking to his dead son, exclaims, "Sleep, then, child,—sleep till I sleep and waken to a baby voice and the ceaseless patter of little feet—above the Veil" (Dubois, pg. 131).

After the death of his son, W.E.B. Dubois's fame continued to grow, his achievements including his work with the NAACP as editor of their official magazine *The Crisis*, as well as other important historical books he authored. He also was an activist on behalf of African American troops during World War I and after their return home. He would also make several trips to Europe and the Soviet Union and eventually came to believe that socialism might be more beneficial for members of his race than capitalism. Though DuBois sympathized with many communist ideals, he himself was more pragmatic and never fully accepted the Soviet Union system of governance. However, because of his travels and associations, DuBois did become involved in the McCarthy anti-communist hearings and was himself brought to trial, with the result that his case was dismissed in 1951. In 1960 DuBois and his wife traveled to Ghana in Africa to celebrate that country's independence, and subsequently stayed here to work on an African encyclopedia at the behest of Ghana's government. He subsequently died in Accra, Ghana, in August 1963 and was there buried, far from his childhood home in western Massachusetts.

For years after his death, even into the 21st century, W.E.B. Dubois has remained a polarizing figure in his hometown. His works are well-studied in the Great Barrington schools, but when the idea of naming a school in his honor was proposed in 2004, the issue was hotly debated, and in the end no such honor came to pass. Likely the deciding factor was DuBois's perceived communist ties or anti–American sentiments, but no matter what the case, the failure to name the school in his honor painted the town in an unfavorable light. In 2005, after the school-naming controversy was over, the idea was put forth that perhaps the town could erect signs on the major roads leading into Great Barrington denoting it as the birthplace of DuBois. This idea, at first, was rejected by the town selectmen, but was later reversed after a public vote on the matter was approved by a large majority, and the signs were subsequently erected. Today, the town seems more comfortable in embracing DuBois as one of their own, highlighted by the fact that the DuBois Center was opened here in 2006, its location adjacent to this cemetery where so many of DuBois's relatives have been laid to rest.

African American GAR Plot
Hope Cemetery
119 Webster Street
Worcester
www.friendsofhopecemetery.com

This large garden-style cemetery, consisting of 168 acres, was established in 1852 and is the largest burial site in the city. Due to both its design and many prominent inhabitants, it is now on the National Register of Historic Places. While many prominent white Worcester-area residents are interred here, including political and military leaders, as well as early rocket pioneer Dr. Robert Goddard, many African Americans are also buried here. These include veterans of both the American Revolution and the Civil War, including Jeffrey and Alexander Freeman Hemmenway.

Jeffrey Hemenway (the name is variously spelled with one or two "m"s) was of mixed heritage and was born free about 1737 in Framingham, Massachusetts. He served in both the French and Indian War and the American Revolution; in the latter war he marched on the Lexington Alarm on April 19, 1775, as a minuteman in the Framingham militia. He later joined the Continental Army, serving under Col. John Nixon (whom he had also served under in the French and Indian War) and may have fought during the Battle of Bunker Hill. Hemenway continued his service in 1776 when he served in the 4th Continental Regiment commanded by Lt. Col. Thomas Nixon during the New York campaign, his captain being killed at the Battle of White Plains.

After this service ended in December 1776, Hemenway returned to Massachusetts and moved to Worcester by 1778, where be bought a small house on May Street (Quintal, Jr.,

Grand Army of the Republic (GAR) plot, Hope Cemetery, Worcester, Massachusetts. Veterans' gravestones in the GAR plot, Hope Cemetery, Worcester, Massachusetts.

pg. 130). Later on, in 1778 and 1779, Jeffrey Hemenway enlisted again for militia service, serving in Rhode Island and New York, and in 1780 joined the Continental Army yet again, serving once more under Col. Thomas Nixon for five months. In 1781 Hemenway saw his final service in the army before receiving his final discharge in November 1781.

Afterwards, Hemenway practiced the trade of a carpenter; his first wife was Susanna Wright, with whom he had two children, his daughter and his wife later dying in a smallpox epidemic (Quintal, Jr., pg. 131). His second wife was Hepsibeth Crossman, a Native American woman of the Nipmuc tribe, whom he married in 1792 and had eight children with, at least one of whom died while still young. Jeffrey Hemenway died in Worcester in 1819 and was buried in the Mechanic Street Cemetery, likely in a segregated portion of the grounds. When the occupants of this cemetery were later moved to Hope Cemetery, so too was Jeffrey Hemenway, though his stone was still set a distance from the others. Hepsibeth Hemenway (1763–1847), who outlived her husband for years, worked to support herself as a laundress and was known for the cakes she baked.

Jeffrey and Hepsibeth Hemenway's son, Ebenezer Hemenway (born 1804), married Betsy Crossman and had at least one child, Alexander Freeman Hemmenway (1834–1896). Alexander was married to Emily Thomas in 1855 and with her had two children, Ebenezer and Emma. He was practicing the trade of a barber in Worcester when he joined the 54th

Massachusetts Regiment during the Civil War in April 1863 (his first name incorrectly recorded in some records as "Augustus"). Hemmenway served until after the war in August 1865, starting out as a private and rising to first sergeant. While little is known about Alexander Hemmenway, his achievement of higher rank was almost certainly due to both his good character and his more mature age, 28, at the time of his enlistment, as well as his fighting abilities. Though he never knew his grandfather, it is highly likely that he heard stories about his service in the Revolutionary War from his father and grandmother, and thus may have been inspired to seek military service. Among the battles he fought in was the assault on Fort Wagner, South Carolina, where the 54th's regimental commander, Col. Robert G. Shaw, was killed. After the war, Hemmenway continued to live in Worcester and was married a second time to Josephine (a native of Florida whose parents were from France and Africa).

Like many other Civil War veterans found here in Hope Cemetery, Alexander Hemmenway is buried in one of the GAR (Grand Army of the Republic) plots which occupy a prominent spot marked by a large flagpole and a tripod sculpture made of three large cannons. One of these plots, the oldest one, was reserved solely for white veterans, while the new GAR section, dedicated on Memorial Day in 1892, contains the graves for all of the African American veterans, as well as white veterans. All of these veterans were members of Worcester's GAR, George Ward Post #10, an indicator of how the GAR attempted to recognize the service of all its members, without regard to color. It is notable that this free section is adjacent to the other free sections set aside for residents of the homes for aged women and men in Worcester.

Among the marked buried in this new GAR section are 12 members of the 54th Massachusetts, plus two men, George Rome and Henry Toney (whose stone is a modern government issue), who served in the all-black 55th Massachusetts, and one man, Jacob Brinton, who served in the 8th U.S. Colored Troop, a regiment raised from men living in Pennsylvania

Left: **Sylvester Mero, 54th Massachusetts.** *Right:* **Sergt. George L. Bundy, 54th Massachusetts.**

Left: Andrew W. Jackson, 3d Class Boy, U.S. Navy. *Right:* 1st Sgt. Alexander F. Hemmenway, 54th Massachusetts.

and Delaware. Brinton (1830–1912) was born in Delaware and joined the service in September 1863; a year later, on September 29, 1864, he was wounded in action at Laurel Hill, Virginia, during the fierce Battle of New Market Heights, an engagement notable for the many black soldiers who earned the Medal of Honor for their valiant service. After the war, Brinton moved to Worcester and practiced the trade of a hairdresser.

Yet another burial here is that for a Navy veteran, 3rd Class "Boy" Andrew Jackson. Among the marked burials for veterans of the 54th Massachusetts in this section, most are for Vermont African Americans who moved to the area after the Civil War, including four men from Rutland (George Storms, Charles Mero, George Scott, and James Quow), two men from Bristol (Amasa Peters and Mark Roberts), and Sylvester Mero from Woodstock. The other men from the 54th here were Massachusetts natives, including Joseph Bosley and George Bundy from Worcester, Charles Reed from nearby Barre, and Emery Phelps from New Bedford.

George L. Bundy, like Alexander Hemmenway, was a local barber who rose to become a sergeant, serving in Company A; he was wounded in action during the 54th's famed assault on Fort Wagner, one of the few African Americans buried here known to have been wounded in battle.

Navy veteran Andrew Jackson (1837–1907) was a native of Virginia, born enslaved on a plantation on Christmas day in Henrico County, who joined the Union Navy for a three-year term in June 1862. Jackson was among fifteen slaves who had ran away from their master's plantation near Richmond at night and were found by the crew of a Union gunboat patrolling the James River. Offered a chance to enlist, they did; Jackson was among three men who were given weapons and given the duty of patrolling the banks of the river before being brought aboard the ship the next day and being formally enlisted. His position as a 3rd Class "Boy" meant that he was employed serving the captain or other officers of the ship and, during battle, was probably engaged as an ammunition handler and runner serving on the ship's gun deck. Jackson saw quite a bit of sea action, including duty aboard the USS *Shenandoah* (1863–64) cruising the New England coast, and later off Wilmington, North Carolina, in search of Confederate raiders and blockade runners. He later served aboard the 12-man tug USS *Cohasset* off Norfolk, Virginia, (1864), and finally aboard the steam frigate USS *Minnesota* (1864–65), taking part in the two amphibious campaigns against Fort Fisher, North Carolina. He was here discharged from the service in June 1865. After the war, Jackson returned to the plantation where he had been employed, and with the help of his former master, was able to find his wife, Martha (Twine) Jackson, who had been raised with him on the same plantation and had been married to him since 1858. The couple subsequently lived in and around Richmond for a decade before moving to New England. Like most of the black veterans from other states who moved to Worcester, Jackson was probably attracted by the many job opportunities available in this large manufacturing city, as well as its vibrant African American community and freedom from the harsh Jim Crow laws of the reconstructed South.

In addition to the GAR section, there are many other veteran burials located throughout Hope Cemetery. Notable among them is that for Civil War veteran Amos Webber (1826–1904), a native of Philadelphia, who joined the all-black 5th Massachusetts Cavalry and rose to the rank of quartermaster sergeant. Like many African Americans, Webber and his wife Lizzie moved to Worcester to gain steady employment and after the war made the city their home, even going so far as to have the body of their deceased son Harry (died 1858) moved to Hope Cemetery from Philadelphia. Webber was noted for his active involvement in local veterans' groups and civic organizations and was the prime mover in organizing reunions of the all-black 54th, 55th, and 5th Cavalry regiments. He has left behind some of his writing in his so-called memory books, in which he recorded events in his life beginning in the 1850s. These books are covered in detail in Nick Salvatore's book *We All Got Memory* (1996). The Webber family all lie next to each other on a hillside facing Aspen Avenue and, like the GAR section, is featured in a visitor's guide and map for the cemetery.

Yet another interesting story for a black veteran buried in this cemetery is that of Alexander H. Johnson (1846–1930), who was nicknamed "The Major." He was a native of New Bedford, Massachusetts, the son of mixed African and Native American heritage parents Henry and Hannah Johnson, and practiced the trade of a seaman before enlisting in the 54th Massachusetts Regiment in March of 1863. While official records give his age at the time of enlistment as sixteen, his obituary claims that he was fourteen at the time of his enlistment. Early on, the young Johnson, who served as a musician in Company C, had nineteen dollars taken out of his pay for losing his musician's dress sword and scabbard. One of the sergeants under whom he served was future Medal of Honor recipient William Carney (also of New Bedford). Johnson fought with the rest of his regiment at Fort Wagner, South Carolina, Olustee, and Honey Hill as a company drummer; he was said to have had his drum hit six times by enemy fire and have been wounded once in the leg (not noted in his service records). After the war, Johnson moved to Worcester by 1869 and here organized a drum corps; being proud of his military service, Johnson often wore his soldier's cap and eventually gained the nickname "Major." Interestingly, the black drummer depicted on the bronze monument erected at the State House in Boston in honor of regimental commander Col. Robert Gould Shaw is said to be a likeness of Johnson.

The Hope Cemetery is an easy one to find, and as an active place for burials, it is manned by helpful city staff members during normal business hours. The grounds are well maintained and cared for, and the cemetery really is a historic gem for the Worcester area. The cemetery and its GAR sections are particularly striking when they are all decorated for Memorial Day. The status of this cemetery is enhanced by the group Friends of Hope Cemetery, which routinely sponsors historic events that are both informative and entertaining. If it should come to pass that Worcester ever develops its own black history trail, as previously discussed, Hope Cemetery will most certainly be one of its feature sites.

Prince Walker Burial Site
Walker Family Cemetery
Off Gilbert Road
Barre

To visit this burial site, located in the woods close by the Burnshirt River, is a unique experience; the quiet solitude of the place is a reminder to us today that free African Americans were often relegated to the fringes of New England society both figuratively and, in this case, quite literally. This humble historic site is also a reminder that sometimes history with wide-ranging implications is made not just in the big cities where the most people live, but sometimes in small towns too.

Prince Walker (1776–1858) was born enslaved in Barre, Massachusetts, and was, by most accounts, the son of the enslaved Quock (sometimes spelled "Quork") Walker (born 1753). Quock Walker was himself born enslaved, the son of Mingo and Dinah Walker, slaves of the Caldwell family. While a young man, Quock was promised he would be granted his freedom in 1778 when he reached the age of 25. When his master James Caldwell died in 1763, his widow not only stated that she would keep this promise, but promised he would be freed at age 21 in 1774. However, the widow Caldwell married Nathaniel Jennison, who, after her death in 1772, was solely in charge of Walker's fate and ultimate freedom. Despite the widow's promise, Jennison refused to free Quock Walker in 1774. Fed up with his continued status as a slave, Walker ran away from Jennison in 1780 and went to live and work on the farm owned by the brothers of his former master.

After Jennison tracked down Walker, he took him home and gave him a severe beating, which resulted in Walker's suing his master for assault and battery. In the summer of 1781 a series of trials took place, with Jennison winning his case against the Caldwell brothers for causing Walker to run away. This verdict was later overturned on appeal, but, more important, not only did Walker initially win his assault case against his master, he was also granted his freedom because his lawyers successfully argued that slavery was contrary to the principles laid down in the new Massachusetts State Constitution of 1780. While this case did not result in freedom being granted to all Massachusetts slaves, it did set a precedent that would hasten the end of the institution of slavery. All of this took place in and around Barre in Worcester County, but little is known of Quock Walker afterwards, even his year of death. It is known that he continued to live in Barre, not far from the town common, where a historical marker has been erected in his honor. Of his son, Prince Walker, however, much more is known.

Prince Walker, too, was born in Barre; it is said that after his father Quock Walker gained his freedom, Nathaniel Jennison, surely sensing that he might lose all his slaves and gain nothing in return as a result of his court cases, sold the remainder of his slaves to Connecticut interests. Where or how this occurred is unknown, but at some point Prince Walker gained his freedom and returned to Barre, where he would live the remainder of his life.

In his early years, Prince earned a living, as many free blacks did, by performing odd jobs and working at seasonal labor. His first wife, Betsy Daws, he married in 1805, but she was dead by 1816, when Prince married his second wife, Anna Morse. Local lore states that Prince had ten children altogether, six of whom, Nancy, Prince, John, George, Enoch, and Sally, are mentioned in his will. Though Prince Walker led a hard life that was typical of many free blacks at this period, he later became somewhat renowned as the being the last man in town who had once been enslaved.

He eventually earned enough money to purchase just over seven acres of land in the Burnshirt Hills, just a few miles from the Caldwell's place where he was born. Here Walker built a small house with only a partial cellar and a stone chimney and a small barn just large enough to hold a few farm animals. Walker farmed a small piece of land down the hill and just beyond a small brook. Town lore states that the neighboring white farmers helped out Walker and his family during lean times, and that "Prince was industrious, honest, friendly, and always wore a smile" (Harwood, *Barre Gazette*, Jan. 1, 1958).

In between his home and his field, at the crest of a ravine, was where Walker established his family cemetery and lay to rest his first wife about 1816. Shortly before his death, Prince Walker in October 1854 deeded "a certain piece of land for a burying ground containing four square rods" to the "Inhabitants of the town of Barre," stating that he had here "buried several of my Family" (Prince Walker deed, October 30, 1854—Walker File, BHS). It is perhaps for this reason that this site has survived all these years when other like sites have vanished. Interestingly, Prince Walker's father, Quock Walker, may also be buried here, but there are only five stones in this cemetery, of which only one, that for Prince, is professionally carved. All the other stones are simple fieldstones with no markings, so it is impossible to say for certain who else is buried here, but Betsy Walker, as well as several Walker children, are the most likely candidates.

Of all the historic African American burial sites listed here for the state of Massachusetts, this one is the hardest to find. In fact, unless visitors are familiar with the area, help from local guides, such as members of the Barre Historical Society, will be needed to find the Prince Walker family cemetery. The trailhead to this site is off to the left of Gilbert Road, approximately 200 yards down from Rte. 62. The trail heads in a westerly direction for about a three-quarters of a mile, winding through woods and several dense patches of brush. Markers to this trail were present in early 2014, but were very faint and easy to miss. Because of its wooded seclusion, this site is best seen in the fall, and though it takes some work getting there, the trail itself is not overly difficult. Once there, facing the cemetery, look beyond the crest of the hill and you can visualize where Prince Walker's house (long gone by the 1930s) once stood, while looking below you can see the small stream which once supplied the Walker family with water. Imagine, too, a landscape that was once open space and farmland, and has now reverted to a wilderness that has almost, but not quite yet, swallowed up the Walker family legacy.

This site now lies on land owned by the state's MDC (Metropolitan District Commission) because it is part of the land encompassing the Quabbin Reservoir Watershed System, though the cemetery is under the nominal control of the Barre Cemetery Commission. Its remote site, however, has resulted in only sporadic maintenance efforts, the cemetery site being last overhauled via a local Eagle Scout project in 1986. Since that time, the site has again become endangered, with Prince Walker's stone down on the ground and in danger of being further damaged or lost.

Gill Slaves burials
Meetinghouse Cemetery
Mountain Rd., off Rte. 62
Princeton

This well-maintained and quaint cemetery is a classic example of a New England burial ground. Not only is it filled with elaborately carved gravestones depicting the soul effigies that symbolized the Puritan theology of the day, it is also in an otherwise rural area surrounded by the quintessential stone wall. While these attributes in and of themselves make this a historic place worthy of a visit, the several stones found here for Thomas, Flova, and Nero, the slaves of the Gill family, make it an even more interesting and unusual site.

As previously discussed, Moses Gill, a prominent Massachusetts businessman and politician, was married in 1759 to Sarah Prince, the daughter of the Rev. Thomas Prince of Boston's Old South Church. The Reverend Prince was a founding father of the town of Princeton, and after his death in 1758, Moses and Sarah Gill inherited his large landed estate in Princeton consisting of some 3,000 acres. On this estate, of which many acres were actively farmed, was a large mansion with four chimneys, a smaller but still sizeable farmhouse, and a connected coach house and large barn, the entire spread surrounded by an ornamental fence. The Gills, however, did not reside in Princeton year round; as Moses Gill was actively involved in state politics and served briefly as governor, he spent much of his time in Boston, and it was there where he died and was buried in 1800. In fact, while there are many Gill family members found in this cemetery, neither Moses Gill or his two wives are buried here. Over the years, the Gill family owned at least four slaves, perhaps more; two of them, Flova (also called "Flora") and Jack, were willed to Rebecca Gill (Moses's second wife) in 1771. Thomas (1693–1782) had probably served the Gills for many years, perhaps since their marriage in 1759, while Flova (1737–1778) only served Gill and his second wife for seven years until her death at an early age. Where Jack is buried is unknown, but there is a heavily damaged (though once elaborate) stone here for a man whose name is thought to have been Nero (1737–1776); nothing is known of this slave.

This cemetery is unusual in that the three Gill slaves buried here, all interred between 1776 and 1782, are not buried in segregated or stranger's ground at the back of the cemetery,

Meetinghouse Cemetery, Princeton, Massachusetts.

Left: Gravestone, Thomas, "negro man servant" to Moses Gill, 1783, Meetinghouse Cemetery, Princeton, Massachusetts. *Right:* Gravestone, Flova, "a Negro woman Servant" to Moses Gill, 1778, Meetinghouse Cemetery, Princeton, Massachusetts.

but rather in the front portion, amidst other prominent individuals who were white. Though speculative, this prominent final resting place for the Gill
slaves, Nero, Flova, and Thomas, is perhaps indicative of both the Gills' high status overall in Princeton, and of the respect and affection that they held
for these individuals, in particular Mrs. Rebecca Gill,
who probably had the most interaction with several
of them. Finally, the gravestones themselves for the
Gill slaves are some of the finest Colonial-era carved
gravestones to be found for African Americans in
central and northern New England. Though the
"Honorable" Moses Gill's status as the owner of
these "servants" is prominently carved on each of
these stones and is most noticeable at first glance, as
is the fact that all three are described as being "Negro,"
the visitor will be rewarded by taking a closer look
at these stones. Note that the stone for Flova clearly
depicts a female soul effigy with coiffed hair that,
though not a carved likeness of the slave, at least pre-

Gravestone, N___ (likely Nero), "Negro
man Servant" to Moses Gill, 1776, Meetinghouse Cemetery, Princeton, Massachusetts.

serves her female identity. In contrast, the stone for Thomas, a personal manservant to
Moses Gill, clearly depicts a male soul effigy that is totally bald. Such gravestones as these
were also carved by the stonecutter for his white patrons, an indicator of the expense Moses
Gill was willing to incur to mark his slave's gravesites, with the wording ("Negro" and "servant") in their brief epitaphs used to identify their proper place in society.

Lovejoy and Coburn Burial Sites
South Church Cemetery
41 Central Street
Andover

This cemetery is located in an in-town setting and is an example of the many picturesque public burying spaces found in the larger towns of New England. This cemetery has
been referred to as Andover's oldest museum, as it was established in 1709 when the parish
itself was established, with the first recorded burial taking place in December 1710. The
land for the cemetery was donated by Deacon John Abbott, a son of one of Andover's first
settlers, and is thought to have originally been the private burial lot for the family. The oldest stones now found here date to 1723 and the site continued as the main public burying
space in town until a second burying ground was established in the west parish in 1791.
Even after this time, burials continued here for many years. About one hundred yards behind
and to the right of the church may be found what was originally the rear portion of the
cemetery where people of color and lesser individuals in society were buried. While this
cemetery now appears to have been an integrated one, a look at the dates on the gravestones

South Church Cemetery, Andover, Massachusetts. The original black burial section here is at lower right, near the grouping by the American flag.

surrounding and to the rear of those for several early free African American residents clearly shows that their graves were isolated for many years before gaining some new "neighbors."

The oldest marked gravestone extant here for an African American is that for Pomp Lovejoy (1724–1826), "Born in Boston, a slave; died in Andover a freeman ... much respected as a sensible, amiable, and upright man." His stone is a finely carved slate of a quality typically purchased by middle- and upper-class whites and sports the willow tree and urn motif that was then in common usage. By the time of his death at an advanced age, Lovejoy was, as his epitaph suggests, a well-respected man. Pompey Lovejoy, or "Pomp," as he was known, had been the slave of Capt. William Lovejoy, who had purchased him in Boston about 1733 and brought him to Andover. Interestingly, Pomp's master was not only a captain, but also a church deacon for South Church, and is also buried here. Pomp Lovejoy worked for his master for years, and continued as a slave until he gained his freedom after William Lovejoy died in March 1762. In his will, Capt. Lovejoy willed his property to various members of his family, "except the negro man Pompey—to him, freedom from all slavery and servitude" (Abbott, pg. 69).

After becoming free, Pomp lived on land owned by his former master and here built a home on Abbot Road in the Ballardville part of Andover, near a pond once known as

Ballard Pond. It is now known as Pomp's Pond due to Pomp Lovejoy's long residence in the area, though few people today realize just how this pond got its name. When Pomp's house burned down in 1773, neighbors and friends helped him build another one, in which he and his wife Rose (Coburn) Lovejoy, would live for the rest of their lives. Of Rose Lovejoy (1727–1826), little is known; like her husband, she was also a slave, owned by the Coburn family (whether in Andover or nearby Dracut is uncertain). She was known for the cakes and root beer she made for the voters on Election Day.

Gravestone, Pomp Lovejoy, 1826, South Church Cemetery, Andover, Massachusetts.

Pomp earned a regular living assisting local butchers, as well as driving a bakery cart. He was also known for his fiddle playing during town social events, especially on Election Day. When the American Revolution began in 1775 with the Lexington Alarm, Pomp Lovejoy, now in his fifties, was among the town's minutemen who marched from Andover to join the fight against the British at Concord, fighting alongside his fellow white soldiers commanded by Captain Henry Abbot. Though Pomp Lovejoy is buried in the South Church Cemetery and may have attended church services here, there is nothing in church records to show that he ever officially joined the church by making a profession of faith and being baptized.

In addition to the Lovejoys, there are several other African Americans, all former slaves, buried here. One of these is Lucy Foster, the former slave of Job and Hannah Foster (later Chandler). As I've discussed in detail elsewhere, Lucy served the Foster family, then the widow Hannah for years until her mistress died in 1812 and Lucy was given her freedom. She continued living in Andover for years and died here due to an asthma attack in November 1845. From the time she gained her freedom until she died, every year Lucy was given some form of relief by the South Church, of which she had become a member in 1793, the year after her son Peter was baptized. This amount ranged anywhere from one to five dollars a year, with the largest amounts given between the years 1837 and 1845 when she could no longer support herself. Though likely buried near to Pomp and Rose Lovejoy, there is no stone marking her final resting place now, and probably never was.

Two other African American graves, that for Rose Coburn and Colley Hooper (the daughter of Titus Coburn), are marked here, though these markers are recent replacements erected in 2002. The most significant is that for Rose (her name given as Roxana or Roseanna in death and military pension records) Coburn (1767–1859); she was the last former slave in Andover at the time of her death just a few short years before the Civil War. Rose was born into slavery in Andover and served the prominent Frye family in Andover prior to gaining her freedom. Her father was named Benjamin, her mother Phyllis, a native of Africa.

Her master was Joshua Frye, and after his death, his widow Sarah Frye became the mistress to Rose and three other slaves, Juba, Cato, and Priscilla. Her 1776 will gave Rose and Juba to her son John, "if I do not sell them before I die" (Abbott, Frye family records, pg. 46), as well as Cato and Priscilla. She also states, "My wish as to servants is that they be sold as soon after my death as such persons can be found to purchase them as will intreat [*sic*] them well, with that justice and humanity which is due such servants—and the proceeds shall be shared by my sons" (Abbott, Frye family records, pg. 46).

When exactly Rose gained her freedom is unknown, but by the 1790s she was free. On September 6, 1792, in Wilmington, Massachusetts, she married Titus Coburn, also a former slave, who had served for nine months in the Revolutionary War in 1778–79. He had enlisted in the Massachusetts Continental regiment commanded by Col. Michael Jackson, assigned to Captain Pierce's company, stationed primarily at West Point, New York, performing garrison duty.

While Rose and Titus Coburn had no children together, Titus had a daughter named Colley Hooper (1786–1857) from a prior relationship who was raised by Rose, the two women living together later on from the 1820s to the 1850s. Titus worked as a laborer to support his family, but life was hard for the Coburns; when Titus, now with a bad rupture and in poor health, applied for a government pension in 1818 due to his military service, the family owned no land of any kind and their belongings of value were meager, including

Gravestones of the Coburn Family, 1857–1859, South Church Cemetery, Andover, Massachusetts. The gravestone at left is a modern replacement for the original, which had the same lengthy epitaph. The gravestone at right is also a modern-day replacement, with the added notation regarding Titus Coburn's burial.

a hoe, a shovel, an axe, some old chairs, a looking glass (mirror), a chest, a pair of tongs, a scythe, a pitchfork, all valued at a total of $5.32, and not including the debts he owed. Titus and Rose at this time were also supporting their daughter and Rose's mother Phyllis, who was aged 90 at the time. Luckily, this pension was granted, but gave relief for only a short time, as Titus Coburn died in May of 1821. He is buried in an unmarked grave, according to his daughter Colley Hooper's gravestone, "elsewhere," but where is unknown. If not buried here, then he could be buried in North Andover's Second Burying Ground, which has an established black section (see below).

Rose Coburn survived without her husband or a pension for over three decades, but in the later years of her life received help from local citizens, including fellow African American Barzillai Lew, Jr. (himself the son of a Revolutionary War soldier) in getting a widow's pension. After her death, Rose Coburn's grave was originally marked, but the stone was replaced in 2002 after it had become damaged or lost.

African American Section
Second Burying Ground
Academy Road
North Andover

This cemetery was established in 1817 and, as its name implies, was the second public burying ground established in the parish of North Andover. There are many fine slate stones here, most of the willow-and-urn variety, found for prominent local families, including at least twenty-five veterans of the American Revolution. The burial ground is fronted by a stone wall of later origin and is distinguished by a mound found in the back third of the cemetery where some family tombs are located.

The real interest here, however, is the clearly defined section set aside for African Americans, known in older days as the "Negro Quarter," in the far right rear corner of the cemetery in a section overgrown by weeds and thorny bushes. Indeed, outside of such larger towns as Boston and Newport, the Second Burying Ground has one of the most obviously defined black sections to be found in any early New England cemetery. While the marked burials in this section for black residents, numbering seven in all for members of the Freeman, Lew, and Francis families and dating from the 1840s to the 1860s, are clearly visible and the professionally carved gravestones well preserved, there are probably a number of other earlier unmarked burial sites for black individuals from the 1820s and 1830s who could not afford the luxury of a gravestone purchase.

Perhaps the most prominent of the known African Americans to be buried here is Cato Freeman (1768–1853); he was formerly enslaved by the Rev. Samuel Phillips and was the son of Phillips's slaves Salem and Reina. Cato was well treated by the Reverend Phillips; he was taught to read and write, and became free after the passage of the Massachusetts State Constitution in 1780. For nearly nine years afterward, Cato continued to work for the Reverend Phillips as a paid servant, but in May 1789 he decided to go his own way; upon his departure he wrote a letter to the reverend that thanked him "for your care over me, your kindness to me, also for your timely checks, your faithful reproofs, necessary correction, your wise counsel, seasonable advice" (Bailey, pg. 42). It is significant, however, that though Cato thanked his old master, he did not choose to become known as Cato Phillips, but took on a new identity, one indicative of his independent status as a freeman.

Later that same year, in December 1789, Cato married Lydia Bristow (1765–1854), and together the two had many children, about nine in number. One daughter, Dorcas Freeman, lived with Cato and Lydia for many years after the other children had left home. Cato Freeman earned a comfortable living farming his own land and owned several homes. By the 1850s he owned $500 in real estate, a sizeable sum for the time, and after his death his entire holdings were valued at nearly $1,000, leaving enough to purchase suitable gravestones both for him and his wife Lydia, who died in 1854. Also buried beside them here in Second Burying Ground is their son Jacob Kimball Holden Freeman (1805–1841), who was both born and died on a "fast day," a day of prayer and repentance in old New England.

Buried beside the Freemans here are members of the prominent Lew family, including Barzillia Lew, Jr. (1777–1861), and his first wife Eliza. Barzillia (also spelled as "Barzillai") was the son of the prominent free black man from nearby Dracut, Barzillai Lew (1743–1822) and his wife Dinah Bowman Lew (1744–1837), who was born enslaved. Barzillai purchased her freedom in 1766 for some 400 pounds. She was said to be very fair skinned. The final resting places of Dinah and Barzillai Lew, Sr., are uncertain, but likely in the old Claypit Cemetery in Lowell, Massachusetts. While the elder Barzillai Lew was born free in Groton, Massachusetts, his father Primus Lew was born enslaved; both men served in the various phases of the French and Indian War as fifers in local militia companies, Primus in 1747 and Barzillai in 1760. The elder Barzillai Lew, who practiced the trade of a cooper and

Left: **Gravestone, Cato Freeman, 1853, Second Burying Ground, North Andover, Massachusetts.** *Right:* **Gravestone, Jacob K.H. Freeman, 1841, Second Burying Ground, North Andover, Massachusetts.**

passed this on to his son and grandson, also served in the American Revolution as a fifer in 1775–76 and for a short time in late 1777 and after the war settled in Dracut. Barzillai and Dinah raised a large family, having thirteen children, and all of them acquired musical skills, the family performing together for pay on many occasions, including concerts as far away as Portland, Maine.

Barzillai, Jr., was a prominent man in Andover; he "was well educated, and became a man of some property and consequence ... he owned the largest library in town ... was tall and dignified in appearance ... was remarkably intelligent, refined, and pleasing in his address ... had it not been for the social degradation to which the race to which he belonged had been reduced, he would have been chosen to the first offices in his town, if not in the state" (Hurd, vol. 2, pg. 311). Indeed, Barzillai Lew, Jr., was a leader in the black community, as evidenced by the help he gave to Rose Lovejoy, the wife of the long-deceased Revolutionary War veteran Pomp Lovejoy, in gaining a widow's pension in 1854.

Gravestone, Barzillia Lew, 1861, Second Burying Ground, North Andover, Massachusetts.

In his personal life, Lew had four wives, including his first, Dorcas, whom he married in Dracut in 1801, followed by Sarah and Eliza (who is also buried here), with virtually nothing known of either of these women, and lastly Nancy Riley, a black woman from Boston whom he married in 1823. In keeping with the Lews' position as leaders and helpers in North Andover's black community, a black woman, Ruby Francis, was taken in by the family and lived with them for at least ten years beginning in 1855, if not earlier. After Barzillai, Jr., died in 1861, his widow Nancy Lew and Ruby Francis lived together for at least another nine years. Nancy Lew later moved to 3 Smith Court in Boston and here died in September 1873.

The final black family with marked graves here is that of John (1799–1869) and Ruby Francis (1798–1881). Little is known of them except that they came from either Lowell or Boston, where their children were born. The couple had two children, both of whom are buried here: Elizabeth Francis (1832–1852) was born in Lowell and died of "palsy," while Henry V. Francis (1836–1856) was a common laborer who died of consumption. Little else is known about this family, except that they were closely connected to the Lew family, perhaps John or Ruby having known Nancy Lew in Boston prior to her marriage. Though uncertain, it is possible that John Fran-

Gravestone, Elizabeth A. Francis, 1852, Second Burying Ground, North Andover, Massachusetts.

cis left his wife by the 1850s and moved to Boston, as a man by that name died there of pneumonia. Ruby Francis (1798–1881) lived with the Lew family for many years. Sometime between 1870 and 1880 she left Andover and moved back to Boston, where she resided in the Home for Aged Colored Women in 1880 and died the following year in September 1881.

Finally, though we know something of those black individuals who have marked burials here, there are likely many other burials in this "quarter" for African Americans that went unmarked; the 1820 federal census for the North Parish of Andover, taken just three years after this cemetery was established, shows 23 people of color living here. As mentioned in my previous entry, Revolutionary War veteran Titus Coburn may be buried here, but so too may be Revolutionary War veteran Caesar Frye, who died in town in September 1820. He was formerly a slave, the servant of Col. James Frye of Andover, and is said to have been with him at the Battle of Bunker Hill in June 1775. He may have gained his freedom in early 1776 after his master died from wounds he received in battle, and later raised a family here. Yet another black man who resided in town whose final burial place is unknown is Bristo Johnson, listed as being the head of a family of five individuals in the 1800 census. He died here in 1822, so likely lies in this ground.

The condition of this cemetery is overall generally good, but the African American section, as I've previously discussed, is just the opposite; the area around the Lew, Francis, and Freeman stones currently serves as an apparent dumping ground for cut brush and old tree stumps and is in a shameful condition. This area needs to be fully cleared so that it is better protected and may be better maintained. The town itself, or the local historical society, could also increase this cemetery's status immensely by erecting a historical sign or plaque near its entrance which denotes the significant African American residents buried here.

Primus Stevens Burial Site
Old North Parish Cemetery
Academy Road, at Court Street
North Andover http://www.townofnorthandover.com/pages/nandoverma_bcomm/cemetery.pdf

This is the oldest burial ground in North Andover and is a place where the earliest residents of the current towns of North Andover and Andover are interred. It is a site known for its many early colonial-era gravestone carvings and picturesque rural location. It is also a typical early New England public burying space in regards to the enslaved and free African Americans and provides an interesting contrast to the town's Second Burying Ground, which is located just up the street less than a half a mile away. From the front of this cemetery, look to the rear left area and you will see a large expanse of open ground where few headstones are found. This is almost certainly the area where the enslaved or free blacks of Andover's North Parish were commonly buried until the Second Burying Ground opened up. In this area there remains one stone for a black individual, Primus (1720–1792), the "faithful servant" to Benjamin Stevens, Jr. It is a typical fine slate gravestone of the day, of the kind often purchased by whites.

Though there are no other black burials marked here, the number buried here may be substantial. Black heads of household in town listed in the 1800 federal census include Allen Richardson (died 1812), Prince Walker (died 1816), and Prince (also known as Prime or Primus) Ames (died 1816). All of these men and/or some of their family members (such as Peter Ames, the son of Prince and Eunice who died in 1785) are likely buried here, though some may have been

Gravestone, Primus, "a faithful servant" of Benjamin Stevens, 1792, Old North Parish Cemetery, North Andover, Massachusetts.

buried on their own land. Perhaps the most intriguing possible burial here is that of the Revolutionary War soldier and hero at the Battle of Bunker Hill, Salem Poor (ca. 1742–?). North Andover town history accounts state that Poor was a slave from birth and was purchased at the Salem, Massachusetts, slave market (thus his given name) as an infant by a young woman named Lydia Abbot and was, at the age of five, baptized in the North Parish church. Later on, Salem became the slave of John Poor of North Andover in uncertain circumstances, who in 1769 allowed Salem to purchase his freedom for the sum of 27 pounds. Shortly thereafter, Poor married Nancy Parker, a free black woman of mixed heritage, in November 1771. The couple had one known child, Jonas Poor, who was baptized in September 1776 in North Andover. This is the extent of any knowledge of the personal details of Salem Poor's family.

In 1775 Salem Poor enlisted for service in the regiment of troops commanded by Col. James Frye of Andover, serving in Capt. Benjamin Ames's company. During the subsequent Battle of Bunker Hill on June 17, 1775, Salem Poor took part in the heaviest fighting of the day and gained attention for his brave conduct during the fierce hand-to-hand fighting that took place in the redoubt. In a petition to the General Court of Massachusetts in December 1775, fourteen white officers who took part in the battle recommended Poor for his bravery, stating that "a Negro man, called Salem Poor, of Col. Fryes regiment, Capt. Ames company ... behaved like an Experienced officer, as well as an Excellent Soldier.... Wee Would Only begg leave to say in the person of this said Negro Centers a brave and gallant soldier. The Reward due to so great and Distinguisht a Caracter, Wee Submit to the Congress" (Quintal, Jr., pg. 175).

After the Revolutionary War, Salem Poor disappears from history, though John Poor, Jr., did have one person of color living in his household listed for the 1790 federal census. Nancy Poor is listed as being the head of a two-person household (probably with her son Jonas) in 1800, a likely indicator that Salem was dead and buried by this time in what is now an unknown location.

Cuffee Dole Burial Site
Union Cemetery
East Main Street (Rte. 133)
Georgetown
http://www.georgetownma.gov/public_documents/GeorgetownMA_Admin/
  un_cem_preservation_plan.pdf

This historic cemetery, established in 1732, was the original public burying space for the newly established West Parish of the town of Rowley, which later separated from Rowley and became the independent town of Georgetown. This cemetery started out on a small scale, but expanded to its current size with the additional purchase of lands, and in 1844 became known as Union Cemetery when its management was given over by the town to a private company. However, by the 1970s, the cemetery was little used and was no longer being maintained, so the town took control of the cemetery again. The earliest gravestones found here date to 1732 and are interesting examples of the stone carver's art, but perhaps the most interesting stone here is that for a once-enslaved African American named Cuffee Dole (1743–1816). In his life he experienced the worst excesses that white society in New England had to offer African Americans, but his gravestone demonstrates that by the time of his death he had become, in the eyes of that same, albeit evolved, society, "a respectable man of colour."

The best account of Dole's life, from which the following basic facts are drawn, is Christine Comiskey's book titled *A Respectable Man of Color: Beyond the Legend of Cuffee Dole* (2008), in which she presents a thorough study of Dole and the community in which

Gravestone, Cuffee Dole, 1816, Union Cemetery, Georgetown, Massachusetts.

he was so closely connected. The early life and parentage of Cuffee Dole is undocumented, though anecdotal accounts recorded by 19th century town historian and librarian Henry Nelson state that Dole was born free in the Boston area, but as a young child was placed in the care of a white woman so that his mother could work. This woman, perhaps seeing an opportunity to make some money or tired of caring for the child, sold Cuffee into slavery. He was subsequently purchased in Danvers, Massachusetts, by Moses Dole of Rowley, a farmer who owned over a hundred acres of land in West Parish and elsewhere, in the late 1740s. It is further stated that the white woman who sold Cuffee into slavery gained a conscience while on her deathbed in the late 1760s and contacted Cuffee's master. Cuffee reportedly made the trip to Boston to hear her confession and search for his mother, who by this time was deceased.

Cuffee Dole, who served as farmhand and general laborer for his master along with a slave black woman named Chloe, continued as Dole's slave for several more years, being listed as a servant for life in the Rowley tax rolls for the year 1771. Cuffee Dole seems to have gained his freedom in the spring of 1772, likely having saved up the money to make a down payment to purchase himself, and perhaps signing an IOU promising to pay his full value at a later date. Though Cuffee and Chloe are listed in Moses Dole's will drafted in February 1772 (not to be freed, but to live with one of his children after both he and his wife had died), when Moses Dole died in October 1772, only Chloe was listed as part of his estate holdings (valued at over 33 pounds). Cuffee, on the other hand, is only listed as owing Dole's estate just over 20 pounds.

As a free man, Cuffee Dole worked as a farmer and common laborer in the area of Rowley and Andover. During the American Revolution he served for two brief terms of service, the first time for a four month term in late 1777, serving in the company of Captain Benjamin Adams in Colonel Samuel Johnson's regiment of militia. This unit reinforced the Continental Army in New York and took part in the fighting against the British at Fort Ticonderoga and during the Saratoga campaign in the Battle of Bemis Heights. Later on, in late 1780, Dole enlisted again and served for six months in the New York–New Jersey area, mostly performing garrison duty. After the war he returned to the area and is listed a resident of nearby Andover in the 1790 federal census.

By 1800 Cuffee Dole returned to Rowley West Parish and would here live out the remainder of his life. Early on, Dole lived with the Rev. Isaac Braman, who was ordained at West Parish in 1797, and was likely paid to work Braman's farm as well as perhaps tend to other chores. He was likely uneducated while enslaved, and it was probably Isaac Braman who taught Cuffee Dole to read and write. By 1806 Dole had saved enough money to buy his own farmland, purchasing a 12-acre spread in West Rowley for $650, but apparently still lived with his friend, the Reverend Braman. This land is now owned by the town of Georgetown and is part of the Lufkins Brook Conservation Area on West Street.

Dole worked as a farmer for another ten years, but as old age caught up with him, he sold his farmland in April 1816. With the help of the Reverend Braman, Dole drafted has last will and testament in July 1816, listing Braman as his sole executor and giving all his possessions to various Braman family members, but also stating: "I order my body shall be decently buried" (Comiskey, pg. 19). It is in this small provision, a standard one for most people, that later trouble would arise. When Cuffee Dole died on August 17, 1816, the final disposition of his remains resulted in a unique controversy. The church deacons appeared to be divided on where Cuffee Dole should be buried. Though he was a church member in good standing who had even contributed to the funds to purchase a new bell in 1815, some deacons believed that because of his color he should not be buried among the white town members. Other deacons, led by the the Reverend Braman, believed that Dole's soul was as good as anyone else's and that he could be buried in the West Parish burial ground without restriction. In the end, the two factions had to compromise, with Cuffee Dole being buried at the rear portion of the cemetery in an isolated spot. However, the Reverend Braman had the immediate last word on the topic when he composed Cuffee Dole's gravestone epitaph, not only citing his respectable status, but also writing "White man turn not away in disgust; thou art my brother; like me akin to earth and worms," a statement surely directed at the deacons and townsfolk who disregarded his counsel when it came to Cuffee Dole's final resting place.

In later years the Dole burial controversy, while never entirely forgotten, subsided, likely because of the fact that as the cemetery grew, Dole was no longer buried in an isolated spot, but is now in a nearly central position (his gravesite is not hard to find) in this expanded place. However, the controversy, as evinced by the direct evidence carved on Dole's gravestone, is an important reminder that even after the institution of slavery had died out in Massachusetts, it would take many more decades before African Americans truly gained a fuller measure of respect from their fellow white citizens. The cemetery is well maintained and Dole's finely carved stone is in excellent shape.

One other person of color, from the 1840s or 1850s is also known to be buried here and has a gravestone, but I could not locate it in 2014. As Comiskey points out in her book, it is likely that other African Americans, most of them slaves, are also interred here. According to West Parish church records, ten other individuals of color died in town between 1741 and 1799, including five children; Candace Dole (1740–1760), the servant of Edward Dole; and Delia Paul (died 1799), a free black woman (Comiskey, pg. 22). If buried here, they surely lie in an area not far distant from where Cuffee Dole was laid to rest.

Joseph Brown and Mary Burial Sites
Old Burial Hill
Orne Street
Marblehead
http://www.oldburialhill.org/

This cemetery is one of the oldest and most historic colonial-era burial grounds in all of New England, and one of the most beautiful, with its spectacular view of Marblehead harbor. Visitors could easily spend the better part of a day exploring this place notable for its finely carved gravestones. One of the lesser known aspects of this ancient burial place is its small but significant African American connection; as with most other early Massachusetts seafaring towns, slaves were brought here early on, well before the end of the 17th century. Those who died here were buried in typical fashion, most of them having no markers placed over their graves.

Despite this fact, Old Burial Hill has within its confines what is perhaps the oldest extant gravestone for a slave in all of New England, that for three year old Mary, a "Sarvant" (this term often mistakenly given as her last name), who died in 1699. This stone is found in row 11 in the grouping of graves found between the paths near the entrance on Orne Street. It is a small stone, low to the ground and easy to miss, but it is there, amidst the larger stones for many of the members of the town's prominent white families. No last name is given on the stone, nor are her parents listed (as was common for white children), so it is unknown for certain which family may have owned Mary. This stone is both a touching and stark reminder that many African slaves were brought to New England, literally stolen from their mothers and fathers, and trained in what would become their lifelong duties at a very young age, even before they could care for themselves.

Mary was not the only early black burial in Old Burial Hill; the stone for "Agnis Negro" (1675–1718), a servant woman to Samuel Russell, once stood near the seamen's monument at the top of the hill, but was lost after 1914. Could Agnis have been Mary's mother? While this is certainly possible, there is no way of telling at this late date. These are just several examples of the lost or hidden stories of the early African Americans who lived and worked in old Marblehead. There are likely many other African Americans buried here whose graves have gone unmarked, as the town had at least twelve free black heads of families enumerated in the 1790 federal census, including Cato Payne, Pomp Foster, and London Champlain, with many more unnamed black individuals residing with the masters for whom they worked.

One black individual buried here, however, does have a story that is well known and celebrated in town, namely Joseph "Black Joe" Brown (1750–1834), the husband of Lucretia (1772–1857), or Aunty 'Crese, as she was affectionately referred to by her fellow townsfolk. She was born in Marblehead, the daughter of two former slaves of Captain Samuel Tucker. Joseph Brown has an attractive narrative that fits in with Marblehead's prominent Revolutionary War and maritime history, highlighted by that of native son General John Glover (who is also buried here). Brown himself, the son of a black mother and Gay Head Indian father, was a slave for the first decades of his life, but likely gained his freedom as a result of his service in the Revolutionary War. In January 1776 he enlisted in Captain Francis Felton's company of Marblehead militiamen, which was employed in guarding the Massachusetts coastline, and served until the end of August of that same year.

Brown's later activities or service, if any, during the war are unknown, but by the late 1780s when many blacks, most former slaves, were being warned to depart town, Joseph Brown was gainfully employed. By 1795 he had saved enough money to buy part of a saltbox home for himself and his wife on Gingerbread Hill, which they co-owned with Joseph and Mary Seawood. After Joseph Seawood died, his widow sold the rest of the house to the Browns, and here they would live for the rest of their days.

Brown decided to open a neighborhood tavern which, depending on your outlook, was a famous or infamous establishment, noted for its rough clientele (black and white men alike, many of them fishermen or farmers), drinking (of course), gambling, and dancing. In fact, this building, built in 1691 and still standing today, is said to have some of the original pine floorboards that are still broken due to the excessive dancing that took place, and Joseph Brown's old fiddle hangs in the parlor.

However, it is not just for their tavern that the Browns are remembered, it is also for the tasty treats that Lucretia Brown baked in their home on the aptly named Gingerbread Hill. As with many free African American women, this was one of the few ways that Lucretia Brown could help support their family. Her "Joe Frogger" cookies made of rum and gingerbread, named after her husband, were a favorite with children and adults alike, and because they were said to never go stale, were a favorite among Marblehead fishermen. Her "Sir Switchells," made of molasses, were also remembered for years after her death (Weltner, pg. 2).

After Joe Brown died in 1834, Lucretia Brown lived in their house for another 23 years until her death in 1857. She was buried in the newer Waterside Cemetery in town, where a weather-worn stone marks her grave. Lucretia was remembered for the daily pilgrimage she made to her husband's grave at Old Hill. She supported herself by baking wedding cakes and making a perfume from rose petals that she gathered locally, as well as by receiving a widow's pension for her husband's military service.

The Brown house and tavern remained in their family until it was sold in 1867 by their adopted daughter Lucy Brown Fontayne. It has remained in the hands of the same family ever since, and is marked with a historic sign designating it as Black Joe's Tavern. In fact, the character of Joseph Brown has continued to be maintained in Marblehead to this day; Black Joe's Pond off Gingerbread Hill is one local landmark, while a wooded area surrounding the pond was designated the Joseph Brown Conservation Area in 1973 by town officials, all in addition to the patriotic grave marker erected in his honor after World War II.

Prince Hall Burial Site
Copp's Hill Burying Ground
Hull Street
Boston
http://www.cityofboston.gov/freedomtrail/coppshill.asp

This historic burial site in one of America's oldest cities was established as the second public burying space in 1659 and was originally called Windmill Hill, but gained its current name from the man, William Copp, who once owned the land. Much has been written about this place, a stop on the city's historic Freedom Trail, but one of its more hidden attributes is the number of African Americans, both enslaved and free, who have been buried here over the many years. Sadly, as in most large New England towns, few early black graves are marked here, though the number of burials for African Americans could easily be a thousand or more. In fact, a black community known as New Guinea thrived here for years, with most of their dead being buried on the Snowhill Street area where today there is much open space.

While there are some scattered gravestones for a few blacks, including Pomp Chew (1765–1803), the most important marker here is for the famed Prince Hall (1735–1807), the most prominent black citizen of the day in Boston and a true community leader. Much about his early life, including his birthplace (possibly in the West Indies) is uncertain, and many historians have claimed incorrectly that Prince was an indentured servant rather than a slave. Prince was in Boston by the 1740s and was the slave of William Hall; he married his first wife, a slave woman named Delia Trask, in the 1750s, and his son Prince (also known as Primus) Trask (he later went by Prince Hall, Jr.) was born in 1756. In 1762 Prince Hall joined the Congregational church in Boston and was married a second time to Sarah Ritchie, who was also enslaved. In 1770, after the events of the Boston Massacre and with a revolutionary spirit in the air in Boston, Prince Hall was manumitted by his master. That same year, his second wife having died, Prince Hall married Flora Gibbs of Gloucester.

To make a living, Prince practiced the trade of a leather worker and must have been respected for his work, as he made five leather drumheads for the Boston Regiment of Artillery in 1777. Prince Hall did serve in the American Revolution as well, but the full details of his service are unknown, as there were several different men with his same name.

Despite these interesting details, Hall is best known for his efforts that resulted in the establishment of the African Masonic Lodge beginning in 1775, one of the first African American organizations to be established in America. Ironically, the first efforts began with the help of British troops stationed in Boston, when Hall and fourteen other African Americans were allowed to join a Masonic lodge that was attached to the 38th Regiment of Foot. After the war began in April 1775, and after the British left Boston, Hall organized the African Lodge and continued its activities, but it was not 1784 until that the lodge received a charter from the Grand Lodge in England, with Hall as its Grand Master. While Prince Hall truly believed in the principles the Masons stood for, he was most interested in helping members of his own race; to that end, in January 1777 he was one of eight blacks, four of whom were also Masons, who petitioned the Massachusetts General Court to abolish slavery. His efforts here were not immediately successful, but they certainly helped pave the way for the wording in the 1780 State Constitution that did effectively end slavery.

In 1787 Prince Hall continued to advocate for African American rights, being the signer of a petition to the General Court asking that those blacks who were still enslaved should be

Portrait, Prince Hall, in Grand Master dress of the African Masonic Lodge he founded in Boston.

granted the right to work for themselves one day out of the week so that they could "procure money to transport ourselves to some part of the coast of Africa, where we propose a settlement" (Kaplan & Kaplan, pg. 207). This is perhaps the earliest known document by an African American leader advocating for a return of his people to Africa, the so-called "back to Africa" movement. Though this petition was never acted upon, Hall continued to advocate for the blacks of Boston, including later in 1787 when he sent yet another petition decrying the lack of educational opportunities for blacks, even though they too paid taxes.

Hall would continue to defend his fellow black citizens, whether it was over worker abuse, or free blacks' being sold into slavery, and would continue to do so right up to his death. His significance of the day can be measured in part by the fact that after his death, six Boston newspapers published his obituary. On his original gravestone, which can still be seen here today, Hall's status as the "first Grand Master of the colored Grand Lodge of Masons" is noted, this being followed with the erection of a large granite monument in his memory by the Prince Hall Grand Lodge in June 1835.

Visitors here should plan ahead, as Copp's Hill, like Boston's other historic cemeteries, is closely controlled and is open regular hours. The condition of this cemetery is fairly good considering its size, but it does have many broken stones, and because it sees a lot of tourist traffic, it is at time heavily littered.

Detail, Prince Hall Monument, 1835, Copp's Hill Burying Ground, Boston, Massachusetts.

Despite these shortcomings, Copp's Hill is a must-see and there are a number of historic signs placed here to help guide and inform the visitor.

Crispus Attucks and Chloe Spear Burial Sites
Granary Burying Ground
83 Tremont Street
Boston
http://www.cityofboston.gov/freedomtrail/granary.asp

This historic site on Boston's Freedom Trail was established in 1660, the third of the city's public burying spaces, and was first known as the South Burying Ground. It gained its current name when a grain storage building was built on the site in the 1730s where the current Park Street Church stands. Like Copp's Hill, the Granary has regular visiting hours and is in generally good shape, with signs denoting the historic personages buried here. The cemetery is best known for its Revolutionary War connections, as John Hancock and Samuel Adams, among others, are buried here. Also buried here, with a prominent memorial erected in 1906, are five of the victims of the 1770 Boston Massacre, a pivotal event in American history which helped precipitate the War for Independence. Interestingly, these victims, all of whom were white except for Crispus Attucks, were buried in a mass grave, a stark reminder that sometimes the fight for liberty against the British overrode all other social concerns.

Though the Boston Massacre is a standard in American history studies, a brief account here may serve to refresh the memory of the reader or visitors here. Since 1768 British troops had been sent to the city and were quartered in the homes of Boston citizens without any recourse. They were here to support an ineffective government that was under constant threat by Boston citizens due to the unfair taxation policies they vigorously opposed. This quartering of troops, indeed their very presence in the city, led to rising tensions between the British and Bostonians, which came to a head on the evening of March 5, 1770, when some of the British soldiers who were out and about that evening abused and taunted some citizens on the street and got into a scuffle with several young men. When troops came out of the nearby barracks with their swords drawn, this caught the notice of other citizens in the streets, causing the church bells to be rung, which led to more people pouring into the streets.

The group (some say mob) of citizens proceeded to walk to the Custom House on King Street and here taunted the one soldier on guard duty and pelted him with snowballs. The soldier soon called for help, and a squad of nine soldiers came to his aid; they drew their guns and pointed them at the American citizens. It was then that another citizen group arrived on the scene and had a verbal exchange with the British soldiers, calling them "dogs" and yelling that the soldiers would not dare to fire. The situation turned bloody when Crispus Attucks, according to a slave named Andrew, attacked the British officer, after which the troops fired into the crowd, killing Attucks, Samuel Gray, James Caldwell, Patrick Carr, and Samuel Maverick. Two other men, Christopher Monk and John Clark, were severely wounded and later died.

In the later trial of the British troops involved, defended by none other than John Adams, Attucks was painted as a troublemaker, but many saw him as a martyr.

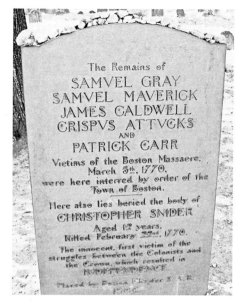

Top: Memorial Stone, Boston Massacre Victims, 1770, Granary Burying Ground, Boston, Massachusetts. *Bottom:* Gravestone, Frank, 1771, Granary Burying Ground, Boston. Little is known about this captive who was "servant" to the wealthy merchant and patriot who would later become the most famous signer of the Declaration of Independence.

But who was Crispus Attucks? He was born into captivity about 1723 and ran away from his master William Brown in Framingham in 1750. An imposing man, he was described as fair skinned and six feet, two inches in height. Attucks seems to have made a living as a sailor, and is said to have served on several whaling voyages; he may have been a free man by the time of his death, but this is uncertain. Local lore states that his father was from Africa and his mother a Native American of the Natick tribe. Indeed, the word "attuck" in their language means "deer" (Kaplan & Kaplan, pg. 8). While there is little known about the life of Crispus Attucks, his death at the hands of British soldiers in 1770 makes him widely regarded as one of the first casualties of the American Revolution, and thus worthy of remembrance.

As with Boston's other public burying spaces, it is unknown for certain how many African Americans other than Attucks may be buried here. While over 5,000 people are known to have been buried here, there are about half this number of gravestones today; many gravestones have undoubtedly been lost, but many graves went unmarked altogether. The site is also known for the many crypts and family tombs that can be found here, and it is within these that some, perhaps many, slaves and former slaves have been laid to rest.

One such known burial of this type to be found here is for the previously discussed Chloe Spear (1750–1815), a boarding-house owner and devout church supporter who chose to be buried in the Bradford family tomb at her death, beside the master who had once whipped her for daring to learn to read on her own. Her funeral was presided over by the well-known black minister Thomas Paul, "whom she was much in the habit of calling her *son*" (A Lady of Boston, pg. 90).

One other even more prominent African American woman with a connection to this cemetery is the poetess Phyllis Wheatley (1753–1784). She was captured in Africa and sold into slavery, purchased by merchant John Wheatley as a servant for his wife Susanna at the age of eight. Phyllis was named after the ship which transported her to Boston and was taught to read and write by the Wheatleys' daughter Mary. The frail Phyllis soon showed great literary ability, and in 1773 accompanied her master's son Nathaniel to England, not only to improve her health (sailing voyages at this time were thought to have a curative effect), but also to have a better chance to get her poems published. Phyllis Wheatley's poems were a great success both abroad and in New England. She published a volume of poems in England later in 1773 titled *Poems on Various Subjects, Religious and Moral*; in 1775 she sent to George Washington a poem she had written about him, and she met him in 1776 in Cambridge while he was busy organizing the Continental Army. By John Wheatley's will of 1778, Phyllis was legally freed and later that year married a black grocer named John Peters.

Though she was highly talented, the war years put an end to Phyllis's career, and life was hard for the young couple. Their first child died in infancy, and Phyllis attempted to support the family by publishing another volume of poetry; but the times were simply not right and the book never came to pass, though several poems

Portrait, Crispus Attucks, date unknown. This is a speculative view of what Attucks may have looked like.

were published in local newspapers. The couple did have another son, but times became even more difficult when John Peters was imprisoned for the debts he owed in 1784, leaving Phyllis to support their infant by working as a maid at a boarding house. Phyllis always seemed to have a frail constitution and the heavy burden of domestic work made her sickly; she died on December 5, 1784, and was followed just hours later by her young son. Despite the enduring mark she left on American literature, Phyllis Wheatley Peters's final resting place is unknown. Because her master John Wheatley is buried here at the Granary, many believe that Phyllis is also buried here, but there is nothing in the records to confirm or deny this.

Finally, perhaps the most intriguing marker here for an African American is that for Frank, the slave of merchant trader, patriot, and famed signer of the Declaration of Independence, John Hancock. Frank, who died on January 23, 1771, was one of a handful of household servants to the Hancocks, but little is known of his life. John Hancock grew up in a wealthy family and was used to the slave presence in his household. While he was in London on business for his uncle, he wrote home to his brother Ebenezer Hancock on December 27, 1760, inquiring about his family, including the household slaves. In this letter, he asks, in the flourishing handwriting for which he is famed to this day, "How is Molly, & how does Cate behave. Is Agniss a breeding, Is Prince as gouty as ever, & Hannibal as peevish as formally tell him I think of him, as he was the last of the family I saw on the Wharf. How is Thomas & in short all." While John Hancock, after taking over the family's successful merchant business, would also own slaves like Frank, he did not take direct part in the slave trade and later on, albeit after Frank's death, held antislavery views. Like many of the New England revolutionaries, his ideas on the subject of slavery, in light of the fight with England, had evolved. It should be noted that though Frank was given a decent burial with a properly marked grave, there are no terms of endearment on his gravestone, nor was he buried in the Hancock family tomb, where John Hancock was buried, but rather apart and separate from them. As one of the characters in Roy MacGregor's children's fiction book stated in stark fashion when viewing Frank's stone, "They didn't even give him a last name.... Just Frank, like he was the family dog or something" (MacGregor, *The Boston Breakout*, pg. 35).

African American Burial Site
Colored Cemetery
Off North Mill Street, behind Nantucket Cottage Hospital
Nantucket Island
http://www.nha.org/library/cemeteries/infomillhill.htm

This historic cemetery on Mill Hill was in use prior to 1805, when the town proprietors formally granted permission for the one-acre section to be fenced in and given to "the Black People" as a burying place. Since then it has always been known as the burying place for "Black People" or "People of Color," usually shortened to its present name. In 2008 the town board of selectmen debated the official name of this cemetery, and though some advised that the word "historic" be added to the name, they ultimately decided against what they felt was an example of so-called "political correctness." The cemetery, whose oldest stone dates to 1798, is close to the African Meeting House located downhill at Five Corners, which was built in the 1820s and served as a church and a school for the black community here. Since 2002 the cemetery has been fully documented and photographed and is in good condition, though some of the stones, because they are made of marble or limestone (originally a bright white in color, now often turned gray or black), have become weather-worn and lichen-stained, making some of them illegible. The wide expanse of open area here is indicative of the fact that many more individuals are buried here than the surviving 126 stones would indicate.

In the 1790 federal census there were 76 African Americans and individuals of mixed heritage enumerated for Nantucket, but by 1800 that number had jumped to 185, including the families of Seneca Boston (household of 6), Dinah Pompey (household of 2), Ephraim Simons (household of 3), Matthew Ross (household of 2), and Edmund Jones (household of 2), all of whom have family members with marked burial sites here. Though the influx of black residents on Nantucket after 1800 has usually been attributed to the abolitionist beliefs of the Quaker religion, which predominated on Nantucket from its earliest settlement, slavery did exist here well before this time, as early as 1659. It should also be noted that though this site is known as the Colored Cemetery, individuals of Native American heritage, primarily the Wampanoag people, as well as those of mixed Native and African American heritage (commonly called "mulattoes"), were also interred here due to the close relations that existed between these two minority groups. A final ethnic group that also has burials here are those from the Pacific islands, most of them men who had served as crewmembers on Nantucket whaling ships.

There are many interesting stories to be found in this cemetery that highlight the black history of the island. Among the burials here are four Civil War veterans, including Sampson Pompey (1830–1909), the son of Stephen and Sylona Pompey, whose military-issue headstone denotes his naval service. Pompey served in the early years of the war, in 1861–62, as a seaman on the receiving ship *Ohio*, followed by duty aboard the barque USS *Kingfisher*, which was based out of Key West as part of the Gulf Blockading Squadron. During this time, Pompey and the crew captured four enemy blockade runners and made several shore raids, losing two men. The ship returned to Boston in late 1862 due to an outbreak of scurvy, which event marked the end of Pompey's service. Within less than two months after the end of his service, Pompey married young Susan Kelley (1844–1904), and afterwards worked as a mariner for many years. Susan Kelley Pompey is also buried here. Yet another Pompey family member whose stone may be found here is Captain Edward Pompey (1800–1848); he was a mariner as well as a leader in the island's abolitionist movement, working closely with his fellow captain, Absalom Boston. He was well read and likely had one of the largest private libraries on the island.

Gravestone, Olaudo H. Boston, 1836, Colored Cemetery, Nantucket, Massachusetts. This young boy was likely named in honor of Olaudah Equiano, a freed slave who championed the abolitionist cause and gained worldwide fame for the narrative of his extraordinary life (courtesy John Speer).

In speaking of the Boston family on Nantucket, they too were a historic black family in terms of their achievements here; the most famous of them was Captain Absalom Boston (1785–1855), the father of former slaves Seneca and Thankful Boston. In 1822 he captained the whaling ship *Industry*, which he manned with an all-black crew, the first whaling vessel ever to be so manned, for a six-month cruise that netted 70 barrels of whale oil. Later on, Boston was a tavern owner on the island and was a leader in the abolitionist movement. His portrait is in the holdings of the Nantucket Historical Society, donated by Sampson Pompey in 1906 several years before his death. This portrait passed to the Pompey family after the death of Hannah Boston, Absalom's wife, in 1857. While there are marked burials for eleven members of the Boston family, those for Absalom and Hannah are unmarked.

Another interesting set of burials here are those in the family plot for the Rev. Arthur Cooper (1790–1853) and his wives, Mary Cooper (1785–1826) and Lucy Gordon Cooper (1798–1866). Arthur Cooper was a fugitive slave from Virginia (born in the Washington, D.C., area) who arrived on the island in 1820, along with his wife Mary, who was a free-black born in Massachusetts. They lived in safety here for two years, until in October 1822 agents for Cooper's former owner finally tracked him down and attempted to take not only him, but also his wife and children back to Virginia as slaves. With the help of the Nantucket Quakers, the agents' plan was obstructed and the Coopers were hidden in the houses of local residents. After his first wife died, Arthur Cooper married Lucinda "Lucy" Gordon (1798–1866) in October 1827. In 1832, Arthur Cooper was a founding member and served as pastor of the newly established African Methodist Episcopal Church, known as Zion Church, the second black church established on the island.

Despite these fascinating biographies, perhaps the most interesting and historic of the burials here is that for Eunice Ross (1823–1895); she was the youngest child of Mary Sampson Ross and James Ross, who was born in Africa and was prominent in Nantucket's black community, donating the land for Zion Church in 1832. As a young woman, she attended the African School in the African Meeting House located on York Street (today a stop on the Nantucket Black Heritage Trail) that had been established for black children by the African American community by 1827. By the time she was fifteen, Eunice Ross was probably the star student of the school's beloved young white teacher Anna Gardner (whose parents back in 1822 had hidden Arthur Cooper and his family in their home from fugitive slave hunters), and by age 16 in 1839 had aspirations to become a teacher herself.

While Ross had reached the limit of the educational opportunities available to black students of the day, with Anna Gardner's encouragement she applied for admittance to Nantucket High School, which had only recently been established in 1838. Eunice Ross was the only person of color among the eighteen students who took and passed

Gravestone, Eunice Ross, 1895, Colored Cemetery, Nantucket, Massachusetts (courtesy John Speer).

the entrance exam in 1840 and, not surprisingly, was the only student denied admission. This event ignited a racial conflict on the island that would last for seven years and have a wide-ranging impact beyond Nantucket's shores. While racism on one hand worsened on the island in the immediate aftermath of the decision against Ms. Ross, with the town library now off-limits to African Americans, the African American community was angered and rose to action, aided by white abolitionists. At this time, too, Anna Gardner quit her teaching position at the African School after four years of service, perhaps forced to resign by the town's white school committee.

In 1842 a motion to integrate the island's schools was passed at town meeting, but the very next day the decision was reversed. Abolitionists were able to gain positions on the school committee, and in 1843, after much maneuvering, they went ahead and integrated the school on their own without town meeting approval. The African School was renamed the York Street School, and hereafter students were to attend the school in their district, regardless of their color. But this was a short-lived success. In 1844 the citizens of Nantucket who opposed integration rose up and made their wishes known at town meeting in no uncertain terms, kicking many of the abolitionists off the school committee. The schools on Nantucket were again segregated, with all black students being sent back to the school on York Street.

This action precipitated a black boycott of the school, with Edward Pompey as a leading organizer, that lasted into 1845. Six petitions were subsequently sent to the Massachusetts State House seeking redress, the last one signed by Eunice Ross herself and describing her ordeal in being turned away from attending high school. Less than a month later, the State House passed a bill outlawing school segregation in all of Massachusetts, not just Nantucket. Ross and the black community, by their strong efforts and perseverance, had made history. However, equal opportunities were still slow in coming, and Ross was still unable to attend high school; incredibly, Nantucket officials ignored the law altogether and continued their segregationist policies, while the black community continued their boycott of the York Street School.

Finally, the schools on the island became integrated in 1846 after all the segregationist school committee members were voted out of office and were replaced with those in favor of integration. It was not an easy fight, and one has to wonder how it affected Eunice Ross; while fifteen students were subsequently admitted to the high school, and many assume that she was one of them, there is no evidence that Ross, now aged twenty-four, actually went back to school. Nor did she ever become a public school teacher, perhaps the greatest sacrifice that came about as a result of this controversy that otherwise gained blacks school educational equality.

Ross's later life is something of a mystery. She loved to read and was fluent in the French language, and it is possible she worked as a tutor (a black youth, William Miller, is recorded as living with her in the 1860 federal census). Anecdotal accounts state that Eunice Ross lived with her older sister Sarah, who supported the two by working as a domestic (Karttunen, pg. 1). No occupation is listed for Ross in any of the census records in which she appears, and she died from the effects of blood poisoning in February 1895. Though she is now widely celebrated and recognized for the part she played in getting the Nantucket schools integrated, for years she was largely forgotten except by the African American community.

IV. New Hampshire

Langdon Slaves Burial Site
Langdon Slave cemetery
1035 Lafayette Road, adjacent to Christ Episcopal Church
Portsmouth

This site, located right off busy U.S. Rte. 1 (Lafayette Road), is passed by thousands of cars a week; few of their occupants likely realize that this direct connection to slavery in the state is so near at hand. This small site, enclosed by a stone wall, contains the graves of at least fifteen individuals, each marked by a simple, unlettered fieldstone. While there is no documentary evidence to prove that this is a slave cemetery, oral tradition has long identified it as such.

The Langdon family is one of Portsmouth's and New Hampshire's most revered, as well as one with long connections to the state that date back to at least 1656. The best known of the Langdon family members is John Langdon, who was a wealthy ship captain and merchant involved in the triangular trade, and later an early U.S. senator and governor of New Hampshire, as well as an important leader during the American Revolution. His father John, Sr., grandfather Captain Tobias Langdon, and great-grandfather Tobias were all slave owners. The family was well established in the Sagamore Creek area of the southern part of Portsmouth by the 1690s and here had a large estate that was extensively farmed with the help of slave labor.

The various branches of the family owned a number of slaves over the years, beginning as early as 1699, when Captain Tobias Langdon purchased a young male slave (Sammons & Cunningham, pg. 41). Just how many slaves the Langdons owned over the years is unknown, but there are at least five mentioned in the records; in addition to the individual mentioned above, there was Hannah (purchased in 1716), Pomp (purchased 1743), Nanne (purchased 1763), and Violet (purchased 1773). It is likely that all of these individuals are buried here, though no burial records were kept, as was typical of the time in regards to slaves. Just when this cemetery was established is unknown, but it was probably established by the mid–1700s at the latest.

In addition to the slaves listed above for earlier generations, for many years beginning in 1783 prior to his death in 1819, Governor John Langdon had employed former slaves Siras Bruce and his wife Flora at his new mansion on Pleasant Street, built in 1784. While

Slave burial ground of Langdon Family Cemetery, Portsmouth, New Hampshire.

Flora died in 1798 during an outbreak of yellow fever in Portsmouth and is likely buried elsewhere, it is entirely possible that Siras Bruce, though not enslaved, is also buried here due to his close connection with the family, but this cannot be proved and his burial place remains unknown. In direct contrast to this site, which is on a distant corner of the original Langdon estate, is the Langdon family cemetery (located off Elwyn Road on what is now the grounds of the Urban Forestry Center); this site contains graves that are splendidly marked with finely carved slate gravestones. The dichotomy of these two sites for blacks and whites is typical of New England in general, and is entirely in keeping with the tradition of burial separation established by the owners of large landed estates in the larger slave-owning states of Rhode Island and Connecticut.

The Langdon slave cemetery is well maintained and protected by its location next to Christ Church, the site further enhanced by an informative historical marker erected by the Portsmouth Black Heritage Trail.

Slaves Burial Site
African Burying Ground Memorial Park
125 Court Street
Portsmouth
http://www.africanburyinggroundnh.org/

This historic place, which is both a burying ground and a monument to the many unknown individuals buried here, is one of the most interesting in all of New England and truly the most unusual in its presentation. The cemetery on this site, formerly called the "Negro Burying Ground," was established by 1705 and is the third oldest cemetery in this old colonial seaport. Its establishment in a location that was at one time on the far edges of the town settlement (then centered at the Strawberry Bank area right along the Piscataqua River) is an indicator of the growth of slavery and the corresponding growth of the black population in Portsmouth. How the town fathers came up with the idea of a totally separate burial ground for blacks is unknown and unique in New England, as most towns merely segregated a portion of their entire burial ground rather than establish a separate yard altogether. Indeed, this arrangement is more akin to the then prevailing private family burial practices, whereby families that held slaves had one burial ground for white family members, and one for their slaves. Whatever the case may have been for its establishment, the Negro Burying Ground continued in use for about 100 years until it fell out of use after 1803, though just as the first burial to take place here is unknown, so too is the last burial.

For many years, this area of town on Chestnut Street (once called Prison Lane and intersected by the appropriately named Fetter Lane) between State Street and Court Street (once called Jaffrey Street), was what we would today call the "bad part" of town. One local paper described the area thusly in 1853: "The old negro burial ground occupied that part of Chestnut street, and spread out rather indefinitely into both of them. The jail stood near, and made a kind of Golgotha of that then neglected part of town. Few bodies have been buried there for the last sixty years: it is said one person was buried there about fifty years ago" (*Daily Morning Chronicle*, June 24, 1853). Just as this burying ground was established for reasons of race and separation, so too was the site eventually taken over and erased; what was once deemed worthless land became much more valuable as the town of Portsmouth expanded and grew, and so it was that what was once land that was set aside for black burials (and likely the indigent as well) was taken back by its white residents and built over with paved streets, homes, and places of business. Whether this burial ground ever had any grave markers is unknown, as no markers were ever noted as being discovered when roadwork was done on the site over the years. It is likely that graves here were marked by simple fieldstones or wooden posts, or perhaps delineated by small stones, and that no professionally carved markers were placed here. At the time this burial site was being used, Portsmouth had no stonecutter practicing the trade and gravestones were imported largely from Massachusetts-based stonecutters.

Once this site was leveled and built over, it was largely forgotten, though evidence of its existence came to light from time to time. These various rediscoveries first occurred during the years when Portsmouth grew and became a modern town, with water lines, sewer lines, and electrical lines being laid. Indeed, from the 1850s onward, the discovery of coffins and human remains was a common occurrence during these municipal projects, and while these discoveries were sometimes noted, the remains appear to have either been discarded or reburied, without any further thought or investigation.

Since the 1960s, the knowledge that a black burial ground was located at or near Chestnut Street was commonplace, and was of great interest to historians and the local African American population as well. The dean of Portsmouth's black historians, Valerie Cunningham, included the site on the Portsmouth Black Heritage Trail after its establishment in

1995, marking it with a bronze plaque. However, the site remained buried until October 2003, when utility work in the area uncovered what would turn out to be the remains of thirteen individuals, both men and women and possibly children as well. Most of these remains were fragmentary in nature, some consisting of a single tooth only, though one nearly complete skeleton (burial #2) of a male, aged 21–26 at the time of death, was recovered. In addition, some artifacts, previously discussed in this work, were also recovered, including coffin fragments with eight of the burials.

This archaeological site, the only such example of its kind in New England, was extremely important for the information it yielded, but its study was also deliberately limited in scope. After the excavations of 2003, the site at Chestnut Street was filled in and the area repaved so that the street and sidewalk areas could be used as before. The remains were temporarily stored at a facility at the nearby Strawberry Banke Museum, and were later transported to a lab set up by the city of Portsmouth for further cleaning, processing, and study. All of these activities were handled with the utmost respect and in cooperation with

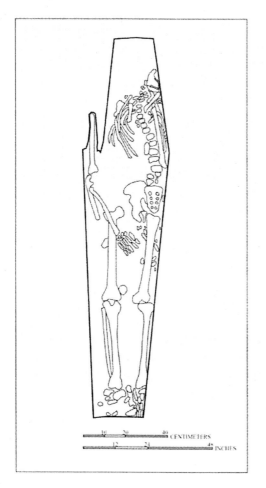 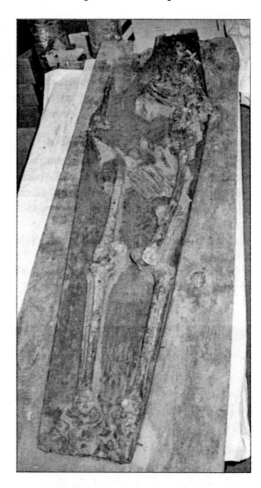

Plan and Photograph, Burial #2, African Burying Ground, Portsmouth, New Hampshire. This burial was the most intact set of remains recovered at this historic site. Illustration from "Archaeological Excavation at the Portsmouth African Burial Ground" (courtesy City of Portsmouth).

local black organizations. For instance, the lab room where the remains were processed was initially "dark and drab" (Marlatt, Wheeler, and Provost, pg. 46), but with the help of members of the Portsmouth Black Heritage Trail and others, the room was turned into a solemn and respectable place, the walls hung with tapestries and muslin cloth draped over the coffins and exposed piping in the rooms, while the Rev. Arthur Hilson of the New Hope Baptist Church visited regularly to offer prayers for the unknown deceased.

A further excavation of the burial site was made in November 2008 to determine an appropriate place for the erection of memorial stones, during which seven new graves were discovered in a very quick time. Upon consultation with members of the black community, it was decided by all parties involved that any further excavations would be halted and that these graves would be recovered and not further disturbed, though an examination of these new remains was also made. This decision was typical, in fact, of the amount of cooperation and trust that existed between all parties, especially the city of Portsmouth and the African American community, involved in the African Burying Ground project.

In addition to the archaeological work that was done, the city also established the Mayor's Blue Ribbon Committee on the African Burying Ground in late 2003, its mission being that of determining the best way to honor those buried at the site and what form any monument or memorial might take. Public meetings were held so that the voices of those in the community could be heard. This committee was (and still is) led by Vernis Jackson, the founder and president of the Seacoast African American Cultural Center. Public meetings were also held regarding the proposed memorial for the site, while the city council also had to approve what was being done. Two key members of the design team were Roberta Woodburn, the landscape architect, and artist and sculptor Jerome Meadows. The African Burying Ground Memorial Park is unlike any other public burial place in the city. Rather than just marking the spot with headstones, it was felt by the Committee members and design team that something more was needed, "a public place of reverence ... so that we will never again forget those buried beneath." The plan for the memorial park was finalized in 2008, and fundraising commenced by early 2009 with the establishment of the African Burying Ground Trust. While the city, through an Urban Development Action Grant, provided much of the funding, still more was needed, and this was provided by donations large and small from individuals, businesses, and organizations in Portsmouth and beyond. The funding effort was delayed by the economic downturn that began in 2008, but finally, in August 2014, work began on the memorial park. It was completed in the spring of 2015, when the remains excavated in 2003 were finally re-interred in a solemn and moving ceremony.

This site, open to the public, is entered from the Court Street side and features at its entrance a female and male figure sculpted in bronze, each on opposite sides of a granite slab, standing over seven feet, their hands nearly touching at the edge. From here, a red line cast in concrete leads toward the burial vault at the opposite end of the park, this line featuring some of the notable phrases from the 1779 petition for freedom by twenty of the enslaved from Portsmouth. Near the burial vault, where the previously discovered remains have now been reburied, there are life-size sculptures which depict men, women, and children, reflecting the Portsmouth community and its coming together to honor and remember those who are buried here. These figures are lit up at night and, whether day or night, give the site a unique human touch. In addition to these key features, the site is highlighted by decorative plantings and some key African cultural components that remind us, in part, that the individuals buried here were not only denied their freedom, but also their cultural heritage. These elements include a Sankofa symbol in mosaic tiles on top of the burial vault cover and a curved metal railing at the State Street end that features the designs found on traditional Kinte cloth from Africa. The site is a compelling one and offers a different side of Portsmouth history.

While, as has been previously stated, we will never know for certain who is buried here, the consecration ceremonies held at the site on August 17, 2014, proved to be an eye-opener for many in the public. While the ceremony was replete with rituals, prayers, and singing in the African tradition, it ended with a sobering event, the reading of over 200 names of African Americans (not including those enslaved, who were just known by their first names) who are likely buried here. This really hit home to those who were present just how large and important this burial site is; among the names that were read were Nero Brewster, Pharaoh Shores, Quam Sherburne, and Seneca Hall, all of them signers of the 1779 petition to the New Hampshire government asking for the abolition of slavery in the state.

African American Section
North Cemetery
Maplewood Ave. near North Mill Pond
Portsmouth

This picturesque cemetery, located adjacent to the historic North Mill Pond area of the city, was established in 1753 and is known for the burials of some of Portsmouth's most historic figures. These include General William Whipple, a wealthy merchant, slave trader, and one of New Hampshire's signers of the Declaration of Independence, as well as Governor John Langdon and Abraham Isaac, the town's first Jewish citizen. For about the first forty-three years of the cemetery's existence, no people of color are known to have been buried here, most of these individuals being buried in the "Negro Burying Ground" (now the African Burying Ground; see above) established by 1705. However, after this cemetery was apparently abandoned by the late 1790s, African Americans began to be buried here. Just how many were laid to rest here is unknown, but there are four marked black burial sites here for the Whipple and Spring families that give some indication as to the location in which these burials were assigned at the rear left portion of the cemetery, near the tomb of John Langdon.

Perhaps the first African American buried here was Prince Whipple (ca. 1756–1796), a former slave of General William Whipple, Revolutionary War soldier, and a recognized leader in Portsmouth's African American community. He was born at Amadou on the Gold Coast of Africa. Tradition states that he and his brother Cuffee Whipple (died 1820), also enslaved in Portsmouth, were the sons of an African prince who were sent to the colonies in America to be educated but were instead treacherously sold into captivity at Baltimore by the ship's captain. Prince and Cuffee eventually ended up being purchased by merchant William Whipple and were brought to Portsmouth about 1765 at the age of ten.

Black section, North Cemetery, Portsmouth, New Hampshire. At far right near the flagpole is the tomb for John Langdon.

Prince soon became a trusted slave for Whipple, and when the American Revolution broke out, he served two terms of military service with his master in 1777 and 1778. While African American historian William Nell wrote that Whipple was serving in the army in 1776 and was one of the men in Washington's army who made the historic crossing of the Delaware River on Christmas day in 1776, leading to the victory at the Battle of Trenton, this has been proven to be inaccurate. Prince instead first served with his master during the Saratoga campaign in the fall of 1777, and once again in 1778 in his master's militia regiment during the Rhode Island campaign of 1778. One other inaccurate piece of folklore surrounding Prince Whipple is the supposed sulky demeanor he exhibited when going off to war with his master, and his master's promise that, if Prince served well, he would be a free man at war's end. In fact, this is a myth, as Prince remained a slave until 1784, well after the time his service ended.

In addition to his military service, Prince was active on the home front advocating for the freedom of his people; on November 12, 1779, he was one of twenty Portsmouth slaves to sign a formal petition which was sent to the New Hampshire government asking for the abolition of slavery and that they be granted their freedom. This petition, of course, was tabled and never acted upon, but was nonetheless a historic moment.

After the war, Prince Whipple continued to serve General Whipple until being given his freedom in 1784; sadly, he would not experience a free life for long. While he and his brother Cuffee, now also free, bought a small house and had it moved to a parcel of land on the Whipple estate on which they were allowed to live, Prince died in 1796 at the young age of forty and was buried at North Cemetery. His grave since the late 1800s has had only a government-issue military headstone, and it is uncertain as to whether or not he had a previous grave marker.

Prince left behind a wife, Dinah Chase Whipple, whom he had married in 1781, and six children who were born between 1784 and 1794. Of his children, one died in 1791 and may also be buried here, while his daughter Esther Whipple Mullineaux is buried here and has a headstone. Prince's widow Dinah is also likely buried here, but has no gravestone to mark the location; she was nearly as prominent in the African American community in Portsmouth, as she, along with Cuffee Whipple's wife Rebecca Whipple, established the first school for black girls in town, called the Ladies Charitable African School. However, in her later life, decades after Prince's death, Dinah Whipple, like many widowed black women of the day, had a difficult time supporting herself. She received charitable assistance from North Church beginning in 1825, and later on in the 1840s until her death in 1846. It was the North Church that paid for Dinah Whipple's funeral expenses.

Prince and Dinah's daughter Esther Whipple Mullineaux (1784–1868) is buried here and has her own gravestone marker. She married a black sailor named William Mullineaux in 1801 and with him had two children, William and Anna. After her husband failed to return from a voyage, Esther assumed he was dead or missing and remarried in 1815, but when the North Church (of which congregation she was a devout member) learned in 1817 that Esther was still legally married, she was reprimanded by the leadership. She was forced to make a public confession of her sins, which she did on December 6, 1817, asking that God "wash me thoroughly from mine inequity" (Sammons and Cunningham, pg. 115). Nothing is known of Esther's second husband, so it may be possible that this marriage was annulled. Esther Mullineaux, described as a widow by 1827, lived with her children and other likely members of William Mullineaux's family, but by the 1830s was living with her mother Dinah in a small house on Pleasant Street. While Esther did received some charitable support from the North Church in the 1840s, she worked as a washerwoman to support herself and saved up enough money to buy a small house on Walden Lane in which she lived for the rest of her life. At her death, she left all of her estate, less funeral expenses including a suitable stone (now well-worn) that still marks her burial site, to the North Church with stipulations that it be used for missionary work.

The second black family with known burials in North Cemetery is that of Pomp (1763–1807) and Candace (1762–1807) Spring. Both were formerly enslaved; little is known about Pomp, but he was almost certainly the slave of the Rev. Alpheus Spring (born in Watertown, Massachusetts) of Kittery, Maine, and his wife Sarah (Frost) Spring, a native of York, Maine. The couple was married in 1769, a year after the Reverend Spring was ordained in that parish of Kittery that is now the town of Eliot. Pomp may have either been purchased after this time or could have been a part of Sarah Frost's dowry or even a wedding present. The Spring family had two individuals of color, probably Pomp and his mother Phyllis, living with them at the time of the 1790 federal census, but in June 1791 the Rev. Alpheus Spring died suddenly, and it is probably at this time that Pomp Spring and his mother either became free or left their former master's household and moved across the river to Portsmouth.

Soon thereafter, in November 1793, Pomp Spring married Candace Wentworth, a former slave from Somersworth. She had two brothers, Thomas and Scipio Fyal, who worked as laborers in the surrounding area, while Pomp had a sister married to his friend (and executor of his will) Caesar Whidden (Sammons and Cunningham, pg. 99). Pomp Spring not only supported his family as a baker, no doubt helped in great part by Candace, but was also a leader in Portsmouth's black community, being president of the African Society. He earned enough money by 1799 to purchase a house on Church Lane, and it was here the Springs would live the remainder of their short lives. Both died in 1807, just four months apart, with Pomp stipulating in his will that his body be decently interred. The gravestones for both Pomp and Candace are typical for the period and resemble those carved for whites

Gravestone, Candace Spring, 1807, North Cemetery, Portsmouth, New Hampshire.

found elsewhere in North Cemetery. They were carved by stonecutter Samuel Treat, a Connecticut native who had only recently come to town; his shop was located on Deer Street, not far from the Spring residence, and it is likely the two men were acquainted with one another. What became of Pomp and Candace Spring's various relatives and where they may be buried is unknown.

The North Cemetery is also the likely site of many other black burials, as the African Burying Ground was out of use by about 1800, but the names are unknown. It is also known that many victims of the 1798 yellow fever epidemic were also buried at the back of the cemetery, among them several individuals of color. The cemetery today is well-maintained and in good condition, with many stones repaired and reset since 2000 under the guidance of the Mayor's Blue Ribbon Cemetery Committee. The military headstone for Prince Whipple, however, is quite weather-worn and in need of a modern-day replacement. The cemetery also has both an informative historical sign and a New Hampshire state historical marker in place to orient visitors. At various times throughout the year it is host to a walking tour, making it a destination for historically-minded tourists and local residents alike.

African American Section
Winter Street Burial Ground
Front Street (Rte. 111) between Winter St. and Railroad Ave.
Exeter
http://exeternh.gov/recreation/cemeteries-national-historic-sites

This public burying space was established in this old colonial town, which served as the state's Revolutionary War–era capital, in 1742 when the land was deeded to the town by Col. John Gilman, though it had previously been used for Gilman family burials. The cemetery remained in active use for about 100 years before falling into gradual disuse after another town cemetery was established in 1844. This site for many years, up until the early 2000s, was in pretty sad shape, with many broken stones and seeing but little upkeep for some years. It has since 2006 been refurbished and is now in generally acceptable condition, though many broken stones remain.

Because of its origins, you will here, towards the front, see some finely carved stones for members of the Gilman family, who first arrived here in 1664 and whose descendants have served over the years as judges, government officials, and town ministers. However, if you go to the back of the cemetery (to the far left from the entrance gate off the Winter Street side), you will also see the black section, where the graves of several prominent members of Exeter's early African American families, including the Tashes, Halls, and Cutlers, as well as others for the Hitchings and Huso families, can be found. These gravesites speak to Exeter's prominence as one of the largest centers of black population in New Hampshire, second only to Portsmouth, after the end of the American Revolution, but also likely represent just a small number of the African Americans who are really buried here, most of them without any grave markers.

Perhaps the most well-known African American known to be buried here is Revolutionary War soldier Jude Hall (ca. 1755–1827). His original stone was once located here but was lost after 1900. A replacement stone was erected in his honor in 2000 which gives details of his life. Hall, who was a large man, standing about six feet tall, and very strong, was enslaved in nearby Kensington, owned by Philemon Blake. But when Blake sold him to another master, Hall resented the sale and ran away to the southwestern part of the state

Monument stone, Jude Hall, Winter Street Cemetery, Exeter, New Hampshire.

in 1775. When Hall gained his freedom is unknown for certain, but it was likely as a result of his enlistment for military service on May 10, 1775, in Captain Jacob Hinds' (a resident of Chesterfield, New Hampshire) company in Col. James Reed's 3rd New Hampshire Regiment. Hall subsequently served in the army for the entire war from 1775 to 1783, and was one of New Hampshire's longest serving and most battle-hardened soldiers.

Right from the start, Jude Hall was in the thick of things, taking part in the Battle of Bunker Hill on June 17, 1775; his regiment played a vital part in this battle, manning the rail fence at the base of Breed's Hill and bearing the brunt of the initial British land assault along with Stark's 1st New Hampshire Regiment. During this battle Hall was nearly hit by a cannonball that struck nearby; he was thrown some distance by the blast, but survived and continued the fight. He and the others in his regiment beat back the right wing of the British assault before running low on ammunition and being forced to withdraw. Hall would continue to serve in like fashion during the rest of the war, and while the details are too extensive here to note, he later gained renown and the nickname "Old Rock" for his service in the grueling Battle of Monmouth in June 1778 with the 2nd New Hampshire Regiment under Col. George Reid.

After the war, life for a free Jude Hall, as with so many other free blacks, was a difficult one. Shortly after his return home, in November 1785, he was warned to depart Exeter, but in January 1786 he married Rhoda Paul (born 1765). A native of Exeter, she was probably the sister or a close relation of the famed African American Baptist minister Thomas Paul (1773–1831) of Boston, who was born here. Between 1786 and 1802 Jude and Rhoda had ten children and lived in various locales in order for Jude to find work, including Stratham (likely in the Guinea Road area), on the Enoch Rowe place in Exeter for over a decade, and later in a cabin in the woods near a body of water known as "Jude's Pond," near present day Drinkwater Road. The Hall family was largely viewed as undesirable, being warned to depart Exeter twice more in 1795 and 1817, but the family gained some relief when Hall received a pension for his military service beginning in 1817.

Tragedy always seemed to be a part of the Halls' life; three of their sons, James, Aaron, and William, were kidnapped and sold into slavery, with only the last known to have survived the ordeal, later becoming a captain of a collier in England. Late in life, in 1822, Jude Hall was in the public eye when he became a key eyewitness in a local murder trial, the deed having taken place in the woods near Jude's home. After his death in 1827, Hall was buried in the old Winter Street Yard, while his wife Rhoda went to live with their daughter Rhoda Cook in Belfast, Maine, collecting a widow's pension until her death in 1844. The progeny of Jude and his later descendants were numerous in the New Hampshire Seacoast area; two grandsons, Moses and Aaron, no doubt influenced in part by Jude's military service, served in the Civil War, the former in the 3rd U.S. Colored Troop Regiment, the latter in the famed 54th Massachusetts Regiment.

As to the other black families with burials here, Tobias (1758–1834) and Dorothy (1775–1835) Cutler are also notable. Tobias was formerly enslaved in the town of Rindge, New Hampshire and gained his freedom after his service during the Revolutionary War from 1781 to 1784, performing mostly garrison duty. At war's end a now free Cutler moved to the seacoast area, where he met and married Dorothy Rollins of Stratham, the daughter of former slaves Caesar Paul and Lovely Rollins. The couple had two children, Mary and Rufus (1797–1864), the latter notable for being the secretary of the first society for people of color to be established in the state, an effort organized at Exeter in 1817 by Revolutionary War veteran London Daily and Rufus Cutler. The gravestones for both Tobias and Dorothy Cutler

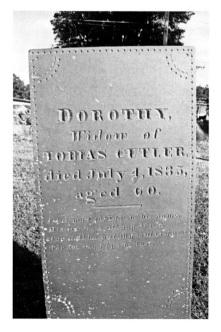

Gravestone, Dorothy Cutler, 1835, Winter Street Cemetery, Exeter, New Hampshire.

can be seen today, though Tobias's stone was defaced some time ago with what appears to be a black, tar-like substance.

Another notable black family with burials here is that of Oxford Tash (died 1810), the slave of Col. Thomas Tash of neighboring Newmarket. Oxford first saw military duty during the French and Indian War and later seems to have gained his freedom as a result of his service in the Revolutionary War beginning in early 1776. The full extent of Tash's service for New Hampshire during the war is uncertain, though he is known to have been at Fort Ticonderoga and there contracted smallpox. In early 1777, records show that he enlisted again for service, this time in the 11th Massachusetts regiment. He took part in the battles of Saratoga and Monmouth during his three year term, during which he was wounded in the thigh, the musket ball staying in his thigh for the rest of his life (Knoblock, pg. 234). After the end of his service in early 1781, Oxford Tash returned to New England, marrying Esther How Freeman, a native of the Cape Ann area of Massachusetts, at Newburyport, Massachusetts, in November 1781. After 1790 the couple returned to the area, living in Exeter for the rest of their lives. Esther Tash died in 1844 at the age of 86, having outlived her husband by over thirty years. While both are buried here, neither of their graves are marked.

The Tash family was a large one, the couple having eight children between 1784 and 1799. One son, Charles Tash (1794–1864), does have a marked grave here; this not surprising, as he was a man of some wealth, albeit also a tragic figure. He was a successful businessman who in 1847 advertised for sale nine properties that he owned, including four houses, but also fell in love with a white woman. When the relationship ended, he tried unsuccessfully to kill both himself and the woman he was involved with; a broken Gothic-style stone, now well-worn, marks his grave.

Gravestone, Mary Jane Hitchings, 1848, Winter Street Cemetery, Exeter, New Hampshire.

Finally, to end our discussion of the black families buried here we should notice those who came to town a bit later: Sarah Huso (1796–1879), a black woman of mixed heritage born in New Hampshire, about whom little is known; and Mary Jane Hitchings (1819–1848), the wife of George Hitchings. At last check Huso's gravestone, previously severely broken into six pieces and lying on the ground, has gone missing. Huso may have come from nearby Barrington, likely related to the Elsa Husow who married Revolutionary War veteran Cato Fisk there prior to 1792. Sarah's early life is largely a mystery, though marriage records for a son, Arles, born in 1828, married in Newburyport, Massachusetts, in 1857, by trade a hairdresser, indicate her husband's name was Ephraim. The 1860 federal census records her as living with a number of other family members, including Ephraim, John, and Thomas Husoe, all sailors and all likely her sons, as well as a woman, possibly her daughter, Ann Husoe, along with two children, George and Granville. Also listed for the household is a black sailor, a native of Pennsylvania named George Hitchings. He married a Portsmouth native, "negro" Mary Jane Usan, in 1837, but the marriage ended with her death eleven years later. In the 1870 census Huso is listed as a housekeeper living in Exeter with George Hitchings and his second wife Elsie and their daughter Sarah, with none of her family present in the home.

Wentworth Cheswell Burial Site
Cheswell Family Cemetery
Rte. 152, South Main Street
Newmarket

Unlike many of the small cemeteries described in this section, this family lot is located on a busy town road and is passed by many motorists and pedestrians almost every day. This cemetery was once an ordinary and neglected part of the town landscape; while many came close to its confines, which features an elaborate wrought-iron entrance gate, few people knew of Wentworth Cheswell and his importance to the town in the decade before the American Revolution and for over thirty years after America gained her independence. From the elaborate entrance gate to the site, perhaps the passerby had an idea, if a thought vwas even given, that here a man or family of importance was interred, but likely even fewer

Cemetery Gate, Cheswell Family Cemetery, 1861, Newmarket, New Hampshire.

people knew that Wentworth Cheswell was an African American. This has changed since 2002, when Newmarket resident and self-made town historian Richard Alperin took an interest in this cemetery. Alperin not only got it cleaned up and restored, but also led the effort to get a New Hampshire State historical marker placed here, which was done in 2007. So what about Wentworth Cheswell? What made him such an important figure that a town whose citizens are largely white would want to commemorate him 186 years after his death? Cheswell's life is in fact one that is both fascinating and one of historic import.

The Cheswell story in this part of New Hampshire begins with Wentworth's grandfather, an enslaved man known as Black Richard, sometime in the late 1600s. In 1707, his master, David Lawrence of Exeter, drafted a deed promising to give Black Richard his freedom in two years, in September 1709. How long Black Richard may have been enslaved prior to 1707 is uncertain, but he did gain his freedom at the time he was legally promised such, and quickly took the name Richard Cheswell (also given as "Caswell" or "Cheswill"). While little is known of his subsequent life, Richard Cheswell in 1717 bought, and soon after sold, a twenty-acre parcel of land in Exeter, making him the first ever African American landowner in New Hampshire.

Richard never formally married, but he did live with a white woman as man and wife and had a son named Hopestill Cheswell. This man, Wentworth Cheswell's father, grew to manhood and practiced the trade of a carpenter, building extensively in the area, including a building that would later serve as the Bell Tavern in Portsmouth. Hopestill also owned large tracts of land in Newmarket (which became a separate town from Exeter in 1737) and was quite well off. He married his wife, Catherine Keniston Cheswell, who was white, before 1746, the year of Wentworth Cheswell's birth.

There can be no doubt that Hopestill and Catherine Cheswell, like any parents, had high hopes for their son; they sent him to the prestigious Dummer Academy in Byfield, Massachusetts, to gain a formal education, rare for all but young boys from upper-class families in that day, and likely that school's first student of African descent. By the time he was a young man, Cheswell was a substantial property owner, having purchased from his father (who likely planned the transaction) a tract of land and some buildings at a young age. In 1767, now aged 21, Wentworth (who was named for New Hampshire's royal governor, perhaps yet another sign of his parents' aspirations), married Mary Davis, who was white, from nearby Durham. They settled down in Newmarket, where Cheswell had a fine mansion home, as well as a farm in his wife's hometown. Because of his mixed heritage, Cheswell was usually referred to early on as a mulatto, or as "the yellow man" due to his sallow complexion; despite his different look, however, race did not seem to be an issue with his fellow town citizens.

Wentworth Cheswell, indeed, was accepted as an active participant in the town's Revolutionary War affairs on many different fronts. He served as dispatch rider (a la Paul Revere) carrying patriot messages between his town and Exeter in 1775, and in April 1776 was one of the men in town, despite his mixed-race heritage, to sign the Association Test pledging his loyalty and support of the patriot cause. He was one of only two African Americans in the state, along with George Blanchard of Wilton (see below), allowed to sign this important show of political support. In 1777 Wentworth Cheswell also saw a brief stint of military duty for thirty days when he signed on as a private in Col. John Langdon's regiment of volunteers (consisting of mostly wealthy men), raised to support the American army in New York during the Saratoga campaign. It is for this reason that within the Cheswell family cemetery, in addition to his regular gravestone, there is also a government-issue military headstone.

After this service, Cheswell continued as an important figure in the town for three decades; in 1778 he was elected as a town delegate to the state constitutional convention (but apparently did not serve), and in 1780 was voted a town selectman, making him New Hampshire's first elected African American town official. In the following years Cheswell would serve the town in many capacities as an assessor, town clerk, town meeting moderator, and even as coroner. By all accounts, Cheswell was one of the most prominent and learned men of his time, owning a large personal library which served as the basis for the town library, which he helped to establish. He was also an avid town historian who gathered and organized manuscripts and data about the town. Among the individuals Cheswell had correspondence with regarding historical matters was none other than Jeremy Belknap, the former minister of Dover and New Hampshire's premier early historian.

Wentworth and Mary Cheswell had a long and prosperous life together, raising a family of eleven children, and losing two who died shortly after being born. Known as "Esquire" at the time of his death in 1817, Wentworth Cheswell died from the effects of typhus fever, while Mary survived as his widow for twelve years. Both are buried here, as are their children Sarah, Martha, William, Mary, and Mehetable, as well as some other related family members. Interestingly, Cheswell's daughters Nancy and Martha are given the title of "Lady" in the

Gravestone, Wentworth Cheswill (1817) and Mary Cheswell (1829), Cheswell Family Cemetery, Newmarket, New Hampshire. The stone on the left is a modern day replacement for the broken original.

1860 federal census, an indicator of the family's continued prominence in town for many years after Wentworth's death, and had an estate valued at nearly $9,000, greater than all but the town's wealthiest merchants and town officials. It was "Lady" Martha Cheswell who had erected the wrought-iron entrance gate, which features her name and an eternal flame motif, to the cemetery in 1861 six years before her death. Today, there are still descendants of Wentworth Cheswell living in the surrounding area, and though they are white in appearance, they take great pride in their African heritage and Cheswell's lifetime achievements.

The Cheswell family plot, with its eighteen marked burials, is one of the largest early African American family lots in northern New England. For many years prior to 2002 it was little maintained due to its status as a private cemetery, and many of its stones were broken. Along with many other individuals led by Alperin's efforts, the author took part in helping to clean up the cemetery and reset the stones in place. In 2004 a new stone for Wentworth Cheswell was crafted and set in place, with the original remnants now a part of the Newmarket Historical Society's collection. The cemetery is now well maintained and has an enhanced status as a historic site since the erection of the New Hampshire State historical marker (#209).

Moses Dustin Burial Site
Beech Grove Cemetery
Province Rd. (Rte. 107), near junction of Providence Rd. (Rte. 140)
Gilmanton

This cemetery is located in a historic village in the Lakes Region of the state and is a typical example of the cemeteries established in the first decades of the 1800s in New England. The site, still used for burials, was taken over by the town in 2009 and is well maintained, consisting of two sections, the first immediately visible upon entry, the second located straight back from the entrance beyond the first section and up the hill to the left. Most of the gravestones in this cemetery are not particularly distinguished, but there is one gravesite that is oddly placed compared to other burials from the same time frame: that for Moses N. Dustin (1830–1895), an African American man, native to the state, who served in the Civil War in the 54th Massachusetts Regiment. This pair of gravestones, the original government-issue military stone backed by one that was placed in modern times, stood alone on the far edge of the cemetery (it is now surrounded by several modern burials) almost outside the cemetery, and can easily be located by the granite bench which sits close by. The presence of a black veteran of the famed 54th located this far north in New Hampshire is unusual in and of itself, as few African Americans made their home in this part of the state, but what catches the eye even more is its lonely placement, far away from any other marked gravesites in Beech Grove. In fact, Dustin's burial site is a blatant example, hidden in plain sight, of the racism that still existed in New England at this late date, and, more specifically, demonstrates that segregation in public burying places was a common practice into the 20th century.

Of Moses N. Dustin's life, we know very little, as efforts to find out the names of his parents have proven unsuccessful. In some accounts he is confused with another man of the same name from Franklin, New Hampshire. Our Moses Dustin was born in Canterbury and was living there when he enlisted for service in the Civil War on August 19, 1863, in the 54th Massachusetts Regiment. Listed as being a farmer and married (his spouse's name is unknown, possibly Rose or Rosie), Dustin joined Company D of the regiment, serving alongside four other black soldiers, including fellow farmers Joseph Reed of Plymouth, George Cogswell of Laconia, and James Haskell of Warner, who joined the regiment from New Hampshire (only eight men from the state served in this regiment overall). Dustin joined the regiment after its heroic efforts to capture Fort Wagner and served until his discharge sometime after August 1864 at Penacook, New Hampshire, due to problems with varicose veins in his legs.

Gravestone, Moses Dustin, 1895, Beech Grove Cemetery, Gilmanton, New Hampshire. This view shows the original stone that marked Dustin's grave, while the modern replacement on the opposite side differs in that it gives this soldier's birth and death dates and the words "Civil War."

After the war, Moses Dustin continued to work as a farm laborer to earn a living. Between 1870 and 1880, according to federal census records, and probably later, he was employed as a farm laborer and servant in the home of John Kimball, a farmer of Canterbury, New Hampshire. No wife is listed in any census records for Moses, so it seems likely that she was out of the picture by 1870, and when and why Moses came to Gilmanton is unknown. Moses Dustin may have had at least one child, a son also named Moses N. Dustin, who enlisted in the U.S. Navy at Boston in October 1872, and possibly two others. This second Moses N. was listed as being "negro," seventeen years old, and was born in nearby Laconia, New Hampshire. A son of a Moses and Rosie Dustin, named Elvin, died in Manchester in March 1880 but was described as being "white," while a daughter of Moses and Rosie, described as being "black," named Lula Dustin, died in Manchester in January 1884. It is unknown if these were the children of the first or second Moses N. Dustin.

Just as his personal life is a mystery, so too is his time in Gilmanton; depending on what you read or who you talk to, local tradition states two variants of the same story. One has it that because of his color, no one wanted to associate with Moses Dustin when he was alive, and the same was true after he died, thus his remote burial. There is also given a variant of this account, with no evidence to back it up, stating that Dustin requested the remote burial because he said he didn't want to be near others from the town since they didn't like him when he was alive. Either way, while there is nothing in the records to show that Moses Dustin lived anything but a normal life ... that is, a "normal" life for a black man in rural New England. The results of this racial divide are still clearly evident today in the placement of his gravestone.

Interestingly, the placement of Moses Dustin's modern military headstone (which differs only in that it has Dustin's birth and death dates) is also indicative of the changing attitudes towards race in the 1960s. It was ordered by a local resident, Charles Sawyer, in the late 1960s or early 1970s "when Civil Rights legislation was still fresh" because he was "a little pissed that he [Dustin] was on the other side of the wall" (Daigle-Sawyer email correspondence, September 2012). Moses Dustin's original gravestone was removed at the time this new stone was erected and was subsequently left propped up against the side of a local home on Rte. 107 for years before being returned to Beech Grove in 2012. This cemetery can be difficult to find, as it is located at the end of a narrow, tree-lined dirt road that has no signs at its entry point. It is close to house number 567 and is on the east side of Province Road. This road is also only maintained seasonally and is inaccessible by car once snow accumulates and sticks around for the winter and early spring months.

Richard and Sally Potter Burial Site
Potter Family Cemetery
Rte. 11, Potter Place Village, adjacent to the train depot
Andover

This small family cemetery that contains but two graves is a little gem of history tucked away in scenic rural New Hampshire. At first glance, you might not even notice this cemetery, as it is located near a historic train depot complete with a rail car, while a cursory second glance might reveal a pair of seemingly ordinary gravestones. However, upon close inspection you will find that things get more interesting, as buried here is "The Celebrated Ventriloquist" Richard Potter (1783–1835), with his wife Sally Harris Potter (ca. 1783–1836) by his side. Not only that, but Richard Potter, a true wizard of the magical arts long before anyone ever heard of Harry Potter, was also of mixed African American descent and lived an exciting life as a renowned entertainer in early 19th century New England and beyond.

Potter's origins are uncertain and, like his career, somewhat exotic. He was born in Hopkinton, Massachusetts (not New Hampshire, as is often mistakenly stated), and was the son of slave Dinah Swain (who had five children while a slave servant), who was sold in Boston to Sir Charles Frankland, an official of the British Crown government employed as a tax collector in Boston (Tomlinson, pg. 403).

Potter Family Cemetery, Potter Place Village, Andover, New Hampshire.

The identity of Potter's father is somewhat of a mystery; church records give his father as one George Simpson, a white man, while others speculate that Frankland was his father. How and when Potter gained his surname is unknown, but he lived on the Frankland estate until he shipped out as a cabin boy on a sailing ship heading toward England at the age of ten.

Here, through unknown circumstances, Potter joined up with a Scottish magician named John Rannie (also given as "Rennie"), became interested in magic, and soon learned the so-called "black art" of magic. He worked with Rannie for some six years and returned with him to America in 1800, the two joining a traveling circus, a common form of entertainment of the day. Rannie and Potter continued together for the next eleven years; Potter became a noted ventriloquist, and is said to have been the first performer to use a dummy.

In 1807 while performing in Boston, Potter met a dancer from Roxbury named Sally Harris, and the two (both listed as being black) were married there in 1808. The couple had two sons, Henry and Richard, Jr., one of whom later lived in Portsmouth, New Hampshire, and worked as a magician. The couple also had one daughter, Anganet Potter, born in 1815.

Gravestone, Richard Potter, 1835, Potter Family Cemetery, Andover, New Hampshire. This stone was once broken in three pieces but has been repaired.

When John Rannie retired in 1811, Potter inherited all his props and equipment and worked as a performer for over the next twenty years; he was famed for his performances in Boston at the Exchange Coffee House and the Columbian Museum, but also performed as far south as New York City; Raleigh, North Carolina; Baltimore, Maryland; and possibly even in Alabama, earning on his engagements a thousand dollars, enough to make him a well-off man. While Richard Potter, recognized not just as America's first black performing magician, but also as America's first celebrated magician overall, performed many magic tricks, some of them scientific in nature, he concentrated on his ventriloquist skills most of all, and by 1833 had discarded magic from his act altogether (Tomlinson, pg. 403).

At the time of his death, which was followed soon thereafter by that of his wife, Potter was buried in a small cemetery in front of the 175-acre estate the couple had purchased in Andover, New Hampshire, in 1814, which was later sold by their children. Though the house, which had a wide open second-floor area where the Potters are said to have entertained their guests, later burned down, the cemetery was moved to its current location when the railroad was built in 1849. The gravestones for the Potters were once knocked down and broken, but have been repaired and the fenced in site is in good condition and well-maintained. The Potters' presence in Andover was relatively brief, lasting but 22 years, but the legacy and lasting impression of this once-famed performer has magically lived on; in

1871 the area in which they lived was renamed Potter Place Village, and the name has continued to this day.

Silva Marcy Kimball Burial Site
Webster Place Cemetery
End of Holy Cross Road
Franklin

Here, in this secluded cemetery that was originally part of the town of Salisbury (Franklin was not established as a separate town until 1828), is a small gravestone, the oldest contemporary stone to be found here, for a "black" girl that is representative of several things; most importantly, Kimball's final resting site offers direct evidence of the presence of the institution of slavery in northern New Hampshire, and New England, long after the end of the American Revolution. It is also the most northerly known burial site of an individually identified slave in New Hampshire. The presence of Kimball's grave has also presented some mysteries that may never be solved. So, who was Silva Kimball? Her elegantly carved gravestone has this epitaph;

In memory
of
Silva Marcy Kimball,
A faithful black servant
in the family
of
Thomas Thompson, Esq.
She died Decr 28, 1800
in the 14 year of her age.
She lived esteemed and
Died lamented.

This is all that is known about her for certain. As her stone states, Kimball was a servant in the home of lawyer Thomas Thompson, along with his wife Elizabeth. Thompson was a native of Boston who graduated from Harvard in 1786 and moved to the wilds of Salisbury, NH in 1794, here establishing a successful law practice. He is most notable for having been mentor to a young Daniel Webster, a native of Salisbury and future famed politician and orator. Several years after arriving in Salisbury, Thompson married Elizabeth Porter on December 25, 1796. Though virtually nothing is known of Silva Kimball's life, this event likely marked her arrival in Salisbury, for Elizabeth Porter was the daughter of Col. Asa Porter of Haverhill, NH, the largest slave-owner in northern New Hampshire. In the 1790 Federal Census, Asa Porter, who, as previously mentioned, was known to whip his slaves, is listed as having three slaves in his household, as well as one free, non-white individual, one of these slaves likely being Silva Kimball. It is very likely that upon her marriage to Thomas Thompson, Elizabeth Porter received Kimball as a gift, as was the custom for many years in New England among the wealthy, to help her in running her new household. It may even be that Elizabeth Porter had known Silva from her youngest days and that Silva was her personal attendant. While this scenario is most likely, it is also possible that Silva was a wedding present to the new couple from Samuel Thompson, Thomas' brother. He was a tobacco merchant in Newburyport, MA and through his business would have had direct access to the slave markets in such tobacco growing states as Virginia and Maryland. As to Silva's name itself, this also presents something of a mystery ... was she previously owned by someone named Kimball (likely), and, if so, where? Once again, we are presented with several possibilities, but no solid evidence, as Kimball families are found in both Haverhill and the area surrounding Salisbury, as well as in Newburyport. While some have speculated that Silva Kimball may have been simply a free-black working for the Thompson family, this seems unlikely as her own gravestone, purchased by them and made to their order, mentions first and foremost her status as a "servant," as previously discussed a polite euphemism in New England for household slaves. However, despite this status, there is ample evidence, the words carved in stone on her marker, that Silva

Gravestone, Silva Marcy Kimball, 1800, Webster Place Cemetery, Franklin, New Hampsire.

Kimball was indeed an intimate part of the Thompson household. Silva's final acts of service to the family probably came in acting as a helper to Elizabeth Thompson, who was about eight months pregnant when Silva died. We can imagine Silva taking on more and more responsibility as Elizabeth Thompson was coming to term, so her death was certainly a blow to the family, both emotionally and physically. Sadly, the Thompson family would endure further tragedy when their infant daughter Caroline, born just eleven days after Silva's death, would die on January 19, 1801, having lived just eleven days. Interestingly, both of the gravestones for Silva and Caroline are nearly identical, having been carved by the same stonecutter, either Paul or Enoch Noyes, in Newburyport, MA and later transported to Salisbury, all at considerable expense. There can be little doubt that both stones were ordered, purchased and erected at the same time, the two girls being laid to rest close to one another in an area that was once an isolated portion of the cemetery, but is now in a front center portion of a cemetery that has since grown in size, the closet gravestone near these two dating over three decades later. That Silva would have been an important caregiver for the infant Caroline Thompson is almost a certainty, so it is perhaps fitting that these two girls, though separated by color, would be united in death as they would have been in life.

This cemetery, located not far from the old homestead of Daniel Webster's family, lies at the end of a dirt road and is well-cared for, offering a spectacular view of the surrounding countryside.

African American Burial Site
Town Hall Cemetery
2 Main Street
Amherst

In this town, within its noted historic district, may be found the Town Hall Cemetery (also known as the Old Burial Ground). As its name implies, the cemetery lies directly behind the Amherst town hall, which was built in 1825, and, as events would later prove, actually covers a rear portion of the original burial ground. This cemetery is one of the finest Colonial-era burying grounds in southern New Hampshire and is known for its fine slate stones.

However, when new town hall construction was undertaken in August 2003, workers discovered the partial remains of three individuals (one adult female, one child of undetermined sex, and another adult of undetermined sex) that were buried in apparently unmarked graves sometime between 1770 and 1830. The remains for the adult female, upon examination by archaeologist Dr. Kathleen Wheeler, principal investigator for Independent Archaeological Consulting (the company hired to examine the site) and osteological analysis by Dr. Marcella Sorg at the University of Maine, Orono, were determined to be of possible African heritage, with further speculation based on proximity that this female may have been the child's mother. While there was much initial excitement and speculation about this discovery, the find was soon, within several months, overshadowed by the discovery of the African Burying Ground in Portsmouth, New Hampshire.

Ultimately, the findings in Amherst were indeterminate. Was this an African American mother and child who had been discovered in a section of the old burying ground that was once reserved for the enslaved or free people of color? The institution of slavery was well-practiced in Amherst before and even after the Revolution, and many free African Americans made this important town their home in the years after independence was gained, with 33 persons of color living here at the time the 1800 federal census was taken (most of them living in white households). Local records, however, make virtually no mention of these individuals or their burial sites, and even the town history only mentions one black family, that of Caesar Parker (who later died in Newport, Rhode Island, in 1858). That this find was a case of an unmarked grave that was forgotten by 1825 is clear, but the reasons for such remain uncertain. However, we must ask the question: who is it that was likely buried in this unmarked grave at the far back of the cemetery and was forgotten by the community? As experts have commented, an "African woman, arriving in Amherst with no other family, would be such a person easily overlooked" (Wheeler and Chan, pg. 7).

What is most curious is the town of Amherst's apathy toward this discovery. Town officials decided not to pursue DNA testing on the remains (though samples were taken) for reasons of cost, and by 2007 the remains were reburied with a simple stone stating "Remains Uncovered and Reburied August 2007." What might have been a unique chance to examine a different aspect of Amherst's historic past instead turned into a possible lost opportunity, and to this date the circumstances surrounding this particular burial site are little known in town and have been virtually forgotten. Samples of the remains collected in 2003 for

DNA testing remain in a laboratory in Massachusetts and have yet to be tested after over a decade, though their heritage could have been easily determined if the town of Amherst had desired such back in 2003.

In 2014 the author contacted the lead genetic scientist handling the remains, Dr. Bruce Jackson of the Boston University Medical School, a co-founder of The Roots Project, a molecular anthropology study begun in 2001, and Dr. Jamie Wilson, a post-doctorate fellow in the Department of Biochemistry at Boston University, about the status of these remains and enquired about the possibility of DNA testing. As of this writing this testing is yet to be performed. If the remains are in fact discovered to be of African origin, what further historic actions might be taken by the town of Amherst, if any, to highlight this belated discovery remains to be seen.

As to the possible African American identities of these individuals, records for the time frame in question are scant at best, with death records incomplete, warning-out records only fragmentary, and records of the poor and town support thereof almost entirely lacking. However, we do have some clues offered by census records. The 1800 federal census for Amherst identifies four independent black families, including those for Peter Lovejoy, head of a household of seven, and Jack Snow, head of a household of three. Snow likely arrived in Amherst from Andover, Massachusetts, where he paid highway taxes in District 14 in the year 1793. Both families disappear from Amherst by the time of the 1810 census, with Snow by then living in Hopkinton, New Hampshire, with no family members, making it a possibility that the people living with him in 1810, perhaps a wife and a child, had died by this time. Is it Jack Snow's wife and child who are buried in an unmarked grave here? The other possibility is that the burials here are for a member of the Lovejoy family, who also disappear from Amherst after this time. In either case, just as these African Americans lived lives that went largely unrecorded, so too will their final resting place remain uncertain.

Humphrey Parker Burial Site
Meadow View Cemetery
Foundry Street
Amherst

This cemetery is located near the center of Amherst and is a latter-day public burying space that was established after the Town Hall Cemetery became full. Only one early African American burial site is known to exist here, that for Humphrey Parker (1807–1861). Parker's gravestone, which was "erected by his friends" (black or white is unknown) is the only tangible remaining evidence of the most prominent black family to live in old Amherst. Caesar Parker (ca. 1756–1855), Humphrey's father, was originally from Boston and came to the area from Litchfield, New Hampshire, where he had been enslaved for some years. When he gained his freedom is unknown, but this was likely by 1800, about the same time that he married his wife, a white woman named Margaret Spear (1769–1854) from Weare, New Hampshire. The couple lived in the southern part of that portion of Amherst that became the independent town of Mont Vernon in 1803 and were enumerated in the federal census for that town between the years 1810 and 1850. Caesar and Margaret Parker had seven children (5 boys and two girls), Humphrey being the second eldest.

The family was supported by their small farm, but also relied on the kindness of their neighbors and fellow town citizens when times were tight. Caesar was said to be a fixture at any town celebration and was described as being "a jolly, good natured African, black as the ace of spades" (Secomb, pg. 907). There are also the standard stories in the Amherst town history that speak of Caesar's petty theft activities and the fact that the boys in town teased him, but it is interesting to note that Caesar Parker was respected enough that when he died in Rhode Island in 1855, his obituary was printed in *The Farmer's Cabinet* (February 22, 1855, pg. 3), a prominent regional newspaper published in Amherst. Caesar had gone to Newport, Rhode Island, likely to live with his daughter (who was married to a Baptist minister) in the months after the death of his wife. Caesar Parker was subsequently buried in the North Cemetery in Providence, Rhode Island, where his broken gravestone can still be seen today.

As for his son Humphrey Parker, described in most records as being "Mulatto," little is known of his life except that he lived with his parents on the family farm at least until their deaths, and possibly afterward, and earned a living as a common laborer. He died due to the effects of heart disease, but though he was likely a man of but little means, he had enough friends who saw fit to give him a properly marked grave. His gravestone, which faces away from the cemetery, can be found on a hillside at the far left edge of the cemetery, toward the back in an isolated area that was likely reserved for burials for the indigent, people of color, and others of low standing in the community.

Gravestone, Humphrey Parker, 1861, Meadow View Cemetery, Amherst, New Hampshire.

Blanchard Family Burial Site
Elm Street Cemetery
Elm Street (Rte. 101A), across from Mill St.
Milford

This old cemetery (established in 1788), now located in a heavily traveled area, is a pleasant and, once you enter its confines, quiet spot to visit, filled with many interesting slate gravestones dating from the late 1700s and the early 1800s. Of course many of the town's early families have interments here, but so, too, does a prominent African American family, that of George Blanchard. The finely carved stones for Blanchard and his immediate relatives are all located in the back right corner of the cemetery as you make your entrance directly off Elm Street. There is also an access point from the rear of the cemetery, and if you enter here, you will find them immediately on your left. As in every New England ceme-

Blanchard Burials, Elm Street Cemetery, Milford, New Hampshire.

tery of the same age as this one, the Blanchards were clearly buried in segregated ground at the back of the cemetery, but unless you know something about the family, there is nothing otherwise to indicate their color. This is due in part to the fact that the Blanchards had enough wealth to purchase their own gravestones and thus could control what was carved upon them.

The patriarch of this family was George Blanchard (1741–1824), who was first a resident of the neighboring town of Wilton before the 1770s. Nothing is known of his early life and whether or not he was once enslaved, but it seems likely that he was, as there were enumerated in the 1790 federal census twelve different Blanchard families in Wilton, all but one, that of George, being white. No matter what his prior status may have been, Blanchard was well-respected in Wilton by the time of the American Revolution. He not only practiced the trade of a veterinarian (a key part of any rural farming community), but also saw militia service for several months beginning in late 1775, being stationed at Winter Hill near Boston from December to January 1776, serving in Captain Benjamin Taylor's Amherst company. Blanchard's wartime service ended in 1776 when he hired a substitute to take his place in a voyage to Quebec (Knoblock, pg. 83), something that was mostly done by affluent whites. However, this practice was an accepted one and no one thought the worse of George Blanchard; he demonstrated his patriotism in another manner when he signed the New

Hampshire Association Test on June 3, 1776. This was an important step towards independence, as the signers of the Association Test were making a commitment to the cause, and sticking their necks out if the revolution were to fail. While blacks and Indians (as well as "idiots and lunatics") were prohibited by law from signing the test in New Hampshire, Blanchard, along with Wentworth Cheswell of Newmarket, was a rare exception.

George Blanchard was married either before or during the American Revolution and had one child, Hannah (born 1778), but his first wife Hannah died in December 1779. Within a short time Blanchard was married for a second time, to Elizabeth, and they had ten children (all born in Wilton), beginning in 1781 with James, who died after living only 35 days, followed by George Washington (1785–1812), John (1786–1828), Anna (1788), Hepsibah (1790–1867; died in Salem, Massachusetts, as Hepsibah Johnson), Timothy (1791), Ruth (1793–1872; died in Salem, Massachusetts, as Ruth Ruliff), and Sally (1795). Several of the Blanchard children are buried here, as well as two of Timothy Blanchard's children. In 1804 the Blanchards moved to Milford, living on a farm in the Mile Slip area, and in 1805 purchased a blacksmith shop on Union Square. Here George continued as a veterinarian, passing the trade on to his son Timothy, before his death in 1824, the same year that Timothy married Dorcas Hood. Elizabeth Blanchard (1750–1832) survived her husband by eight years before passing away.

Interestingly, the Blanchards may have been the most prominent black family of their day in Milford, but they weren't the only one. Also born here was future African American writer Harriet E. (Adams) Wilson (1825–1900), whose 1859-published work *Our Nig*, a semi-autobiographical account of her time spent in Milford as a young indentured servant, made her the first African American novelist in America. She was born free but was sent into servitude with a Milford family while young after becoming an orphan and worked in slave-like conditions until the age of eighteen. Her literary work was largely forgotten within a short time of being published, and it was not rediscovered until 1982. The work is now

Left: Gravestone, George Blanchard, 1824, Elm Street Cemetery, Milford, New Hampshire. *Right:* Gravestone, George Washington Blanchard, 1812, Elm Street Cemetery, Milford, New Hampshire.

considered a classic account of the racism that existed in New England even after the days of formal slavery had ended. While Wilson later moved to Massachusetts and died in Quincy, a statue in her honor was erected in Milford's Bicentennial Park in 2006 and is well worth a visit. It has been speculated, though no proof exists, that Harriet Adams may have been known by the Blanchards, perhaps being born on their Milford farm at a time when veterinarians like Timothy Blanchard also sometimes served as doctors to those of lesser status.

Amos and Violate Fortune Burial Site
Old Burying Ground
Rte. 124 (Mountain Rd.)
Jaffrey Center
http://town.jaffrey.nh.us/Pages/JaffreyNH_Bcomm/Cemetery/about

This cemetery and its immediate surroundings, which includes the picturesque 1775-built Jaffrey meetinghouse and 1810-constructed horse sheds, is one that is quintessentially New England in appearance. The well-maintained and neatly kept cemetery has many fine slate gravestones with interesting epitaphs and carvings, and at its entrance there is posted a sign showing a map of the cemetery and a listing of the prominent individuals buried here (a feature more historic cemeteries should consider).

Perhaps the most famous of the Jaffrey citizens buried here are Amos and Violate Fortune. Both were formerly enslaved in Massachusetts before coming to Jaffrey in 1781, just as the Revolutionary War was ending. The story of the couple's life in Jaffrey is an interesting one, and because of it the Fortune family legacy has loomed large in this town for many years and continues to this day. In 1946 the town became host to a summer lecture series entitled the Amos Fortune Forum (www.amosfortune.com), which offers free lectures to the public on a wide variety of current interest top-

Old Burying Ground, Jaffrey, New Hampshire. The gravestones for Violate and Amos Fortune are in the foreground.

ics, and in 1950 children's author Elizabeth Yates penned the classic story *Amos Fortune: Free Man*, which won the Newberry Medal for its distinguished contribution to children's literature. All of these attributes have made this site a popular destination for many visitors over the years.

As his finely carved gravestone states, Amos Fortune (ca. 1710–1801) "was born free in Africa" and, at an unknown time, became "a slave in America." The details of the first half of his life are scant indeed, as he does not appear in any records until 1752, when he was listed in the will of Ichabod Richardson, a tanner in Woburn, Massachusetts, and is promised his freedom within six years of his master's death (Lambert, pg. 5). This arrangement did not appear to come to pass, as in 1769 a Simon Carter of Woburn, an heir to Richardson, made an agreement to manumit Amos in return for several yearly payments, which were completed by Amos in 1770. How Fortune supported himself in the early years of his life as a freeman are uncertain, but he likely worked as a tanner, perhaps in his former master's tannery. In 1774 he purchased a small tract of land in Woburn and built a house.

The elder Fortune, desirous of companionship no doubt, had two known wives. His first wife was Lydia Somerset, an enslaved widow of color (much younger than Amos) with three daughters, whom he purchased from her master for fifty pounds in 1778 and soon thereafter married. Sadly, Lydia Fortune died just three months later in October 1778. Amos Fortune's second wife was Violate Baldwin (ca. 1729–1802), who was also enslaved; Amos purchased her from her owner in Woburn on November 9, 1779, for fifty pounds, and married her the very next day. As I've discussed previously, Amos Fortune's purchase of his two wives did not make Amos a slave-holder even if he did not formally manumit the women, as they were to him "his beloved wife" (Lambert, pg. 50). This is in direct contrast to the poorly chosen words used on Violate's gravestone.

The couple lived in Woburn for about a year and a half before moving to Jaffrey in the summer of 1781. It is unknown why the Fortunes made the move; perhaps it was at the encouragement of others or for better economic opportunities, perhaps to make a new home for themselves away from the locale in which they had been held in bondage for so many years, or maybe a combination of all these reasons. The Fortunes first settled on town land that was reserved for the minister (which the town did not have at the time) along modern-day Rte. 124. Like many new arrivals in town, they were, within a month or two, "warned" to depart the town. Town selectmen also warned incoming white families to leave town as a matter of course, as this was a standard practice at this time in many New England communities to avoid the poor from relying on the town for their support. But it seems likely that there was real concern about Amos Fortune, and probably not based on just his color, but whether or not this seemingly aged man would be able to support his family. The Fortunes, of course, ignored the warning and stayed in Jaffrey for the remainder of their lives, becoming well-regarded and active town citizens.

Amos and Violate Fortune lived on the land that later became the property of the Rev. Laban Ainsworth after he was hired by the town in 1782. They remained here until 1789, when Amos purchased a twenty-five acre lot of land (on what is now called Amos Fortune Road) on Tyler Brook. Here he built a house and barn (still standing today) and dug pits for his tanning business, which he operated for many years with a good reputation and success. At this same time, Fortune had help in operating his business, including a black man from Woburn named Pompey Freeman (aka Pompey Blackman), who died in 1790 and is likely buried here in an unmarked grave. Fortune also took on two apprentices in succession to learn the tanning business, the first being a black man named Simon Peter; the second, beginning in 1793, a white boy named Charles Toothaker. While these young men helped an aging Amos Fortune in his business, they received in turn the skills to become tanners themselves, as well as room and board at the Fortune homestead.

Also staying with the Fortunes were two black girls; one was named Polly Burdoo, whose father Moses had died, leaving her mother destitute and without the resources to care for her own children. Sadly, this girl died within a short time in 1793 and is likely buried in this cemetery but without a stone to mark her grave. Also a resident in the Fortune household from about 1785 onward was a girl named Celyndia, whom Amos called his "adopted daughter" (Lambert, pg. 17). This girl's parentage is something of a mystery, but she may have been the daughter of his first wife Lydia. In any event, she survived Amos Fortune and was taken care of in his will drafted in 1801 not long before his death.

These connections, along with his business dealings and his church membership (though likely he sat in a balcony on the second floor in an area set aside for black worshippers), made Amos Fortune an involved citizen in the town of Jaffrey, also highlighted by his participation in the founding of the town's first library in 1789. In his will, Amos Fortune did not forget the town of Jaffrey, directing that a "handsome present" be made to the church, while any money left in his estate after caring for his beloved wife Violate and purchasing gravestones to mark their graves was to go to the town to support the school in his district (Lambert, pg. 8). Both of these wishes were accomplished with the money that

Left: Gravestone, Amos Fortune, 1801, Old Burying Ground, Jaffrey, New Hampshire. *Right:* Gravestone, Violate Fortune, 1802, Old Burying Ground, Jaffrey, New Hampshire.

went to the town directly being used into the 1970s, not a bad legacy for a man and woman once held in captivity.

While Amos and Violate Fortune did indeed have their graves properly marked as directed by Amos's will, it is important to note that their graves are located at the far back center portion of the cemetery in what was then (1801–1802) an isolated portion of the cemetery, as was typical for most African Americans at this time period throughout New England. Though the site appears to be an integrated one, all of the marked graves surrounding the gravestones for the Fortunes were erected many years later.

V. Vermont

The Vermont in the Civil War website (http://vermontcivilwar.org/cem/) has an excellent cemetery database that highlights some of the veteran's burials at a number of the sites listed below.

Turner Family Burial Site
Village Cemetery
Middletown Road, just off Rte. 121
Grafton

Here, in this quaint village cemetery where burials date back to the late 1700s, you will find the dual monument for Alexander (1845–1923) and Sally Ann (1855–1933) Turner. This monument is of a standard modern type, likely erected after Sally's death in 1933. This stone, in and of itself, is not particularly interesting, and there is no indication from it that the Turners were any different from the town's other period residents. Despite this appearance of relative anonymity in this corner of Vermont, town lore tells a different story, for the Turners were a black family who arrived in Grafton after the Civil War and created for themselves and their descendants an amazing legacy that exists to this day in a town that is otherwise largely white.

This story begins in Africa, where Alexander Turner's father, Robert, the son of an African prince and an Englishwoman who was shipwrecked off the coast of Ghana, was captured and sold into slavery at Port Royal, Virginia. Here, on the large Golden Plantation, sometime after the 1820s, Robert married a Cherokee woman named Rose Berkeley. One of their children born into captivity was Alexander Turner, who as a teenager during the Civil War ran away from the plantation to the Union lines in Virginia and ended up with the 1st New Jersey Cavalry near Fredericksburg. With this unit the young Turner became an assistant cook, afterwards serving as an assistant to the regiment's surgeon, Ferdinand Dayton, who later served in the 2nd New Jersey Cavalry. Turner acted as a stretcher-bearer, carrying the wounded to the hospital, and was himself wounded in the hip during the Battle of Brandy Station in June 1863. Also in 1863, family tradition states that Turner guided his unit to the plantation where he has been cruelly treated and killed the overseer.

After the war, Alexander Turner moved northward to work in a quarry near Williamsburg, Maine, afterwards moving back south to work in Boston. Here he worked until 1872, when two sawmill operators from Grafton, Vermont, on a recruiting trip for workers, encouraged Turner to come to their town. This Turner and his family did in the fall of 1872, settling on Bare Hill, with Alexander working in the lumber trade. He eventually saved enough money to purchase several lots of land over the years, amounting to 150 acres, and established a farmstead on the Townshend Road that became known as "Journey's End."

Alexander Turner's wife, Sally Early Turner, was likely owned by the family of Confederate General Jubal Early. Together she and her husband had fourteen children, including their oldest son William (who served in the army during World War I); an infant son who died in 1882; a daughter Carrie who died at the age of eleven in 1888 (their burial sites are unknown); and their last child, Enough Turner. Members of Sally Turner's family also came to Vermont and lived nearby in Grafton, including her brother William Early and her sisters Zelma and Florida. The Turners attended the local Baptist church and were well-known and respected in town, with their white farmer neighbors treating them respectfully, a far cry from the treatment received by some early African American settlers like Jeffrey Brace.

While Alexander was a lumberman, the family also earned a living later on by boarding and entertaining summer tourists, many from Boston, at their farmstead. The Turners, indeed, became a vital part of the fabric of life in Grafton, their children attending school alongside their white classmates, and their family members still live in the area today. Alexander Turner suffered from the effects of rheumatism for years, and in 1916 attempted to gain a government pension for his military service, even though he had not been formally enlisted. At his death he was described in his published obituary as "a respectable citizen" and may have been the first African American to be buried in the Village Cemetery.

While there is not enough space here to devote to the entire Turner family story, no account of them is complete without mention of their daughter Jessie N., known as "Daisy" Turner (1883–1988). At her death, she was Vermont's oldest citizen and had been known for her dramatic storytelling for years in Grafton. Indeed, the importance of the stories she had to tell of her family's life in Grafton was not lost on local historians. As a result, some 60 hours of interviews were recorded with Daisy Turner and are now part of the Vermont Folklife Center's archival holdings at Middlebury, Vermont. However, the results of these interviews are also available locally at the Grafton Museum, which is located just down the road from the Village Cemetery. In fact, no trip to Grafton would be complete without a visit here, which features many pictures of the Turner family and homestead, as well as a well-produced video about Daisy and her family. As a result of this history, Grafton is a featured site on the Vermont African American Heritage Trail, and while the Turner farmstead buildings are no longer extant, the land upon which they lived has now become the Turner Hill Wildlife Management Area.

Finally, for those who want to see even more, take the short and scenic drive up Rte. 121 (Houghtonville Road) to nearby Houghtonville and turn left on Cabell Road; here you will find the Houghtonville Cemetery, where Daisy Turner and her sister Zelma (Turner) Grant are buried at the far back center, up against the fence. Quite fittingly, Daisy's monument has the simple epitaph "Journey's End."

Burdoo Family Burial Sites
Baileys Mills Cemetery
Baileys Mills Road, near Whitmore Rd.
Reading

This small, two-acre cemetery has burials dating back to the 1760s, but marked graves are only found here dating back to the early 1800s. One of the earliest of these is that for Betsey Burdoo (1743–1816), who was one of the town's first free black settlers, the wife of Revolutionary War veteran Silas Burdoo (1748–1837). Also buried here nearby is Silas Burdoo and his second wife Rosannah Burdoo (died 1836). This plot is one of the earliest known marked burial sites that have survived intact for free African Americans in the entire state and is indicative of the growing black presence in Vermont immediately after the American Revolution.

The Burdoos were a family of free blacks from the Boston area whose history has been well documented; their patriarch was Phillip Burdoo, a native of Africa who was likely enslaved but had gained his freedom by 1704 when he married Ann Solomon in Medford. This couple soon afterwards moved to Lexington, Massachusetts, and had six children, including Phillip (born 1709) and Aaron (born 1712), all of whom were born here and baptized in the church. Silas Burdoo was the son of Phillip and Mary Burdoo, one of four children, including one who died in infancy.

How Silas Burdoo made a living is unknown, but he likely first worked as a laborer, eventually making enough money to buy and farm his own land. He purchased land in Jaffrey, New Hampshire, in 1773, but still lived in Lexington. When the Revolutionary War broke out on April 19, 1775, in his own town, Silas Burdoo took part in the fighting later on that day along Battle Road, perhaps with a minuteman company from nearby Woburn. This was not the first time a Burdoo had seen military service, for Silas's uncle, Moses Burdoo, had served during the French and Indian War.

Soon after this initial service, Burdoo formally enlisted for service in the 9th Massachusetts Regiment in May 1775, commanded by Col. Samuel Gerrish, the unit largely performing guard duty in and around Boston. When Burdoo's service ended in December 1775, he declined to enlist again, instead living a civilian life before enlisting for a final time in September 1781 in Webb's regiment of Massachusetts militiamen raised for garrison duty in New York. Once this service ended in December 1781, Burdoo returned to civilian life for good.

Burdoo moved to his land in Rindge, New Hampshire, for a short time, but within a few years, by 1784, had moved further west to Reading. In the 1790 federal census he is listed as the head of a household of three, which included his wife Betsey (about whom nothing is known), and likely a child. What prompted this move to Vermont is unknown; perhaps it was the availability of inexpensive land, but Silas Burdoo was not the only black family to move to Reading, for his cousin Aaron was also here by 1790, also the head of a household of three. Together, the Burdoo families constituted the only black population in Reading at the time. Also buried here is Aaron Burdoo's first wife, Phebe Burdoo (1744–1818); he would marry a second time in October 1821, this time to Rebecca Dexter.

While little is known of Silas Burdoo and his time in Reading, it seems evident that he was well accepted by his fellow townsmen; he signed petitions regarding land allotment and road construction in 1807 and 1824, and when he applied for a pension in 1833 based on his Revolutionary War service, his good character was attested to by several neighbors and town officials. Little is known of Burdoo's first wife, though his second wife Rosannah (Brackey) Burdoo was a resident of Chester, Vermont, when they were married there in February 1818. Despite a dearth of knowledge about the details of their lives, their burial

sites in a major town cemetery are both indicative of the acceptance they gained in Reading, as well as their economic standing, reflected in the ability to purchase professionally carved gravestones on multiple occasions. Even after the death of Silas Burdoo, the presence of the family continued in the area for at least another seventy years; a namesake nephew, Silas Burdoo (1826–1900) was born to Aaron and Rebecca Burdoo. He served in the 54th Massachusetts Regiment during the Civil War, perhaps inspired by the service of his uncle, and later lived in South Woodstock for many years. His gravestone can be seen there in the Walker Cemetery, for which family he worked for over forty years.

Gravestone, Betsy Burdoo, 1816, Baileys Mills Cemetery, Reading, Vermont.

African American Section
River Street Cemetery
River Street, between Mountain Ave. and North Street
Woodstock

This quiet and well-maintained cemetery is an important site on the Vermont African American Heritage Trail and is perhaps the only tangible reminder of the small but thriving black community that existed in this historic town beginning in the early 19th century. Prior to 1800, few blacks lived in Woodstock; the 1790 federal census enumerated one unnamed black, likely a servant, in a white household, and the three person household of Cato Boston. However, by the 1830s and 1840s a small number of black families had moved to Woodstock, most of them coming from New Hampshire and Massachusetts. The arrival of these families no doubt coincided with the many incidents in those states involving the kidnapping and selling of free blacks into slavery in the deep South in the decades prior to the Civil War. The state of Vermont was perceived by many blacks as a safe haven due to both its northerly location, and the perceptions regarding its state constitution and the partial abolition of slavery.

Among the most prominent of the African American families living in Woodstock were the Wentworths and the Hazards, though they were not the only ones. Both of these families have burials in this cemetery, but unless someone today knew that they were African Americans, their burial sites would offer but few clues to this fact. However, the full acceptance of these families as full-fledged members of society must also be questioned. Safe though these families were from slave hunters in this quiet town, they were still seen as residents of lesser status, as indicated by their burial positions at the far back of the cemetery in a center section that was obviously reserved for people of color.

One of the most interesting of these black families of Woodstock was that of Charles B. Wentworth (1814– 1893). He was the son of Charles and Jane (Barrett) Wentworth, who were likely former slaves. They were married in Londonderry, New Hampshire, in October 1802 and later moved to Hanover, where Charles worked

Gravestone, Charles B. Wentworth, 1870, River Street Cemetery, Woodstock, Vermont.

at Dartmouth College as a janitor. His son Charles B. Wentworth was born in Hanover and later learned the trade of a barber. He married his wife Mary (Little) Wentworth (1809– 1893), a Vermont native, in Windsor, Vermont, in 1836, she likely being the daughter of Joseph Little (born 1785 in New Hampshire). The couple would subsequently raise four children, including William, Charles B., Jr., Frank, and Christiana. Like their father, Charles B. Jr. and William Wentworth also learned the trade of a barber.

Interestingly, all three Wentworth men would fight in the Civil War; they were among a number of black men from town, also including Austin Hazard, who first joined the Woodstock Light Infantry Company that was raised early on and became a part of the First Vermont Brigade, not as soldiers, but as waiters to the officers. These men served far from home for some months in Virginia, but when the decision was made to allow black men to serve in the army in segregated units, all of them joined the famed 54th Massachusetts Regiment in late 1863 and served until the end of the war in August 1865.

Charles B. Wentworth, Sr., who was an old man among Civil War recruits, was nicknamed "Old Duke" and served in Company B; he became stricken with illness, possibly sunstroke, during an inspection in September 1864 when the regiment was stationed at Folly Island, South Carolina. It later was reported that Wentworth's brain was still "mildly sensitive" to sunlight when his service ended in 1865. Despite this affliction, Wentworth lived a civilian life for many years before his death at the age of 79.

However, his son Charles B. Wentworth (1842–1870) was not so lucky. He was assigned to Company K of the 54th and served not just as a soldier (being charged fourteen cents for two mess plates he lost in 1864), but in February 1865, by Special Order #48, was assigned as a clerk in the Union Army's headquarters in South Carolina by Brigadier General John P. Hatch. In July 1865 Special Order #150 assigned Wentworth for "special duty" in the

Union Army's Ordnance Department under Capt. James Grace, in which department Wentworth ended his service. Neither of these positions was with the all-black 54th Regiment, but at a higher level involving the entire Union Army command in the area, a sign not only of Wentworth's reading and writing abilities, but also surely a measure of his hard work and trustworthy character. After his service ended, Charles B. Wentworth, Jr., survived but five years, becoming stricken with tuberculosis and dying at the age of 27 in 1870. His military-issue headstone, an early one for an African American in the state, was erected in 1879.

As for William Wentworth's (1838–1883) military service, he became a member of Company I in the 54th Massachusetts in November 1863, was detached for service as a boatman from March to May of 1864 in Florida and South Carolina, and in early 1865 was docked twenty-five cents from his pay for "ordnance lost through carelessness." His non-military life details are less well known; he was married to a black woman, Rhoda Maria Talbot Wentworth (1826–1906), in 1860 and the couple had five children, including at least one daughter. In 1906 Rhoda Wentworth, now widowed, was living with her daughter Louisa Robbing (born 1868) in Worcester, Massachusetts. In 1870, William and Rhoda Wentworth were living with her father, Sampson Talbot (born 1800 in Maine), a farmer in Boxborough, Massachusetts, with William employed as a farmhand. Both William and his widow Rhoda have standard period gravestones in the River Street Cemetery.

Another of the black families with marked burials here is that of the Hazards, including Austin (1829–1886) and James (1831–1890), as well as their sister, Roxanna Hazard Park (1827–1915). These burials are indicative of the family's long presence in Woodstock, all of them the children of Thomas and Belinda Hazard. The couple also had another daughter named Mary and another son named Thomas. Thomas Hazard (1800–1866) the elder, was born the son of Peter and Lucy Hazard in Shirley, Massachusetts, and lived in Barnard and Windsor, Vermont, before moving to Woodstock to practice the trade of a butcher. His father Peter Hazard (also born in Shirley) died in 1880 in Groton, Massachusetts, at the age of 101, and was known as "Uncle Peter" to his fellow town citizens. Thomas married his wife Belinda (Lewis) Hazard (1796–1894) in December 1824 in Norwich, Vermont; she was born in Sutton, New Hampshire, the daughter of former slave Caesar Lewis. In various census records over the years Belinda Hazard is referred to as "Lindy" or "Matilda" Hazard. Thomas Hazard did not have a long life like his father but was a well-liked man in Woodstock who had the nickname (not surprising for the time) "Uncle Tom." Belinda's father Caesar Lewis, like Thomas's, lived a long life; he was listed a resident of the poorhouse in Sutton, New Hampshire, in the 1860 federal census, his age given as 105 years.

Two of the Hazards' sons (both born in Barnard, Vermont), Austin and James, served in the Civil War in the 54th Massachusetts Regiment, both of them enlisting for service in the regiment in December 1863 after first serving as servants to officers of the Woodstock contingent in the First Vermont Brigade. Like his father, Austin practiced the trade of a butcher, but also worked as a day laborer. He lived in Pomfret, Vermont, as a young man, but by 1860 was married and living in Woodstock with his wife Rhoda and five daughters, Lucy, Julia, Frances, Harriet, and Emma. In 1863 Austin Hazard was working as farmer in Barnard, Vermont, when he registered for the draft. During the course of his service in

Company B of the 54th, Hazard was a cook, but also was frequently ill due to a severe chest cold he suffered as a result of the march the unit made from Jacksonville, Florida, during the Olustee campaign, in which the soldiers had to wade through a river at night in order to get to their camp (Fuller, pg. 141). Even after the war, Austin Hazard would suffer from the effects of his service, dying of rheumatism. In December 1868, Austin Hazard was married for a second time in Woodstock, this time to Martha Miller. It is unclear if his first wife Rhoda had died or if the couple was divorced.

Gravestones, Austin Hazard (1886) and James Hazard (1890), River Street Cemetery, Woodstock, Vermont.

As for James Hazard (1833–1890), he worked as a laborer in Woodstock in the area for years and by 1860 was married to Sarah Talbot Hazard (the sister of Rhoda Talbot Wentworth) and had five children, Sylvester, Ellen, William, Allen, and an unnamed infant. James Hazard became a member of the 54th Massachusetts in December 1863, but it is unclear if he was one of Woodstock's black men who served as a waiter in the First Vermont Brigade before being allowed to join the war effort as a true soldier. While subsequently serving in Company G, Hazard was stationed near the Union cannon positions at Fort Wagner, South Carolina, and suffered hearing problems after the war as a result (Fuller, pg. 142).

After the war, James and Sarah had two more children, Clara and John, between 1868 and 1871, but Sarah died in May 1871, probably during or shortly after giving birth to John. In the census for 1880, James Hazard has his two youngest children John and Clara, as well as his mother "Lindy," listed in the household. By one account, James, or "Jim" as he was usually called, was a landmark about the town of Woodstock for many years, being well-liked and one of the best workers. He died in tragic circumstances on July 18, 1890, in Grantham, New Hampshire; he and Charles Pratt had gone to Lebanon, New Hampshire, the previous day to watch a baseball game between the towns of Woodstock and Lebanon, and the next day went fishing in a local pond. During the outing the men's boat capsized and James Hazard subsequently drowned. His body was recovered by his fellow townsmen Frank Wentworth and Tom Mero after word of the accident was sent back to Woodstock. Hazard's body was subsequently brought home for burial, his grave in River Street Cemetery next to his brother Austin going unmarked until a military-issue headstone was erected around July 1897. A local paper published his obituary, stating: "A good citizen was Jim and people will miss him on the street" (*Vermont Standard*, July 24, 1890).

The other black Woodstock families that have members buried here are the Meros, the Parks, and the Harts. Hezekiah and Harriet Mero, both New Hampshire natives, were married in Woodstock in 1826 and lived here for many years. Among their children were four sons, Andrew, Charles, Edward, and Sylvester, who all fought in the Civil War in the 54th Massachusetts Regiment. Andrew Mero (1836–1870) is buried here, having died from tuberculosis just a few years after his service had ended, while two of his brothers, Charles and Sylvester, later moved to Worcester, Massachusetts, and are buried in the GAR plot in Hope Cemetery (see above). Also to be found here is Henry Park (1823–1908), also a member of the 54th Massachusetts; his family lived with the Hazards for a time before the war, and Henry would later marry Roxanna Hazard.

A final burial here of note is that of George Hart (ca. 1837–1917); he was a former slave from Louisiana who joined the 54th Massachusetts in December 1863, and after the war came to the state with an officer in the 7th Vermont Regiment, which had been stationed after the war in Louisiana. Hart, who was slightly injured by a fall during the Olustee campaign in Florida in 1864, would stay in the Green Mountain State for the rest of his life and, like many of the town's black veterans, was an active member of the local GAR post #82. Hart married Mary Ann Wentworth, the daughter of veteran Charles B. Wentworth, in 1866 and worked in town as a mason and laborer for many years prior to his death (Fuller, pg. 139). As can be seen from the preceding accounts of all these black families in Woodstock, all knew each other well and marriages between them were a common occurrence.

Finally, it should be noted that not all of Woodstock's African American soldiers survived their military service. Another man, Elisha Braddish (1833–1865), was a native of the town and may also have been one of those men who accompanied the First Vermont Brigade as a waiter to the town's officers in the early period of the war. He enlisted for military service in December 1863 and joined the 54th Massachusetts at Jacksonville, Florida. Braddish took part in the regiments fighting as part of Company K in the Olustee campaign and thereafter in South Carolina. After surviving this action, he subsequently died due to yellow fever at the Union Army Post Hospital in Charleston, South Carolina, in August 1865; it is unknown if Braddish's body was brought home for burial, as there is no gravestone or monument here to mark his possible final resting place. While the town recorded Braddish's death in their records, no mention is made of any possible burial site.

African American Burial Sites
West Street Cemetery
West Street (Rte. 4), next to railroad tracks
Rutland

This historic cemetery was established in 1817 but fell into disuse after nearby Evergreen Cemetery (see below) opened in 1861. By the late 1800s the cemetery was in such bad shape that many burials here were relocated to Evergreen, including several members of black veteran John Fuller's family (see below). Just how many of the town's black citizens are buried here is uncertain, but the West Street Cemetery is notable as having marked bur-

West Street Cemetery, Rutland, Vermont. The marked burials for African American veterans Pierson Freeman and William Scott are at far right, second row.

ial sites for two African American veterans, and is located in what was once called the West Parish of town. Its church was presided over by a noted African American minister for some thirty years beginning shortly after the end of the American Revolution.

The latest dated African American burial site here is that for William Scott (ca. 1821– 1870). He was a runaway slave from Maryland who settled in Rutland, married first to Adaline Scott, and by 1860 to Harriet Scott. He had five known children, including Margaret, John, Warren, George, who also served in the Civil War, and a daughter, Mary, who was married to black Civil War veteran John Fuller after the war. William Scott, who made a living as a farm laborer, enlisted for service in the 54th Massachusetts, along with his son, in December 1863, certainly one of the older enlistees. He was subsequently wounded in action during the Olustee campaign in Florida in 1864, sustaining a head wound that was the cause for his discharge from the service in May 1865. He lived for another thirteen years making a good living in partnership with his son George as a truckman, while his wife Harriet worked as a housekeeper. The 1870 federal census lists the Scotts as having an estate valued at $2,600, a tidy sum for the time for any citizen.

William Scott's gravestone lists his age as being seventy, and if true (former slaves were not always sure of their birth years), his service as soldier at such an advanced age is even more remarkable. Scott's gravestone, not of government issue but a private purchase, is indicative of the comfortable wealth of his family, and is also notable for its patriotic theme. The epitaph at the bottom (now partially obscured) reads "I have fought my last battle, I have gone to rest," a fitting sentiment not just for his military service, but perhaps for his life as a whole.

Close to William Scott, the visitor to this cemetery will find the gravestone for Revolutionary War veteran Pearson Freeman (1761–1847), a former slave from Massachusetts and the best known African American resident of the day in Rutland. His gravestone is of modern-day government issue and one of many such stones placed here during cemetery restoration efforts for all veterans in the 1970s. It is unknown if Freeman previously had a gravestone marking this exact burial site, but that he was buried somewhere in this cemetery is likely.

Pearson Freeman was born a slave in Connecticut and was sold several times before gaining his freedom as the result of his service during the American Revolution. At the age of nineteen in the spring of 1780, he was living in Waterbury, Connecticut, when he enlisted for three years of service in the 1st Massachusetts Regiment, serving first as a waiter to a Captain Ransom, and later in the Wagon Department under Major Amos Coggswell. Though Pearson saw no direct battle action, he traveled throughout New York and New Jersey as a wagoneer, including stops at Verplanck's Point and White Plains in New York, and spent the winter of 1781-82 at the Connecticut huts at Morristown, New Jersey. His most memorable service was participating in the transport of ten cannons, requiring ten yoke of oxen, from Peekskill, New York, to Philadelphia, and from there to Head of Elk, Maryland. There he remained with his unit until after the surrender of the British Army under Lord Cornwallis at Yorktown, Virginia, in October 1781. Freeman also recalled serving as a wagoneer for Moses Hazen's 2nd Canadian Regiment and General Samuel H. Parsons's brigade in New Jersey. Indeed, Freeman's travels took him many places to help keep the army supplied; he later stated in his pension application that he "knew generals Washington, Sullivan, Lafayette, Lee, Baron Steuben, and many other continental officers."

After his service ended in 1783, Freeman remained in Connecticut for a time, where he married his wife, Rebecca Moody Freeman (1766–1863) at Kent in 1790. Freeman also lived in Gilmanton, New Hampshire, and Woodbury, Connecticut, before moving to Rutland, Vermont, possibly as early as the spring of 1792 by one recollection, and no later than early 1793. Here he would raise a family and live the rest of his life.

Gravestone, Pearson Freeman, 1847, West Street Cemetery, Rutland, Vermont. This is a modern replacement stone.

Having learned the potash and soap-making trade in Connecticut, Freeman was employed in this line of work for several men in town when he first arrived. In 1795 the Freemans purchased land on North Main Street, where Pearson established his own potash or "ashery" business, making a living making soap and dyeing cloth. He later, by 1799, purchased additional land on which he built a home. The Freemans had eight known children: Roxanna, Rebecca, an unnamed infant son who died in 1799, Pearson Toussaint (1800–1830), Charity, an unnamed infant child who died in 1803, Henry (1804–1822) and Sampson (1806–1808), who died of whooping cough (Swan, pg. 142).

Pearson Freeman, without a doubt, was a colorful personality, and took pride in his heritage. In 1817 he placed a humorous newspaper advertisement for his dye business, stating: "The underwritten at his old stand, in Rutland ... not withstanding some fairer complexioned people, who pretend to make *all blue*, may assume to know more of dark hues, still continues to Dye Cotton, Linen and Sheep's Woolen Yarn Blue; and from twenty years' experience thinks that he knows how to fix this colour" (Hance, pg. 516). Two years later, when a competing business tried to sabotage his potash business in December 1819, Freeman placed an ad in the local paper claiming that the deed was done by "some malicious person with a view to injure the reputation of the chief of the *African Band*" (Hance, pg. 511). Both these advertisements offer interesting insights to the competition that sometimes existed between free blacks and whites in early New England.

In addition to his potash and dye business, Pearson Freeman was also something of a musician, his 1817 advertisement also mentioning that he had plenty of music and "every musical instrument" available. This love of music he obviously passed on to his namesake son, Pearson Toussaint Freeman, who in 1829 "would inform his friends and the public, who are fond of music and dancing, that he is at home and will furnish music for Cotillion Parties, Balls, Dancing Assemblies, &c, on the violin and flute.... He will likewise give instructions on the Violin, Bass Viol, Clarinet, Flute" (*Rutland Herald*, December 22, 1829).

After his death in 1847, Pearson Freeman was survived by his wife, Rebecca "Aunt Becky" Freeman for many years. A picture was taken of her several years before her death and was exhibited at the Rutland centennial in 1870. Like many widows, Rebecca Freeman had a hard life. She attempted to gain a widow's pension based on her husband's service, guided by the help of her daughter Rebecca; sadly, while Pearson Freeman had a pension for the last fifteen years of his life, his widow was denied the same benefit because she could not provide proof of her marriage to Pearson. In her pension application to the federal government, one white fellow townsman, Lott Keeler, wrote in 1847 of the Freemans, "They were colored people but very much respected."

The Freemans had many grandchildren, and the name survived in Rutland for many years after Pearson and Rebecca had died. One of the most notable of these grandchildren is Martin Henry Freeman (1826–1889), the son of Charles and Patience Freeman. Nothing is known of Charles Freeman, though historians speculate that he may have been an older son of Pearson and Rebecca, perhaps born in Connecticut. Their son Martin Henry Freeman became a prominent achiever, graduating with honors from Middlebury College in Vermont in 1849 and later becoming the nation's first black college professor at the Allegheny Institute in Pittsburgh in 1850. A notable figure in the field of African American education, Freeman also became a proponent of the back to Africa movement in the years before the Civil War. In 1864 he moved to Liberia, taking his family with him and working as a college professor at Liberia College in Monrovia. Freeman returned to the U.S. for a brief period in 1867–68, during which time he accepted the presidency of his alma mater, now called Avery College, making him America's first black college president. However, he returned to Liberia in 1868 and would remain there for the next twenty-five years, serving as the driving force behind Liberia College. Freeman returned to America due to health reasons in 1887 and stayed with his son in Pittsburgh, but also returned to Vermont one last time in November 1887. He subsequently returned to Liberia, arriving in early 1888. Martin Freeman died in Liberia in March 1889, his last words being "I can teach no longer" (Irvine, pg. 96). He was buried in that country.

In addition to the burials here for William Scott and Pearson Freeman, there are other Freemans buried here toward the back portion to the right that may also be related to Pearson Freeman. It can also be speculated that other black residents in town who died during the time this cemetery was in use were also buried here in graves that were unmarked. One final note about the West Street Cemetery and its African American connections is the fact that some of the first burials here, whether they were for white or black citizens, were likely presided over by the noted black minister Lemuel Haynes. He was installed as the minister of Rutland's West Parish in March 1788 and preached here for thirty years before his dismissal in 1818, the year after the West Street Cemetery was established. Noted for his Calvinistic doctrine, Haynes was the first black minister in America to lead a white congregation, first doing so in Torrington, Connecticut, and then in Rutland, where he was a beloved figure for many years. Of the 5,500 discourses he wrote and preached here over the years by his own count, some 400 were funeral sermons (Cooley, pg. 199). Whether or not the Reverend Haynes had any association with Pearson Freeman or his musically inclined son Pearson T. Freeman is unknown (and unmentioned in Haynes's 1836 biography), but likely; Haynes was an ardent supporter of music in his church, the parish having a choir and an organ, and the younger Freeman later gave bass viol lessons, an instrument commonly used in church services at the time.

Visitors to this cemetery need to plan ahead: its gate is always locked, with the keys available at town hall during normal weekday business hours. Weekend visitors may need to make some special arrangements to gain entrance. This cemetery has suffered from neglect and a lack of maintenance over the years; though it is in better shape as of this writing, with many broken or missing stones, especially those for military veterans, being replaced in the 1970s, much more needs yet to be done to restore it to its former glory.

The Rev. Lemuel Haynes, portrait, 1838, from Cooley's *Sketches of the Life and Character of the Rev. Lemuel Haynes.*

African American GAR, Veteran, and Pauper Burial Sites
Evergreen Cemetery
465 West Street
Rutland

This large cemetery, established in 1861, is yet another indicator of the historic presence of African Americans in Rutland. This burying place was a successor to the West Street Cemetery and was designed to have a park and garden-like appearance that was the hallmark of the rural cemetery movement begun in the first decades of the 19th century. The most evident of the African American burials here are those for four Civil War veterans and their families. A less obvious reminder of the many Rutland residents who were on the lowest rung of the town's socioeconomic ladder, both black and white alike, is this cemetery's pauper section, highlighted by its closely packed graves marked with simple stones that have no name carved upon them, but only a number.

Of the four Civil War veterans known to be buried here, two of them were buried in different parts of the cemetery, while two others were buried in or near the GAR plot reserved for Civil War veterans. Nathan Hayes (ca. 1817–1907), buried in section 18 in the far left front of the cemetery, has a patriotic gravestone with a flag emblem that denotes his wartime service in Company H of the 54th Massachusetts Regiment. He was born in Vermont and was practicing the trade of a teamster in Rutland when he enlisted for military service in December 1863 at the age of 45. Although he was in good shape at the time of his enlistment, his advanced age made his military service very arduous. Not only was he injured (non-combat related) while performing his duties, but he also suffered from the heat and exhausting conditions, tough even for recruits in their twenties, during the campaign in Florida. Hayes would later be discharged due to his disabilities and later received a disability pension.

For many years after the war he continued as a teamster. He and his Portuguese-born wife Margaret had several daughters, including Rhoda and Harriet, who later married a black veteran of the war from Woodstock, Sylvester Mero. Hayes was visiting his daughter in Worcester, Massachusetts, at the time of his death, his body subsequently shipped back to Rutland for burial. Hayes's wife Margaret is also buried here, as is his daughter Rhoda Hayes Brown.

Also buried in Evergreen Cemetery (section 29B) is veteran Cyrus Williams (ca. 1845–1896). He was married to Emily Dolby Williams of Middlebury, Vermont, in 1866 and with her had four children, George, Hattie. Elsie, and Louisa. Cyrus was the son of Cato and Eunice Williams and moved to Rutland from Pittsford, Vermont, with his parents by 1860. He enlisted for service in the war in December 1863, his father consenting to his enlistment because of his age. Cyrus Williams, soon after joining, contracted typhoid fever and would suffer the effects of this illness during the course of his service and after the war ended. He supported himself as a laborer and a janitor at Trinity Church while Emily worked as a domestic. In 1880 the couple was living in Troy, New York (where both of their parents were born).

The Evergreen Cemetery, like many burying places in larger New England towns and cities, established a GAR veterans' burial plot (located far back and to the right from the main entrance) sometime after the end of the Civil War, distinguished by its flagpole and enclosed by wrought iron chains connected to granite posts. This area of the cemetery has burials for two African American veterans who were active members of the town's GAR Post #14; buried within the confines of this enclosure is John Watson Williams (1842–1899), the son of Cato Williams and the older brother of Cyrus Williams.

In 1863, just before going off to war, John Williams married Helen Quow, and would later serve with her brother James Quow (buried in Hope Cemetery, Worcester, Massachusetts; see above) in the 54th Massachusetts. Williams enlisted in December 1863 and served

Grand Army of the Republic (GAR) plot, Evergreen Cemetery, Rutland, Vermont. The gravestone for black veteran John Williams can be seen at far left, with a GAR cast-iron marker beside it.

until after the war ended in August 1865. He worked as a farm laborer for many years after the war and died at a relatively young age due to pneumonia.

Not far away from the GAR plot may be found the monument for John C. Fuller (1842–1904), which is the largest grave marker for an African American in all of Rutland. Fuller's place of birth is uncertain, as census records list both Virginia and Pennsylvania, while his military records state that he was born at Rockingham, Vermont. Now aged 21 and practicing the trade of a farmer, Fuller enlisted for service in the war in Woodstock, Vermont, on January 5, 1864, and subsequently joined his regiment at Jacksonville, Florida, in time to take part in the Olustee campaign.

After the war, Fuller married Mary Scott of Rutland (whose father William Scott served in the war; see above). The couple had three children, Fred, Mary, and Anna, who all died before their father and are buried under the Fuller monument. John's wife Mary and his daughter Mary both died of tuberculosis on the same day, July 25, 1883, and were originally buried in the West Street Cemetery before being moved to Evergreen in 1896. Anna Fuller (1870–1885) died of typhoid fever in 1885 and was also buried in the West Street Cemetery before her removal here in 1896. The Fullers' son Frederick (1866–1895) died in Boston, but it is unknown if his body was brought back home for burial or just memorialized on the Fuller monument. Despite the tragic deaths of his entire family, John Fuller married

Pauper's Section, Evergreen Cemetery, Rutland, Vermont.

his second wife, Julia Williams, about 1885 and worked as a laborer and janitor in Rutland for many years prior to his death.

Finally, the Evergreen Cemetery is also notable for its paupers' burial site annex, located toward the back left area in a clearing separate from the main cemetery that is about the size of a football field. These burials were for those individuals who died while being cared for or supported by the town, and whose burials were also paid for by the town. As was the case in many towns throughout New England, these pauper graves were marked with simple stones that had no name, but merely a number that was recorded in public records to identify who was buried here. Sadly, in many locales these records were poorly kept and later were often lost, leaving the identity of these individuals a mystery. This same is true for Rutland, and while town poorhouse reports regarding those in town care who had died were published in Rutland on a yearly basis, the identities of those paupers buried at Evergreen Cemetery are uncertain. While most of these poor individuals buried here were white, some of them were also likely to have been African Americans, possibly including the previously mentioned Rebecca Freeman, the wife of Pierson Freeman. However, because the records for these pauper burials are scant and incomplete, the names of all those buried here will likely never be known for certain.

The Evergreen Cemetery is a beautiful and well-maintained cemetery, most of its gravestones and monuments in good repair. This is a large cemetery, so finding individual monuments can be challenging. The cemetery does have an office, but it only seems to be sporadically manned. For an index to burials and their locations, should this office be closed, the visitor should check out the nearby Rutland Free Library, located at 10 Court Street; their local history room (open on a regular basis) has materials which document this cemetery's burials. The holdings of the Rutland Historical Society, located in the old firehouse at 96 Center Street (open limited hours) also offer good resources for this cemetery.

African American Veterans Burial Sites
Old Greenwood Cemetery
Route 7, between Nason and Upper Gilman streets
St. Albans

This large, thirteen-acre cemetery, the main burying place for St. Albans and the surrounding area for ninety years until the opening of Mt. Calvary Cemetery in 1895, is notable for the many prominent local family members buried here, some of whom have local streets and roads named in their honor. However, located to the back and side of this cemetery, which is still active, are the graves for six black Civil War veterans, members of the famed 54th Massachusetts Regiment. While these graves in this northern Vermont city, located close to Canada and far from the famed battlefields of the so-called "war between the states," may seem unusual to those who are not Civil War enthusiasts, they are actually quite fitting. In a way, the soldiers' gravesites here in Greenwood, for both blacks and their more numerous white counterparts, combined with the fact that the war's northernmost land action, the Confederate raid on St. Albans in October 1864, was also fought here, brings together all the war's New England participants in this one small spot.

In all, at least four black families have soldiers represented here: the Braces, the Princes, the Phelpses, and the Garrisons. Many of these families lived in this town for years after the war ended and some still have descendants in the area today. In fact, most of these families were closely related, with several marriages taking place between them, and most lived close to one another in town. That these burials are located in close proximity to one another, several in the same row, in an area that was once at the back of the cemetery and was clearly reserved for black burials, is not surprising, as this was typical for the time, even after 1900. While these burials are well integrated within the current confines of the cemetery, a quick look at the surrounding stones clearly shows that most of them were placed here decades or more after these black veterans had died.

The most historically important black family represented here is the Brace family. Peter Brace (1848–1913) was the son of Theodore and Sarah (Prince) Brace and was the great-grandson of Jeffrey Brace, the former slave from Connecticut who served in the American Revolution and made Vermont his home afterward. As has been previously discussed, Jeffrey Brace, a native of Africa originally named Boyrereau Brinch, lived in several towns in the southern part of Vermont and was subject to harassment by an intolerant neighbor in Poultney before moving northward to Georgia, Vermont. In 1810 in St. Albans, Jeffrey Brace's memoir, titled *The Blind African Slave, or Memoirs of Boyrereau Brinch, nick-named Jeffrey Brace*, was published, giving an account of his life in Africa, his many years of captivity, and his travails as a freeman in Vermont.

Brace had at least three children, including his sons Jeff and Ishmael; Peter's father was the son of Jeff and Diana Brace (Winter, pg. 83). Theodore Brace, employed as a laborer and known in St. Albans for his talented fiddle playing, had several sons with his wife, including Peter, Jeffrey (who married Mary Phelps), Wyron (named after the first Jeffrey Brace's father), and Ethan Allen. Many of the Brace family members lived on LaSalle Street in St. Albans.

Peter Brace, like many of the men in the family, earned a living as a laborer; he enlisted for service in the 54th Massachusetts, possibly inspired by his ancestor's Revolutionary War service, in December 1863. He fought in the Olustee campaign in Florida in early 1864, and on November 30, 1864, was slightly wounded in the face during the Battle of Honey Hill in South Carolina. After his service ended, Peter Brace married Louisa Woodbeck, also of St. Albans, the couple having at least four children, Laura, Richard, Anna, and Bell, and possibly several others. Peter's wife Louisa, either deceased or divorced, was gone by 1885 when Peter Brace married for a second time to Rebecca Johnson.

Also known to be buried in this cemetery are three soldiers from the several Prince families that lived in the area: Abel Prince (ca. 1828–1890), Daniel Prince (1843–1913), and Isaac Prince (1844–1898). Abel Prince was the son of Henry (born 1790) and Hannah (born 1810) Prince and was born in St. Albans. He was employed as a laborer when he enlisted for military service in July 1863. Abel Prince joined his regiment at Morris Island, South Carolina, and subsequently served for the remainder of the war, participating in the Florida and South Carolina campaigns. For several months Abel served as a member of the regiment's Pioneer Corps, a specialized unit employed in both destroying enemy fortifications and railroads and cutting roads and building or repairing bridges so that the unit's soldiers could advance. At Camden, South Carolina, he became ill from the effects of sleeping on cold, swampy ground and would, as a result, suffer from rheumatism for the remainder of his life (Fuller, pg. 155).

After the war, Abel Prince continued to work as a laborer, supporting his aged father Henry Prince, with whom he was living by 1880. Abel Prince seems to have been a lifelong bachelor. Two other Prince men, possibly Abel's cousins, also served in the war for St. Albans. Daniel Prince, the son of George and Caroline Prince, enlisted for service in December 1863 and joined his regiment at Jacksonville, Florida, in January 1864 in time to take part in the Olustee campaign. He was subsequently mustered out of service after the war ended in August 1865. Shortly after his return home he married Esther Boucher, and with her had two children, Daniel, Jr. (born 1867) and Hattie. Before his death in 1913, Daniel Prince worked in the town for many years as a common laborer. The last man named Prince known to be buried here is Isaac Prince (ca. 1848–1890); this man's life details have been confused with another man by this same name that enlisted for Charlotte, Vermont, and is buried in Burlington. The Isaac Prince who enlisted for Saint Albans was born in Sheldon, Vermont, also the son of George and Caroline Prince. He was living in St. Albans when he enlisted for the war in December 1863, and because he was just eighteen years old, his legal guardian and brother, Daniel Prince, had to give his consent. Issac was a participant in all of the 54th's 1864 and 1865 campaigns, and his service ended in August 1865. Details surrounding his later life are uncertain, though he is known to have been married in January 1883 and likely worked as a common laborer until his death in January 1885. His wife Margaret (Gordon) Prince began collecting a widow's pension in 1890.

Finally, also buried here are William Phelps (1845–1905) and Alexander Garrison (1838–1883), who was married to Peter Brace's younger sister Dianthia Brace. William J. Phelps (born 1845) was the son of William and Rosannah (Prince) Phelps. He was working as a laborer when he enlisted for military service in March 1863 as one of the first members of the 54th Massachusetts Regiment from Vermont. Phelps took part in the unit's famed assault on Fort Wagner in South Carolina on July 18, 1863, as a member of Company C and lived to tell the tale, though he afterwards had docked from his pay the expenses for gun and equipment "lost at the charge on Wagner," totaling the hefty sum of $21.25. Later, in December 1863, Phelps was again charged for losing his Enfield rifle and bayonet and other accoutrements through his own "carelessness." Phelps was subsequently discharged from the service in August 1865 at Charleston, South Carolina, having served for nearly three and a half years and taking part in some of the hardest fighting in the war. After the war, Phelps returned to Saint Albans, marrying Mary J. Blanchard (listed in census records as being black), a native of New York, in June 1879. The couple had one child, Cythnia (born 1893), who married a member of the Prince family.

Alexander Garrison is the only black soldier buried here who was not a Vermont native. He was a native of Patterson, New York, and was living in Brooklyn by 1860, the son of George and Lucinda Garrison. He was working as a tinsmith apprentice when he enlisted for service in the 54th Massachusetts at New York City in April 1863 and subsequently served for the duration of the war. He served for a time as the cook for Company F and, like many of his fellow soldiers who took part in the assault on Fort Wagner, was charged for the loss of his Enfield musket and other equipment as a result of the battle. He was discharged from the service at Charleston, South Carolina, in August 1865, and by 1870 was a resident in Saint Albans, working as a laborer and married to Dianthia Brace. The couple had three children, Sarah, Arthur, and Ethan Allen, born between 1871 and 1880 before Garrison's early death in 1883.

The Greenwood Cemetery is in a quiet and beautiful setting, and though there have been incidents of vandalism as recently as 2013, the town has received financial help from outside groups to help pay for repairs. The gravestones within the cemetery are in generally good shape and are well maintained.

African American Burial Sites
Lakeview Cemetery
455 North Avenue
Burlington
http://www.enjoyburlington.com/Cemeteries.cfm

This 30-acre cemetery, established in 1871, is one of the most beautiful of the garden-style cemeteries to be found in all of northern New England. In addition to its stunning view (hence its name) of Lake Champlain, this cemetery is also notable for its many plantings, historic gate and chapel, as well as three fountains. This cemetery is also particularly notable for its many military burials, including those from the Civil War and World War I, some of whom are Medal of Honor recipients. Even the War of 1812 is represented here in the Tomb of the Unknowns, the final resting place for remains dating to that time that were uncovered during city street construction. Because Burlington was (and is) Vermont's major urban area, this cemetery also features sections that were set aside for paupers (the stones here numbered instead of named) and destitute or orphaned children. In short, this cemetery, containing over 4,000 burials (and still in use today), represents all facets of Burlington society from the 1870s onward.

The black community in Burlington in the 19th century in terms of numbers, as with other northern New England cities, was never large, averaging about one-half of one percent of the entire population, with the peak numbers, some 116 individuals in all, living in the city from 1880 to 1900 (Whitfield, pg. 103). In terms of percentage, however, the fifty-three blacks who comprised one and a half percent of the city's 3,526 residents in 1830 was the high-water mark, and from here, within fifty years, that population doubled as the city's white population grew at an even faster rate. Despite this significant African American population in the last decades of the 19th century, there are almost no reminders of this black presence to be found in the city today; no black church was founded here and Burlington is not featured on Vermont's African American Heritage Trail. However, there is one place in Burlington with some hidden reminders of its African American history, and that is here in Lakeview Cemetery. Here are found the burials for at least fifteen black individuals (and likely many more) from nine different families, not including those buried in unknown paupers' graves and those from later generations of black families who lived after 1900. As might be expected, many of these burials are for veterans, five who served in the Civil War, while another is for a member of the all-black 10th Cavalry Regiment that was stationed at nearby Fort Ethan Allen (see below). The rest of the known early burial sites are for some individuals who were Vermont-born and others who came from places as far away as South Carolina and Virginia.

Perhaps the first African American to be buried in Lakeview Cemetery was the Civil War veteran Israel Freeman (1844–1871); he served in the 43rd Regiment of U.S. Colored Troops, enlisting for service in December 1863 and joining his unit at Camp William Penn in Philadelphia in early 1864. He was born in Cavendish, Vermont, and had practiced the trade of a butcher before going off to war. At first Israel Freeman showed great promise as a leader and was promoted to sergeant, but in October 1864 was reduced to a private "on account of drunkenness," though by war's end had risen in rank again to a corporal. Freeman took part in his regiment's action during the war, including the disastrous Battle of the Crater at Petersburg, Virginia, in July 1864, and later on in other actions around Petersburg and Richmond. At war's end, he was at Appomattox Court House, being present when General Robert E. Lee surrendered, effectively ending the war. After the war, Freeman worked as a laborer, living with his mother Clarissa and his brother Leander Freeman, until he was murdered on October 26, 1871, in unknown circumstances. Freeman's marker was provided by the local GAR post, but at last check was down on the ground and quite weather-worn. Also buried here is Israel Freeman's mother, Clarissa Freeman (died 1893).

Another Civil War veteran buried here is Isaac Prince (1842–1898). He was the son of Isaac and Rhoda (Smith) Prince, born in Bristol, and was living in Charlotte, Vermont, when he enlisted for service in Company H of the 54th Massachusetts Regiment in August 1863. By this time Prince was married and had a young son named George (born ca. 1863), but the name of his wife is unknown. Also enlisting in the same company at this time with Isaac was his brother Henry Prince. One of the regiment's many replacement recruits after the assault on Fort Wagner, Isaac Prince saw action with the regiment for the remainder of the war in Florida and South Carolina. On April 18, 1865, just days after President Lincoln was assassinated, Isaac Prince was wounded in the right shoulder and foot at the Battle of Boykin's Mill in South Carolina. He was subsequently discharged from the service in July 1865 and returned home to Vermont, marrying for the second time to Maria Barney in June 1872. The couple had three children together, Walter, Alice, and Eva, and also raised Isaac's son George from his previous marriage. Isaac Prince was employed as a laborer in Shelburne and Burlington until his death in 1898. He is buried in the so-called "Free Ground" (lot 242) part of the cemetery; his gravestone was likely provided by the local GAR post and, at last check, was overgrown and obscured by plant growth.

Of the three other Civil War veterans buried here, Leander Freeman (1841–1917), was the brother of Israel Freeman and was one of the most well-known black men in Burlington during his day. He was born at Lincoln, Vermont, and was employed as a laborer in Burlington when he joined the 54th Massachusetts Regiment in July 1863, serving as a member of Company F. Like his brother, he was wounded in the Battle of Boykin's Mill in South Carolina near the war's end and was discharged due to his disability in June 1865. He would return to Vermont, where he worked as a laborer in a lumber yard and elsewhere in Burlington for the rest of his life. He was also very active in the local GAR post and took part in many Memorial Day parades (Fuller, pg. 136). In 1892 he married his wife, Marion Davis Freeman (the daughter of veteran William Davis); the couple had one child, Hortense. Interestingly, when Marian Freeman died in 1913, her gravesite in Lakeview was marked with a finely cut stone with a shield that nearly resembles those of government issue provided for veterans.

Also buried in Lakeview is yet another 54th Massachusetts Regiment veteran, William A. Davis (1828–1903); he was born in Castleton, Vermont, and was one of the older enlistees to serve in this regiment. Davis, a barber in his civilian life, joined the war effort at St. Albans in December 1863 and took part in the Florida campaign. By August 1864 had become so sick and unable to withstand the rigors of the field that he was hospitalized and transferred to the base hospital at Beaufort, South Carolina, where he remained a patient for the rest of the war until his release in June 1865. After the war, Davis continued the trade of a barber; he and his wife Elisabeth (1830–1891) had four children,

Gravestone, Marion Freeman, 1913, Lakeview Cemetery, Burlington, Vermont.

Marian, Frank, Anson, and Henry. A number of the Davis family members are also known to be buried here, in addition to Marian, including Elisabeth Davis and her son Anson.

A final Civil War veteran known to be buried here is former slave Thomas Green (1837–1905), aka Thomas Marais. He was a native of Virginia who was sold south to New Orleans to a wealthy slave dealer named Marais, to whom he became a trusted valet; learning to speak French, he accompanied his master on several trips to Paris. When the war broke out and the Union Army captured New Orleans, Green went to the Union camps to gain his freedom and soon became the servant of a Vermont officer, later going to Vermont with him (Fuller, pgs. 78–79). While at Leicester, Vermont, Marais joined the 41st U.S. Colored Troop Regiment in August 1864 (later changing his name back to Green). Green joined his regiment at Camp William Penn near Philadelphia and subsequently took part in the fighting at Fair Oaks, Virginia, and that around Petersburg and Richmond. On April 3, 1865, the men of the 41st U.S.C.T. were among the first Union troops to enter the captured Confederate capitol, of Richmond, and days later were present during the surrender at Appomattox Court House. The regiment was later sent for duty in Texas, where Green became ill and was discharged in September 1865. He then returned home to the South, later living and working in Maryland. However, Green returned to Vermont by 1890 at least, living first in Leicester and later Burlington, where he worked as a laborer and handyman, and was very active in the local GAR post. Green was married and had relatives in Virginia at the time of his death, but few details are known about these individuals. There are several other Greens buried here with marked graves, including a child (Ida Green) in the section for destitute children, that may be related to Thomas Green. Thomas Green's gravestone was donated by the local GAR post.

Yet another forgotten black veteran who is buried in Lakeview is Beverly Thornton (1846–1922); he was a native of Virginia, the son of Paul and Mary Thornton, who registered for the draft while living in Washington, D.C., during the Civil War, but apparently never served. He later graduated from the Hampton Normal and Agricultural Institute in Virginia in 1888 and worked as a schoolteacher in Hampton and Gloucester, Virginia, for some years. He joined the U.S. Army by the late 1890s, serving in Troop K of the all-black 10th Cavalry as cook; he retired by 1913 as a trained sharpshooter, having attained the rank of sergeant. Thornton served with his regiment both out west at Fort Robinson, Nebraska, and during the Spanish-American War in Cuba and the Philippines. In Cuba his unit took part in the Battle of San Juan Hill. A well-educated and respected man in his regiment, Thornton was an advocate for African American development and even gave lectures while stationed at Fort Robinson. He served with his regiment when it relocated to Vermont, and here retired in 1913 when the 10th Cavalry was reassigned. He first worked as a cook and lived in Colchester with his wife Sallie Conley Thornton (1862–1931), a native of Alabama and the sister of Thornton's fellow 10th Cavalry trooper, Quartermaster Sergeant Paschall Conley. Also living in the Thornton household were members of the Scruggs family, including his brother-in-law, Zan Scruggs, who is also buried in Lakeview. The Thorntons would late in life buy a farm in Winooski, where Beverly Thornton died; his grave seems to have gone unmarked until his wife Sallie died in 1931.

Of course, veterans and their families are not the only representatives of Burlington's African American population buried in Lakeview Cemetery; also to be found here are regular citizens, many of whom migrated here from the South after the Civil War. Their life stories are less glamorous and the details of their lives largely unknown, but are nonetheless important and indicative of the black presence in Vermont. Why these families came here is unknown, but was likely due to a search for greater economic opportunities and almost certainly to escape the oppression of the Jim Crow laws of the South. We can only imagine today the difficulty of making such a life-changing move so far from home, and are left to wonder sometimes at the outcome; were these black families satisfied at the new life they made in the Green Mountain State, or were they disappointed with their strange new surroundings?

Gravestone, Beverly (1922) and Sallie (1931) Thornton, Lakeview Cemetery, Burlington, Vermont (courtesy Barb Destromp).

Madison Paxton (1838–1925) was a native of Virginia, living here with his wife Jennie (a New York native). He worked at a lumberyard, while their daughter Frances worked as a machine operator in a shoe factory. Also found here are the graves for James and Ella Wyatt. James Wyatt (1839–1900) was also a native of Virginia; he and his wife Hattie, employed as a washerwoman, had two children, including Ella Nora (1869–1877) and a son named John, who was employed as an errand boy. Ella died due to diphtheria on Christmas Eve. Another black family with burials here is that of Abial (1839–1938) and Clara (1853–1916) Anthony, according to one historian "one of the more prominent and stable black families in late-nineteenth-century Burlington" (Whitfield, pg. 101). Abial was a native of Burlington, the son of Thomas and Amanda Anthony, and here married Clara Smith, a native of South Carolina, in June 1868. The couple had three children, Nettie, Albert, and Grace. Abial first worked as a barber for George Williams, and later opened his own barbershop, which he operated for many years.

The Lakeview Cemetery is city-owned and is still used for burials today. The cemetery office is open regular weekdays and the staff is very helpful. Many of the African American burials here are located on the southern edge of the cemetery. Lakeview Cemetery is well maintained, and though there are some broken stones in need of repair, restoration efforts appear to be ongoing. Though not a standard tourist destination for this vibrant city, historic walking tours are sometimes available.

African American Veterans Burial Sites
Fort Ethan Allen Cemetery
College Parkway (Rte. 15), near Fletcher Allen Hospital
Colchester
http://www.uvm.edu/~vtbufalo/

This military cemetery was established beginning about 1894, the same time when Fort Ethan Allen was built as a cavalry post for the U.S. Army. The army post, for the first fifteen years after its establishment, led a quiet existence, but this all changed in July 1909. It was then that the 10th Cavalry Regiment, one of four segregated African American regiments in the U.S. Army, arrived at their new post in Colchester, Vermont, a town neighboring the large city of Burlington. This city had been a center of abolitionist activity in Vermont decades earlier, but by 1900 Burlington had fewer than 120 African American residents, while Vermont as a whole reported but 826 black residents in the 1900 census. Virtually overnight, with the arrival of the 10th Cavalry, the black population swelled to over 1,500 individuals, including not only the soldiers but also their families and other camp followers. As one historian has written, this arrival "sent Burlington into demographic shock" (Work, pg. 65).

The reaction to this large influx was mixed at first; one Burlington newspaper opposed the arrival of the regiment, while another supported the 10th Cavalry. The same was true of the city's residents, with some worried about disorderly behavior and a rise in crime, while other whites supported the soldiers, who from the start were model citizens. The locals resented their state being portrayed like the South, "a stubbornly, bigoted, narrow-minded, rural people" (Work, pg. 67). While segregation did occur in Burlington, in that businesses and saloons that catered to the soldiers became quickly established, there was no official segregation or Jim Crow laws passed limiting their presence in public places or on railroad cars. In fact, the area quickly grew to accept the soldiers, who enjoyed displaying their military drills to the public and became active members of the community. The fort's baseball team even played white teams from nearby towns and factories, as well as the University of Vermont and Dartmouth College in neighboring New Hampshire.

When the regiment's duty at Fort Ethan Allen came to an end in 1913, the Vermont press praised the soldiers for their courteous conduct and spoke of the "good will that now existed between the regiment and the people of the state" (Work, pg. 74). Indicative of this acceptance is the fact that a number of the members of the 10th Cavalry later made Vermont their home, residing in the area where they were once stationed and where their arrival had caused such an outcry. Most settled in the town of Colchester or nearby at Burlington or Winooski. Four of these Buffalo Soldiers who remained in the area—William Thacker, Andrew Hale, Silas Johnson, and Willis Hatcher—are buried here, their gravestones a quiet and largely unknown testament to racial tolerance in this small corner of New England known as the Northeast Kingdom.

William Thacker (1862–1924) was a native of Anderson County, Kentucky, and was employed as a teamster when he enlisted for service in the 10th Cavalry on December 10, 1886, at Lexington. He remained in the service for over thirty years, rising to the rank of 1st sergeant, and was always rated an "excellent" soldier. After his retirement about 1920, Thacker became a Vermont resident and was living in Essex when he died in 1924.

Andrew J. Hale (1867–1952) was born in Whitesburg, Tennessee, and first joined the 9th Cavalry Regiment in 1892, later transferring to the 10th Cavalry. He too was rated an "excellent" soldier and rose to the rank of 1st sergeant in Troop M. Upon his retirement, Hale became a Vermont resident and lived in Colchester upon his retirement from the army in 1919; he is listed in that town for the 1920 census, but afterwards disappears from the records. His government-issue headstone application shows that he had a wife who survived him (Mrs. Andrew Hale), but also states that there is no record of his burial.

The other two Buffalo Soldiers buried here, however, are much better known. Willis Hatcher (1865–1943) was born in Farmsville, Virginia, the son of former slaves Merrit and

Amanda Hatcher and the grandson of Sampson and Amy Hatcher. Willis worked as a farm laborer until he joined the army in December 1888 at Cincinnati. Hatcher served with the 10th Cavalry for the next twenty-five years and was a Spanish-American War veteran who was wounded during the Battle of San Juan Hill. He later accompanied his regiment to Vermont, and would stay in the Green Mountain State the rest of his life. Hatcher retired from the military on September 28, 1913, as a sergeant before the regiment left Vermont, and he moved to the town of Winooski. Soon after his retirement, and perhaps the reason for his remaining in Vermont, Hatcher married Mary Ward Hatcher (1894–1952), a black girl, aged nineteen and a native of Tennessee, who also resided in Winooski. Willis Hatcher was a well-respected man about town, known for his bowler hat and smart appearance, living with his wife and daugh-

Gravestone, Andrew Hale, 1952, Fort Ethan Allen Cemetery, Colchester, Vermont.

ter Mary on LaFountain Street for many years. Both his wife and daughter are also buried in this cemetery.

Finally, there is Silas Johnson (1865–1935), a native of Caroline County, Virginia, the son of Leonard and Lucy Johnson. He was working as brickmaker when he enlisted for service in the 10th Cavalry in January of 1886; he would serve in the army for the next twenty-seven years, rising to the rank of 1st sergeant. In addition to his soldiering duties, Johnson was also a farrior, his job to shoe the horses upon which his regiment and troop rode, and was early on in his military service noted for his "excellent character." In addition to the Indian War in which the men of his regiment fought, Johnson also saw service in Cuba and the Philippines during the Spanish American War. In September 1898, while aboard a ferry with other members of his regiment in New York harbor, Johnson personally met and spoke with President William McKinley, who was no doubt impressed by Johnson's appearance in his canary-colored uniform and thanked him for the fine fighting his regiment had done. Silas Johnson married his wife Fannie Welch Johnson, who is also buried here, in 1904; the couple had three children, Milton, Beatrice, and Gertrude, all but the first being born in Vermont. With the pending departure of the 10th Cavalry from Vermont, Silas Johnson decided that here he would stay and retired from the army on March 28, 1913. Silas and his wife subsequently purchased a home on Franklin Street in Colchester and would live there the rest of their lives. Their family members would subsequently live in the area for many decades after their decease.

Like most military cemeteries, the Fort Ethan Allen Cemetery is well-maintained and its stones are in good condition; in recent years ground-level stones have been placed near the regular grave markers for some of these men, identifying them as African Americans of the 10th Cavalry Regiment.

VI. Maine

"Negro" Sailor Burial Site
First Congregational Church Cemetery
23 Pepperrell Road (Rte. 103)
Kittery Point

This historic cemetery overlooking Pepperell Cove was established in 1714, situated across the road from the 1732-built First Congregational Church and adjacent to the 1662-built John Bray mansion, the oldest extant house in the state. The most unusual marker found here is a slate gravestone/monument that depicts a storm-tossed ship in peril approaching a rocky shore. This stone was erected for six un-named sailors of the *Hattie Eaton*; they perished when the brig went ashore on nearby Garrish Island during a storm on March 21, 1876. The vessel was commanded by Captain James Cook and manned by a crew of seven men. It had been bound from Cuba to Boston with a cargo of sugar and molasses when the storm hit and drove the *Hattie Eaton* ashore. Only First Mate W.C. Lebarron would survive the shipwreck; those who lost their lives in addition to Captain Cook were Second Mate John Atwood (Maine), and crewmen William Fitzpatrick (Ireland), Peter Bokers (Grenada), Jeremiah Stevens (St. Kitts), William Brewcanon (Tobago), and Joseph Alhan (residence unknown) (*The Daily Graphic* [New York], March 22, 1876, pg. 177). One of these sailors, whose names are not recorded here, is identified on the gravestone as being a "negro," a small indicator of the fact that blacks were commonly involved in the maritime trade of New England from colonial times to the end of the sailing ship era. While the exact identity of the "negro" who died in this shipwreck is unknown, the man about whom the least is known (information presumably supplied by the surviving first mate), Joseph Alhan, is a possible candidate.

African American Section
Eastern Cemetery
224 Congress Street
Portland
http://www.portlandmaine.gov/603/Historic-Cemeteries

This waterfront cemetery, situated at the base of Munjoy Hill and chartered in 1668, has over 3,800 burials and was declared a National Historic Landmark in 1974. The marked

Above: Sailors' burial site, First Congregational Church Cemetery, Kittery Point, Maine. *Right*: Gravestone, Brig *Hattie Eaton* shipwreck victims, 1876, First Congregational Church Cemetery, Kittery Point, Maine.

burials here date from the early 1700s, with known African American burials not taking place until after the American Revolution. The black portion of this cemetery is located at the intersection of Congress and Mountfort streets at what was once the rear of the cemetery. The current cemetery gate is off Congress Street, with the so-called "Colored Ground" located immediately within on the far left. Here are located the marked graves for five men, four of them soldiers in the American Revolution, the other a sailor who served in the War of 1812. These, along with several other stones for the children of the Driver and Ruby families and several plaques erected by the Portland Freedom Trail, of which this cemetery is a featured site, constitute the only visible black presence in this cemetery.

Of the veterans buried here, little is known of their lives, but almost all of them were

Top: "Colored Ground," Eastern Cemetery, Portland, Maine. *Bottom:* Gravestone, Lewis Shepherd, 1833, Eastern Cemetery, Portland, Maine.

formerly enslaved. Lewis Shepherd (1751–1833), "a soldier of the Revolution," has the only contemporary stone for an African American veteran in Eastern, perhaps indicative of his social or economic standing. He came from nearby Scarborough and, if enslaved, was freed on the eve of the war and married his wife Elizabeth in that town in July 1774. His service in the Revolutionary war began in January 1777 when he enlisted in Capt. Clark's company in Col. Benjamin Tupper's 11th Massachusetts Regiment (Maine was still a part of Massachusetts at this time). Shepherd's service lasted through December 1779; he took part in the regiment's actions during the Saratoga campaign in New York, the defense of Philadelphia, and the Battle of Monmouth in New Jersey in 1779. After the war, Shepherd returned to Maine and was living in Gorham, the head of a household of six blacks in 1790. He later moved to nearby Portland and little is known of his remaining life, though his wife did outlive him by several years.

All of the other veterans with marked graves in Eastern Cemetery have government-issue military headstones that have been erected in modern times. Two of them, Cato Shattuck and Plato McLellan, served together in the company of Cumberland County men commanded by Capt. Paul Ellis, a unit in Col. Timothy Bigelow's 15th Massachusetts Regiment. Both men enlisted in May 1777 for a three-year term, their service ending in December 1779. Both men took part in the regiment's actions at Saratoga, the defense of Philadelphia, the Battle of Monmouth, and the Rhode Island campaign in 1779. While McLellan, who was formerly enslaved by Lt. Cary McLellan in Gorham, served as a regular soldier, Shattuck is notable for being the company fifer. Shattuck's owner is unknown, but there were several well-known families with this name living in Portland and Falmouth. Little is known of these men's lives after the war, including their death dates. McLellan was living in Gorham in 1820, but later moved to Portland and was likely deceased before 1830.

The final Revolutionary War veteran with a stone here is James Bowes (1764–ca. 1835). Whether or not he was enslaved is unknown, but he was a farmer living in Plymouth, Massachusetts, when he enlisted for service for the town of Bridgewater, Massachusetts, in February 1781. Bowes joined the company of Capt. Abraham Watson in Col. John Greaton's 3rd Massachusetts Regiment but saw no real action while stationed in the Hudson Highlands of New York. How or when Bowes decided to come to Maine is unknown, but he was in Portland by 1820, head of a household of three blacks, one of them his wife, the other likely a son named Charles, who is listed in the 1840 Census for Portland. James Bowes died sometime around 1835, though his gravestone incorrectly gives a death date of 1800.

The final black veteran known to be buried here is Richard Hill (ca. 1792–1861). His government-issue headstone is the most recent in Eastern Cemetery, having been erected in 2012. He was born in the state of Maine according to census records and was living in Portland by 1830. Richard Hill served aboard Gunboat 47, part of the New York flotilla, during the War of 1812 as an ordinary seaman (OS). Gunboats such as Hill's, which were small schooner- or sloop-rigged vessels that were about fifty feet long, were manned by a crew of about 40 and carried several guns. The gunboats of the New York flotilla saw quite a bit of action in Long Island Sound, and some of them, possibly including Hill's vessel, were present at the Battle of Fort McHenry in Baltimore on September 14, 1814, the British bombardment inspiring Francis Scott Key to write the song that would later become our national anthem. After the war, Hill's whereabouts until 1830 are unknown, but it seems likely he served as a sailor. He was married by 1830 and had at least one child, a son named Richard, and worked as a laborer in the city. Richard Hill, a veteran of the War of 1812, was a widow by September 12, 1861, the day he was shot to death by his troubled son, who had previously served jail time for

Gravestone, Richard Hill, 1861, Eastern Cemetery, Portland, Maine. The death date on this stone is incorrectly stated.

robbing a store. Richard Hill remained a forgotten man until local historian Larry Glatz began researching Mainers who had fought in the war. It was his efforts that led to the erection of Hill's military headstone, though the death date on his stone is incorrect, off by 20 years.

Because Eastern was the main cemetery for the city in the first decades of the 19th century, and due to its location close to the first black church in Maine, the Abyssinian Meeting House (built 1829) on nearby Newbury Street, many of the African American burials here have gone undocumented. However, it is certain that many other African American residents of Portland have been buried here over the years until this cemetery fell out of use by the 1860s. Among such burials are those for the Ropes brothers, George, David, and Joseph, who owned a hardware and crockery store and served as conductors on the Underground Railroad. Also buried here is Christopher Emanuel (1781–1845), an immigrant from the Cape Verde Islands who was employed in town as a barber; his gravesite next to his wife Sophia (Ruby) Manuel went unmarked until 2006. Finally, among the other marked graves here is that for William, the infant son of Reuben and Janet Ruby. Reuben Ruby, a native of Gray, Maine, was a founder of the Abyssinian Meeting House and was Portland's most important antislavery activist and Underground Railroad Conductor. He is buried in an unmarked grave in the Forest City Cemetery in South Portland.

The Eastern Cemetery once had an abandoned air to it and was, several decades ago, in poor condition, being overgrown and strewn with broken stones. The cemetery is in much better condition today, although broken stones still abound. Sadly, the record keeping for this cemetery was virtually nonexistent for most of the time it was in operation, and thus many early burials have gone undocumented. This cemetery used to be locked at all times, but is now usually open during daylight hours.

Neptune Stephenson Burial Site
South Street Cemetery
Rte. 114, near Junction of Rte. 4
Gorham

This small cemetery, located in the heart of Gorham center, was established by the 1760s and has marked burials dating back to 1774. Interred here are some of the town's founding families, including the Gorhams, the McLellans, and the Elders. However, at the far back left corner of the cemetery, in an area devoid of any stones but one, may be found the gravesite for a former slave in town, Neptune Stephenson (his name misspelled on his grave stone as "Stephenon"). This 1824-dated stone is the oldest for an African American in Gorham, a town closely associated with Portland, its larger neighbor. Neptune was the slave of Captain John Stephenson, a native of New York who first came to Portland (then known as Falmouth) by 1770, and later moved to Gorham when that town was attacked and burned by the British fleet in October 1775. Whether or not Capt. Stephenson was involved in the slave trade is unknown, but his slave Neptune's given name suggests that perhaps he was employed as a sailor, or perhaps Neptune was the name of the vessel which carried him as part of his cargo.

The age of Neptune Stephenson at the time of his death in 1824 suggests that he was born in 1780, which is intriguing; if this date is accurate, it means that Neptune was either purchased as an infant at a time when most masters in Massachusetts (of which Maine was a part) were freeing their slaves, or was born to a slave woman already owned by Capt. Stephenson. However, it is more likely that Neptune's exact birth date is unknown, and that a young Neptune accompanied his master to Maine from New York. Little is known of Neptune Stephenson's life as a freeman, except that he married Mary Pollard in 1807 and that, by

Gravestone, Neptune Stephenson, 1824, South Street Cemetery, Gorham, Maine.

the epitaph on his gravestone, that he was "a pious man" and likely a regular church attendee. The large amount of open space in the area where Neptune was buried makes it likely that this was an area of the so-called "Old Yard" where people of color, and perhaps paupers, were buried, but if this is the case, their names have gone unrecorded.

McLellan Family Burial Site
Eastern Cemetery
Rte. 25, near Junction Rte. 4 and Elizabeth St.
Gorham

This large cemetery was first established in 1830 and was referred to as the "New Yard" for many years. It size was expanded with the addition of several parcels of land over the years and the site now has over 4,000 burials. The oldest burials here are located at the back of the cemetery off New Portland Rd. However, the first burial within the confines of what would become the Eastern Cemetery took place as early as 1800 before it was even established, for here is buried Prince (ca. 1729–1829), the former slave of William McLellan, as well as his two wives, Dinah (died 1800) and Chloe (died 1827).

Prince was a native of Africa who after his capture was sent to the West Indies. Sometime before the American Revolution, Prince was purchased at Antigua as part of a venture by Mrs. Rebecca McLellan, and was transported to Portland from there by Captain Joseph McLellan. However, Prince evidently cost more than Mrs. McLellan had intended to pay, and thus a further settlement was required. To complete the transaction, it was agreed that a load of shooks (the wooden boards used to make casks or barrels) would be sufficient, and thus it was that one of Prince's first jobs as a slave in America was to bring this cartload of shooks from Gorham to Portland. Prince's master William McLellan would later, before 1776, purchase a slave woman named Dinah to be Prince's wife.

However, when his master went off to war, joining the Continental Army in January 1776 (and serving through August of that year), Prince took the opportunity to run away, and subsequently served as a sailor in the Revolution. He ran away to Portland and may have here served on a privateer, a privately armed merchant vessel, early on. Later, Prince joined the crew of the Continental Navy frigate *Deane* (later renamed *Hague*) at Boston, first under Captain Samuel Nicholson, later under Captain John Manley. While it is uncertain how long Prince served, it was likely from 1779 to 1782, during which time the ship saw much action and captured fourteen enemy vessels before being decommissioned at Boston in 1783.

According to his weather-worn gravestone, Prince was discharged from the navy at Boston and subsequently returned home, at which point he was freed by his master. Upon gaining his freedom, Prince was also given ten acres of land by his old master and here lived for the rest of his life in Gorham. When his first wife Dinah died in 1800, he subsequently married Chloe (possibly also a former slave of the McLellans). In 1818 Prince applied for and received a pension based on his naval service which helped support him in the years leading up to his death.

Prince's detailed gravestone, made of either marble or limestone, was probably paid for by the McLellan family, and for many years was the only marked burial in this part of the cemetery. It is now quite worn and should probably be removed to preserve what is left and replaced with a replica. It is found at the far back portion of the cemetery from the main entrance off Rte. 25.

Gravestone, Prince McLellan and his wives Chloe and Dinah, 1829, Eastern Cemetery, Gorham, Maine.

Phebe Ann Jacobs and Freeman Family Burial Sites
Pine Grove Cemetery
Junction of Rte. 24 (Bath Rd.) and Pine Street
Brunswick
http://www.curtislibrary.com/wp-content/uploads/2013/08/Pine-Grove-Cemetery-searchable.pdf

This historic cemetery was established beginning in 1821 when the land was donated by Bowdoin College, with the stipulation that the college could take back the land if it was not used as a cemetery. It is for this reason that Pine Grove is adjacent to Bowdoin College today. The first burials here took place in 1825, this two-acre plot of land serving as Brunswick's second public burying space after the town built a new church in the area away from the First Parish Church Burying Ground on Maine Street. This new cemetery, as was quite common, quickly became the favored burial spot in town, with some prominent families relocating earlier burials to new plots in Pine Grove. In fact, there are many prominent individuals buried here, including Bowdoin College officials, along with several Maine governors, including the famed Colonel (later General and Governor) Joshua Chamberlain, the commander of the famed 20th Maine Regiment during the Civil War that helped save the Union Army during the Battle of Gettysburg. However, one of the most interesting of the burials here is that for a humble and devout woman, Phebe Ann Jacobs (1785–1850), a former slave of the families of the presidents of two renowned New England colleges, Dartmouth and Bowdoin.

Phebe Jacobs was born into slavery in the north at Beverwyck Plantation in Morris County, New Jersey (modern day Parsippany), owned by planters from the Danish West Indies. This plantation was about 2,000 acres in size, with excavations on the site in 2003 uncovering several shackles inside the remains of a slave dwelling. While still a young girl, Jacobs was given as a present to the Wheelock family in New Hampshire and became the personal attendant of Maria Wheelock, the granddaughter of the founder of Dartmouth College. In 1812 Maria Wheelock married the Rev. William Allen, then the pastor of the First Congregational Church in Pittsfield, Massachusetts, and Phebe Ann Jacobs accompanied her to become a part of their household. The Allens would subsequently have eight children before Maria's death in 1828 and though the details of her life are unknown, we can be sure that Phebe Ann served her mistress as an attendant at each of these births, perhaps even acting as a midwife. Before the Allens moved to New Hampshire in 1817, Phebe joined the church in Pittsfield and thereafter became a devout Christian. The Allens' time in Lebanon, New Hampshire, was relatively short, with William Allen serving as a professor at Dartmouth, and for a short time as the college's president after the death of his father-in-law, John Wheelock. In 1820, the Allen family, Phebe included, moved to Brunswick, Maine, where Allen served as Bowdoin College's president for most of the years between 1820 and 1838.

Interestingly, though Phebe Ann Jacobs was certainly loved by the Allens and treated well, she was still a slave, and remained so, despite the Missouri Compromise of 1820. This act set the dividing line between the slave states in the South and the free states in the North when it came to the issue of slavery, but also admitted Missouri into the union as a slave state, and Maine (formerly a part of Massachusetts) as a free state. And still, Phebe Ann Jacobs, now aged 35, remained a slave in Brunswick. She would continue to serve the Allens until at least 1828 and joined the Congregational Church in Brunswick in 1823. It is unclear when Phebe gained her freedom, some historians speculating that she may have become free based on a provision in Maria Allen's will, while others believe that she continued serving William Allen as a slave. She may have chosen to remain in the Allen household as a free woman, but certainly became free when William Allen decided to retire and left Brunswick to live in Pittsfield, Massachusetts, in 1839. We know not the conditions of her separation from William Allen, except that it was on friendly and respectful terms; he may have given her the money that enabled her to buy a small home.

Phebe probably could have remained with Allen but instead made the decision to be free and stay in Maine, even if it meant her life would be more difficult. Phebe Ann Jacobs subsequently supported herself by working as a seamstress and washerwoman for Bowdoin College students and faculty and remained a devout member of the church in Brunswick for the rest of her life, renowned as a constant attendee of prayer meetings and a studious

Bible reader. She was also highly respected by the white members of the congregation and had a great concern for both their physical and spiritual needs.

Though we know little of her life within the small black community that thrived in Brunswick, Phebe was almost certainly an admired and respected figure, and though she lived alone, she is known to have cared for at least one black girl for several weeks at a time. However, though respected for her devout beliefs, Phebe was also a black woman in an overwhelmingly white society and was subject to abuse, she on occasion being "rudely spoken to, and her feelings wounded" (Upham, pg. 2). It was then that she turned to God for comfort.

The night that Phebe Ann Jacobs died, she visited the house of her pastor, George Adams, to check in on his ill wife. Both women died that same evening, February 27, 1850. It says something of Phebe's character that the Reverend Adams gave her funeral sermon and presided over her services before doing the same for his wife the next day. As I've previously discussed, the Reverend Allen and his daughters returned to Brunswick for Phebe's large and well attended funeral, her pallbearers including a Bowdoin College professor and former Maine governor Robert Dunlap. According to Phebe's own desire, she was buried next to her beloved mistress, Maria Allen, in the Allen family plot (located at the far right front of Pinegrove) and was given a fine gravestone to mark her final resting place.

Phebe Ann Jacobs's story might have been forgotten except that it was recorded and published in the form of a religious tract by a white woman, Phebe Lord Upham, who knew Jacobses well. This small, 8-page work was published in London about 1850 and had several titles, including *Narrative of Phebe Ann Jacobs* and *Happy Phebe*. This is a significant work in more ways than one, for not only does it preserve some of the life details and character of a black slave woman living in Maine, it may have also served as an inspiration to Harriet Beecher Stowe, the famed abolitionist and author of *Uncle Tom's Cabin*. Phebe Upham was the friend of Stowe during her time spent in Brunswick when her husband taught at Bowdoin, and it is believed by some scholars that the instances of Phebe Ann Jacobs's piety that are portrayed in the tract book served as an inspiration and model for Uncle Tom's piety and good character in Stowe's book.

Gravestone, Phebe Ann Jacobs, 1850, Pine Grove Cemetery, Brunswick, Maine.

In contrast to Phebe Ann Jacobs, there are also four other African American burials here at Pine Grove, including those for Isaiah Freeman (1830–1866) and his children Eugene (1851–1853), Alzada (1862–1863), and Louisa Freeman (1856–1873). The Freemans were one of the largest and most important of the black families living in Brunswick and the surrounding area at this time. These family members are buried at the back of Pine Grove Cemetery, to the right of the main entrance. Their stones are typical ones for the time, nothing but their location giving any hint that here were buried some of Brunswick's black citizens.

Isaiah Freeman was born in Maine, as was his wife Abigail (Abby) Freeman (1834–1870). He was living in Topsham, Maine, and working as a teamster before moving to Brunswick by 1863, where he registered for the draft during the Civil War and was listed as a laborer. In addition to their children mentioned above, the couple had two others, Ann and Simeon. The Freemans were married in Bath, Maine, in October 1851. Isaiah was one of eight children of Samuel and Priscilla Freeman, and Abigail the daughter of Adam and Nancy Freeman. There are no records surviving that detail why Isaiah's children died at such young ages, though Isaiah died as the result of a railroad accident (Price and Talbot, pg. 66). Abigail Freeman also died young in May 1870, her daughter Louisa recorded as living with a related black family, that of

Gravestone, Louisa Freeman, 1873, Pine Grove Cemetery, Brunswick, Maine.

Henry and Julia (Freeman) Johnson, in Brunswick later that year. Julia Johnson was Isaiah's sister. Abigail Freeman's final resting place may be near that of her family, but if so it has gone unmarked.

Malaga Island Residents Burial Site
Pinelands Patients' Cemetery
Rte. 231 (Intervale Rd.), just past Pineland Farms
New Gloucester
http://www.malagaislandmaine.org/

This small cemetery is located behind Webber cemetery, whose sign is clearly visible from the road, and is also adjacent to the relatively new Pinelands Cemetery. This arrangement of cemeteries may seem confusing, but that for the patients held at the Maine School for the Feeble-Minded, later called the Pinelands Hospital, is a separate entity altogether and was a place for the burial of unclaimed bodies of individuals who died while being held there. Most of the graves here were marked in very simple fashion and it is only in recent years that gravestones with the patients' names have been erected. As well, there is no official sign designating this burial site, though there is one small memorial stone here and a sign, placed by Bath Middle School students in 2008, that details this cemetery's connection with Malaga Island. It is this connection to a small island off the coast of Phippsburg that has given this site a great degree of attention and notoriety over the years, much to the chagrin of Maine's state government.

The story of Malaga Island, and how some its residents came to be buried in this forlorn location begins in the 1790s, begins when a black man named Benjamin Darling appears

Pinelands Patients Cemetery, New Gloucester, Maine.

on the tax rolls for Georgetown, Maine (which Phippsburg was then a part of). He was a mariner and former slave of a Portsmouth, New Hampshire, ship captain, and seems to have earned his freedom in the early 1770s after saving his master's life in a shipwreck off the coast of Ireland. Darling, by 1793, owned Horse Island (now Harbor Island), which is just south of Malaga Island, and here settled down to raise a family. Little is known of the personal details of his life, his marriage (possibly to a white woman), or his interaction with locals, but he seems to have been a hardworking man. His descendants populated the area and intermarried among the local white population.

Malaga Island in 1860 was just one of hundreds of little islands, many of them rocky and of little value, that dotted the Maine coast; sitting at the mouth of the New Meadows River in Casco Bay and 41 acres in size, this island's first known resident was a black man and Maine native named Henry Griffin. By the 1870s, other black or mixed-race families began to move here, including that of James McKenney (a white man later called "the King of Malago"), Robert Tripp, John Easton (also spelled "Eason"), and William Johnson, as well as members of the related Marks and Darling families. All of these black families are represented in the Pineland's Patients Cemetery. This community was largely left on its own for several decades, many of the men employed as fishermen or farm laborers on the mainland, while the island's women were employed in digging clams and taking in laundry and mending from whites on the mainland. However, by the 1890s things changed when many of the Malaga Island residents had fallen on hard times and were forced to rely on the town of Phippsburg for support as paupers. By 1900, town officials were tired of this costly upkeep, and so apparently were their fellow white residents. The settlement on Malaga was now branded both a lazy and degenerate one, this last claim based on the mixed race relations that existed among the island's small black and white population. The town of Phippsburg even tried to stop paying for the poor on Malaga by insisting the island belonged to neighboring Harpswell, but were foiled by a state ruling in 1903 that deemed the islands to be a part of Phippsburg.

It was not just forces at the local level that were working against the poor Malaga Island residents, but those on a regional and national level also played a huge part. First and foremost was the growing tourist economy on the Maine seacoast; more and more tourists from outside the state were coming to Maine every summer to escape the crowded cities of New York and Boston to enjoy its beautiful and rugged coastline, picturesque lighthouses and port cities. Malaga Island was seen as a blot on the Maine coast, with its black residents and the tattered dwellings they occupied, and the community's wild and undeserved reputation for degeneracy. Things got worse in 1901 when the nearby city of Bath prohibited the islanders and other Phippsburg residents from clam-digging in their waters, taking away a major source of revenue. In 1902 the island was hit by a measles epidemic that killed an unknown number of people (Price and Talbot, pg. 72).

Postcard, "The Tray of Spades, Malago ID, New Meadows River, Maine," ca. 1900. Racist postcards with views of Malaga Island were widely distributed throughout New England. This card depicts three members of the Tripp family, one of the young children being Perlie Tripp; she watched her mother die after the family was evicted from Malaga Island.

In 1905, after much debate, the Malaga Island residents were made wards of the state of Maine, absolving Phippsburg residents from paying for their support outright, a seemingly good move that, at least early on, helped those on Malaga. A Massachusetts missionary group came to the island and built a one-room schoolhouse that did great service, while other mainland groups donated food and other necessities. However, these efforts, though well meaning, fell short in the end, and Malaga Island residents remained at the very bottom of the socioeconomic ladder in every single aspect imaginable.

As it turns out, too, the state of Maine seems to have had little of the stomach or patience required to help the Malaga Islanders for the long term; after just six years of oversight, Maine Governor Frederick Plaisted, having made an inspection tour of the island in 1911, sided with local white residents and decided to have the settlement on Malaga Island removed altogether. In December 1911 a local doctor, in conjunction with a member of Governor Plaisted's Executive Council, forcibly committed eight islanders, seven of them members of the Marks family, to the Maine School for the Feeble-Minded on the mainland. That same month, the state purchased Malaga Island (probably illegally, as Henry Griffin had earlier purchased the item but lost his documents) and issued eviction notices to all the remaining residents, giving them until July 1912 to leave, along with a small amount of money to compensate them for their lost homes. After the islanders departed their homes, the state destroyed all traces of the settlement there, razing houses and even evicting the dead. State workers disinterred those buried in the island cemetery in October 1912, placing the remains in five caskets and taking them to the mainland, where they were buried in the Pinelands Patients' Cemetery in an unmarked grave the following month.

Of the evicted residents still living, most had a difficult time finding accommodations, let alone making a living. At least one person, Laura Tripp, the wife of Robert Tripp, died of tuberculosis, caused by exposure and starvation, while living aboard their houseboat, her husband rowing to the mainland in vain during a storm to gain help for her. As for Malaga Island itself, as journalist Allen Breed has stated, "Now, no one else will ever be from Malaga" (Price and Talbot, pg. 75). The island has never again had any residents or even any development, and after a series of outsiders owned the island, in 2000 it was sold to the Maine Coast Heritage Trust for $200,000.

While the Malaga Island saga is a story of shameful intolerance, racism, and greed all rolled into one, there are also other aspects of this story that are even more disturbing that relate to the bad social science of the day known as "eugenics." The application of this science to the Malaga Island residents has also been perceived, and rightfully so, by many as being a form of ethnic cleansing. The pseudo-science

RECORD OF A DEATH

Name, *Annie Parker*

Place of Death, *New Gloucester*

No. .... Street.

Ward, ... Village, ...

How long a resident, *5 yr 5 mos, 15 dy*

Previous residence, *Malaga Island*

Date of Death: Year, *1916* Month *May* Day, *29*

Death Record, Annie Parker, 1916, New Gloucester, Maine. Parker was the elderly woman who was forcibly removed, along with many of the Marks family, from Malaga Island by the state in late 1911 and committed to the Maine Home for the Feeble-Minded, where she died less than five years later.

of eugenics attempts promoting superior human genetic traits by reducing the rate of procreation among the so-called undesirable elements of society and increasing the procreation rate for those deemed to have superior human traits. Such ideas have been around for centuries, but gained an official name and many scientific followers in the 1880s. By the time the Malaga Island settlement was destroyed, the science of eugenics was on the rise and near its height of popularity, with an international conference on the topic held in 1912 in London. By the 1930s, though many American institutions, like the Maine School for the Feeble-Minded, had forced sterilization programs for their inmates, the science of eugenics was on the decline. The heightened application of this so-called science by the Nazi regime in Europe during World War II ended the widespread acceptance of eugenics, but many aspects of this science were practiced in American institutions into the 1960s.

As for the seven Malaga Island residents who were committed to the Maine School for the Feeble-Minded (founded in 1908), all but two of them were kept here for the rest of their lives, all deemed to be mentally defective. It is unknown if any of the Marks family members were forcibly sterilized here, which procedure was authorized by Maine law beginning in 1925 and continued up to 1963. While this institution was labeled as a "school," classroom education was actually a very small part of what went on here; the primary goal was to separate these so-called defective, low-intelligence individuals from the rest of society.

However, institutes like the Maine School for the Feeble-Minded (its name changed to the Pownal State School in 1925, and Pinelands Hospital in 1953) also became a dumping ground for the elderly who could not care for themselves, as well as for orphaned children. Thus it is that many of those buried here, not just the African Americans from Malaga Island, were some of Maine's most vulnerable and forgotten citizens. The dubious care given to those held at the Maine School for the Feeble-Minded is highlighted by the fact that of the Malaga Islanders (see below) who died here, several succumbed to disease within months after their transfer, while three others died before reaching the age of 36.

Of the Malaga Island black families who were either inmates at the Maine School for the Feeble-Minded or had their relatives' bodies re-interred here and marked with a stone, below is a brief account of their lives.

The Marks family: only two of the seven members of this family who became inmates ever gained their freedom again, namely Abbie Marks (1861–1944), the wife of Jacob Marks, and their daughter Charlotte "Lottie" Marks (1894–1997). They were released in 1925 and lived together for many years, Lottie supporting her mother by working as a housekeeper in Bath. Both of them are buried in the Growstown Cemetery in Brunswick, Maine. As for the rest of the family: the head of the family, Jacob Marks (1852–January 1912), died within a month of being committed due to a medical condition, while his son James Marks (1892–May 1912) survived just a few months longer before succumbing to a disease that affected his face and scalp. Three other Marks children also died here: Lizzie (1886–1921), Etta (1897–1825), and William "Willie" Marks (1909–1928). Hannah Marks (died 1908), the mother of Jacob Marks, was buried on Malaga Island, her body disinterred and reburied here at Pinelands in November 1912.

Annie Parker (1853–1916): This black woman, about whom I've been able to discover but little information, was a widow and was the elderly resident of Malaga Island who was committed to the Maine School for the Feeble-Minded at the same time as the Marks family in December 1911. She may have been born on Malaga Island, but records are lacking. Labeled as senile at the time of her death, Parker died from the effects of bronchitis in 1916.

The Tripps: The relationship of the two individuals, Laura and Calvin, for this family buried here, both identified on the same gravestone, are uncertain. They were likely the children of Robert (1872–1948) and Lara Darling Tripp and probably died at an unknown time before 1912. The Tripps had three children, according to the 1910 federal census, the last one in which Malaga Island residents appear. They were Abbie (born 1899); a son, Linnie (born 1903); Perlie (born 1904); and Harold (born 1907). It was Robert Tripp's wife, Laura, who died during a storm after they were evicted from Malaga Island; she bled to death due to the effects of tuberculosis alongside her daughter Perlie and another of their children while Robert Tripp went off to find a doctor. Robert Tripp lived in the area for many years after leaving Malaga Island, earning a living as a laborer, and died in Harpswell.

The Griffins: Eight members of this family are buried here, including one of the patriarchs of the family, George Griffin (1818–1906). Practicing the trade of a fisherman, he was likely one of the Malaga Island's first settlers in the 1860s. Other Griffin heads of families who lived on Malaga Island include Henry Griffin (born 1809) and his wife Fatima (born 1809), and William H. Griffin (born ca. 1840), who practiced the trade of a sailor, and with his wife Ellen (born ca. 1842) had at least three children, Emma (born 1869), William (born 1872), and Eliza (born ca. 1864). Eliza was remembered for her fishing skills that rivaled those of the men on the island, as well as the fact that she wore pants and lived in a salvaged schooner cabin (Price and Talbot, pg. 71). There is one stone here at Pinelands for Roxanna and Ellen Griffin, both of whom died before 1912, likely William's wife and one of their daughters.

Henry Griffin (ca. 1843–1921), is also important in this story as he seems to have owned Malaga Island, making the purchase by 1870, but subsequently lost proof of the sale in a land transaction that went unrecorded, not surprising given the fact that most whites deemed Malaga Island useless and of no value. He was the son of the first Henry Griffin, though his mother is listed as being Minny Darling Griffin. Henry married Ellen Darling Griffin (born 1844) about 1870 and they would have five children together, all of whom died before 1912 and were re-interred here. Three of these children were dead by 1900, with only William Griffin (born 1873) recorded in the census records for that year. The names of the other Griffin children are uncertain. After being forced to leave Malaga Island, Henry Griffin lived in Harpswell, where he practiced the trade of a fisherman before dying due to "acute intestinal indigestion" in 1921. Interestingly, death records identify him as a white man, an indicator of the lighter skin color of some of the residents of Malaga.

The Johnsons: Lucy Marks Johnson (born ca. 1855) died before November 1910 on Malaga Island and was one of those individuals whose body was exhumed and reburied here in November 1912. She was the daughter of Hannah Marks; her siblings were her brother Jacob Marks, and sister Ellen Marks Griffin (died 1904), both of whom are also buried here. Lucy married North Carolina native and Civil War veteran William H. Johnson

These individuals were originally buried on Malaga Island, but were disinterred from the island's cemetery after their living relatives were evicted, and were reburied without ceremony here in New Gloucester in November 1912.

(ca. 1828–1914) and with him had seven children, only one of whom, a daughter named Sadie (born ca. 1896) was alive in 1900, according to census records. However, when William Johnson was admitted to the Home for Disabled Soldiers in Togus, Maine, in November 1910, his daughter's name was given as Sarah Johnson, and she was still living on Malaga Island. Johnson died at this soldiers' home in 1914 and is buried in the Togus National Cemetery, Plot L, #3221. William Johnson was a resident of Brunswick, Maine, and employed as a seaman when he enlisted in the 54th Massachusetts Regiment in November 1863, serving in Company I. Enlistment records show that Johnson was married at this time, so it is likely that Lucy Marks, given their age disparity, was his second wife, but this is not known for certain. The couple was married by 1900, and William Johnson earned a living as a fisherman while living on Malaga Island.

The Eastons: Three children of John (1849–1947) and Rosilla (1863–1941) Easton (also given as "Eason") are buried here at Pinelands. John Easton was the son of former slaves and his wife is said to have been a full Native American. He made a living as a mason and, in his later years after being forced off Malaga Island, as a plasterer. He was said to have been a well-spoken man with a fine singing voice and may have served as the island's preacher when one was needed. In his later years, when he and his wife lived on Cundy Harbor Road in Harpswell, he was affectionately known as "Uncle John." Of the Easton children, little is known; two of their children were Robbie (born 1884) and Hattie (born 1886), who was living with the Griffin family on the island in 1900. I have been unable to find any records of these children in later years after 1900, so they may have died by 1911, their bodies subsequently relocated to Pinelands. The identity of the other Easton child buried here is also uncertain.

The erased settlement on Malaga Island has an interesting and varied postscript that took many years to play out. Those residents who were not committed to the state school eventually, after much hardship, found new places to live in surrounding towns on the Maine coast. Indeed, many of their descendants still live in New England to this very day, including those of the Darling and McKenney families in nearby Portland and those of the Tripp family in Connecticut, so the story of what happened on Malaga Island wasn't entirely forgotten. However, as far as everyone else was concerned, especially the state of Maine, what happened on Malaga Island passed into the realm of an unpleasant history that was but little discussed or even documented and largely forgotten.

This began to change when interest in what happened on Malaga Island was fueled by an article that appeared in the popular regional magazine *Down East* in November 1980, titled "The Shameful Story of Malaga Island." Written by William D. Barry, it was the first major account of the settlement to appear in modern times, and from that time interest in this terrible episode in Maine's recent past began to grow. Calls by civic organizations for the state of Maine to make an official apology to the Malaga Island residents also began to grow, but these efforts for many years were met with official silence. However, with the release of more books, articles, and a 2009 radio and photo documentary titled *Malaga Island: A Story Best Left Untold*, it became clear that the state could no longer ignore what happened on Malaga Island.

Influenced by this increasing interest, as well as the election of America's first African

American president, Maine Democrats formulated an official bill offering an apology on behalf of the state in 2009. The Maine state legislature after much negotiation unanimously passing an apology bill on April 7, 2010, in the last hours of its session. This bill received virtually no publicity, and to those with an interest in Malaga Island it appeared as yet another bungled attempt by the state to deal with this issue of racial intolerance. Based on this new controversy, the state finally did the right thing when Governor John Baldacci in September 2010 made the journey to Malaga Island and here met personally with nearly forty of the island's descendants and made a heartfelt apology for what had happened so long ago. It was also at the end of this ceremony that a Maine Freedom Trails marker was also unveiled, standing as a reminder of the island's historical significance.

Malaga Island in recent years has been the subject of archaeological excavations that have helped detail what life was like for its residents, and in 2012 an exhibit about the Malaga Island settlement was opened at the Maine State Museum in Augusta. Today the island is a protected entity but is open to boaters for recreational use. Some descendants of the islanders have expressed a desire to have those remains that were disinterred here in 1912 returned for burial on the island, but this has not yet happened. The Pinelands Patients' Cemetery is in good condition, well maintained and easily accessible, though a more detailed historical plaque documenting this site's significance would be an appropriate addition. All of the Malaga Islanders who were reinterred here have gravestones bearing the date of November 1912, reflective of the date when they were placed here, not their actual dates of death. In addition, some of the headstones for others buried here contain inaccurate information, including several for the Marks family; that for James Marks (1892–1912) incorrectly gives his name as Jane, while that for Jacob Marks (1868–1912) incorrectly gives his name as James.

African American Burials
Peterborough Cemetery
Sandy Shores Road
Warren

The Peterborough Cemetery, located just off Rte. 1, about four-tenths of a mile from the Maine Central railroad tracks on the left, is a site that is indicative of the development of a black community tucked away on the mid–Maine coast which got its start in the late 1700s. The earliest burials, likely including those for founders Amos and Sarah Peters, are marked by the simple unlettered fieldstones that can be seen at the far left portion of the cemetery and probably date to the first decade of the 1800s. In fact, had this black community not been sustained for over 150 years, this cemetery would surely have been lost, the simple fieldstone-marked burial sites being plowed under or simply fading into wilderness. However, the professionally carved gravestones here, the earliest of which are dated from the 1850s and are typical for the times, instead reflect this community's success and perseverance in an otherwise overwhelmingly white area.

Among the most interesting stones here are those for veterans of the Civil War, the U.S. Navy, and even a World War I serviceman, all native to Warren. Among the veterans buried here who have government-issue military headstones are Abram Peters (1846–1900), a barber who served in the Navy during the Civil War; Samuel S. Peters (1844–1914), the son of Isaac Peters, also a Navy veteran who served aboard the wooden steam sloop USS *Richmond*; Charles E. Peters (1855–1921), who served in the Navy during the post–Civil War peacetime years; and Francis Olney (1836–1880; name misspelled as "Oney" on his gravestone), a seaman by trade who joined the 43rd U.S. Colored Troop Regiment in July 1863 and trained as a soldier at Camp William Penn near Philadelphia. In fact, Olney was one of at least nine black men from Warren who saw service in the war, all but Olney members of the Peters family. William H., Dexter, Reuben, and Daniel Peters all served in the 43rd U.S.C.T. in Company B, with Reuben dying during the course of his service at Philadelphia in January 1865. Of the other Peters men who served in the war, Merrill Peters served in the Navy, while Emerson Peters served in the all-black 5th Massachusetts Cavalry. None of these men, however, are buried here, since many of them moved to Massachusetts after the war. Yet another veteran buried here is William F. Peters (1888–1963), the son of Charles Peters and a veteran of World War I, serving in the 546th Service Battalion Engineer Corps. In addition to these veterans, other black families with burials here are those for the Mink, Griffin, and Carter families, many of whom were related by marriage.

While theories abound as to where the early residents of Peterborough may have come

Peterborough Cemetery, Warren, Maine.

from, with some speculating that they were runaways from the South (Price and Talbot, pg. 77), most came from Maine. Among the black families living here in 1860, in addition to ten different Peters households, who were all native to Maine, according to the federal census, were Lorenzo D. Carter (also given as "Lorenzo DeCaster" in the 1850 census), a seaman and native of Philadelphia, and his Maine-born wife Lucy; Samuel Mink, also a mariner, and his wife Sarah; and Reuben Mink, a day laborer, all Maine natives; day laborer Henry Seco and his wife Priscilla; and washerwomen Jane Griffin and Elanson (Eleanor?) Johnson, who were both also born in Maine; as well as two young children from the Sewall and Talbot families. No Southern-born individuals are noted as being residents of Warren in either the 1850 or 1860 census. Some of these families have marked burials here, and it is highly likely that many other members of this community are buried here in unmarked graves.

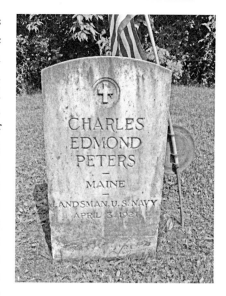

Gravestone, Charles Edmond Peters, 1921, Peterborough Cemetery, Warren, Maine.

This cemetery, whose wooden sign is visible from the road, is easily found by walking down a grassy path leading from the road for about fifty yards and is located in a small clearing. It is a well-maintained and peaceful place featuring a flagpole and serves as a beautiful and fitting tribute to an otherwise vanished black community.

London and Eunice Atus Burial Site
Court Street Cemetery
Corner of Court St. (Rte. 1A) and West Street
Machias

The historic black presence in northern Maine is often difficult to find, but this Downeast town offers several examples of this aspect of their heritage. The most immediately identifiable of these sites, at least for those "in the know," is located in the Court Street Cemetery. Here, at the far back of this cemetery, there is one black-colored slate gravestone for London Atus (died 1843) and his wife, a white woman, Eunice (Foss) Atus (died 1854). This couple had twelve children and gave the black community in Machias, later known as Atusville, its start in 1791. London Atus (ca. 1760–1843) was the slave of the Rev. James Lyons and arrived in Machias with the reverend, the town's first minister, and his wife when they came here from New Jersey in 1772. Lyons had graduated from Princeton College in 1762 and had preached beforehand in Halifax, Nova Scotia, and in New Jersey. He was in Boston when he accepted the call to preach at the Congregational Church in Machias; it is unknown how long London, who was born in New Jersey, had been his slave beforehand.

London, who was usually referred to by his master's surname as London Lyons, is best remembered for the role he played in June 1775 when Machias patriots captured the British armed sloop *Margaretta*, which vessel was in the town's harbor to serve as an escort for supplies provided by a loyalist merchant in town. The town's patriots seized the British ship by force in the first naval battle of the war, but what role London played in the event is a mystery to this date. Though there are no official records of which townsmen participated in this action, some anecdotal accounts state that London helped in the capture, while yet others state that he inadvertently alerted the British to the patriots' plan because he had not been told of their plans in advance to capture the *Margaretta*. However, London Lyons's later actions suggest that perhaps the latter story is untrue, for he did serve in the Revolutionary War and was granted a pension for this service. London served in the local artillery regiment commanded by Col. John Allen and made a privateering voyage on the sloop *Winthrop*.

Local lore also suggests that London was an accomplished mariner, serving as a sort of messenger for the Machias patriots, as well as bringing food in past the British blockade of Machias harbor and distilling salt from seawater on Salt Island, bringing this commodity in to the town when it was badly needed (LiBrizzi, pgs. 22–24). Local tradition further states that London used the pay he earned from his naval service to buy his freedom; he likely became free by 1790 and subsequently took the surname of Atus, its meaning and origin unknown. London Atus would later, in 1792, marry Eunice Foss, a white girl who had served as a maid, but he had known her for at least several years before this.

In March 1791 Eunice Atus was summoned to appear before a local justice of the peace and pay a fine for the sin of fornication, having in February 1791 given birth to Louisa Atus out of wedlock. Despite this illegal beginning to their life together, the couple seems to have had a normal existence in Machias in the following decades, though little is known of their lives in detail. Their son John Atus did serve in the War of 1812, and others of their children (including Susan Atus) and grandchildren married locally, their descendants prominent in the area down to the 1960s.

While the gravestone for London and his wife was not erected until after the Eunice's death in 1854, it is unknown if London's burial was previously marked; some locals believe that London may not even be buried here, instead interred in the Atusville Cemetery (see below) in an unmarked grave (LiBrizzi, pg. 44).

The Court Street Cemetery is town owned and maintained and in generally good condition and is open during daytime hours.

African American Community Burial Site
Atusville Cemetery
North Main Street (Rte. 1A),
Machias

This four-acre parcel of land located on a hillside in the middle of an area of town once known as Atusville is now heavily wooded and nearly unrecognizable as a cemetery. However, this was not always the case, and it is now recognized as a historic site by the Maine Historic Preservation Commission. It was sold to the town in 1841 with the express intent of using it as a burial ground, and may indeed have already been used as an informal burying place. The town subsequently built a wall on the highway side of the lot. Oral tradition states that, though there are no gravestones, there were a number of burials made here which were clearly evident even as late as the 1940s by the mounded graves that were scattered about. Local residents recall that these mounds were spread out over the hillside, perhaps numbering twenty or more, and anecdotal accounts suggest that some black residents of town, whose burials are listed as being in the nearby Court Street Cemetery, are actually buried here (Librizzi, pgs. 44–45). This site is really the only tangible, on-the-spot reminder of a black community that existed in this far northern town. Oral traditions state that the Atusville section of Machias had strong ties to the Underground Railroad network to aid runaway slaves on their trek northward to Canada and that there may even be a secret tunnel, possibly constructed by London Atus, to aid in that purpose that runs close to this site down to the Machias River (LiBrizzi, pgs. 56–58). Among the black residents here were local mariners, as well as those who had moved here from the South.

Interestingly, in 1853 a school for the black children of Atusville was constructed within the confines of this cemetery, its building necessitated by the assaults made by white children upon the black children attending the regular schools in town (LiBrizzi, pgs. 59–60) This fact makes the Atusville burial ground, even if no visible traces remain, an even greater historical site and a hidden symbol of the institutionalized racism that once existed in Maine.

This burial site was nearly lost by the 1990s, but interest was revived when the town proposed to use the site as a gravel pit. Fortunately, this did not happen; the site has been left as is, and has been marked with a historical plaque since 2005. Just how many individuals are buried here will probably never be known, as records for the site are nonexistent and the town of Machias has not allowed any archaeological digging. Ground-penetrating radar surveys have revealed just a few depressions suggestive of interments, but there is much about this site that will probably always remain a mystery.

Bibliography

Abbott, Charlotte H. "Early Records and Notes of the Lovejoy Family of Andover," Andover, MA: typed manuscript, n.d.
_____. "Early Records of the Frye Family of Andover," Andover, MA: typed manuscript, n.d.

Adams, Catherine, and Elizabeth H. Pleck. *Love of Freedom: Black Women in Colonial and Revolutionary New England*. New York: Oxford University Press, 2010.

Aldrich, George. *Walpole as It Was and as It Is*. Claremont, NH: Claremont Manufacturing, 1980.

Aptheker, Herbert. *The Negro in the American Revolution*. New York: International Publishers, 1940.

Arlington Historical Society (MA). "Prince Hall Cemetery." Accessed online at http://www.arlingtonhistorical.org/learn/prince-hall-cemetery/.

Armstrong, Douglas V., and Mark L. Fleischman. "House-Yard Burials of Enslaved Laborers in Eighteenth-Century Jamaica." *International Journal of Historical Archaeology* 7, No. 1 (March 2003).

Arnold, James N. *Vital Records of Rhode Island 1636–1850, First Series,* vol. 7. Providence, RI: Narragansett Historic Publishing, 1896.

Arpin, Iva. "Cemetery Rescues in Voluntown & Griswold, CT." Accessed online at http://www.ctgravestones.com/CTprojects/kinne.htm.

Avery, Vicky. "Great Caesar's Ghost in NH." Accessed online at http://www.seacoastnh.com/Black-History/Black-History/great-caesars-ghost-in-nh/?showall=1.

Bailey, Sarah Loring. *Historical Sketches of Andover*. Boston: Houghton Mifflin, 1880.

Baker, Vernon G. "Archaeological Visibility of Afro-American Culture: An Example from Black Lucy's Garden, Andover, Massachusetts." In *Archaeological Perspectives on Ethnicity in America*, Robert Schuyler, ed. Farmingdale, NY: Baywood, 1980.

Batignani, Karen W. *Maine's Coastal Cemeteries; A Historic Tour*. Camden, ME: Downeast Books, 2003.

Benson, Judy. "Digging unearths more on Venture Smith." *The Day* (New London, CT), December 6, 2009.

Bentley, William. *The Diary of William Bentley, D.D., Pastor of the East Church Salem, Massachusetts,* vols. 1–4. Salem, MA: Essex Institute, 1906–1914.

Benton, Josiah H. *Warning Out in New England*. Boston, MA: W.B. Clarke, 1911.

Bicknell, Thomas W. *A History of Barrington, Rhode Island*. Providence, RI: Snow & Farnham,1898.

_____. *The History of the State of Rhode Island and Providence* Plantations, 2 vols. Providence, RI: American Historical Society, 1920.

Bingham, Lucretia. "Hallowed Ground; An Investigation of Old Grave Sites in New England Is Unearthing Hard Truths About Yankees and Slavery." *Smithsonian Magazine* (November 2001).

Blakey, Michael, Lesley Rankin-Hill, Warren Perry, and Jean Howson, eds. *The New York African Burial Ground: Unearthing the African Presence in Colonial New York*. Washington, D.C.: Howard University Press, 2009.

Bontemps, Arna, ed. *Five Black Lives: The Autobiographies of Venture Smith, James Mars, William Grimes, The Rev. G.W. Offley, James L. Smith*. Middletown, CT: Wesleyan University Press, 1971.

Boston Parks and Recreation Department. "Historic Burying Grounds Initiative Newsletter-Funerary Practices in Early Colonial Boston". Accessed online at http://www.cityofboston.gov/images_documents/HBGI%20October%202013tcm3-40815.pdf.

Brattleboro History (VT). "Alexander and Sally Turner." Accessed online at http://brattleborohistory.com/slavery/alexander-turner.html.

Brewster, Charles. *Rambles About Portsmouth-First Series.* Portsmouth, NH: Lewis Brewster, 1873.

Brown, Barbara W., and James M. Rose. *Black Roots in Southeastern Connecticut 1650–1900.* New London, CT: New London County Historical Society, 2001.

Browne, Katrina. *Traces of the Trade: A Story from the Deep North* (film). Public Broadcasting System, 2008.

Bullen, Adelaide K., and Ripley P. Bullen "Two Burials at Tiverton, Rhode Island." *Bulletin of the Massachusetts Archaeological Society* 8, No. 1 (October 1946).

Caron, Denis R. *A Century in Captivity: The Life and Trials of Prince Mortimer, a Connecticut Slave.* Hanover, NH: University of New Hampshire Press/University Press of New England, 2006.

Caulkins, Frances M. *History of New London, Connecticut.* New London, CT: H.D. Utley, 1895.

_____. *History of Norwich, Connecticut.* Norwich, CT: Thomas Robinson, 1845.

Child, David Lee. *The Despotism of Freedom: A Speech at the First Anniversary of the New England Anti-Slavery Society.* Boston: Boston Young Men's Anti-Slavery Association, 1834.

Christianson, Scott. "Dubois comes home from the grave." Accessed online at http://theberkshire edge.com/du-bois-comes-home-grave/.

Cleary, Calista K. "Little Egypt: Black History in Three New England Towns." Easton, CT: Barton L. Weller Scholarship Foundation research paper, 1989.

Comiskey, Christine. *A Respectable Man of Color: Beyond the Legend of Cuffee Dole.* Georgetown, MA: Georgetown Historical Society, 2008.

Comstock, Cyrus B. *A Comstock Genealogy.* New York: Knickerbocker Press, 1905.

Cooley, Timothy M. *Sketches of the Life and Character of the Rev. Lemuel Haynes, A.M.* New York: Harper & Brothers, 1838.

Daggett, John. *A Sketch of the History of Attleborough.* Attleboro, MA: S. Usher, 1894.

Davis, Paul. "Rhode Island's Slave History: The Unrighteous Traffick." *Providence Journal,* accessed online at http://res.providencejournal. com/hercules/2006/slavery/text/.

Deetz, James. *In Small Things Forgotten: The Archaeology of Early American Life.* New York: Anchor Books, 1977.

Denehy, John W. *A History of Brookline, Massachusetts.* Brookline, MA: Brookline Press, 1906.

Dinan, Michael. "Future of 1735 Ferris Hill Road Home Concerns New Canaan Preservationists." Accessed online at http://newcanaanite.com/ tag/onesimus comstock.

Drisko, George W. *Narrative of the Town of Machias.* Machias, ME: Press of the Republican, 1904.

DuBois, W.E.B. *The Souls of Black Folk.* New York: Dover, 1994.

Eastman, John R. *History of the Town of Andover, New Hampshire.* Concord, NH: Rumford Printing, 1910.

Eldridge, the Rev. Joseph, and Theron W. Crissey. *1744–1900 History of Norfolk, Litchfield County, Connecticut.* Everett, MA: Massachusetts Publishing Co., 1900.

Emilio, Luis F. *A Brave Black Regiment: The History of the 54th Massachusetts, 1863–1865.* New York: Da Capo Press, 1995.

Essex Institute (MA). "Historical Visitation on Andover 1863, Part Two." *Essex Institute Historical Collections,* vol. 44, 50–64, 1912.

Fowler, William C. *The Historical Status of the Negro in Connecticut.* Charleston, SC: Walker, Evans, and Cogswell, 1901.

Friends of Hope Cemetery. "Hope Cemetery Visitor Guide and Map." Worcester, MA: n.d.

Fuller, James. *Men of Color to Arms! Vermont African-Americans in the Civil War.* San Jose, CA: iUniversity Press, 2001.

Garman, James C. "Viewing the Color Line Through the Material Culture of Death." *Historical Archaeology* 28, No. 3 (1994).

Garrison, Will. "Col. John Ashley and His Web of Commerce." *Sheffield* (MA) *Times,* November 25, 2003.

Gidwitz, Tom. "Freeing Captive History: The Hunt for Evidence of Slavery in the North." Accessed online at http://www.tomgidwitz.com/ main/slavery.htm.

Gillon, Edmund V., Jr. *Early New England Gravestone Rubbings.* New York: Dover, 1966.

Greene, Lorenzo J. *The Negro in Colonial New England 1620–1776.* New York: Columbia University Press, 1942.

Guyette, Elise A. "Black Lives and White Racism in Vermont 1760–1870." Master's thesis, University of Vermont, October 1992.

_____. *Discovering Black Vermont: African American Farmers in Hinesburgh, 1790–1890.* Hanover, NH: University of Vermont/University Press of New England, 2010.

Haas, Genevieve. "The Brief but Courageous Life of Noyes Academy." *Dartmouth Life,* December 2005.

Hall, Edwin, ed. *Ancient Historical Records of Norwalk, Conn.* Norwalk, CT: James Mallory, 1847.

Hall, M.O. *Rambles About Greenland in Rhyme.* Boston: Alfred Mudge & Sons, 1900.

Hance, Dawn D. *The History of Rutland, Vermont.* Rutland, VT: Academy Books, 1991.

Hanson, John W. *History of the Town of Danvers.* Danvers, MA: n.p., 1848.

Hartford in the Civil War. "Silent Sentinels: Civil

War Headstones." Accessed online at http://hartfordinthecivilwar.com/wordpress1/2013/07/03/silent-sentinels-civil war-headstones/.

Hoffbeck, Steven R. "Remember the Poor (Galatians 2:10): Poor Farms in Vermont." *Vermont History* 57, No. 4 (Fall 1989).

Holloway, Karla F C. *Passed On: African American Mourning Stories*. Durham, NC: Duke University Press, 2002.

Irvine, Dr. Russell W. "Martin H. Freeman of Rutland: America's First Black College Professor and Pioneering Black Social Activist." *Rutland Historical Society Quarterly* 26, No. 3 (1996).

Jamieson, Ross W. "Material Culture and Social Death: African American Burial Practices." *Historical Archaeology* 29, No. 4 (1995).

Johnson, Clifton H. "The *Amistad* Case and Its Consequences in U.S. History." Accessed online at http://www.amistadresearchcenter.org/Docs/Johnson%20-%%20Amistad%20Case%20and%20Its%20Consequences.pdf.

Johnson, Tim. "A museum and botanical garden rolled into one." Accessed online at http://archive.burlingtonfreepress.com/article/20130525/LIVING20305250003/A-museum-botanical-garden-rolled-into-one.

Johnston, William D. *Slavery in Rhode Island, 1755–1776*. Providence, RI: Rhode Island Historical Society, 1894.

Jones, Miss Electa F. *Stockbridge, Past and Present*. Springfield, MA: Samuel Bowles, 1854.

Kaplan, Sidney, and Emma Nogrady Kaplan. *The Black Presence in the Era of the American Revolution*. Amherst, MA: University of Massachusetts Press, 1989.

Karttunen, Frances. "Nantucket Places and People—James Ross and His Legacy." *Yesterday's Island, Today's Nantucket* 38, No. 20 (September 2008).

King, Henry M., ed. *Historical Catalogue of the Members of the First Baptist Church in Providence, Rhode Island*. Providence, RI: F.H. Townsend, 1908.

Kingston Improvement Association (RI). "Fayerweather House." Accessed online at http://kingstonimprovementassociation.org/fayerweather.html.

Knoblock, Glenn A. *Cemeteries Around Lake Winnipesaukee*. Charleston, SC: Arcadia Publishing, 2006.

_____. *Historic Burial Grounds of the New Hampshire Seacoast*. Charleston, SC: Arcadia Publishing, 2006.

_____. *Portsmouth Cemeteries*. Charleston, SC: Arcadia Publishing, 2005.

_____. *"Strong and Brave Fellows": New Hamp-shire's Black Soldiers and Sailors of the American Revolution, 1775–1784*. Jefferson, NC: McFarland & Co., 2003.

Kruger-Kahloula, Angelika. "History, Memory, and Politics Written in Stone: Early African American Grave Inscriptions."Accessed online at http://www.wm.edu/sites/middlepassage/documents/MBA_Kruger.pdf.

"A Lady of Boston." *Memoir of Chloe Spear, A Native of Africa*. Boston: James Loring, 1832.

Lambert, Peter. *Amos Fortune: The Man and His Legacy*. Jaffrey, NH: The Amos Fortune Forum, 2000.

Lancaster, Jane. "'I Would Have Made Out Very Poorly Had It Not Been for Her': The Life and Work of Christiana Bannister, Hair Doctress and Philanthropist." Accessed online at http://www.rihs.org/assetts/files/publications/2001_Nov.pdf.

Landi, Lauren. "Reading Between the Lines of Slavery: Examining New England Runaway Ads for Evidence of an Afro-Yankee Culture." *Pell Scholars and Senior Theses*. Paper 78, 2012. Accessed online at http://digitalcommons.salve.edu/pell_theses/78.

Lawrence, Robert F. *The New Hampshire Churches*. Claremont, NH: Claremont Power Press, 1856.

Lemire, Elise. *Black Walden: Slavery and Its Aftermath in Concord, Massachusetts*. Philadelphia, PA: University of Pennsylvania Press, 2009.

LiBrizzi, Marcus. *Lost Atusville: A Black Settlement From the American Revolution*. Orono, ME: The Maine Folklife Center, 2009.

Little, George T., ed. *Genealogical and Family History of the State of Maine*. New York: Lewis Historical Publishing, 1909.

Locke, John L. *Sketches of the History of the Town of Camden, Maine*. Camden, ME: Masters & Smith, 1859.

Lord, Charles C. *Life and Times in Hopkinton, NH*. Hopkinton, NH: Republican Press, 1890.

Lord, John K. *A History of the Town of Hanover, N.H.* Hanover, NH: Dartmouth Press, 1928.

Luti, Vincent F. *Mallet & Chisel: Gravestone Carvers of Newport, Rhode Island in the 18th Century*. Boston, MA: New England Historical Genealogical Society, 2002.

MacGregor, Roy. *The Boston Breakout*. Plattsburgh, NY: Tundra Books, 2014.

Main, Jackson T. *Society and Economy in Colonial Connecticut*. Princeton, NJ: Princeton University Press, 1985.

Maine Coast Heritage Trust. "Malaga Island—An Overview of Its Natural and Cultural History." Accessed online at http://mcht.org/preserves/docs/Malaga%20overview%203-9-09%20final.pdf.

Malloy, Tom, and Brenda Malloy. "Slavery in Colonial Massachusetts as Seen Through Selected Gravestones." *Markers XIV.* Worcester, MA: Association for Gravestone Studies, 1994.

Marlatt, Ellen, Kathleen Wheeler, and Shannon Provost. "Archaeological Excavation at the Portsmouth African Burial Ground." Portsmouth, NH: Independent Archaeological Consulting, 2005.

Mason, George C. *Reminiscences of Newport.* Newport, RI: Charles Hammett, Jr., 1884.

Massachusetts Historical Commission. "Form E-Burial Grounds—Woodcock Cemetery," North Attleboro, MA, ca. 1990.

Mattatuck Museum (CT). "Burial Locations; Waterbury's Early Cemeteries." Accessed online at http://www.fortunestory.org/religionand slavery/burial.asp.

McCain, Diana Ross. "Connecticut African American Soldiers in the Civil War, 1861–1865." Accessed online at http://www.ctfreedomtrail.org/data/files/resource-library/reports/CT-African-American-Soldiers-in-the-Civil-War.pdf.

McDuffee, Franklin. *History of Rochester New Hampshire,* vol. 1. Manchester, NH: John Clarke, 1892.

McLellan, Hugh D., and Katherine B. Lewis, eds. *History of Gorham, ME.* Portland, ME: Smith & Sale, 1903.

Metropolitan Museum of Art (NY). "Heilbrunn History of Art Timeline—Figure (gravemarker), 20th century Kenya; Giryama people." Accessed online at http://www.metmuseum.org/toah/works-of-art/1993.522.

Minardi, Margot. "Chloe Spear: Leaving a Legacy, Listing a Life." Accessed online at http://www.royallhouse.org/chloe-spear-by-margot-minardi/.

Mitchell, Steve. *The Shame of Maine.* Brunswick, ME: n.p., 1999.

Mollan, Mark C. "Honoring Our War Dead: The Evolution of the Government Policy on Headstones for Fallen Soldiers and Sailors." *Prologue* 35, No. 1 (Spring 2003).

Moore, George H. *Notes on Slavery in Massachusetts.* New York, NY: D. Appleton, 1866.

Munro, Wilfred H. *The History of Bristol, R.I.: The Story of the Mount Hope Lands.* Providence, RI: J.A. and R.A. Reid, 1880.

National Park Service. "African American Heritage Sites in Salem." Accessed online at http://www.nps.gov/sama/historyculture/upload/Salem AfAmsitessm.pdf.

Nell, William C. *The Colored Patriots of the American Revolution.* Salem, NH: Ayer, 1986.

Nemitz, Bill. "After 98 years, an apology long overdue." *Portland* (ME) *Press Herald,* September 17, 2010.

New York Times. "The President's Arrival." *New York Times,* September 3, 1898.

Nichols, Joan H., Patricia L. Haslam, and Robert M. Murphy. *Index to Known Cemetery Listings in Vermont,* 5th ed. Barre, VT: Vermont Historical Society, 2012.

Noyes, Sybil, Charles T. Libby, and Walter G. Davis. *Genealogical Dictionary of Maine and New Hampshire.* Baltimore, MD: Genealogical Publishing, 1996.

Oat, David. "Old Norwichtown Burial Ground" (brochure). Norwich, CT: Norwich Tourism Office, 1997.

Orcutt, Samuel. *History of Torrington, Connecticut.* Torrington, CT: J. Munsell Printer, 1878.

Pfeiffer, Dr. John. "Slavery in Southeastern Connecticut: A View from Lyme." Accessed online at http://www.oldlymehistoricalsociety.org/docs/slavery_in_lyme.pdf.

Piersen, William D. *Black Yankees: The Development of an Afro-American Subculture in Eighteenth-Century New England.* Amherst, MA: University of Massachusetts Press, 1988.

Pilgrim Hall Museum. "Beyond the Pilgrim Story: Long Road to Freedom, African-Americans in the Old Colony." Accessed online at http://www.pilgrimhallmuseum.org/long_road_to_freedom.htm.

Pjepscot Historical Society (ME). "Pine Grove Cemetery of Brunswick, ME." Accessed online at http://pinegrovebrunswick.blogspot.com/search/label/Pine%20Grove%20Cemetery%20History.

Prentiss, Benjamin F. *The Blind African Slave, or Memoirs of Boyrereau Brinch, Nick-named Jeffrey Brace.* St. Albans, VT: Harry Whitney, 1810.

Price, H.H., and Gerald E. Talbot. *Maine's Visible Black History: The First Chronicle of Its People.* Gardiner, ME: Tilbury House, 2006.

Price, Hugh B. "The Search for Nero Hawley." *American Legacy* (Fall 2008).

Princeton (MA) Historical Society. "Honorable Moses Gill." Accessed online at http://www.princetonmahistory.org/people-groups/residents/honorable-moses-gill.

Quimby, Beth. "War of 1812 veteran gets his due, late." *Portland (ME) Press Herald,* September 15, 2012.

Quintal, George Jr. *Patriots of Color: "A Peculiar Beauty and Merit."* Boston, MA: National Park Service, 2002.

Roads, Samuel (the younger). *A Guide to Marblehead.* Marblehead, MA: M.H. Graves, 1881.

Robinson, Caroline E., and Daniel Goodwin, ed. *The Gardiners of Narragansett.* Providence, RI: Daniel Goodwin, 1919.

Romer, Robert H. *Slavery in the Connecticut Valley of Massachusetts.* Florence, MA: Levellers Press, 2009.

Saint, Chandler B., and George A. Krimsky. *Making Freedom: The Extraordinary Life of Venture Smith*. Middletown, CT: Wesleyan University Press, 2008.

Salvatore, Nick. *We All Got History: The Memory Books of Amos Webber*. New York: Times Books, 1996.

Sammons, Mark J., and Valerie Cunningham. *Black Portsmouth: Three Centuries of African-American Heritage*. Hanover, NH: University of New Hampshire Press/University Press of New England, 2004.

Seacord, Stephanie. *In Honor of Those Forgotten: The Portsmouth, New Hampshire African Burying Ground*. Portsmouth, NH: Brown, n.d.

Secomb, Daniel F. *History of the Town of Amherst, Hillsborough County, New Hampshire*. Concord, NH: Evans, Sleeper, & Woodbury, 1883.

Sedgewick, Miss (Catherine). "Slavery in New England." In *Bentley's Miscellany*, vol. 34, London: Richard Bentley, 1853.

Seeman, Erik R. "Sources and Interpretations; Reassessing the '*Sankofa* Symbol' in New York's African Burial Ground." *William and Mary Quarterly*, 3d Series, 67, No. 1 (January 2010).

Sewall, Samuel. *Diary of Samuel Sewall, 1674–1729*. Boston, MA: Massachusetts Historical Society, 1882.

Sheldon, George. *History of Deerfield, Massachusetts 1636–1886*. Deerfield, MA: E.A. Hall, 1896.

Shipton, Clifford K., ed. *Sibley's Harvard Graduates*, vols. 7–12. Boston, MA: Massachusetts Historical Society, 1945–1962.

"Shudder Island." *Portland Magazine* (October 2004).

Slavenorth.com. "Slavery in the North," accessed online at http://slavenorth.com/slavenorth.htm.

Smith, James A. *The History of the Black Population of Amherst, Massachusetts 1728–1870*. Boston, MA: New England Historic Genealogical Society, 1999.

Smith, S.F. *History of Newton, Massachusetts*. Boston, MA: American Logotype, 1880.

Smith, Venture, and H.M. Selden. *A Narrative of the Life and Adventures of Venture, a Native of Africa*. Middletown, CT: J.S. Stewart, 1897.

Spender, Wilbur D. *Burial Inscriptions and Other Data of Burials in Berwick, York County, Maine to the Year 1922*. Sanford, ME: Averill Press, 1922.

Sprague, John F. "Slavery in the District of Maine." *Sprague's Journal of Maine History* 4, No. 3 (October 1916): 224.

Stark, Bruce P. "RG 003, New London County Court African Americans and People of Color Collection Finding Aid." Accessed online at http://www.cslib.org/archives/Finding_Aids/RG003_NLCC_AA.html.

Steiner, Bernard. *History of Slavery in Connecticut*. Baltimore, MD: Johns Hopkins Press, 1893.

Sterling, John E. *North Burial Ground, Providence, Rhode Island Old Section 1700–1848*. Providence, RI: Rhode Island Genealogical Society, 2000.

Sterling, John E., Barbara J. Austin, and Letty R. Champion. *Newport, Rhode Island Colonial Burial Grounds*. Hope, RI: Rhode Island Genealogical Society, 2009.

Stiles, Ezra, and Franklin B. Dexter, eds. *The Literary Diary of Ezra Stiles*. New York: Charles Scribner & Sons, 1901.

Stiles, Henry R. *The History of Ancient Wethersfield Connecticut*, vol. 1. New York: Grafton Press, 1854.

_____. *The History of Ancient Windsor, Connecticut*. New York: Charles B. Norton, 1859.

Swann, Marrel G., and Donald P. Swann. *Early Families of Rutland, Vermont*. Rutland, VT: Rutland Historical Society, 1990.

Tashjian, Ann, and Dickran Tashjian. "The Afro-American Section of Newport, Rhode Island's Common Burying Ground." In *Cemeteries & Gravemarkers; Voices of American Culture*, Richard E. Meyer, ed. Logan, UT: Utah State University Press, 1992.

Temple, J.H. *History of Framingham, Massachusetts*. Town of Framingham, MA: 1887.

Thomas, Miriam S. *Flotsam and Jetsam*. N.p.: published by the author, 1973.

Thompson, Mary P. *Landmarks in Ancient Dover, New Hampshire*. Durham, NH: Durham Historic Association, 1973.

Thoreau, Henry David. *Walden and Civil Disobedience*. New York: Sterling, 2012.

Tolman, George. "John Jack, the Slave and Daniel Bliss, the Tory." Concord, MA: Concord Antiquarian Society, 1902.

Tomlinson, Charlie. "Richard Potter (1783–1835)." In *African American National Biography*, vol. 5. Henry L. Gates, Jr., and Evelyn B. Higginbotham, eds. New York: Oxford University Press, 2008.

Toner, Mike. "Digs unearth plantations holding slaves in 'free' North." *Baltimore Sun*, March 9, 2003.

United States Department of the Interior. "National Register of Historic Places Inventory—Nomination Form." Griswold, CT: Kinne Cemetery, 2001.

_____. "National Register of Historic Places Inventory—Nomination Form." Newport, RI: Common Buying Ground and Island Cemetery, 1974.

_____. "National Register of Historic Places Inventory—Nomination Form." Providence, RI: North Burial Ground, 1977.

Upham, Mrs. T.C. *Narrative of Phebe Ann Jacobs.* London: W.& F.G. Cash, ca. 1850.

Vermont, State of. "Vermont African American Heritage Trail" (brochure). N.p., April 2013.

Vida, Christina. "Nancy Toney's Lifetime in Slavery." Accessed online at http://connecticut history.org/nancy-toneys-lifetime-in-slavery/.

Wardner, H.S. "Judge Jacob and his Dinah: A Story of Windsor." *The Vermonter* 19, No. 5–6 (May-June 1914): 80–88.

Warner, Robert A. *New Haven Negroes: A Social History.* New York: Arno Press and the New York Times, 1969.

Washburn, Emory. *Historical Sketches of the Town of Leicester, Massachusetts.* Boston: John Wilson and Son, 1860.

Weintraub, Elain Cawley. "The Triumph of Captain William A. Martin." Accessed online at http://mvafricanamericanheritagetrail.org/williammartin.html.

Weltner, Linda. "Black Joe; A Mythical, Musical, and Unforgettable Man on Gingerbread Hill". Accessed online at http://www.legendinc.com/Pages/MarbleheadNet/MM/Articles/BlackJoe.html.

Wepman, Dennis. "Cinque (c. 1814–c. 1879)." In *African American National Biography*, vol. 2. Henry L. Gates, Jr., and Evelyn B. Higginbotham, eds. New York: Oxford University Press, 2008.

Weston, Thomas. *History of the Town of Middleboro, Massachusetts*, vol. 1. Boston: Houghton Mifflin, 1906.

Wheeler, Edmund. *The History of Newport, New Hampshire from 1766 to 1878.* Concord, NH: Republican Press, 1879.

Wheeler, Kathleen, and Alexandra Chan. "Recovery of Human Osteological Remains at the Amherst Public Cemetery." Portsmouth, NH: Independent Archaeological Consulting, 2005.

Wheeler, Kathleen, with Marcella Sorg. "Addendum No. 1: Archaeological Excavations at the Portsmouth African Burial Ground." Portsmouth, NH: Independent Archaeological Consulting, 2009.

White, Barbara. *A Line in the Sand: The Battle to Integrate Nantucket Public Schools, 1825–1847.* New Bedford, MA: Spinner Publications, 2009.

_____. "The Integration of Nantucket Public Schools." *Historic Nantucket* 40, No. 3 (Fall 1992).

White, David O. *Connecticut's Black Soldiers 1775–1783.* Chester, CT: Pequot Press, 1973.

Whitfield, Harvey Amani. "African Americans in Burlington, Vermont, 1880–1900." *Vermont History Journal* 75, No. 2 (Summer-Fall 2007).

"Who Was Moses Dustin?" Gilmanton, NH: newspaper clipping, n.d., ca. 2008.

Wilcoxson, William H. *History of Stratford Con-necticut 1639–1939.* Stratford, CT: Stratford Tercentenary Commission, 1939.

Williamson, Jane. "African Americans in Addison County, Charlotte, and Hinesburgh, Vermont, 1790–1860." *Vermont History Journal* 78, No. 1 (Winter-Spring 2010).

Wilson, Harriet E. *Our Nig: Or, Sketches from the Life of a Free Black.* New York: Vintage Books, 2002.

Winter, Kari J., ed. *The Blind African Slave: Memoirs of Boyrereau Brinch, Nick-Named Jeffrey Brace.* Madison, WI: University of Wisconsin Press, 2005.

Work, David. "The Buffalo Soldiers in Vermont, 1909–1913." *Vermont History Journal* 73 (Winter-Spring 2005).

Wright, Robert K., Jr. *The Continental Army.* Washington, D.C.: U.S. Army, G.P.O., 1989.

York County (ME) Registrar. *York Deeds*, 18 vols. Portland, ME: Maine Historical Society/Maine Genealogical Society, 1887–1910.

Youngken, Richard C. *African Americans in Newport: An Introduction to the Heritage of African Americans in Newport, Rhode Island, 1700–1945.* Newport, RI: The Rhode Island Black Heritage Society and the Newport Historical Society, 1998.

Zernicke, Kate. "Slave Traders in Yale's Past Fuel Debate on Restitution." *New York Times*, August 13, 2001.

Miscellaneous Archival Records

Record Group 002, Failed Bills, Connecticut State Archives, Connecticut State Library (Hartford).

Record Group 003, African Americans and People of Color Collection, New London County Court, New London, CT.

Rockingham County (NH) Probate Records, County Courthouse, Brentwood, NH.

Strafford County (NH) Deeds, County Courthouse, Dover, NH.

Warning Out Notices, Amherst, NH (file), State of New Hampshire, Division of Records Management and Archives (Concord).

Newspapers

Barre Gazette (Barre, MA).

Boston News-Letter.

Bridgeport Spirit of the Times (CT).

Bridgeport Telegram (CT).

Columbian Centinel (Boston).

Daily Morning Chronicle (Portsmouth, NH).

Exeter News-Letter (NH).

Exeter Watchman (NH).

Farmer's Cabinet (Milford, NH).
Hartford Courant (CT).
New Hampshire Gazette.
New London Gazette (CT).
Providence Gazette (RI).
Providence Journal (RI).
Rutland Herald (VT).
Vermont Standard (Woodstock, VT), July 24, 1890; December 13, 1894.

Online Records

The following source records were accessed online via the subscription service ancestry.com:

Barbour Collection-Connecticut Birth, Death, and Marriage Record Abstracts, Pre-1870.
Connecticut Church Abstract Records 1630–1920.
Connecticut, Hale Cemetery Inscriptions and Newspaper Notices, 1629–1934.
Connecticut Revolutionary War Military Lists, 1775–1783.
Maine Birth and Death Records, 1617–1922.
Massachusetts Birth and Marriage Records, 1620–1850.
Massachusetts Birth Records, 1840–1915.
Massachusetts Soldiers and Sailors of the American Revolution.
Massachusetts State Census, 1855, 1865.
Massachusetts Town and Vital Records, 1620–1988.
New England Historical and Genealogical Register, 1847–1900.
New Hampshire Death and Burial Records Index, 1654–1949.
Revolutionary War Pension and Bounty-Land Warrant Application Files, 1800–1900.
Rhode Island State Censuses, 1865–1935.
Suffolk County (Massachusetts) Court Records, 1671–1680.
U.S. Civil War Draft Registrations Records, 1863–65.
U.S. Civil War Pension Index, 1861–1934.
U.S. Colored Troops Military Service Records 1863–65.
U.S. Federal Census Records for Connecticut, Maine, Massachusetts, New Hampshire, Rhode Island, and Vermont, 1790–1880 and 1910–1940.
U.S. Headstone Applications for Military Veterans.
U.S. National Homes for Disabled Volunteer Soldiers, 1866–1938.
U.S. Naval Enlistment and Rendezvous Records, 1855–1891.
U.S. Pensioners, 1818–1872.
Vermont Vital Records, 1720–1908.
Vital Records of Rhode Island, 1636–1850, first Series, births, marriages, and deaths.

Index

Slaves identified in sources or on gravestones by first name only, but whose masters are known, are indexed under their master's name, indicated by the use of parentheses. This is not the case for slaves or former slaves who are referred to in these same sources as having taken their master's or another surname. Those individuals whose last names are not indicated in sources are indexed under their known given name, i.e., Phyllis, Tituba, etc. Numbers in **bold italics** indicate pages with photographs.